D1298986

CROP SCIENCE PRINCIPLES AND PRACTICES by Mullen, Russ. © 2005
Reprinted by permission of PEARSON LEARNING COLUTIONS.

R.E. Mullen

Crop Science

Principles and Practice

Russell E. Mullen
Iowa State University
Ames, Iowa

Fourth Edition

Pearson
Custom
Publishing

Copyright © 2003 by Pearson Custom Publishing.
All rights reserved.

Permission in writing must be obtained from the publisher before any part of this work
may be reproduced or transmitted in any form or by any means, electronic or mechanical,
including photocopying and recording, or by any information storage or retrieval system.

Printed in the United States of America

10 9 8 7 6 5 4 3

Please visit our web site at www.pearsoncustom.com

ISBN 0–536–72100–9

BA 996388

PEARSON CUSTOM PUBLISHING
75 Arlington Street, Suite 300, Boston, MA 02116
A Pearson Education Company

Contents

For more detailed reference use the Topical Index on the following pages.

Topical Index

Acknowledgments

In dedication to Detroy Green and Donald Woolley... As books evolve and change so do authors. The present author is indebted to Dr. Detroy Green and Dr. Don Woolley, co-authors of the first edition of *Agronomy— Principles and Practice*. The present edition goes forth upon their foundation. Their contributions and friendship are greatly appreciated.

Gratitude is extended to the many colleagues, former and present graduate instructors, teaching assistants, and students who have provided invaluable ideas, assistance, and feedback upon which the former and present editions have depended.

The author is also indebted to colleagues who have served as reviewers and provided valuable suggestions for improvement of this edition: Mike Lauer, Pioneer Hi-Bred Int.; Brent Pearce, Dick Carlson, Tom Loynachan, Rick Cruse, Arden Campbell, Al Knapp, Mike Owen, John Obrycki, and Ed Braun, Iowa State University; Steve DeBroux, Delaware Valley College; and Mary Holmes, Iowa State University, who provided the input and guidance for integration of environmental issues and sustainable agriculture concepts in the text. Their help is gratefully acknowledged.

Special thanks are extended to Marilyn Clem, Larry Barr, Karen Kuenzel for the preparation of illustrations retained from prior editions and to Shari Vogl, illustrator for the new edition. Gratitude is also extended to the Iowa State University Seed Science Center and the United States Department of Agriculture for permitting and providing illustrations of seeds and plants. The typist for this edition was Evelyn Kruse, whose patience and assistance were gratefully appreciated. The author wishes to thank Burgess International Group, Inc. for their assistance and support in the preparation of this manuscript.

I would like to affectionately acknowledge the support and understanding of my wife, Michele, and family, whose help and patience made this endeavor possible.

Preface

Crop Science—Principles and Practice is a spiral bound, "working textbook". It is the result of continued efforts to provide students with textual material that emphasizes fundamental concepts underlying crop science and production. The first edition entitled, *Agronomy—Principles and Practice,* evolved from the introductory course in crop production at Iowa State University. The second edition continues that evolution.

The new edition, in addition to updating and revision of chapters, also represents efforts to integrate concepts of sustainable agriculture and environmental awareness throughout written materials. It is designed to embrace concerns and questions related to agriculture, environment, and protection of our natural resources rather than ignore them. The text purposefully emphasizes basic principles illustrated with crop examples. It was not designed to be a large reference manual of crop statistics and information lest students lose sight of the principles in a sea of information. The text allows the instructor to enhance the student's understanding and application of material to different agricultural regions using lecture, discussion, or other instructional formats.

Crop Science—Principles and Practice was written with the following goals:
1) To help students develop the fundamental vocabulary used in crop-, soil-, and climate-related sciences and industries.
2) To emphasize the basic principles and relationships among crops and their environment and production.
3) To help students learn and apply the broad sciences of botany, anatomy, taxonomy, physiology, soil, climatology, genetics, entomology, and pathology, that are intrinsically involved in crop production.
4) To develop a textbook that is flexible for student learning and instructor use. The text is written in outline form to help students identify, follow, and learn concepts. The text was designed and written for students with or without an agricultural background. The text can be used alone, as a lecture supplement, for individualized study, or for remedial learning of basic crop science principles.

Chapter Videos Available:

Through the financial support of the Leopard Center for Sustainable Agriculture, Media Resources Center, College of Agriculture, and Department of Agronomy at Iowa State University, video tutorial tapes were developed for each chapter in the textbook. The videos were instructionally designed and professionally produced to help students learn and visualize textual material and to increase their awareness of the environmental issues and sustainable concepts in agriculture. Videos are 25-60 minutes in length and can be obtained from the Instructional Technology Center, Iowa State University, Ames, IA 50011-1010 (phone: 515-294-8022).

Chapter 1

Crop Plant Anatomy

WHY STUDY ANATOMY?

A knowledge of crop plant anatomy is basic to the agronomist for describing and identifying different species and types of plants. Crop anatomy is essential in communication among farmers, entomologists, pathologists, weed scientists, or anyone involved in crop production. Farmers in seed, grain, fiber, or forage production frequently use plant anatomy to distinguish crop pests, to identify optimum management practices and to aid in production decisions. Determining when to replant, optimum hay cutting schedules, and trouble shooting nitrogen deficiency in legumes are just a few examples of where a knowledge of crop anatomy can play an important role in making the right decision.

In this chapter and others, comparisons are frequently made between cereals and legumes. Agricultural crops are frequently subdivided into two broad categories. Monocotyledonous plants (commonly referred to as "monocots" or "grasses") are those that contain one seed leaf (one cotyledon). Cereal crops are grass crops grown for their seed. Dicotyledonous plants (commonly referred to as "dicots" or broadleaf plants) are those that contain two seed leaves (two cotyledons). An important group within dicots are legumes (podded crops that have nitrogen fixation ability in the root system) and can be grown for their seed (pulse crops/grain legumes) or forage (forage legumes). The various crop classifications are discussed in more detail in Chapter 2.

I. THE PLANT CELL

This unit will begin with a review of the plant cell. The cell is the basis for plant life and much of the research in increasing quality and quantity of crop products for the future is involved at the cellular level. Use the following diagram of a plant cell (Figure 1) and the information to help you understand the functions and characteristics of the parts:

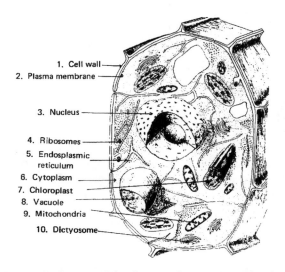

1. Cell wall
2. Plasma membrane
3. Nucleus
4. Ribosomes
5. Endosplasmic reticulum
6. Cytoplasm
7. Chloroplast
8. Vacuole
9. Mitochondria
10. Dictyosome

Figure 1. General features of a young plant cell

After studying the diagram, you should be able to properly label the cell components, give their function and to describe their importance.

Cell Part	Function or Characteristic
1. Cell Wall	Protects the inner parts of the cell and gives rigidity to the cell. Hay quality is influenced by cell wall digestibility.
2. Plasma membrane	Differentially permeable-some materials will pass through this membrane while others will not. Some herbicides kill weeds by breaking down membrane structure.
3. Nucleus	Contains chromosomes which contain the genetic material (DNA) involved in the inheritance of characteristics.
4. Ribosomes	Involved in protein manufacture in the plant.
5. Endoplasmic reticulum	Involved in protein manufacture in the plant.
6. Cytoplasm	Living gel-like material containing the functioning parts of the cell. Cold hardiness in crops is influenced by changes in cell cytoplasm.
7. Chloroplast	A principal type of plastid containing chlorophyll-the site of photosynthesis in the plant cell.
8. Vacuole	A storage region for desirable and undesirable cellular materials. Also acts as an internal balloon to help regulate water pressure within the cell and to maintain proper cell rigidity. Size varies with age of the cell.
9. Mitochondria	Site of aerobic respiration that is the main source of energy for cellular metabolism and growth.
10. Dictyosome	Associated with cell wall formation. (Golgi apparatus)

Plant or Animal Cell?? Based on plant cell characteristics, what cell parts are not found in animal cells? (Hint: animal cells are not rigid, nor do they photosynthesize.)

II. SEED AND SEEDLING ANATOMY

Seeds are miniature plants in an arrested state. Research has shown that seeds can be damaged by rough handling and improper storage. Some seed parts are more vulnerable to damage than others. A knowledge of seeds and seedling parts is important in judging the quality of seeds, estimating seedling vigor and predicting germination and establishment success. In this section cereal crops (i.e. maize, wheat, rice, etc.) are compared with legume crops (soybeans, peanuts, alfalfa, etc.).

From the following information you should be able to label and describe functions of the parts of:

    A.   Cereal seed and seedlings

    B.   Legume seed and seedlings

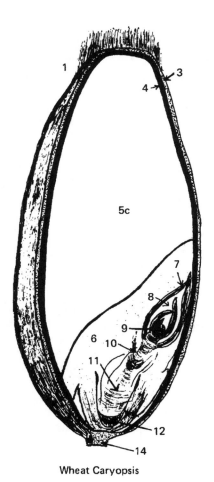

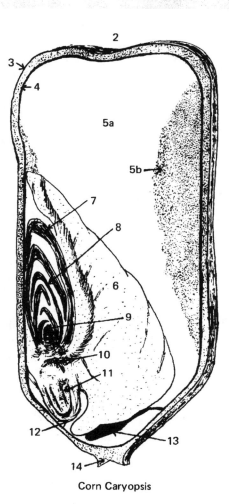

1. Brush
2. Dent
3. Pericarp
4. Aleurone
5. Endosperm:
   a. Starchy
   b. Flinty
   c. Gluten
6. Scutellum (Cotyledon)
7. Coleoptile
8. Epicotyl
9. Apical meristem
   (Growing point)
10. Scutellar node
11. Radicle
12. Coleorhiza
13. Black layer
14. Tip

Wheat Caryopsis

Corn Caryopsis

Figure 2

A. **Cereal Caryopsis Anatomy**

Kernel Part	Function or Characteristic
1. Brush	Tuft of persistent hairs on tips of wheat kernels.
2. Dent	Found on tops of corn (maize) kernels (in dent corn). Forms because soft starch in the center of the kernel shrinks more on drying than does the flinty endosperm along the outside of the kernel.
3. Pericarp	Primarily ovary tissue (maternal tissue) which protects the caryopsis (kernel). The caryopsis is a ripened ovary (fruit) because of the presence of the pericarp and therefore, is not a true seed (ripened ovule). Red color in some corn seed is found in the pericarp. Pericarp characteristics are determined by the mother plant.

3

4. Aleurone layer — The outer, few cellular layers of endosperm. Unlike the pericarp in that aleurone characteristics are determined by both the female and male parents. Secretes enzymes that help break down endosperm material for germination. Colorless in normal dent corn; blue in blue corn kernels.

5. Endosperm — Mostly starch and comprises the bulk of the mature cereal grain. Energy source for the germinating seed and seedling. Endosperm can be further classified as starchy (soft) or flinty (hard) depending on texture and color.

   a. Starchy endosperm-soft, white starch
   b. Flinty endosperm-hard, vitreous (glasslike), yellow in yellow dent corn -reddish brown in hard, red wheats. The presence or amount varies in varieties or types of cereals.
   c. Gluten-a proteinaceous matrix which gives dough its sticky, elastic quality in bread making. Wheat, rye and triticale are the only cereals whose endosperm contains gluten.

6. Scutellum (cotyledon) — Primary function is enzyme secretion for breaking down endosperm and transporting food to the developing seedling. The grass caryopsis has one cotyledon (scutellum), so grasses are known as monocotyledonous plants.

7. Coleoptile — The topmost part of the embryo axis (embryonic root and shoot) that serves as a protective sheath for young leaves and growing point during seedling emergence.

8. Epicotyl — Also called plumule and is the embryonic leaves and shoot.

9. Apical meristem — Located immediately above the scutellar node. Stalk and leaf tissue develops (growing point) from the growing point. If the growing point is destroyed, further plant development is prevented.

10. Scutellar node — Point of attachment of the scutellum to the embryo axis.

11. Radicle — Embryonic root found in the lower part of the embryo axis.

12. Coleorhiza — Protective sheath surrounding the radicle. Helps seal and prevent disease from entering the kernel through the rupture made by the elongating radicle during germination.

13. Black layer — Forms near the tip of the corn kernel. Indicates physiological maturity (maximum kernel dry weight).

14. Tip — The point of attachment of the kernel to the flower stalk. Botanically called a pedicel.

B. Cereal Seed Germination and Seedling Establishment

Seedling anatomy, germination and establishment characteristics of cereals are important especially when damage occurs at the seedling stage and replanting decisions must be considered. Cereals such as wheat, rye, maize, oats and rice have hypogeal type emergence. This means that the cotyledons (and food supply) of the cereal plants remain below the soil surface during emergence.

Use the following diagrams to identify seedling parts at different stages in germination and establishment.

Germination and Emergence

Wheat	Days from Planting	Comments	Maize (Corn)

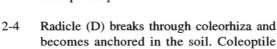
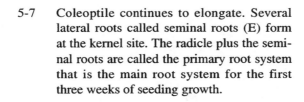
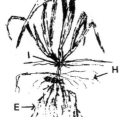
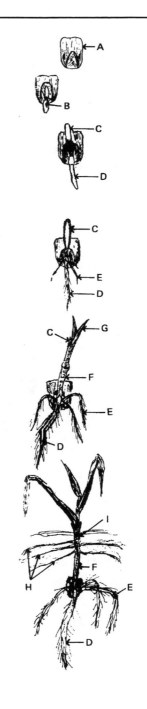

0-1   Pericarp (A) inbibes water, becoming soft and elastic.

1-2   Coleorhiza (B) elongates slightly emerging from pericarp.

2-4   Radicle (D) breaks through coleorhiza and becomes anchored in the soil. Coleoptile (C) elongates.

5-7   Coleoptile continues to elongate. Several lateral roots called seminal roots (E) form at the kernel site. The radicle plus the seminal roots are called the primary root system that is the main root system for the first three weeks of seeding growth.

7-14   The first internode, called the mesocotyl (F), elongates in corn (and oats) but usually remains inactive in wheat (also in barley and rye). Mesocotyl and/or coleoptile elongation begins to cease when the coleoptile emerges from the soil surface. The first leaves (G) break through the coleoptile, turn green and begin to photo-synthesize.

14-21   Coronal roots (H), also called crown or adventitious roots, develop immediately below the soil surface. Coronal roots are the secondary root system of grasses and become the principal absorbing roots after about three weeks of seeding growth. The growing point (1) is located just above the top node and remains below the soil surface for approximately 30 days.

1. Why does corn (maize) dent?

2. In what parts of the maize kernel are the following colors carried?

    Yellow   White   Red   Blue

3. Why is the wheat kernel called a caryopsis?

4. Why is wheat rather than maize used for bread making?

5. What are the following parts?

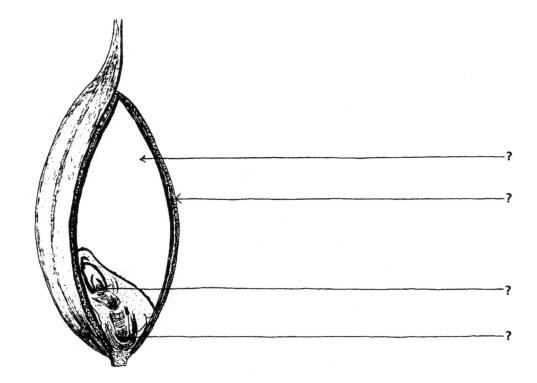

    ?

    ?

    ?

    ?

6. What is the function of the scutellum in oat kernels?

7. Rice germination and emergence is hypogeal. What does this mean?

8. What are the functions of the:

    a. coleoptile?
    b. mesocotyl in corn?

9. Why will maize survive a killing frost until it is about 12 inches tall?

10. Why does a pop-up fertilizer (placing fertilizer near the seed) result in only a short term effect on corn growth?

C. Legume Seed Anatomy

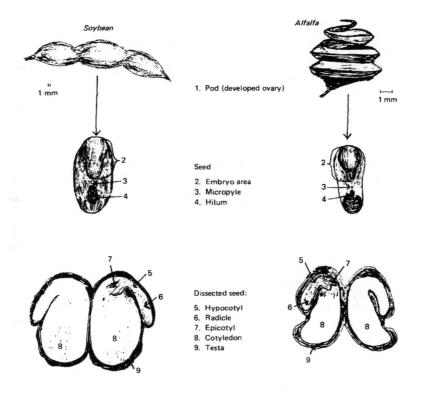

Figure 3

Seed part	Function or Characteristic
1. Pod	The legume pod with enclosed ovules (seeds) is called a legume. When legume seeds are threshed from the pod (developed ovary), the remaining seed are actually mature ovules. Thus, the term legume "seed" is botanically correct.
2. Embryo area	This is the area of the embryo axis which develops into the legume seedling and is in a very vulnerable position for mechanical damage. Therefore, seeds should be handled as gently as possible in threshing and conditioning.
3. Micropyle	Point of entry of the pollen tube into the ovule as fertilization took place.
4. Hilum	Point of attachment of the seed to the legume pod. The seed receives its food during its growth and development through this attachment. The hilum may vary in color (ex. soybeans), thus providing one method of variety identification.
5. Hypocotyl	The stem tissue between the epicotyl and the radicle. In most legumes the hypocotyl elongates during germination to cause emergence of the seedling.
6. Radicle	The embryonic root found in the lower portion of the embryo axis. Upon germination and emergence it develops into the central axis of the root system.
7. Epicotyl	The embryonic shoot and leaves. It contains, the growing point (apical meristem) and the first two (unifoliolate) leaves. The stem and future vegetative growth forms from the growing point.
8. Cotyledon	Each "half" of a legume seed is a cotyledon. Therefore, legumes are known as dicotyledonous plants. Cotyledons are seed leaves and serve as a food supply for the seedling during germination and emergence. Soybean cotyledons contain approximately 20% oil and 40% protein.
9. Testa	The true seed coat of a legume seed. The testa develops from the fertilized ovule and acts as protective tissue for the internal seed parts.

D. Legume Seed Germination and Seedling Establishment

The seedling anatomy, germination and establishment characteristics of legumes differ from those of cereal grasses. These differences are important in applying management practices to ensure adequate germination and seedling establishment. Replanting decisions may vary for legumes and cereal grasses based on differences in seedling characteristics.

Most legumes have epigeal type emergence such as soybeans, field beans, alfalfa and red clover. The cotyledons are pulled above the soil surface due to the elongation of the hypocotyl. Peas and hairy vetch are examples of legumes with hypogeal germination in which the cotyledons remain below the soil surface.

Use the following diagrams to identify seeding parts at different stages in germination and establishment.

Germination and Emergence

Soybean	Days from Planting	Comments	Pea
	0-2	Testa (A) allows water to be imbibed by the seed, swells, and becomes elastic. Hormones stimulate the growth of the radicle (B) which ruptures the testa and penetrates the soil.	
	3-4	In most legumes the hypocotyl (C) begins to elongate pulling the cotyledons toward the soil surface. However, in peas the hypocotyl does not elongate and cotyledons remain below ground. Emergence of the pea seedling is accomplished through the elongation of the embryonic shoot called epicotyl (D).	
	4-6	The curved, upper portion of the hypocotyl is called the hypocotyledonary arch (E) and straightens when the seedling emerges. The testa usually falls off the cotyledons (G) or remains in the soil. The soybean seedling on the left is in the "crook" stage of emergence. The elongation of the pea seeding is slowing down and new vegetative growth is continuing. Branch roots (F) are developing from the main root.	
	6-12	As the hypocotyl straightens, the cotyledons (G) (soybean) unfold allowing sunlight to reach the young leaves in the epicotyl. The leaves turn green and begin to photosynthesize. The cotyledons will also turn green (chlorophyll formation) after receiving sunlight and serve as photosynthetic organs for several days following emergence. The first vegetative leaves to appear after emergence in soybeans are unifoliolate (a leaf consisting of a single leaflet) (H). In the pea, unifoliolate leaves are scale-like, have no petiole and remain below ground.	
	12-18	Leaves consisting of three leaflets called trifoliolate leaves (I) are forming in soybeans. Other leaves (J) in peas have one or more leaflets per leaf with large leaf-like stipules. Swollen, knotlike nodules (K) are becoming visible on the legume roots. Nodules contain bacteria *(Rhizobium)* which convert nitrogen to a form available for plant use. Axillary buds (L) are present at each node (joint) above the soil surface. These buds can give rise to vegetative or reproductive growth. The apical bud (growing point) (M) is the topmost bud on the stem and is enclosed in the youngest developing leaf. Growth can resume from axillary buds if the apical bud is destroyed.	

9

1. Based on the following diagram, what type of germination would cotton have?

2. Label parts A, B, and C.

   Cotton

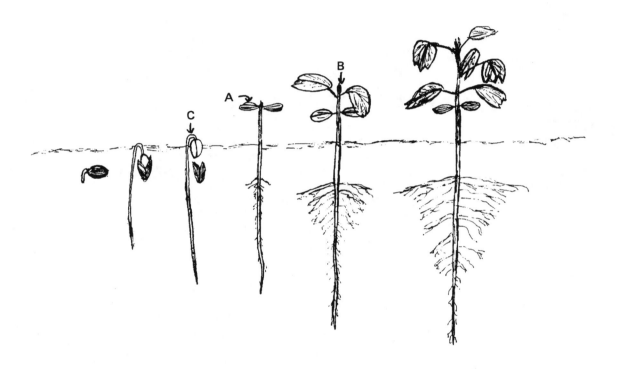

3. What are the functions of parts A, B, and C?

4. How would the soybean plant react under each of the following conditions?

   a) Clip the hypocotyl just below the cotyledons.

   b) Clip the epicotyl just above the cotyledons.

5. Why has seed treatment with a fungicide generally improved emergence of corn and small grains but seldom results in increased emergence percentage in soybeans?

6. Why will corn usually emerge from greater depths than will soybeans?

7. Why will 2-month old soybean plants survive the destruction of the growing point on the main stem, when 2-month old corn plants will not?

III. PLANT LEAVES

A. Leaf Anatomy

Leaves arise from buds and are appendages from the nodes of the plant stems or branches. The major functions of leaves are photosynthesis and gas exchange between the plant and the atmosphere. Leaves are generally classified under one of the two following categories.

1. Parallel-veined leaves-These leaves contain veins about equal in size and running parallel. Growth of grass leaves takes place by elongation near the base.

example: grasses

2. Netted-veined leaves-These leaves have a few prominent veins from which a large number of minor veins arise.

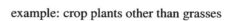

example: crop plants other than grasses

Study the following diagrams of cross sections of typical dicot and monocot leaves showing cells and tissues. Understand the functions of the various leaf parts.

Dicot Leaf

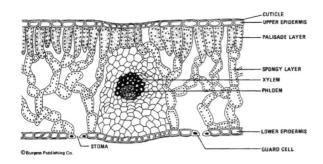

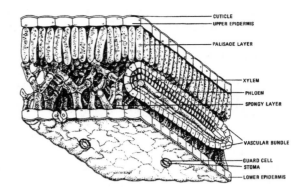

Monocot Leaf

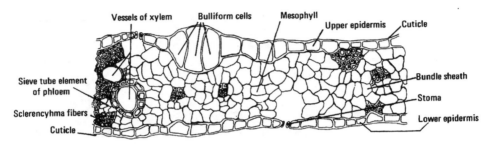

From *Botany, 5th edition,* by Carl L. Wilson, Walter E. Lomis and Taylor A. Steeves, 1971. Holt, Rinehart and Winston.

Figure 4. Cross section of dicot and monocot leaves

A major difference between the monocot leaf and dicot leaf is that dicot leaf has palisade parenchyma cells while the monocot leaf does not. The mesophyll cells of the monocot leaf are not as regularly arranged.

Characteristics and Functions of Various Leaf Cells and Tissues

1. Cuticle-Composed of a waxlike material (cutin) that acts as protection and helps prevent evaporation through the epidermal layer of the leaf. Cutin also prevents water droplets from adhering to plant leaves.

2. Epidermis-Made up of cells that act as a protective covering for the leaf.

3. The mesophyll is composed of the palisade and spongy parenchyma cells.
   a. Palisade parenchyma-cells arranged in a uniform "side by side" manner. They contain chloroplasts and are active in photosynthesis.
   b. Spongy parenchyma-Irregularly shaped cells that usually have large intercellular spaces between them. These intercellular spaces allow for gas movement in the leaf.

4. Vascular bundle-Contains the translocation tissue of the xylem and phloem.

   Xylem-Elongated pipe-like cells (non-living) conducting water and minerals, primarily upward, through the plant from the roots.

Phloem-Elongated, specialized cells (living) translocating photosynthate (sugars) and other materials in both upward and downward movement to all parts of the plant.

5. Bundle sheath-A specialized ring of cells found in some plants encompassing the vascular bundle and believed to be involved in storage of photosynthetic materials.

6. Stoma-An opening in the lower or upper surface of the leaf. Two guard cells regulate the size of the stoma, thus influencing the rate of CO_2 movement into the leaf and water evaporation from the leaf (Note Figure 5).

7. Bulliform cells-Enlarged epidermal cells (in longitudinal rows) in leaves of grasses that influence the rolling and unrolling of leaves during drought stress and leaf wilting.

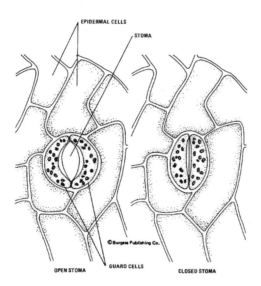

Figure 5. Stomatal apparatus in leaves

1. "Surfactants" are chemicals which help herbicides adhere to leaf surfaces. What leaf part is particularly responsible for the need of using surfactants on weedy plants?

2. Some foliar-applied herbicides are effective on certain weeds because they are translocated to the root. What specialized cells would these herbicidal chemicals move through?

3. What leaf structure is analogous to the human mouth?

B. Leaf Morphology

In many cases, it is nearly impossible to differentiate plant species without using leaf morphology. Some leaves and other plant parts have hairlike structures on the surface called pubescence. Plants with extremely dense pubescence are often damaged less by small insect feeding. Plants without pubescence are called glabrous.

Use the illustrations below to learn the important parts of grass and legume leaves.

1. Parts of the Grass Leaf

Grass leaves are simple (undivided) and have parallel veins.

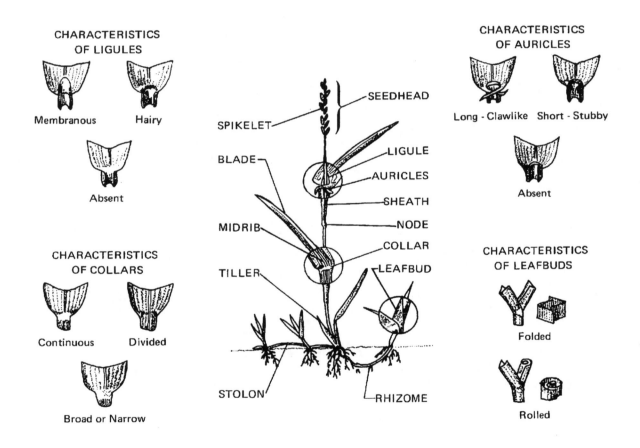

Figure 6. Parts of a grass leaf

2. Parts of the Legume Leaf

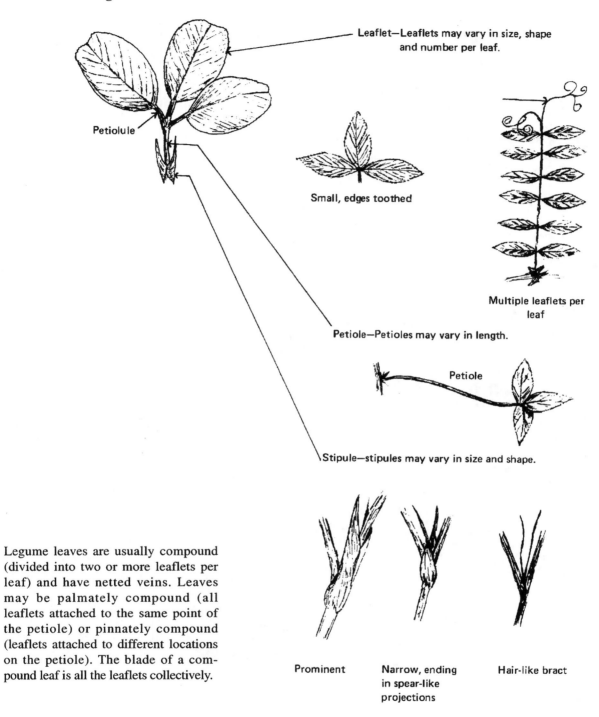

Legume leaves are usually compound (divided into two or more leaflets per leaf) and have netted veins. Leaves may be palmately compound (all leaflets attached to the same point of the petiole) or pinnately compound (leaflets attached to different locations on the petiole). The blade of a compound leaf is all the leaflets collectively.

Figure 7. Parts of a legume leaf

III. PLANT STEMS

A. Functions of Stems

1. Conduction of water and mineral solutes from the roots to other parts of the plant, primarily through the vessels of the xylem.

2. Conduction of synthesized food from the leaves to other parts of the plant, chiefly through the phloem.

3. Support of other plant organs such as leaves and flowers.

4. Storage of food materials as in sugarcane.

5. Manufacture of carbohydrates in stems containing chlorophyll.

6. Propagation of new plants.

B. Stem Anatomy

Carefully study the figures of the typical grass and legume stems on the following pages. Know how to identify and describe the various parts of the stems.

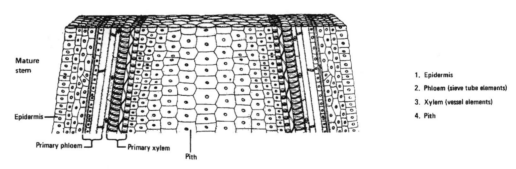

1. Epidermis
2. Phloem (sieve tube elements)
3. Xylem (vessel elements)
4. Pith

From *Botany,* Revised Edition, by Carl L. Wilson and Walter E. Loomis. Copyright 1952, © 1957 by Holt, Rinehart and Winston, Inc. Reprinted by permission of Holt, Rinehart and Winston, Inc.

Figure 8. Longitudinal section of a dicot stem (highly diagrammatic)

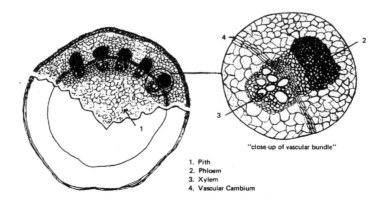

"close-up of vascular bundle"

1. Pith
2. Phloem
3. Xylem
4. Vascular Cambium

Figure 9. Dicot stem anatomy (cross section of a legume stem)

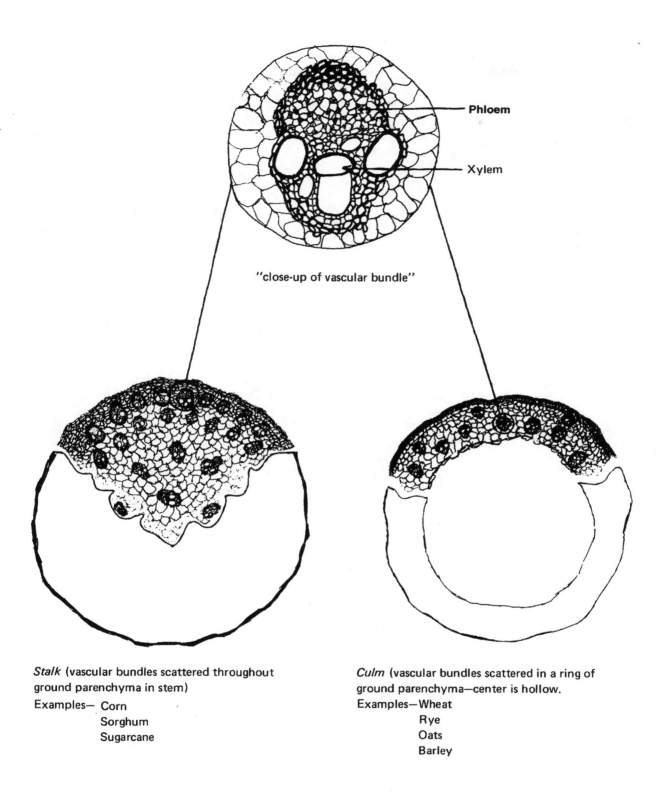

"close-up of vascular bundle"

Phloem

Xylem

Stalk (vascular bundles scattered throughout ground parenchyma in stem)

Examples— Corn
Sorghum
Sugarcane

Culm (vascular bundles scattered in a ring of ground parenchyma—center is hollow.

Examples—Wheat
Rye
Oats
Barley

Figure 10. Monocot stem anatomy (cross-section of a cereal stem)

A major difference in legume and grass stem anatomy is that legumes have a meristimatically active cambium layer that separates the phloem and xylem. The cambium usually forms a ring around the stem giving rise to new phloem on the outside of the ring and new xylem on the inside. This allows legume stems to increase in diameter.

Stem formation and elongation in legumes occurs as the terminal growing point (apical meristem) of each stem continues to form new nodes and internodes. Thus, a young legume plant will have fewer nodes and internodes than a mature plant. However, in cereal grasses, the total number of nodes and internodes is usually determined early in the life of the plant. An intercalcary meristem at the base of each node stimulates internode elongation. In favorable conditions, the grass plant will reach maximum height through internode elongation. Grasses may produce additional branches (tillers) from lower nodes near the base of the plant.

C. Modified Stems

Some plants have stems that are modified to carry out functions such as storage of food materials and/or the development of new vegetative growth and possibly new plants. Several kinds of modified stems are shown in Figure 11.

Stolon—a horizontal stem that grows above the soil surface.

Rhizome—a horizontal stem that grows below the soil surface.

bud

Tuber—an enlarged underground stem (carbohydrate storage) with buds.

Haplocorm—an enlarged internode (carbohydrate storage) at the crown of the plant.

Figure 11

V. PLANT ROOTS

Roots of plants serve to anchor the plant in the soil, to absorb minerals and water from the soil, and to transport water and minerals to the plant stem. Minerals and water are absorbed primarily through the root hairs.

Compare the different regions of a developing root, illustrated in Figure 12.

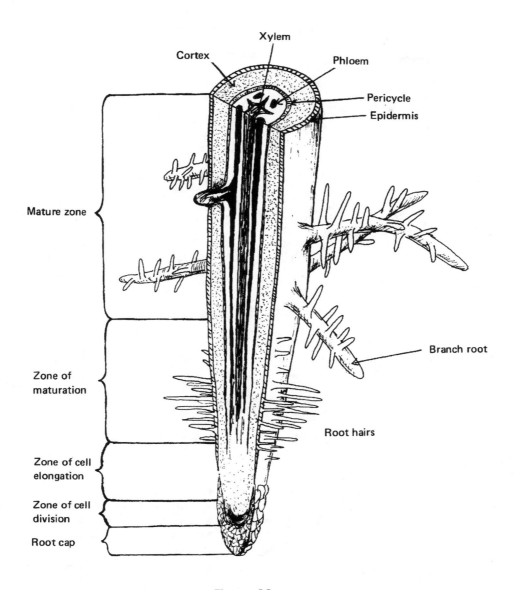

Figure 12

Root Region	Function
Root Cap	protection
Cell Division	forms new root cells
Cell Elongation	newly formed root cells expand
Maturation	cell maturation; zone of root hair formation and maximum water and mineral uptake in root
Mature	cells reach mature stage; formation of lateral (branch roots)

Grasses have fibrous roots (a root system in which the roots are finely divided) and dicotyledonous plants usually have a taproot (a tapering main root from which smaller lateral roots arise). Note Figure 13.

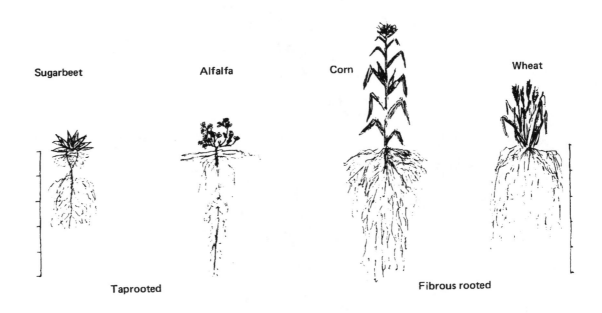

Figure 13. Root systems

VI. GRASS AND LEGUME INFLORESCENCE

Many crops depend upon seeds for the production of a new generation. These seeds are formed from florets which contain the reproductive organs of the plant. A knowledge of floral parts is important in understanding practices used for controlled pollination in developing varieties of crops or in maintaining varietal purity.

In several instances (i.e., cereal and oil seed crops) the product which is of economic value is the seed. The ultimate seed yield of a crop depends upon the number of seeds per unit of land area and upon seed size. Therefore a knowledge of the typical inflorescence of crop plants becomes of interest from the standpoint of understanding seed yield.

In addition, an understanding of the inflorescence is important from the standpoint of plant identification. Grasses and legumes can be identified by differences in seeds, florets, spikelets, or by the general inflorescence arrangement.

A. Parts of a Grass Floret

The floret of a grass plant is composed of a lemma and a palea enclosing the reproductive parts of the plant. The female portion of the floret is called the pistil (gynoecium). The pistil is composed of the stigma, style, and ovary. The ovule (egg cell) is produced in the ovary. The male portion of the floret is called the stamen. The stamen is composed of the anther and filament. The pollen grains are produced in the anther.

The following grass flower shown is perfect (i.e., has male and female parts within the floret). Imperfect flowers are missing either male or female parts. Corn is an example of a monoecious grass plant because it has imperfect flowers with both sexes located on the same plant. The corn tassel contains male flowers and the ear shoot has female flowers. A dioecious plant has imperfect flowers, with male and female flowers on separate plants. Grass flowers are incomplete. They are missing the corolla (petals).

In mature florets the ovary wall is fused to the endosperm and embryo, thus making up the complete caryopsis. The stigma, style, anther, and filament degenerate and are not noticeable in most mature flowers.

The following diagram shows the parts of a typical grass floret:

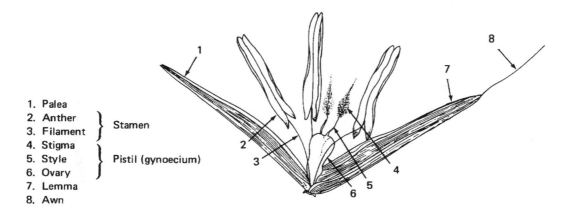

1. Palea
2. Anther ⎫
3. Filament ⎬ Stamen
4. Stigma ⎫
5. Style ⎬ Pistil (gynoecium)
6. Ovary ⎭
7. Lemma
8. Awn

B. Grass spikelet

The unit of a grass inflorescence is the spikelet. The spikelet is composed of two glumes enclosing one or more florets. The central axis of the spikelet is the rachilla.

Learn the parts of a spikelet shown in Figure 14.

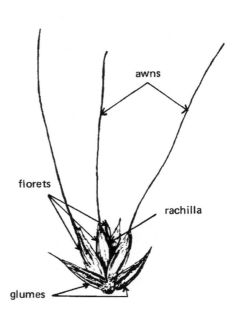

Figure 14

21

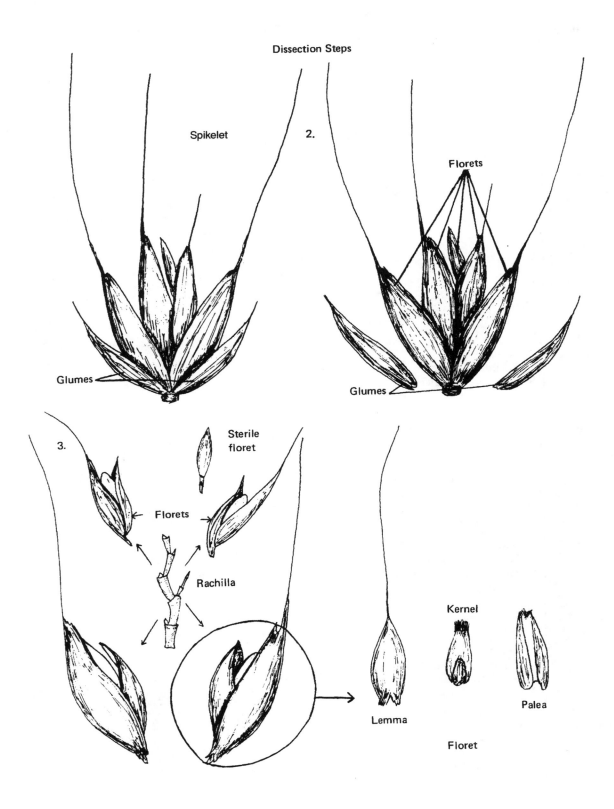

Dissection Steps

Spikelet

2.

Florets

Glumes

Glumes

3.

Sterile floret

Florets

Florets

Rachilla

Kernel

Lemma

Palea

Floret

C. Parts of a Legume Flower

The female portion of the legume flower is called the pistil (gynoecium). The pistil is composed of the stigma, style and ovary. The male portion of the legume flower is called the stamen. The stamen is composed of the anther and filament. Ten stamens are present (one free and nine fused together to form a staminal column which encloses the pistil).

The legume flower is perfect (i.e., has both male and female parts) and complete (i.e., has corolla, calyx, male parts, and female parts. The corolla has five petals: one standard petal, two wing petals and a keel petal (two united petals). The calyx consists of five sepals fused at the base. The perianth consists of corolla and calyx.

Learn to identify the essential parts of the legume flower using the diagrams:

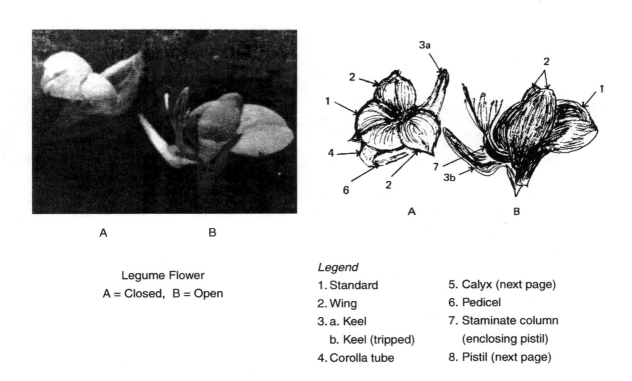

A   B

Legume Flower
A = Closed, B = Open

Legend

1. Standard	5. Calyx (next page)
2. Wing	6. Pedicel
3. a. Keel	7. Staminate column
b. Keel (tripped)	(enclosing pistil)
4. Corolla tube	8. Pistil (next page)

Figure 15

Dissection Steps

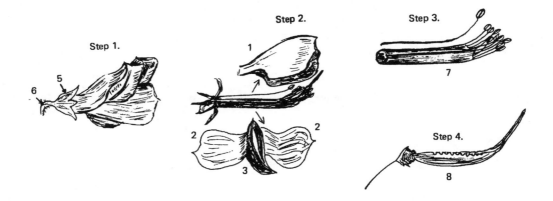

Some legumes such as peanuts have a unique flower structure (Figure 16).

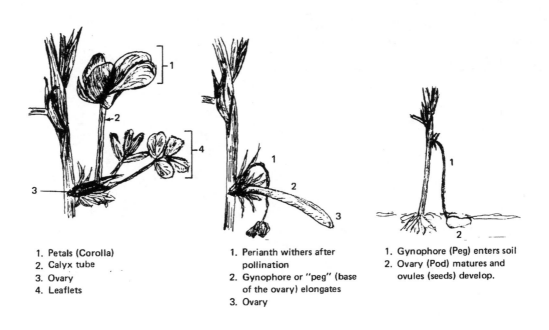

1. Petals (Corolla)
2. Calyx tube
3. Ovary
4. Leaflets

1. Perianth withers after pollination
2. Gynophore or "peg" (base of the ovary) elongates
3. Ovary

1. Gynophore (Peg) enters soil
2. Ovary (Pod) matures and ovules (seeds) develop.

Figure 16. Peanut Flower

D. Inflorescence Types

The inflorescence refers to the flowering structure of a plant. Four basic types of inflorescences commonly found in agricultural crops are: spike, raceme, panicle, and head.

1. Spike inflorescence-The spikelets are directly attached (sessile) to the central stalk of the inflorescence (rachis).

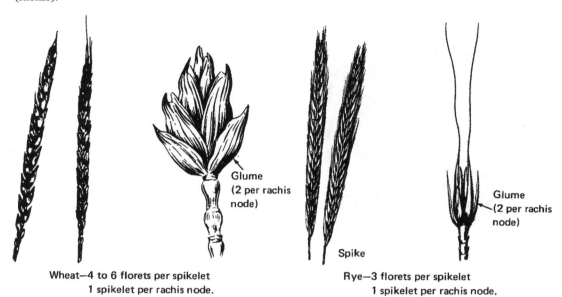

Wheat—4 to 6 florets per spikelet
1 spikelet per rachis node.

Figure 17. Wheat spike

Rye—3 florets per spikelet
1 spikelet per rachis node.

Figure 18. Rye spike

Spike   Glumes (6 per rachis node)   Spike   Glumes (6 per rachis node—
                                                                                2 Glumes are prominent

6-rowed barley
1 floret per spikelet
3 spikelets per rachis node

2-rowed barley
1 floret per spikelet
3 spikelets per rachis node (the 2 lateral spikes are empty (sterile)

Figure 19. Barley spike

2. Raceme inflorescence-The spikelets or flowers are attached to the central stalk (rachis) of the inflorescence by a small stalk called the pedicel. Examples are alfalfa, sweetclover and soybeans.

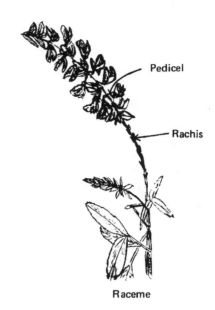

Figure 20. Raceme

3. Panicle inflorescence-The spikelets or flowers are attached to the pedicels, the pedicels are attached to a panicle branch, and the panicle branch is attached to the rachis. Examples are oats, rice, sorghum, and a corn tassel.

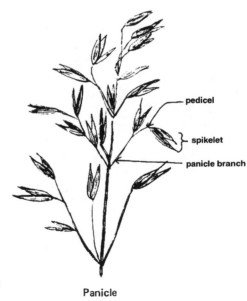

Oats
2-3 florets per
spikelet
1 spikelet per node
of panicle branch.

Figure 21

4. Head-The word "head" is a general term that is often used to refer to many inflorescence types but may be used to specifically refer to an inflorescence whose flowers are clustered and attached to an enlarged, shortened receptacle. Examples are red clover, white clover, and sunflower.

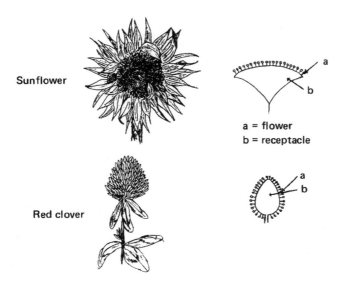

Figure 22

SELF-EVALUATION TEST

Crop Plant Anatomy

Circle letter corresponding to one best answer.

1. The function of the epicotyl is to

    a)   absorb nutrients for the cotyledons
    b)   produce the cotyledons
    c)   develop the above ground portion of the plant
    d)   push the coleoptile to the soil surface
    e)   elongate during epigeal emergence

2. The structure indicated by the arrow on the following drawing is

    a)   a cotyledon
    b)   a hypocotyl
    c)   a mesocotyl
    d)   an epicotyl
    e)   a trifoliolate leaf

3. On the following drawing, the arrow is pointing to the

    a)   seminal root
    b)   radicle
    c)   mesocotyl
    d)   crown roots
    e)   coleoptile

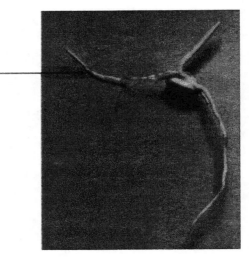

4. The following crop has epigeal emergence:

    a)   wheat
    b)   corn
    c)   barley
    d)   orchardgrass
    e)   alfalfa

5. In the following drawing, the part of the corn caryopsis indicated by the arrow is:

   a) an aleurone
   b) a flinty endosperm
   c) a starchy endosperm
   d) a pericarp
   e) a scutellum

6. The part of the grass floret indicated by the arrow is

   a) lemma
   b) palea
   c) awn
   d) pistil
   e) stamen

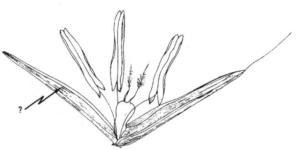

7. The flower parts making up the calyx are the

   a) petals
   b) sepals
   c) standards
   d) corolla tubes
   e) keels

8. The following statement about a legume seedling is true:

   a) The radicle develops into the fibrous root system
   b) The seminal roots develop into the fibrous root system
   c) The coronal roots develop into the primary root system
   d) The radicle and seminal roots make up the secondary root system
   e) The radicle develops into the taproot

9. The flower part indicated by the arrow is the:

   a) keel
   b) wing
   c) standard
   d) calyx
   e) stamen

29

10. The structure indicated by the arrow is:

    a) a petiole
    b) a leaflet
    c) a leaf
    d) an auricle
    e) a petiolule

?

11. A legume leaf:

    a) has parallel venation
    b) has a sheath
    c) is compound
    d) has a ligule
    e) is simple

12. Grass flowers are:

    a) incomplete because they lack the stamen
    b) imperfect because they lack the stamen
    c) incomplete because they lack the corolla
    d) complete because they have both male and female parts
    e) perfect because they have corolla, calyx, and pistil

13. The type of inflorescence shown is a:

    a) panicle
    b) spike
    c) raceme
    d) spikelet
    e) head

14. During the emergence of a corn seedling

    a) the epicotyl pushes the coleoptile upward
    b) the hypocotyl elongates, pushing the coleoptile upward
    c) the coleoptile elongates, pushing the hypocotyl upward, until it breaks the soil surface
    d) the mesocotyl is pushed upward by the coleoptile
    e) the mesocotyl elongates pushing the coleoptile upward

15. The outermost layer of a grass seed is the

    a) aleurone
    b) testa
    c) endosperm
    d) cuticle
    e) pericarp

16. The primary root system of corn functions effectively for

    a) three to four weeks
    b) eight to ten weeks
    c) the entire life of the corn plant
    d) the period from emergence to flowering
    e) one week

17. The soybean, as compared to corn seed, would

    a) have a higher percentage of starch
    b) tend to have less mechanical damage during harvesting
    c) tend to have more mechanical damage during harvesting
    d) have a lower percentage of protein
    e) have fewer cotyledons

18. The primary function of the hypocotyl of most legume seedlings is

    a) food supply
    b) anchorage
    c) photosynthesis
    d) emergence
    e) moisture absorption

19. In what floral part is pollen produced?

    a) anther
    b) pistil
    c) filament
    d) style
    e) calyx

20. The central axis of a spikelet is the:

    a) rachis
    b) pedicel
    c) panicle branch
    d) rachilla
    e) floret

21. Perfect flowers in a panicle type of inflorescence are found in which crop?

    a) corn
    b) soybeans
    c) oats
    d) sweetclover
    e) wheat

22. Sugars which are produced in corn leaves by photosynthesis are translocated to the maturing kernels primarily through the

    a) stomates
    b) esophagus
    c) phloem
    d) spongy parenchyma
    e) xylem

23. Which part of a plant is most likely to give rise to a new plant?

    a) a leaf
    b) a rhizome
    c) a sheath
    d) the culm
    e) the radicle

24. The primary structure through which carbon dioxide enters the plant is the

    a) root
    b) xylem
    c) phloem
    d) stomate
    e) ribosome

25. Root hairs develop in what region of growth in the terminal portion of the root?

    a) zone of root hairs
    b) zone of elongation
    c) zone of maturation
    d) meristematic zone
    e) apical meristem zone

Chapter 2

Crop Plant Classification and Identification

There are hundreds of thousands of different kinds of plants, each of which has a name. To the common plants in a locality we give common names. For instance, "corn" is a common name; unfortunately, "corn" refers to many different grass crops depending on the local custom. As long as people had little need or opportunity to travel from one locality to another, there was no need for a uniform system of naming plants. As knowledge increased concerning the many uses of plants and as plants were transplanted from one area to another, it became apparent that a systematic approach to the naming of the plants must be made. There are many ways of classifying plants. A few of the more important methods are described on the following pages.

I. SCIENTIFIC OR BOTANICAL SYSTEM OF CLASSIFICATION

A Swedish botanist, Carl Linnaeus, is acknowledged as the originator of this system of classification. When the system was adopted in the 18th century, Latin was the written language of science and thus the classification is in Latin. The Botanical System of Classification is given in Table 1 in a synoptic form to include only some categories of the higher plants. All crop species are classified the same from Kingdom through Division. The classification examples given for the categories from class through variety are for *Triticum aestivum* (wheat) and *Glycine max* (soybean).

Table 1. Botanical Classification*

	Kingdom	= *Plantae* ("plan-TEE")- Plants
	Division	= *Magnoliophyta* ("mag-NO-lee-oh-fy-ta") - Flowering Plants
Lilliopsida ("lilly-OP-sah-dah") - Monocot Plants (one cotyledon per seed; parallel veined leaves)	Class	*Magnoliopsida* ("mag-NO-lee-op-sah-dah") - Dicot Plants (two cotyledons per seed; net veined leaves)
Commelinidae ("COM-ah-lin-ah-dee")	Subclass	*Rosidae* ("ROSE-a-dee")
Cyperales ("cy-per-A-lees")	Order	*Rosales* ("rose-A-lees")
Poaceae (Gramineae) ("po-ACE-see-ee") ("gra-MEN-ah-ee")	Family	*Fabaceae (Leguminoseae)* ("fah-BAY-see-ee") ("lay-GUME-in-os-ah-ee")
Triticum ("TRIT-tee-cum")	Genus	*Glycine* ("gly-SEE-nee")
aestivum ("ee-STY-vum")	Species	*max* ("MAX")
vulgare ("vul-GAY-ray")	Subspecies	none
Nugaines	Variety	Corsoy

*No system of classification can be final as long as we are increasing our knowledge of plants. This classification system is thought to represent newer and more natural relationships among plant species discovered in recent years.

A. Important Crop Families

It has been estimated that there are approximately a quarter of a million species of flowering plants, of which nearly 4/5ths are classified as dicots (includes the legume crops) and 1/5th are classified as monocots (includes the grass crops). Within the dicot and monocot classes, there are many plant families represented by the numerous crop species. Of these, the grass *(Poaceae)* and legume *(Fabaceae)* families are by far the most important in food production. Wheat, rice, maize, and barley in the *Poaceae* family collectively account for nearly one-half of the world's total food production. There are approximately 15,000 species in the legume family and 8,000 in the grass family. Some important crop families with the common names of some crops belonging to each are given in Table 2.

Table 2. Important crop families

---

1. *Fabaceae (Leguminoseae)*-("fah-BAY-see-ee"; "lay-GUME-in-os-ah-ee") - Bean or Legume family: nitrogen fixing legumes, e.g., alfalfa, beans, clover, pea, peanut, soybean
2. *Poaceae (Gramineae)*-("po-ACE-see-ee"; "gra-MEN-ah-ee") - Grass family: e.g., maize, rice, sorghum, sugarcane, timothy
3. *Brassicaceae (Cruciferae)*-("BRASS-sah-kay-see-ee"; cru-SIF-fer-ee") - Mustard family: e.g., cabbage, mustard, rape
4. *Solanaceae*-("so-lan-ACE-see-ee") - Nightshade or Potato family: e.g., potato, tobacco, tomato
5. *Chenopodiaceae*-("CHIN-ah-po-dee-ace-see-ee") - Goosefoot family: e.g., sugarbeet, mangel
6. *Linaceae*-("lye-NACE-see-ee") - Flax family: e.g., flax
7. *Polygonaceae*-(po-lig-o-NACE-see-ee") - Buckwheat family: e.g., buckwheat
8. *Asteraceae (Compositae)*-(aster-ACE-see-ee"; com-PAUSE-eh-tee") - Sunflower family: e.g., safflower, sunflower
9. *Malvaceae*-("mal-VACE-see-ee") - Mallow family: e.g., cotton, kenaf
10. *Cannabaceae*-("can-nah-BACE-see-ee") - Hemp family: e.g., hemp
11. *Liliaceae*-("lil-lee-ACE-see-ee") - Lily family: e.g., garlic, onion
12. *Convolvulaceae*-("con-volve-vue-LACE-see-ee") - Morning Glory family: e.g., Sweet potato
13. *Cucurbitaceae*-("cue-curr-bit-TACE-see-ee") - Cucumber family: e.g., cucumber, squash, melon crops
14. *Apiaceae (Umbelliferae)*-("a-pea-ACE-see-ee"; "um-bell-LIFF-fer-ee") - Carrot or Parsley family: e.g., carrot, celery

---

B. The Binomial System of Naming Plants

In addition to developing a system for botanical classification of plants, Linnaeus is also given credit for establishing a system of binomial nomenclature for plants. In this system, the name of every plant consists of a genus name, listed first, and a species name, listed second. Genus is a taxonomic grouping of closely related plants but the group can be further divided into smaller categories called species based on more specific plant characteristics. The generic name is always capitalized, while the species name is not. Both names are always italicized or underlined. The name (or abbreviation of the name) of the person(s) name making the classification follows the species' name. There are usually many species belonging to the same genus. The genus and species names of some important crop plants are listed in Table 3.

Table 3. Some important crops and their scientific names

Common name	Genus	Species	Classifier
Cereals and Grains:			
Barley*	Hordeum	vulgare	L.
Buckwheat	Fagopyrum	esculentum (syn. F. sagittatum Gilib.)	Moench
Millet,*			
Common (Proso)	Panicum	milliaceum	L.
Finger	Eleusine	coracana	L.
Foxtail	Setaria	italica	(L) Beauv.
Pearl	Pennisetum	americanum	(L.) Leeke
Maize (corn)*	Zea	mays	L.
Oats (common)*	Avena	sativa	L.
Rice*	Oryza	sativa	L.
Rye*	Secale	cereale	L.
Sorghum (grain)*	Sorghum	bicolor	(L.) Moench
Wheat (common)*	Triticum	aestivum	L.
Oil and Protein:			
Bean (common or field bean)	Phaseolus	vulgaris	L.
Broadbean	Vicia	faba	L.
Castorbean	Ricinus	communis	L.
Chickpea	Cicer	arietinum	L.
Cowpea	Vigna	unguiculata	(L.) Walp.
Field pea	Pisum	sativum	L.
Flax	Linum	usitatissimum	L.
Lentil	Lens	culinaris	Medik.
Lima Bean	Phaseolus	lunatus	L.
Mungbean	Vigna	radiata	(L.) Wilczek
Peanut	Arachis	hypogaea	L.
Pigeonpea	Cajanus	cajan	(L.) Millsp.
Rape, Oilseed	Brassica	napus	Koch
Safflower	Carthamus	tinctorius	L.
Sesame	Sesamum	indicum	L.
Soybean*	Glycine	max	(L.) Merr.
Sunflower	Helianthus	annuus	L.
Root and Tuber:			
Cassava*	Manihot	esculenta	Crantz
Potato*	Solanum	tuberosum	L.
Sweet Potato*	Ipomoea	batatas	L.
Yams*	Dioscorea	spp.	
Sugar:			
Sugarbeet*	Beta	vulgaris	L.
Sugarcane*	Saccharum	officinarum	L.
Fiber:			
Cotton	Gossypium	hirsutum	L.
Flax Linum	usitatissimum		L.
Hemp	Cannabis	sativa	L.
Jute	Corchorus	capsularis	L.
Kenaf	Hibiscus	cannabinus	L.
Sisal	Agave	sisalana	Perr.
Drug/Medicinal:			
Ginseng	Panax	quinquefolius	L.
Hemp (marijuana)	Cannabis	sativa	L.
Tobacco	Nicotiana	tabacum	L.

332 7840

Forage Legumes:			
Alfalfa	Medicago	sativa	L.
Alsike Clover	Trifolium	hybridum	L.
Birdsfoot Trefoil	Lotus	corniculatus	L.
Crimson Clover	Trifolium	incarnatum	L.
Crownvetch	Coronilla	varia	L.
Hairy Vetch	Vicia	villosa	Roth
Korean Lespedeza	Lespedeza	stipulacea	Maxim
Ladino (White) Clover	Trifolium	repens	L.
Red Clover	Trifolium	pratense	L.
Sweetclover (yellow)	Melilotus	officinalis	(L.) Pall.
Forage Grasses:			
Cool Season Species:			
Bromegrass, Smooth	Bromus	inermis	Leyss.
Crested Wheatgrass	Agropyron	desertorum	(Fisch) Schult.
Kentucky Bluegrass	Poa	pratensis	L.
Orchardgrass	Dactylis	glomerata	L.
Reed Canarygrass	Phalaris	arundinacea	L.
Ryegrass, Italian (annual)	Lolium	multiflorum	Lam.
Ryegrass, Perennial	Lolium	perenne	L.
Tall Fescue	Festuca	arundinacea	L.
Timothy	Phleum	pratense	L.
Western Wheatgrass	Agropyron	smithii	Rydlb.
Warm Season Species:			
Bahiagrass	Paspalum	notatum	Flugge
Bermudagrass	Cynodon	dactylon	(L) Pers.
Big Bluestem	Andropogon	gerardi	Vitm.
Blue Grama	Bouteloua	gracilis	(H.B.K.) Lag.
Buffalograss	Buchloe	dactyloides	Engelm.
Carpetgrass	Axonopus	affinis	
Dallisgrass	Paspalum	dilatatum	Poir
Guineagrass	Panicum	maximum	Jacq.
Indiangrass	Sorgastrum	nutans	(L.) Nash
Little Bluestem	Schizachyrium	scoparium	(Michx.) Nash
Napiergrass (Elephantgrass)	Pennisetum	clandestinum	Hochst.
Pangolagrass	Digitaria	decumbens	Stent.
Rhodesgrass	Chloris	gayana	Kunth
Sorghum (forage)	Sorghum	bicolor	(L.) Moench
Side-oats grama	Bouteloua	curtipendula	Torr.
Sudangrass	Sorghum	bicolor var.sudanense	(Piper) Hitchc.
Switchgrass	Panicum	virgatum	L.

*Most important food crops on a world production basis. The leguminous grain crops (including lentil, peanut, and the various bean and pea crops) collectively constitute a major important group. The top five world food crops in ranked order are wheat(1), rice(2), maize(3), potato(4), and barley(5).

C. Other Categories of Life

Taxonomy (the science and study of biological classification) continues to evolve as new knowledge in biological diversity and similarity are gained. Taxonomists (those who study taxonomy) have proposed different classification schemes and continually revise or adapt existing ones. Previously, taxonomists felt that all living things could be classified into two kingdoms, plant and animal. Now, many taxonomists classify earth's organisms into 5 kingdoms: Monera-bacteria, Protista-protozoa and algae, Fungi-true fungi, Plantae-plants, and Animalia-multicellular animals (insects/worms/mammals). Characteristics of the different categories of life, in addition to the plant and animal kingdoms, are given below.

MONERA—Kingdom for bacteria (prokaryotes, i.e. unicellular organisms that are made up of a prokaryotic cell). Prokaryotic cells have simple interior organization, lack internal compartmentalization and membrane-bound organelles like mitochondria or chloroplasts, and reproduce by simple cell division (binary fission). All other kingdoms have eukaryotic cells (more advanced, highly organized, and compartmentalized cells that organize DNA into chromosomes). Bacteria are the most abundant organisms on earth and are found in most environments. Monera includes non-photosynthetic bacteria and the photosynthetic cyanobacteria (formerly called blue-green algae). Bacteria are usually saprophytes (obtain their essential life needs from dead or dying tissue) or parasites (obtain their essential life needs from living tissue). Bacteria have an important effect on crop production in the following ways:

1. in ecological recycling, such as nutrient recycling and the biological breakdown of crop residue, pesticides, and wastes
2. as causative agents for plant diseases
3. in the improvement of soil structure through organic matter decomposition
4. in nitrogen fixation (conversion of atmospheric nitrogen to organic nitrogen)
5. as disease organisms of insects and weeds, thereby acting in their natural control (biological control)

PROTISTA—Includes unicellular and multicellular eukaryotic organisms of algae and other organisms. Taxonomic classification of multicellular algae is not uniform; some classify multicellular algae under Protista and others under the Plantae kingdom. Most taxonomists agree that protista are intermediate ancestors between prokaryotes and the higher eukaryotic organisms of plants, animals, and fungi. Protista species include non-photosynthetic and photosynthetic organisms and commonly occur in moist or aquatic environments as pond scum, seaweeds of fresh or salt water, and marine plankton. Green algae is believed to be the ancestor of plants. Algae are especially important as the basis of the food chain and overall health of aquatic ecosystems.

FUNGI—Includes unicellular and multicellular eukaryotic organisms of fungi. Fungi do not conduct photosynthesis; can be saprophytes or parasites; and reproduce by fission, by budding (forming a small cell from a larger one), or by spores borne on fruiting structures. The fungal kingdom includes molds, yeasts, mushrooms, and many species that cause plant diseases. Fungi have important effects on crop production in the following ways:

1. in ecological recycling, such as nutrient recycling and the biological breakdown of crop residue, pesticides, and wastes (fungi, together with bacteria are the principal decomposers on earth)
2. as causative agents for many plant diseases
3. in the improvement of soil structure through organic matter decomposition
4. in the natural control of insects and weeds by acting as disease organisms
5. in food utilization through positive (flavor enhancement and food products) and negative (spoilage) ways
6. in improvement of soil mineral uptake by plants through mycorrhizal association (a symbiotic association of fungi and roots that enhances the root absorption capacity of many crop species)

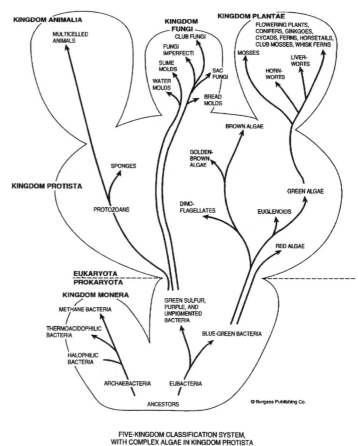

FIVE-KINGDOM CLASSIFICATION SYSTEM, WITH COMPLEX ALGAE IN KINGDOM PROTISTA

VIRUSES—Viruses are an anomaly in biological classification schemes. Many taxonomists classify viruses as non-living because viruses act as inert chemicals outside living cells and only reproduce through an infected host cell. On this basis, viruses are not included in a biological classification scheme; however, they are agriculturally important in the following ways:

1. as causative agents for plant diseases
2. in natural control of insects, weeds, and plant diseases by acting as causative agents of diseases

II. PLACE OF ORIGIN

Closely associated with the botanical classification of plants is their place of geographic origin. The study of plant origin is still very much subject to conjecture and revision. Professor Nikolai Vavilov of Russia advanced the art and science of plant origin more than any single scientist through the use of a very extensive world collection of plants. He postulated that any geographic area possessing a wide diversity of plant types within a species would very likely be the center or origin of that species. With this and other criteria he identified eight centers of origin in the world. These centers, with a species originating in each of them, are given in Table 4.

Table 4. Vavilov's Centers of Origin

Center of Origin	Some Species of the Center
1. Chinese	Soybean
2. Indian	Rice
3. Central Asia	Wheat
4. Middle East	Alfalfa and Small Grains
5. Mediterranean	White Clover
6. Ethiopia	Sorghum
7. Central America	Maize
8. South America	Potato

Other scientists have disagreed with Vavilov as to whether a center of diversity is really the center of origin for a species. Another point of disagreement has been related to the reasons for the existence of the primary and secondary centers of origin. The important thing, from a practical standpoint, is that we know where the centers of diversity are located. These centers of diversity contain a wealth of genetic material that could possibly be used for improved crop varieties in the future. Some characters of crop plants that have already been improved by using plants collected in centers of diversity in breeding programs include: disease resistance, insect resistance, improved quality, and increased yield.

Two broad categories used in classifying plants on the basis of origin are:

Indigenous-plants that are native to the area in question and have evolved as a natural component of that particular environment.
Exotic-plants that have been intentionally or unintentionally introduced into the area in question.

Most of the major crops in the United States are exotic. Some forage species such as western wheatgrass, the bluestems, and buffalograss are native to the U.S.A. Several important crops like corn and beans originated in Central and South America. Table 5 is a partial listing of the many species that are native to the Western Hemisphere.

Table 5. Some Species Native to the Western Hemisphere

Big Bluestem	Eastern Gamagrass	Sand Bluestem
Blue Grama	Gourd	Sand Lovegrass
Blue Wild Indigo	Indiangrass	Sideouts Grama
Brazil Nut	Lima Bean	Silver Bluestem
Buffalograss	Little Bluestem	Sisal
Caco	Maize (corn)	Sunflower
Canada Wild Rye	Papaya	Sweet Potato
Cashew	Peanut	Switchgrass
Common Bean	Pepper	Tobacco
Compassplant	Pineapple	Tomato
Cotton	Potato	Western Wheatgrass
Curly Mesquite	Pumpkin	Wild Strawberry

III. CLASSIFICATION BY AGRONOMIC USE

Crops are grown for many purposes other than their economic value alone. Farmers may use sweetclover as a green manure crop to build up the organic matter and nutrient status of the soil. Oats may be used as a companion crop to control weeds during the establishment of a meadow. Other crop species may be used as a cover crop to help protect the soil from erosion or to provide a better habitat for wildlife. One crop may be grown for several purposes and thus, has several different agronomic classifications. For example, maize can be classified as a cereal, forage, silage, greenchop, and trap crop depending on its use. Crops can be classified according to on- and off-farm use; soybeans can be called a grain crop (on-farm use) and an oil crop (processing use).

There are also different classification terms that describe how crops are agronomically used in different cropping systems (the yearly sequence and arrangement of crops grown on a field). For instance in a double cropping system, soybeans may be used as a double crop in a field of wheat. A list of some important use categories is found in Table 6.

Table 6. Classification of Crop Plants and Cropping Systems

A. **Grain**-any crop grown for its seed for animal feed or human food. Example: beans, buckwheat, flax, maize and the other cereals.

    1. **Cereal**-grass species used for its edible seeds (therefore, buckwheat is a grain but not a cereal, because it is not a grass). Example: barley, grain sorghum, oats, maize.

    2. **Small Grains**-small-seeded species of grain crops. Example: most frequently refers to barley, oats, rye, and wheat but can refer to other small seeded grain crops such as rice and flax.

    3. **Pulse**-legumes species grown for their edible seed. Also called food or grain legumes. Example: chickpea, cowpea, field bean, peanut, soybean.

B. **Forage**-any crop whose vegetative matter, fresh or preserved, is fed to animals.

    1. **Hay**-the herbage (vegetative portion) of grasses and legumes or comparatively fine stemmed plants cut and cured (dried) for forage. Example: alfalfa cut, cured, and baled or stacked.

    2. **Silage**-forage preserved in a succulent condition by partial fermentation in a tight container. Example: maize cut and ensiled (process of making silage).

    a) Haylage-low moisture silage. Example: Ensiling alfalfa at low moisture.

    3. **Greenchop**-a crop grown to be cut and fed in a fresh or green condition (transported to animals immediately after cutting). Sometimes referred to as soilage, soiling crop, and zero grazing. Example: alfalfa and maize used for greenchop.

Table 6. Classification of Crop Plants and Cropping Systems (continued)

C. **Specific Use**- Classifications according to intended use

1. **Catch**-usually refers to crops that replace planned crops that have failed because of pre- or post-plant conditions. Sometimes called emergency crops. Example:buckwheat, early maturing soybean, or sorghum.

2. **Companion ("Nurse")**- a crop that is sown with another crop that is slow to establish and grow. Used to help control soil erosion and weed growth. Example: oats, barley, wheat, or flax.

3. **Cover**-crops grown to protect soil against erosion, leaching of nutrients, and/or to provide cover for wildlife. Example: establishing a cover crop on exposed land.

4. **Supplementary**-usually refers to a crop grown to increase production in unfavorable periods. Example: Sudangrass, millet, etc. grown to supplement forage production during an anticipated hot and dry period of the growing season.

5. **Green Manure**-any crop incorporated in the soil to improve soil fertility and organic matter content. Example: forage legumes such as alfalfa, clovers, etc. are frequently used.

6. **Seed**-any crop grown to produce seed for planting purposes. Example: Wheat grown for next year's planting seed.

7. **Trap**-a crop used to attract certain insects or parasites. Example: a border of early planted maize (trap crop) surrounding a later planted maize crop.

8. **Oil**-Crops grown for their oil content and oil properties. Examples: canola, castorbean, flax, peanuts, safflower, soybean, sunflower.

9. **Rubber**-crops grown for producing rubber . Example: guayule, hevea.

10. **Fiber**-crops grown for paper and textile industries. Examples: cotton, hemp, flax, ramie.

11. **Root and Tuber**-crops whose desirable food product is in the root or tuber. Example: tubers-Jerusalem artichoke, potato, and yam; roots-cassava, sweetpotato.

12. **Sugar**-sugar producing crops whose juice contains high amounts of sucrose (table sugar). Examples: sugarcane, sugarbeet, sweet sorghum (sorgo) for syrup.

13. **Drug/Medicinal/Stimulant**-any crop grown whose extracts are used for drug, medicinal or stimulant purposes. Example: coffee, hops, medicinal herbs, mustard, peppermint, tea, tobacco.

14. **Biofuel**-crops grown to produce fuel. Crops may be used in direct combustion (e.g., burning wood or crop residue for heating) or by converting to liquid fuel (e.g., producing ethanol and methanol from maize).

D. **Classifications and Terms Used in Cropping Systems**

Pertaining To Crop Selection Across Years:

1. **Crop Rotation**-the yearly and planned succession of crops grown on a field over several years. Example: a 4-year rotation of maize-soybean-alfalfa-alfalfa. Rotations may include a year of fallow.

2. **Fallow**-land that is uncropped and maintained free of weedy growth to conserve soil moisture and soil fertility for next year's crop; term used in describing cropping systems and/or rotations. Example: a crop rotation of wheat-fallow-wheat-fallow.

3. **Monoculture**-repeatedly growing the same crop on the same field. Also called continuous cropping. Example: a field planted to sorghum for 4 successive years.

Pertaining To Arrangement and Management of Crops in a Field:

1. **Sole (single) cropping**-a single (sole) crop grown exclusively on a field during the year or growing season. Example: a field planted entirely to peanuts.

2. **Multiple cropping**-growing 2 or more crops on the same field within the same year or growing season; a more intensive cropping system (in time and space) than sole cropping. Multiple cropping can be further divided into two main categories:
   a) **Sequential Cropping**—growing 2 or more crops in sequence (i.e. no overlap of life cycles) on the same field in the same year or growing season. Example: **double cropping** (2 crops in sequence/field/year), **triple cropping**, etc. and **ratoon cropping** (growing crops that allow multiple, separate harvests)

Table 6. Classification of Crop Plants and Cropping Systems (continued)

b) **Intercropping**—simultaneously growing 2 or more crops during all or part of their life cycles on the same field; opposite of sole cropping. Includes the following types of intercropping systems: **Mixed** (no distinct rows), **Row** (at least one or more crops grown in rows), **Strip** (crops grown in narrow, alternating strips), and **Relay** (a second crop is planted in the field after the first crop flowers but before it is harvested i.e. an overlap of life cycles).

IV. LIFE CYCLE

The life cycles of plants provide us with a simple yet universal means of plant classification. All higher plants can be classified as annuals, winter annuals, biennials, or perennials.

Annuals-complete their entire life cycle (from seed to seed) and then die within a year. Annuals can be further subdivided into spring, summer, and winter annuals.

Spring Annuals-primarily utilize spring months for growth and maturation. Harvest may be completed during early summer. Examples: spring barley, oats, spring rye, spring wheat

Summer Annuals-primarily utilize summer months for growth and maturation. May be planted in late spring and harvested in fall months. Examples: corn, peanuts, sorghum, soybeans

Winter Annuals-utilize parts of two growing seasons in completing their life cycle. They are planted in the fall, vernalized (cold temperature exposure that induces flowering and seed production in some plants) during the winter, and produce seed and die the following summer. Examples: winter barley, winter rye, winter wheat

Biennials-normally require two full growing seasons to complete their life cycle. Vegetative growth occurs during the first season primarily as a rosette (low growing circular cluster of leaves). Vernalization occurs during the winter and flowering and seed production occur in the second season. Examples: carrot, sugarbeet, sweetclover, turnip

Perennials-have an indefinite life period and may live several or many years. They differ from the other life patterns in that they do not die after reproduction. Some perennials continue to add new growth each year, such as coffee and cacao trees; others regenerate new vegetative growth each year from plant reserves, such as alfalfa and orchardgrass.

The life cycle of a species is one of the factors that determines its use in a cropping system. How a crop is used in a cropping system may depend upon how it "fits in" with other crops. For instance, in latitudes with long growing seasons, a winter annual may be planted in autumn and harvested in May or June. Then a summer annual, such as an early maturing soybean variety, can be planted to produce a seed crop before frost occurs in autumn. The life cycle of a crop species may also be used to help in the control of plant pests, such as weeds. A winter annual or perennial crop can be used in a rotation with annual crop species in order to control annual weed species that are problems in the annual crops.

The climate of a region may also influence the growth of crops with different life cycles. For example, on a botanical basis, cotton is a perennial and may be grown as such in tropical climates; but, it is usually grown as an annual in temperate regions.

What would be the advantages of using perennial crops, rather than annual crops, whenever possible in our modern cropping systems?

V. IDENTIFICATION OF COMMON CROP PLANTS AND SEEDS

It is sometimes necessary to identify crop plants when they are in the vegetative stage and the inflorescence is not present. In other instances a need arises to identify only the seed of a plant when no vegetative parts are present. Plant identification becomes much easier when vegetative parts, inflorescence, and seed are present. However, the agronomist is seldom faced with conditions which are this ideal. In this section morphological traits that are useful in the identification of broadleaf and grass plants will be reviewed, followed by a general description of common crop plants.

A. Vegetative Plant Identification Characteristics—Broadleaf Plants*

1. Crop plant leaves have been previously described in Chapter 1 as having:

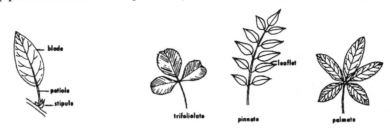

Simple Leaf   Compound Leaves

2. Some common leaf blade or leaflet shapes are:

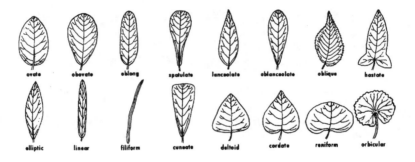

3. Leaf blades or margins are described as follows:

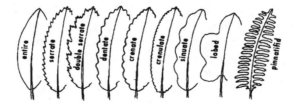

4. Common types of leaf attachments are:

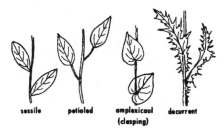

5. The two following leaf arrangements are commonly encountered:

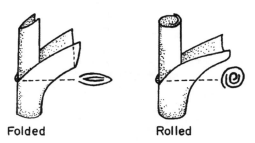

B. Vegetative Plant Identification Characteristics—Grass Plants

1. Vernation - Grass leaves may be rolled or folded in the growing point (bud-shoot).

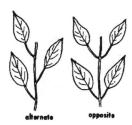

2. Sheath - The sheath is the tubular portion of the leaf that encloses the stem or the leaves that have not yet unrolled. The sheath is usually one of the following forms:

3. Ligule— The ligule is a plant part located on the inside of the leaf at the junction of the blade and sheath. The ligule may be membranous, a fringe of hair or absent as illustrated below:

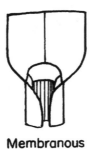
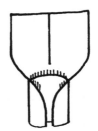

Absent   **Membranous**   **Fringe of Hairs**

The shape of the ligule may be:

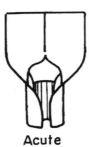
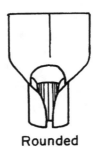
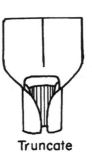

Acuminate   **Acute**   **Rounded**   **Truncate**

4. Auricles—Auricles are clawlike projections that are fastened to the leaf at the junction of the blade and sheath. The auricles extend partially around the stem, often in a clasping manner. Auricles are usually described as being:

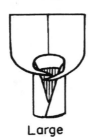
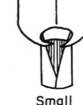

Large   **Small**   **Absent**

C. **Common Flower Types***

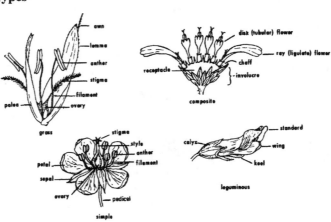

44

D. Inflorescence Types*

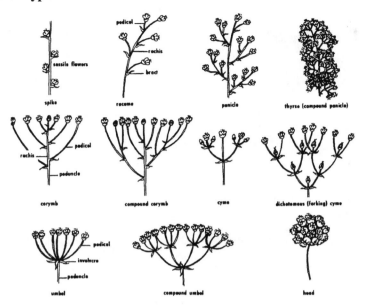

*Figures C. and D. are from: Agriculture Handbook No. 366. 1970, 1976. Selected Weeds of the United States. Agricultural Research Service, United States Department of Agriculture. Descriptions and distribution maps by Clyde F. Reed, research botanist and plant explorer, ARS. Drawings by Regina O. Hughes, scientific illustrator, ARS.

E. Common Field Crops

1. Cereals:
Poaceae (Gramineae) Family

MAIZE (CORN)
Zea mays ("ZEE-uh; MAIZE")

Life cycle - Annual.

Stem - Conspicuous nodes; solid stem (not hollow).

Flower type - Incomplete and imperfect (monoecious-female and male parts at different positions on same plant.)

Roots - Fibrous secondary root system. May extend to a depth of 1 meter or more.

CORN TYPES
Differences are due to:
1. Color in:
   a. pericarp (red, colorless)
   b. aleurone layer (blue, colorless)
   c. Endosperm (yellow, white)
2. Type of endosperm-When a cross section is made of seed, the following can be observed:
   a. Dent corn-flinty endosperm along sides and shoulder, starchy endosperm in the center and near the dent area.
   b. Flinty corn and popcorn-outer perimeter of flinty endosperm.
   c. Flour corn-primarily starchy endosperm, little or no flinty endosperm.
   d. Sweet corn-sugary endosperm results in wrinkled caryopsis when mature and air-dry.

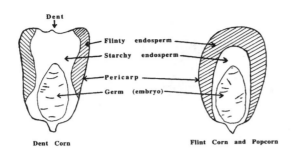

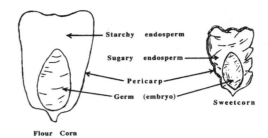

GRAIN SORGHUM

Sorghum bicolor ("SORE-gum; BYE-color")

Life cycle–Annual.

Use– Usually used as a feed grain.

Leaves–Alternate.

Stem–Conspicuous nodes, Solid stem, 60-150 cm tall, 0 to several tillers.

Inflorescence–Panicle, 10-50 cm long, 4-20 cm wide, with few to many branches.

Flower type– Incomplete and perfect, with 2 florets per spikelet-the upper fertile and the lower usually sterile.

Roots– Fibrous 1-3 m deep, with absorption about twice as efficient as corn.

Grain Sorghum

SMALL GRAINS: BARLEY, OATS, RYE, AND WHEAT

General Characteristics of Small Grains:

Trait	Species			
	Barley	Oats	Rye	Wheat
Winter Hardiness	++	+	++++	+++
Inflorescence*	Spike	Panicle	Spike	Spike
Life Cycle	Spring or Winter Annual			
Flower Type	Incomplete and Perfect			
Stem Type	Culm (hollow stem)			
Root Type	Fibrous; reaching depths of 1 to 1.5 m			

*See Chapter 1 for visual comparisons of inflorescences

VEGETATIVE COMPARISONS

Oats - No auricle
  Large ligule
  Pubescence (hairs) at base of leaf blade

Barley - Large clasping auricles
  Small ligule
  Waxy coating on leaves

Wheat - Medium-sized auricles
  Rounded ligules

Rye - Short or small-sized auricles which are not pubescent
  Sheath is pubescent
  Ligules are small

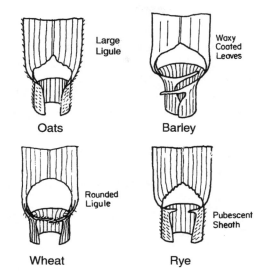

WHEAT
Common wheat-*Triticum aestivum* ssp. *vulgare*
("TRIT-tee-cum; ee-STY-vum; subspecies vul-GAY-ray")
Durum wheat-*Triticum durum* ("TRIT-tee-cum; DUR-um")

Common wheat (*T. aestivum* ssp. *vulgare*) includes the major classes or types of wheat: Hard Red Spring, Hard Red Winter, Soft Red Winter, and White wheat. Durum wheat (*T. durum*) is the other major type. The seed characteristics in the following illustrations are those which should be observed in differentiating between the wheat types.

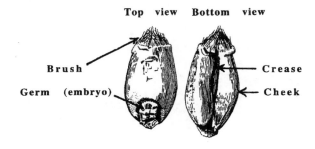

Points to consider in differentiating between hard red winter and hard red spring wheats:
  1. Hard red winter wheat has a larger germ area.
  2. Hard red spring wheat is usually shorter and fatter.
  3. Hard red spring wheat has a larger brush area.
  4. Both have hard starch and are vitreous (glasslike). Hard red spring wheat is usually more vitreous, indicating higher quality.
  5. Hard red spring wheat has a more open crease.

Uses: Both are high in protein and used for bread making. They are known as the 'bread wheats".

Points to consider in differentiating between soft red winter and hard red winter wheats:
  1. Soft red winter wheat usually has smaller brush area.
  2. Soft red winter wheat usually has rounder "cheeks" when viewed from end of seed and a more yellow-orange tint.
  3. When seeds are cut in half and compared, soft red winter wheat has more soft white starch and hard red winter has more vitreous, hard starch.

Uses:
1. Soft red winter-pastry flour, crackers, cake (low in protein).
2. Hard red winter-bread making (higher in protein).

Points to consider in differentiating between white and durum wheats:
1. Durum seeds are larger, longer, more tapered, and arched or curved in the mid-section.
2. When seeds are cut in half and compared, it can be seen that:

   a. Durum is flinty and almost translucent (vitreous, glassy).

   b. White wheat is white and starchy.
3. Durum wheat has no brush.

Uses:
1. White wheat is used in pastries, cake flours, and breakfast cereals.
2. Durum wheat is used in spaghetti, macaroni, etc.

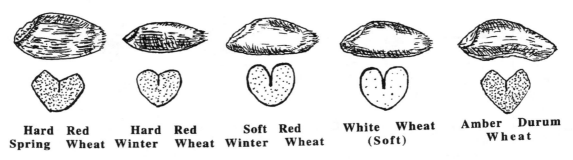

| Hard Red Spring Wheat | Hard Red Winter Wheat | Soft Red Winter Wheat | White Wheat (Soft) | Amber Durum Wheat |

Classes of Wheat - Top View and cross-sectional view

BARLEY
Hordeum vulgare ("HOR-dee-um; vul-GAY-ray")

Two major types of barley are Two-row (*H. distichum*) and six-row (*H. vulgare*) barley. The inflorescences of each can be distinguished according to the number of rows of kernels arranged laterally on the spike. Six-row barley has three developed spikelets at each node on both sides of the rachis while two-row has only one developed spikelet per node on each side of the rachis. Most commonly grown barleys produce seed with tightly attached hulls (lemma and palea remain attached to the caryopsis after harvesting).

Barley seeds are identified by the following characteristics:
1. Shape–normally, six-row barley produces two-thirds of the seed with curved narrow ends; two-row barley produces more uniform, non-curved seeds.
2. Color– yellow or white (common colors) or black.
3. Awned– hooded or smooth.

   Awned–nonbranched projection from tip of lemma.

   Hooded– pointed, forked, or branched projection from tip of lemma.

   Smooth–no projection from lemma (smooth-awnless).
4. Hulless–(lemma or palea not attached to kernel). Hulless (naked) kernels may be confused with wheat, but in contrast to wheat kernels, barley kernels:

   a. have no brush.

   b. are pointed at both ends.

   Uses: Feed, malting.

48

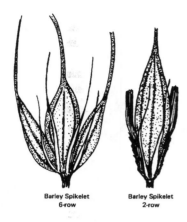

Barley Spikelet
6-row

Barley Spikelet
2-row

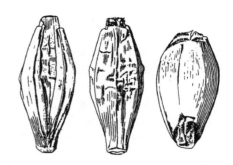

Barley Seed and Kernel
(Iowa State University Seed Science Center)

RYE
Secale cereale ("seh-KAY-lee; sear-ee-A-lee")

There are winter and spring annual types of rye. The winter-hardy varieties of winter rye are the hardiest of the common cereal crops. Kernel characteristics are generally similar among spring and winter annual types. Rye kernels can be distinguished from wheat and other cereal seed using embryo and seed shape and kernel color. Rye kernels have:

1. Pointed embryos and long, narrow kernels.
2. Greenish-brown kernels-somewhat multicolored.

Uses: Feed, food.

Rye Kernel
(Iowa State University Seed Science Center)

A problem may occur when used in feed or food: the grain may contain a fungus (ergot) which causes sickness in livestock and humans.

OATS (Common or Cultivated Oats)
Avena sativa ("ah-VEE-nah; sah-TYE-vah")

Primary and secondary kernels are present in oats. Secondary kernels are usually smaller and are called "pin-oats" if they are not well developed. Most oat seeds have the hulls (lemma and palea) attached to the groat (oat caryopsis). Oat types are distinguished primarily by color of the hulls. Oat types include:

White or yellow oats-used as food or feed. Most widely grown in the U.S..
Gray, Black (rarely grown) and Red *(A. byzantina)* oats- used as feed
Hulless oats *(A. nuda)*-lemma and palea are detached. Used as feed.

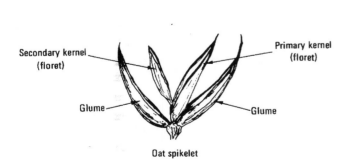

Secondary kernel
(floret)

Primary kernel
(floret)

Glume

Glume

Oat spikelet

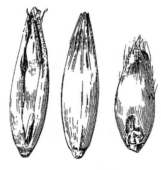

Oat Seed and Kernel
(Iowa State University Seed Science Center)

RICE
Oryza sativa ("o-RYE-zah; sah-TYE-vah")

Life cycle–Annual, adapted to dryland farming (upland types) and to flood-irrigated soils (lowland types; most common in the U.S.).
Use–Cereal grain.
Leaves– borne at an angle on the culm in two ranks (one from each node.) Auricles present; long, pointed ligules.
Stem–Culm type, hollow when mature and finely grooved. Tillers grow out of the main culm. Secondary and tertiary tillers may be present.
Inflorescence–Panicle with secondary and sometimes tertiary branches.
Spikelet–Two very small glumes and one floret.
Floret–Lemma has three nerves on each side. Flower consists of 6 stamens and a pistil.
Grain–Lemma and palea are attached after threshing. Dehulled rice grain (the caryopsis) is known as brown rice. The grain with the pericarp removed is known as polished rice. Grain types are usually classified into long, medium, and short grain types.

2. **Pulse crops:**
    Fabaceae (Leguminoseae) Family

SOYBEAN
Glycine max ("gly-SEE-nee; MAX")

Life cycle–Annual.
Leaf type– Trifoliolate (with petiolule).
Stem type–Inconspicuous nodes; solid stem; 50 to 150 cm tall.
Flower type–Complete and perfect (typical legume flower).
Inflorescence–Raceme or pedicel attached directly to the stem.
Root type– Weak taproot (75 to 150 cm deep).
Seed–Varieties are sometimes identified by hilum color and by seed coat characteristics.

   Hilum Color:
   1. Imperfect black hilum Black center-bordered by brown area
   2. Black hilum
   3. Buff to brown hilum
   4. Clear or yellow hilum
   Seed coat characteristics:
   1. Dull
   2. Shiny (or glossy)

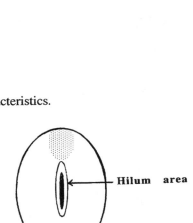

Soybean

PEANUT (Goober, Groundnut)
Arachis hypogaea ("ARE-ak-iss; hypo-GEE-ah")

Life cycle-Annual legume.
Use - Legume seed food, peanut butter, vegetable oil, livestock feed, hay crop.
Plant - Short (up to 50 cm tall), with a central upright stem and numerous branches that may vary from prostrate to upright.
Leaves - Pinnately compound, with two pairs of opposite leaflets and occasionally a fifth terminal leaflet.
Inflorescence - Single or clusters of flowers form in leaf axils. Flowers have long slender calyx tubes with corolla at the end of the tube. After pollination a gynophore (peg) develops and pushes the ovary into the soil where the pod develops.

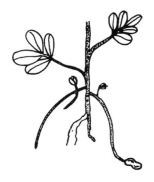

Pod - Usually contains 1 to 3 seeds, approximately 1 to 3
seeds/gram (1,000 seeds/lb). Thin papery testa, usually tan to brick red in color. Cotyledons of the seed are creamy
to white in color.
Root system– A well developed taproot with many branch roots.

OTHER PULSES:

General Characteristics of Some Important Pulse Crops

Trait	Species			
	Cowpeas	Field Beans	Field Peas	Lentils
Primary Use	Food and forage	Food	Food and forage	Food
Plant Type	Upright to viny or semiviny growth	Bushy or viny growth	Viny to semiviny growth	Semiviny to weakly upright growth
Leaf Type	Pinnately trifoliolate	Pinnately trifoliolate	Pinnately compound; 1 to 3 pairs of leaflets ending with a tendril	Pinnately compound; 4 to 6 7 pairs of leaflets usually ending with a tendril
Pods	Smooth, 20-30 cm long; 8-20 seeds per pod	10-20 cm long; 4-6 seeds per pod	7-10 cm long; 4-9 seeds per pod	1-2 cm long; 2-3 seeds per pod
Life Cycle	Summer annual			
Inflorescence	Raceme			
Flower Type	Perfect, Complete - typical legume flower			
Root Type	Leguminous taproot			

Types and Seed Charcteristics:
   There are many types and varieties of cowpeas, field beans, field peas, and lentils used throughout the world
   and are frequently distinguished by seed characteristics. The following is a general description of seeds of each
   species:

COWPEAS
Vigna unguiculata ("VIG-nah; un-guik-u-LAH-tah")

   Seeds—Bean shaped but shorter in proportion to width; may be flattened on
   the ends in some varieties. Seeds may vary from solid to multicolored in colors ranging from white, brown, maroon, to almost black. Some types, such as
   purplehull or blackeye cowpeas, have the distinctive color located in the
   hilum area.

Cowpea

FIELD BEANS (Common bean, dry edible bean)
Phaseolus vulgaris ("fah-zee-OH-lus; vul-GAY-ris")

Field Bean

Seeds–Extremely variable in color and shape among different types of field beans. Seeds range from white, yellow, green, to red or purple or multicolored. Seeds may be rounded or flattened on the ends and short or long. Major types grown in the U.S. are:

1. Navy (white) field bean-white, glossy, small seed.
2. Great Northern field bean-large, white, somewhat flattened seeds
3. Pinto field bean-oblong, medium sized, light tan to buff colored marbled or speckled with brownish streaks and spots.
4. Red Kidney field bean-large, long, somewhat flattened seeds that are dark red at maturity.

FIELD PEAS (Dry Edible Peas)
Pisum sativum ("PIE-sum; sah-TYE-vum")

Field Pea

Seeds - Smaller, more rounded than cowpeas. Color and appearance vary among varieties; may be white, green or mottled with gray and brown. Seed coats may be smooth or wrinkled.

LENTILS
Lens culinaris ("LENZ; coo-lin-AIR-is")

Seeds - Flattened, circular and convex (lens) shaped seed. Color varies from yellow, orange, to brown.

Lentil

3. **Oil Crops:**

SUNFLOWER
Helianthus annuus ("hee-lee-AN-thus; AN-you-us")
Asteraceae Family

Life cycle–Annual.

Use–Two types are grown, one for oilseed production (38 to 50% oil and 20% protein) and one for nut and birdfood markets.

Plant–Stout, erect 1 m to 6 m in height, rough and hairy stem that is 2 to 7 cm in diameter.

Leaves–Petioled, up to 30 cm long with margins

Inflorescence–A head (or disk) that is 2 to 3 cm in diameter. The disk flowers are brown to almost black, surrounded by yellow ray flowers.

Root system–Strongly branched taproot system that may be 3 meters or more deep.

Seed–Oilseed varieties usually have black or dark brown seed and thin hulls that adhere to the kernel (10-13 seeds/gram). Non-oil varieties usually have striped larger seed (5-10 seeds/gram).

Sunflower
(top few nodes
and head)

4. Sugar Crops:

SUGARBEETS
Beta vulgaris ("BAY-tah; vul-GAY-ris)
Chenopodiaceae Family

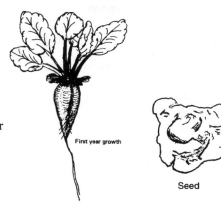

First year growth

Seed

Life cycle– Biennial, grown as an annual for sugar production.
Use–Beets are processed for sugar. The remaining beet pulp is used for livestock feed. The beet tops may also be used as feed for livestock, usually in the form of silage.

First year

> Plant and leaves - Petioled leaves are arranged on the crown in a close spiral. Leaves vary in size from approximately 7 cm x 10 cm to 15 cm x 30 cm.
> Root system - A large, fleshy cone-shaped root (beet) develops. The beet is slightly flattened, with grooves on two sides and may be up to 1-1/2 kg in weight, usually ranging from 10 to 20% sugar content. The beet terminates in a slender taproot.

Second year

> The beets first produce a rosette of leaves (like those of the first year). After about 6 weeks a branched flower stalk develops.

> Inflorescence-A branched (or paniculate) arrangement of spikes. Flowers are perfect and without petals. Seed is borne in a "seed-ball" (a hard irregularly shaped cork-like body).

SUGARCANE
Saccharum officinarum ("sac-CAR-um; oh-fish-ih-NAR-um")
Poaceae (Gramineae) Family

Life Cycle– Perennial, sugarcane fields may last three or more years. Harvests in subsequent years after the first harvest are called ratoon crops.

Use–Stems (stalks) are processed for sugar, syrup, and molasses. By-products of processing include blackstrap molasses for livestock feed, filtering residue (filter-press cake) for fertilizer and bagasse (stalk residue) for fiber and paper manufacturing.

Plant–Tall (up to 5 m or taller) tropical bunch grass that produces many tillers (20-50 or more) per plant.

Leaves– Large, erect or semierect, coarse leaves approximately 1-2 m in length.

Stem–Large stems (2-5 cm wide) with conspicuous nodes. Stalks produce a single bud (eye) at each node and are covered with a fine layer of wax.

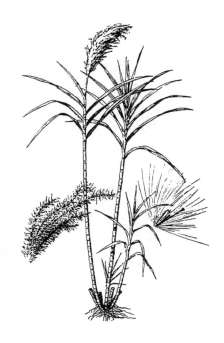

Reproductive Structure–Sugarcane rarely produces seed in the continental U.S. and is established by vegetative propagation using stalk pieces. The inflorescence is a profusely branched, plume-like panicle with small spikelets (3 mm long) and small seeds (1-2 mm long). Florets are perfect and incomplete and are frequently sterile.

Roots–Extensive fibrous root system, 2-3 m deep or more.

5. Fiber Crops:

COTTON
Gossypium hirsutum ("go-SIP-ee-um; here-SUE-tum")
Malvaceae Family

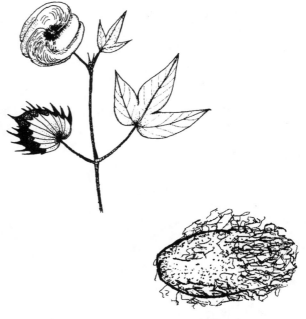

Life cycle–Annual (perennial in the tropics).

Use-Fiber crop. Seeds are used for oil and protein.

Plant–Herbaceous, 50-150 cm tall, usually with many branches from a main stem.

Leaves–Petioled, blade with 3, 5, or 7 lobes, usually covered with fine hairs.

Fruiting–Squares (flower buds), flowers, and bolls arise from the base of the leaf petiole. Three large bracts occur at the base of each flower, above which is a 5 lobed calyx. Corolla has 5 petals that range from white to purple. The fruit is an enlarged ovary with a 3 to 5 loculed boll (capsule). Bolls are 2 cm to 4 cm long. Seeds are covered with lint hairs (fibers). Fibers range from 2 cm to 5 cm long.

Root system–A strong taproot system that may be 3 meters or more deep.

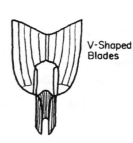

Seed

F. Common Forage Grasses—Vegetative Identification
Poaceae (Gramineae) Family

1. Grasses with Folded Vernation and No Auricles

ORCHARDGRASS
(*Dactylis glomerata*) ("DAK-til-iss; glom-er-A-tah")

Vernation–folded.
Auricles– none.
Leaf Blades–distinctly V-shaped, 5-12 mm wide, tip of blade taper-pointed.
Sheath–mostly split part way.
Ligule– membranous, 3 to 10 mm long, acuminate.
Glabrous plant.
Distinctly a bunch-grass.
Inflorescence–panicle but distinctly bunched.

V-Shaped Blades

KENTUCKY BLUEGRASS
(*Poa pratensis*) ("PO-uh; pray-TEN-sis")

Vernation–folded (shoot apparently flattened).
Leaf Blades– flat to V-shaped, 2 to 3 mm wide, tip of blade is boat-shaped.
Sheath–split with overlapping margins.
Stem–round.
Foliage–bright green.
Auricles–none.
Ligule– short, .2 to .3 mm long.

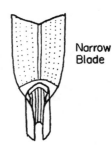

Narrow Blade

SUDANGRASS
(*Sorghum bicolor* var. *sudanense*)
("SORE-gum; BYE-color; variety sudan-EN-see")

Vernation–rolled.

Leaf blades–20 to 40 mm wide.

Sheath–split with overlapping margins.

Ligule– membranous (papery), 3 to 4 mm long and rounded.

Auricles–absent.

Rhizomes and stolons–not present.

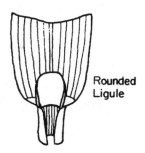

Rounded Ligule

2. Grasses with Folded Vernation and Auricles

PERENNIAL RYEGRASS
(*Lolium perenne*) ("LO-lee-um; per-REN-nee")

Vernation–folded.

Leaf blades–very shiny, 2 to 3 mm wide.

Auricles–clawlike.

Ligule–membranous, .4 to .6 mm long, truncate.

Sheath–often reddish below ground, split, with overlapping margins.

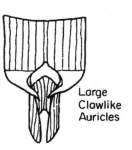

Large Clawlike Auricles

3. Grasses with Rolled Vernation and No Auricles

BERMUDAGRASS
(*Cynodon dactylon)* ("SIGN-a-don; DACK-til-on")

Vernation– rolled.

Leaf blades–2 to 3 mm wide.

Sheath– loose and split with overlapping margins.

Auricles– none.

Ligule–a fringe of hairs, 2 to 3 mm long.

Stolons and rhizomes– present, very strong and dense growth from stolons.

Tufted Sheath

SMOOTH BROMEGRASS
(*Bromus inermis*) ("BRO-mus; in-ER-mis")

Vernation–rolled.

Leaf blades–10 to 15 mm wide, with a constriction in the form of an inverted "W".

Sheath–closed to near top.

Auricles– none.

Ligule– membranous, truncate to rounded, less than 1 mm long.

Rhizomes-present (sod-forming).

Inflorescence– panicle.

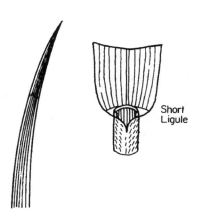

Short Ligule

REED CANARYGRASS
(*Phalaris arundinacea*) ("FAH-lar-iss; a-run-din-A-see-uh")

Vernation– rolled.

Leaf blades– 10 to 20 mm wide, with rough margins, constriction near tip.

Sheath– split with overlapping margins.

Auricles–usually absent (or not clawlike).

Ligule– rounded, occasionally toothed, 2 to 3 mm long.

Inflorescence–bunched panicle.

Rhizomes–present.

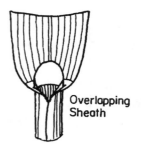

Overlapping Sheath

TIMOTHY
(*Phleum pratense*) ("FLEE-um; pray-TEN-see")

Vernation–rolled.

Leaf blades–5 to 10 mm wide.

Sheath–split with overlapping margins.

Auricles–none.

Ligule– 4 to 5 mm long, membranous, rounded, notched toward sides.

Haplocorm-on lower stem below soil surface.

Rhizomes or stolons - none.

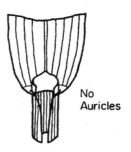

No Auricles

4. Grasses with Rolled Vernation and Auricles

TALL FESCUE
(*Festuca arundinacea*) ("fess-TOO-kah; a-run-din-A-see-uh")

Vernation– rolled.
Leaf blades–5 to 10 mm wide, coarse, deeply veined, margins rough.
Sheaths–split with overlapping margins.
Ligule– membranous, truncate, usually 0.5 mm long.
Auricles– narrow and clawlike, hairy.

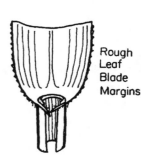

Rough Leaf Blade Margins

ITALIAN (ANNUAL) RYEGRASS
(*Lolium multiflorum*) ("LO-lee-um; mul-tee-FLOOR-um")

Vernation - rolled.

Leaf Blades - midribs off-center, 3 to 7 mm wide.

Sheaths - split with overlapping margins.

Auricles - narrow and clawlike.

Ligule - membranous, truncate, rounded, 1 to 2 mm long.

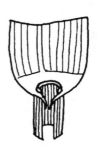

Midrib of Blade Off-center

G. Common Forage Grasses—Useful Seed Identification Characteristics

Morphologically, the "seeds" of cultivated forage grasses and grassy weeds are usually developed florets or spikelets. That is, the lemma and palea and perhaps even the outer glumes remain attached to the true seed. The naked caryopsis is usually found only in the cultivated cereals. Therefore, in forage grass seed identification, the characteristics of the glumes, lemma, and palea afford a means of identification. In species with more than one floret per spikelet, the rachilla often adheres to the floret and may furnish descriptive clues. The characteristics of the lemma are very useful for classification. Lemmas may vary in size, shape, texture, color, number of nerves, and presence or absence of other characters such as keel, pubescence, teeth, and awns. The rachilla may vary as to length, shape, pubescence, and nature of abscission or fracture. These characteristics should be considered in learning to identify the seed which is presented in this unit.

1. Illustration of Grass Seed Parts Used in Identification

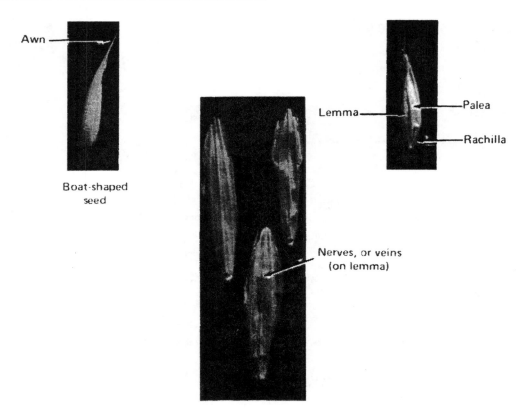

Awn

Boat-shaped seed

Lemma — Palea

— Rachilla

Nerves, or veins (on lemma)

2. Illustration of the Usual Forms of the Rachilla

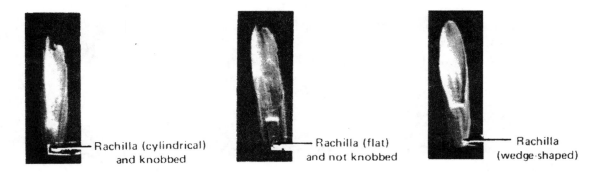

— Rachilla (cylindrical) and knobbed

— Rachilla (flat) and not knobbed

— Rachilla (wedge-shaped)

H. Common Forage Grasses—Seed Identification

1. Grass Seeds with Lemma and Palea Easily Detached

TIMOTHY

Seed–not more than 6 mm (1/4" long), 2,500 seed/gm (1,230,000 seed/lb.)
Shape–somewhat round
Color–usually some hulled, giving a two-color effect

SORGHUM X SUDANGRASS HYBRID

(Same appearance as grain sorghum because the seed is characteristic of the female parent, which is usually grain sorghum)

Seed–0-45 seed/gm (13-20,000 seed/lb.)
Shape– elliptical, hulls absent
Color–white with brown to purple undercoat or reddish brown, all seed usually have lemma and palea detached

2. Grass Seeds with Lemma and Palea Not Easily Detached

a. Large Seed with Prominent Nerves on the Lemma

SMOOTH BROMEGRASS

Seed–more than 6 mm (1/4" long), 300 seed/gm (135,000 seed/lb.)
Shape–seed blunt at top, lemmas distinctly three-veined on backs, seed appear chaffy awns few or absent Color - light to dark brown

b. Seed with a Shiny Texture-Large Plump Seed

SUDANGRASS

Seed–120 seed/gm (55,000 seed/lb.)
Shap– rounded at base and pointed tip, hulls and glumes usually present, pedicels not knobbed
Colo–Common Sudangrass-seed mostly greenish-yellow with some black;
Piper Sudangrass–seed mostly black with some greenish-yellow

FORAGE SORGHUM

Seed–100 seed/gm (40,000 seed/lb.)
Shape– rounded at base and pointed tip, hulls and glumes usually present, pedicels not knobbed.
Color–brownish to black usually with some dehulled, tannish to brown seeds

c. Seed with a Shiny Texture-Small, Slender Seeds

REED CANARYGRASS

Seed–not more than 6 mm (1/'4" long), 1,200 seed/gm. (530,000 seed/lb.)
Shape–boat-shaped
Color–hulls shiny, opaque, and grayish black

d. Seed Boat-Shaped

ORCHARDGRASS

Seed–not more than 6 mm (1/4") long, 1,400 seed/gm. (650,000 seed/lb.)
Shape–boat-shaped, curved and pointed "keel-like" lemma, awned
Color– hulls dull, brownish color

KENTUCKY BLUEGRASS

Seed–not more than 6 mm (1/4") long, 4,800 seed/gm (2,200,000 seed/lb.)
Shape–straight, boat-shaped, awnless
Color– brownish to tannish, hulls dull

e. Seed Almost White

BERMUDAGRASS

Seed–not more than 6 mm (1/4") long, 4,000 seed/gm (1,800,000 seed/lb.)
Shape–seed flattened and irregular, somewhat triangular
Color–almost white

f. Seed with Distinctive Rachilla Characteristics

TALL FESCUE

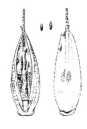

Seed–7 mm (1/4") long or longer, 500 seed/gm (230,000 seed/lb.)
Shape–somewhat flattened, rachilla cylindrical and knobbed, no awns
Color– hulls dull, tannish to brown

PERENNIAL RYEGRASS

Seed–6 mm (1/4") long or longer, 500 seed/gm (230,000 seed/lb.)
Shape–somewhat flattened, rachilla flattened and not knobbed, awns few or absent
Color– hulls dull, tannish to brown

ANNUAL RYEGRASS

Seed– 6 mm (1/4") long or longer, 500 seed/gm (230,000 seed/lb.)
Shape– somewhat flattened, rachilla flat across the top and wedge-shaped, awns few or absent
Color–hulls dull, tannish to brown

I. Common Forage Legumes-Flowering Plant Identification
Fabaceae (Leguminoseae) Family

The legume family is one of the largest in the plant kingdom, containing over 15,000 recorded species.

1. Inflorescence Characteristics

The inflorescence may be a raceme, head, or umbel. The flowers are irregular and many require insect visitation for pollination. The petals, five in number, are the standard, two wing petals and two petals fused together into a keel. These five combined make up the corolla. The male structure consists of ten stamens. These may be all united or nine fused and one free. The female structure has one carpel, but may contain many ovules. When ripened this pod-like structure is called a legume.

2. Terms to Remember

Serrated leaflet – notches or slits in the margins (edges) of leaflets
Petiolule– attaches leaflets to the petiole in non-sessile leaves
Pubescence–hairlike projections
Glabrous– smooth (no pubescence)
Raceme–flowers attached to a pedicel, which attaches to the rachis
Head– individual flowers fastened close together to give continuous appearance (see red clover)
Umbel– an inflorescence in which the pedicels arise from the same level

3. Species with Pinnately Trifoliolate Leaves - Central Leaflet with Elongated Petiolule, Slender Leaflets

ALFALFA
(*Medicago sativa*) ("med-ih-KAH-go; sah-TYE-vah")

Pinnately trifoliolate leaf, central leaflet with elongated petiolule
Outer one-third of leaflets serrated
Raceme type inflorescence, most varieties are blue-purple flowered

Serrations (at tip of leaflets)

SWEETCLOVER
(White-*Melilotus alba*) ("mel-ee-LO-tus; AL-bah")
(Yellow-*Melilotus officinalis*) ("mel-ee-LO-tus; oh-fish-ih-NAL-iss")

Pinnately trifoliolate leaf, central leaflet with elongated petiolule
Entire leaflets serrated
Glabrous plants
Inflorescence–long racemes, white or yellow flowers depending on species
Sweet (coumarin) odor

Serrations (encircle leaflets)

4. Species with Palmately Trifoliolate Leaves-Wide or Rounded Leaflet

RED CLOVER
(*Trifolium pratense*) ("try-FO-lee-um; pray-TEN-see")

Palmately trifoliolate leaf
Many leaflets have inverted "V" markings
Sheathlike stipules
Pubescent (hairy) plant
Inflorescence round or ball-like head (leafy collar at base), reddish flowers

Sheath-like Stipules

60

ALSIKE CLOVER
(*Trifolium hybridum*) ("try-FO-lee-um; HI-brid-um")

Palmately trifoliolate leaf
Stipules long and pointed
Glabrous (not hairy)
Inflorescence–almost spherical (raceme), peduncle is shorter than white clover and longer than red clover, white flowers

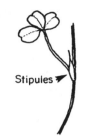

Stipules

LADINO OR WHITE CLOVER
(*Trifolium repens*) ("try-FO-lee-um; REP-ens")

Palmately trifoliolate leaf
Some leaves have inverted V-shaped white markings
Decumbent stems (horizontal with tips becoming vertical)
Leaves and flowers on separate stalks
Stolons present
Glabrous plant
White flowers are borne in terminal heads

Decumbent Stem

KOREAN LESPEDEZA
(*Lespedeza stipulacea*) ("less-puh-DEE-zah; stip-you-LAY-see-ah")

Palmately trifoliolate leaf
Leaflets notched at tip (almost heart-shaped)
Stipules papery and sheath-like, brownish in color
Bluish-white flowers on short racemes toward branch tips

Membraneous
Sheath

BIRDSFOOT TREFOIL
(*Lotus corniculatus*) ("LO-tus; cor-nik-you-LAY-tus")

Palmately trifoliolate leaf
Edges of leaflets not serrated
Large stipules (look like leaflets)
Glabrous plant
Inflorescence umbel-like with yellow flowers

Leaflike
Stipules

5. Species with Multiple Leaflets Per Leaf

HAIRY VETCH
(*Vicia villosa*) ("VICH-ee-uh; vil-LOS-sah")

Pinnately compound leaf with multiple leaflets ending in a tendril
Pointed stipules
Pubescent stems and leaves
Multiple flowers (violet to purple) on an elongated raceme

Tendrils

CROWNVETCH
(*Coronilla varia*) ("cor-oh-NIL-luh; VAR-ee-uh")

Pinnately compound leaf with 9-25 leaflets ending with a leaflet
Leaflets are oblong
Stems are angular and hollow and 30-120 cm long
Flowers are variegated white to purple, arranged in a compressed, umbel-like inforescence
Pods are long and slim with 3-12 seeds

J. Common Forage Legumes-Useful Seed Identification Characteristics

Morphologically, the seeds of forage legumes are ripened ovules; their outer layer is a testa (true seed coat). In nearly all cases (exception: lespedeza) the ovary wall dehisces and the seeds are bare.

The seed is nonendospermic; two cotyledons contain starch and protein food reserves (oil in some species); a large radicle, a hypocotyl, and a small plumule make up the embryo. Useful characteristics for identification are: color, size, texture, and shape.

(1)   Color— this descriptive term is quite useful with new seed, but may be misleading as the seed ages. The pigments may fade to a color resembling some other species. For certain seeds, however, (e.g., alsike clover) this is the first, most readily observed character.

(2)   Size— this also is a relative term which may be modified by the environment during the plant's growth cycle. However, forage seeds that are well filled are not as variable in size as the cereal and oil crops. If the environment was unfavorable, seeds will be shriveled or wrinkled. Number of seeds per gram is indicative of the seed size. It is also useful to refer to this value when determining seeding rates.

(3)   Texture—rough, smooth, shiny. Texture may be seen in some cases, or sensed by handling the sample in other cases.

(4)   Shape is the most useful and reliable character for identification. It is essentially a combination of the presence or absence of three characters: the notch, beak, and groove.
  a.   The notch is an indentation in the region of the hilum. It may be deep to shallow. If the notch is centered in the seed, kidney to bowl-shaped seeds result (bur clover, alfalfa, alsike clover).

LEGUME SEED SHAPES

b. The beak is a pointed protuberance from the notch of the hilum area. It may occur in a notch, as in alfalfa, or on the surface of a rather round seed, like crimson clover.

c. The groove is a trough like indentation leading away from the hilum down the side of the seed, giving the seed a thumb-like, or in some cases, a mitten-shaped appearance.

K. Common Forage Legumes-Seed Identification

ALFALFA

Color– greenish yellow
Size:–440 seed/gm (200,000 per lb)
Texture– dull
Shape–predominantly kidney (may have some mitt- or irregularly shaped seeds with sharply angled grooves)
Other–one-third of seeds will have a small beak in the notch

SWEETCLOVER

Color–greenish yellow
Size–570 seed/gm (260,000 per lb)
Texture– dull
Shape– mitten (longer thumb than red clover and alfalfa; groove is long and not sharply angled)
Odor–coumarin-characteristic only of sweet clover

RED CLOVER

Color–variegated yellow, blending to purple
Size–600 seed/gm (275,000 per lb)
Texture– dull
Shape– mitten (shorter thumb than S. Clover)

ALSIKE CLOVER

Color–green to black
Size–1550 seed/gm (700,000 per lb)
Texture– rough or pebbled (not shiny)
Shape– irregular heart (groove located near the top center portion)

LADINO CLOVER OR WHITE CLOVER

Color–yellow to light brown
Size–1750 seed/gm (800,000 per lb)
Texture–dull (not shiny)
Shape–irregular heart (groove located near the top center portion)

KOREAN LESPEDEZA

Color–brown
Size–500 seed/gm (225,000 per lb)
Texture–rough-calyx lobe and pod present
Shape–flattened oval
Seedlot may contain some black colored seed with pod and calyx lobes detached
Seed with calyx and pod

Seed with
calyx and pod

63

BIRDSFOOT TREFOIL

Color–dark olive green to brown
Size–800 seed/gm (375,000 per lb)
Texture–smooth, shiny
Shape–oblong to round, some with central indentation (bowl-shaped)

HAIRY VETCH

Color–black
Size–3 mm (1/8") or more in diameter
Texture–dull
Shape–irregularly round, hilum is a distinct line

CROWNVETCH

Color– yellow to brown
Size– 3.5 mm long and 1 mm in diameter 250 seed/gm (105,000 seed/lb)
Shape–rod-shaped

STUDY QUESTIONS

Crop Classification and Identification

1. Classify 'Star' Alfalfa and 'Higrow' Oats according to the binomial system by filling in the blanks below:

	Alfalfa	Oats
Kingdom		
Division		
Class		
Subclass		
Order		
Family		
Genus		
Species		
Variety		

2. What do most of the centers of origin have in common?

3. What is the difference between a silage crop and a greenchop crop?

4. Why is flax a grain crop but not a cereal crop?

5. What does "vernalize" mean?

6. The red color of corn is always carried in the _____ (kernel part).

7. What is the "hilum" of soybeans?

8. List five market classes (types) of wheat.

9. A small grain plant has a ligule and long clasping auricles. Name the plant.

10. Using seed shape, identify red clover, sweetclover, alfalfa, and white clover seeds:

SELF-EVALUATION TEST

Crop Plant Classification and Identification

Circle letter corresponding to one best answer.

1. The identification structure indicated by the arrow is

   a) a ligule.
   b) an auricle.
   c) a stipule.
   d) a leaflet.
   e) a petiole.

2. An annual plant would likely

   a) have haplocorms.
   b) have rhizomes.
   c) produce seed for the following generation.
   d) produce only vegetative material during the first growing season.
   e) store carbohydrates for regrowth.

3. The following plant would be properly classified as dicotyledonous:

   a) corn
   b) oats
   c) orchardgrass
   d) barley
   e) alfalfa

4. What does the initial following the genus and species of a crop plant mean? (ex. *Medicago sativa* L.)

   a) center of origin
   b) family
   c) kingdom
   d) classifier
   e) variety

5. Which list of descriptive terms best describes the parts of a floret that is incomplete and perfect?

   a) sepals, petals, stamens
   b) stamens, pistil, rudimentary calyx
   c) petals, stamens, calyx
   d) calyx, corolla, pistil
   e) ovary, calyx, corolla

6. Which of the following is never used to describe a grass seed?

   a) ripened ovary
   b) raceme
   c) groat
   d) caryopsis
   e) kernel

7. The following crop is indigenous to the United States:

   a) western wheatgrass
   b) soybean
   c) wheat
   d) corn
   e) oats

8. Which of the following is correct?

   a) There are many species belonging to the same variety.
   b) There are many genera belonging to the same species.
   c) There are many classes belonging to the same genus.
   d) There are many genera belonging to the same family.
   e) There are many orders belonging to the same family.

9. The following cereal grain would most likely be used for macaroni:

   a) durum wheat
   b) white wheat
   c) white oats
   d) two-row awned barley
   e) rye

10. In the vegetative stage of growth, *Avena sativa* can be identified by

    a) the absence of the blade.
    b) the presence of netted venation.
    c) the absence of auricles.
    d) the presence of a raceme inflorescence.
    e) the absence of nodules.

11. The following crop is correctly matched with its scientific name:

    a) oats-*Hordeum vulgare*
    b) soybeans-*Glycine sativa*
    c) sudangrass-*Sorghum bicolor var. sudanense*
    d) wheat-*Trifolium aestivum*
    e) alfalfa-*Melilotus officinalis*

12. An example of a pulse crop is

    a) oats.
    b) sorghum.
    c) alfalfa.
    d) sunflower.
    e) cowpeas.

13. Which plant is a member of the *Solonaceae* family?

    a) cotton.
    b) sunflower.
    c) sugarbeet.
    d) tomato.
    e) squash.

14. Perennial plants

    a) live three seasons before producing seed.
    b) die soon after setting seed.
    c) have an indefinite life span.
    d) must be used for forage production.
    e) are found only in temperate regions.

15. A red dent corn kernel

    a) has a red pericarp.
    b) has a red endosperm.
    c) has a colorless pericarp.
    d) has a red embryo.
    e) has no flinty endosperm.

16. Which of the following plants is monoecious?

    a) oats
    b) corn
    c) barley
    d) rye
    e) rice

17. The arrow in the figure below, is pointing to a part of the oat spikelet. Identify it.

    a) secondary floret
    b) glume
    c) rachilla
    d) primary floret
    e) receptacle

18. The leaf pictured below belongs to the genus known as

    a) sweetclover
    b) *Medicago*
    c) *Melilotus*
    d) *Gramineae*
    e) *Zea*

19. Which description correctly identifies the seed of *Trifolium repens?*

    a) variegated yellow; dull texture; mitten-shaped
    b) green to black; pebbled texture; irregularly heart-shaped
    c) greenish-yellow; dull texture; mitten-shaped
    d) yellow to light brown; dull texture; irregularly heart-shaped
    e) greenish-yellow; dull texture; kidney-shaped

20. Which description correctly identifies the seed of tall fescue?

    a) awned; wedge-shaped rachilla
    b) no awns; cylindrical rachilla
    c) few awns; flat rachilla
    d) awned; boat-shaped rachilla
    e) no awns; no rachilla

21. Vernation is a term used to designate

    a) breaking of seed dormancy.
    b) shape of the corolla in legume flowers.
    c) arrangement of leaves in grass plants.
    d) arrangement of veins in plant leaves.
    e) a process that stimulates flowering of grass plants.

22. The corn kernel pictured below would likely

    a) be a popcorn type.
    b) be a dent corn type.
    c) be a flour corn type.
    d) have a wrinkled caryopsis.
    e) be used for animal feed.

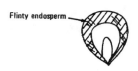

23. Cross sections of two market classes of wheat are shown below. Which statement is true?

    a) Figure A is a hard winter wheat type.
    b) Figure B is a hard winter wheat type.
    c) Figure B is likely higher quality for bread flour.
    d) Neither would be used for bread flour.
    e) Both would be mainly used for cake flour.

A   B

24. Identify the correct statement.

    a) The protista kingdom is made up of entities that are not really alive.
    b) Algae conduct photosynthesis so do not belong to the protista kingdom.
    c) Algae are not important in crop production.
    d) Bacteria are important in the natural control of insects.
    e) Fungi cause plant diseases and have no beneficial effects.

25. Select the entry in which the crop and its use are properly matched.

    a) tobacco-fiber
    b) flax-cereal
    c) alfalfa-greenchop
    d) sunflower-pulse
    e) potato-grain

26. Using a crop to attract and concentrate pest insects into a localized area is an example of a

    a) cover crop
    b) green manure crop
    c) catch crop
    d) trap crop
    e) companion crop

Chapter 3

Crop Physiology

I. IMPORTANCE OF CROP PHYSIOLOGY

Crop physiology is the study of plant functions and responses of crops grown in agricultural environments. It is the underlying science that helps us to understand questions such as:

**What causes a plant to grow?

**Do the largest plants produce the largest yield?

**How is yield related to the environment?

**Why do overcrowded plants grow tall and spindly?

**How is sunlight converted into food?

Knowing why and how crop plants react to their field environment is essential for crop improvement, solving crop management problems, and making good management decisions.

II. YIELD

A. Definition

Yield is the amount of product produced per unit of land area. The amount of product in many agronomic crops is usually expressed as the weight of dry matter (weight of dried product). Water content in plants can commonly vary from 55 to 90%, depending on plant age, environment, and other factors. Thus, wet weight yields (weight of non-dried product) is a poorer indicator of actual organic matter production by the plant than dry matter yields. The unit of land area frequently used in yield measurements is the hectare (metric) or acre (English). Examples of yield measurements are:

Grain yield (maize) = 150 bu/A or 8400 lbs/A (English)
  = 94 q/ha or 9400 kg/ha (metric)

Forage yield (hay) = 6 tons/A or 12,000 lbs/A (English)
  = 13 mt/A or 13,450 kg/ha (Metric)

B. Types of Yield

There are two general types of yield:

1. Biological Yield-The total dry matter produced per plant or per unit area. It includes all of the leaf, stem, grain, and root dry matter produced by the plant.
2. Economic or Agricultural Yield-The volume or weight

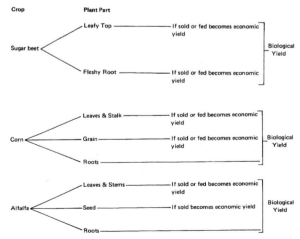

per unit area of only those plant parts that have marketable value. It may refer to seed or grain yield for species like wheat or maize, leaf and stem yield for forage species and root and tuber yield for beets and potatoes. Each species usually has a standardized market moisture content.

Harvest index (the ratio of economic yield to biological yield) is frequently used by scientists to determine the efficiency of crop species and varieties in converting biological yield into an economically desirable product under different management practices or environments. Conditions or practices that promote very high biological yield and low economic yield result in a low harvest index.

C. Components of Yield

1. The economic yield of grain crops is usually determined by the following equation (all other factors being present in optimum amounts):

    YIELD =   Plants/area x Heads/plant x Seeds/head x Weight/seed

    For a given species, each yield component has an optimum level for each level of the other components. Some yield components may affect all of the other components and some may be affected more than another. For example increasing plants per acre may greatly reduce the heads per plant which causes a moderate increase in seeds per head which may cause a slight reduction in the weight per seed.

III. RATE OF GROWTH

A. Plant Growth Curve

The rate of plant growth follows a general pattern altered by environmental factors. This pattern is called the growth curve (see Figure 1). The curve typifies the growth of all organisms or parts of organisms, such as a maize plant, a bacterium, or an ear or leaf on a maize plant. The growth curve is divided into three parts:

1. Logarithmic growth phase-The period of ever increasing rate of growth - includes the germination and vegetative stages.
2. Linear growth phase-The period of constant growth rate - includes the flowering and seed filling stages.
3. Maturation phase-Growth slows and declines with age. Growth eventually ceases.

NOTE: Departure from the optimum curve indicates that dry matter is not being accumulated very efficiently and usually indicates the species is not well adapted to the environment or to a particular geographic location.

B. Plant Growth Regulators

A wide range of plant responses to environment are mediated through plant growth regulators, which are minute amounts of organic substances that influence and regulate plant growth and development. These substances are active within the plant at very low concentrations and may be produced in one plant organ which stimulates or inhibits a response in another location. Plant growth regulators may be naturally produced within the plant ("plant hormones" or "phytohormones") or synthetically produced ("synthetic hormones"). There are five major groups of plant growth regulators:

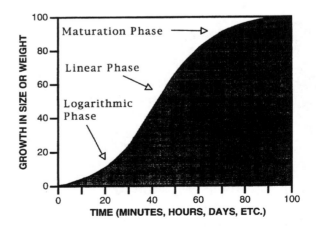

Figure 1. Plant growth curve

1. Auxins –stimulate cell elongation and many other growth responses. Example: indoleacetic acid (IAA).

2. Gibberellins -stimulate cell elongation and many other plant responses similar to auxins. However, gibberellins are chemically different from auxins and act in a different manner. Example: gibberellic acid.

3. Cytokinins (Kinins)– stimulate cell division (cytokinesis), cell differentiation, and many other plant responses. Example: zeatin.

4. Growth Inhibitors–inhibit growth and development and induce dormancy in seeds and plants. Example: abscisic acid (ABA).

5. Ethylene–a gaseous substance that may also be considered a growth inhibitor. Hastens fruit ripening and inhibits many other plant responses.

It is difficult to attribute a particular plant response to just one type of plant hormone. Growth and development is frequently adjusted due to the interaction of 2 or more plant hormones. One hormone may enhance or inhibit the action of another. The amounts and balance of plant hormones within the plant are important regulatory factors. Synthetic hormones have been used for a variety of purposes ranging from weed killers (herbicides), producing seedless grapes, cloning plants, retarding vegetative growth, and stimulating uniform ripening in fruit crops.

C. Measuring Growth Rate

Growth rates of plants or plant parts can be estimated by measuring the progression of length or weight over time. To illustrate differences in growth rates, an experiment using plant growth regulators is shown:

Experimental Objective: To determine the effect of growth regulators on the rate of soybean plant growth.

Method and Materials: Twenty-four soybean plants were planted and grown in the greenhouse for a 21-day period. The plants were divided into 3 groups of 8 plants each. As the epicotyls began to elongate, minute concentrations of growth regulators were applied in a lanolin paste to leaf axils of plants in each group. Treatments were labeled A, B, or C. and consisted of:
Treatment A– control (lanolin paste only).
Treatment B– lanolin paste with phosphon (a synthetic growth inhibitor).
Treatment C– lanolin paste with gibberellic acid (a plant hormone that stimulates cell elongation).

Measurements: The lengths of the unifoliate leaves (in mm) and the first internode (in cm) were measured at the intervals indicated in the table which follows. To obtain measurements for day 0, three soaked seeds were split open. The lengths of the first two true leaves were measured. The lengths of the internode between the cotyledons and the unifoliolate leaves were also measured.

Results: The growth of the plants was recorded in Table 1.

Table 1

Average length of selected plant parts

		Day 0	9	12	15	18	21
Unifoliolate Leaves				-mm-			
Treatment	A	1	10	22	34	35	36
	B	1	9	20	27	28	29
	C	1	11	26	37	39	40
Internodes				-cm-			
Treatment	A	0	2	7	12	13	14
	B	0	1	5	9	10	11
	C	0	3	11	17	19	20

The above data should now be plotted in Figures 2 and 3.

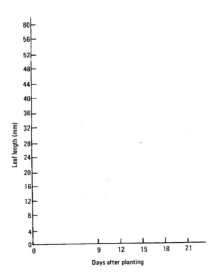

Figure 2. Growth curves of leaf length for A, B, and C treatments

Figure 3. Growth curves of internode length for A, B, and C treatments

Draw smooth lines through the data points plotted in Figures 2 and 3. These lines represent the growth curves for the unifoliolate leaf and for the first internode or epicotyl. The same kind of curve could be obtained for each internode and leaf and also for the whole plant.

Conclusions: The leaves and internode receiving the gibberellic acid had the longest and steepest logarithmic phase. The control or untreated plants had a shorter and less steep logarithmic phase than the gibberellic treatment. The phosphon treatment produced less growth than the control. Gibberellic acid increased cell elongation and the growth rate, while phosphon decreased cell elongation and the growth rate.

Results of the dry weight comparison: The plants in each of the three treatments were clipped (on day 21) at the soil surface. The wet and dry weights of the plants with cotyledons detached were recorded in Table 2. (Calculate the % dry weight using the formula in the table.)

Table 2. Record of plant response

	Treatment		
	A (Control)	B (Phosphon)	C (Gibberellic acid)
Wet Weight (gm)	4.59	3.88	5.81
Dry Weight (gm)	.64	.61	.65
Percent Dry Weight			
[% D.W. = (D.W. ÷ W.W.) x 100]			

Conclusions: The plants treated with phosphon have the lowest dry weight, the darkest green color, and the highest percent dry weight. Plants treated with gibberellic acid have about the same dry weight as the untreated plants but have a higher wet weight, and the lowest percent dry matter.

NOTE: Temperature, moisture, light and perhaps other environmental factors may interact to accentuate or nullify the anticipated results of biochemical reactions.

D. Regrowth

Frost, hail, wind, insects, animals, and machines can cause field plants to lose anatomical parts. The species, size, or age of the plant plays a major role in determining the ability of the plant to survive and to regenerate new growth. In cereal crops, growth of a stem and its leaves is largely determined by the growing point (apical bud) . The cereal crop stem has no lateral buds. Stems of legumes, however, have lateral buds and an apical bud, which can produce new growth if not damaged or removed. Vegetative regrowth can occur as long as one or more meristematic buds remain and remaining leaf tissue and/or stored carbohydrates in the plant can sustain regrowth. When crops are in the seedling stage, the risk of plant death by removing the growing point and all lateral buds is greater because of the low total number of meristematic buds on a young plant. If the growing point of the young plant is removed or injured, regrowth can be completely blocked or reduced. It is important to know where the growing points of the plant are located at all times during the life of the plant. The following demonstrations illustrate the regrowth capacity of young maize and soybean seedlings:

Demonstrations:

Twenty-five soybean and corn (maize) seeds were planted and grown in a greenhouse sandbench for twenty-one days. The following treatments were applied to each group of five plants:

1. Soybeans

Treatments:
1. Removed one cotyledon (day 9)
2. Removed two cotyledons (day 9)
3. Epicotyls removed; cotyledons left intact (day 9)
4. Hypocotyls clipped below the cotyledons (day 9)
5. Normal untreated plants

On day 21, the growth of the treated soybean plants was recorded in Table 3. Try to explain the reasons for the various treatment responses.

Table 3. Growth of soybeans

Treatment Number	1	2	3	4	5
Average stem length (mm) (above cotyledonary node)	62	39	41	0	70

As shown in Table 3, the first 3 treatments stunted the plants to varying degrees but did not kill them. However, clipping stems of soybean seedlings below the cotyledons resulted in plant death.

Why does the removal of soybean cotyledons greatly reduce the amount of seedling growth?

Why were soybean seedlings killed when the hypocotyls were clipped?

2. Corn (maize)

Treatments:
1. Clipped off at day 9 (clipped at 1.25 cm above the soil surface)
2. Clipped off at day 14
3. Clipped off at day 19
4. Normal untreated plants

On day 21, the growth of the maize plants in the above treatments was measured. The average height was recorded in Table 4.

Table 4. Height of corn plants

	Treatments			
	1	2	3	4
Extended height above ground (cm)	12	7	0	23

The maize plants clipped on days 9 and 14 should continue to live and resume growth after the clipping treatment. Those clipped on day 19 may or may not regrow depending on whether or not the growing point was clipped off. Under field conditions the growing point will be above the soil surface in three to six weeks, depending upon the temperature and general growing conditions. In the laboratory, under ideal growing conditions, the growing point will likely be above the soil line in less than three weeks, thus the 19-day clipping treatment should have killed the plants.

If frost, hail, insects, or wind cut young grass plants off at the soil level, the plants will likely be stunted but they will not be killed. If these crop hazards occur later on in the life cycle when the growing point is above the soil surface, the plants will be killed and no regrowth will occur.

IV. PHOTOSYNTHESIS AND RESPIRATION IN CROP PLANTS

Over 90% of all plant dry matter yield is the result of photosynthesis. Therefore, it is important to understand how photosynthesis occurs, and even more important, to learn how photosynthesis can be controlled for efficient crop production. The basic energy and chemical reactions in photosynthesis are shown in Figure 4.

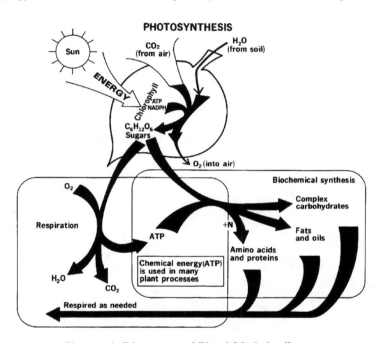

Figure 4. Diagram of Plant Metabolism

A. Terms and Definitions

1. **Photosynthesis:**
   a. The use of light energy to convert non-nutritious inorganic compounds (CO_2 and H_2O) into essential or nutritious foodstuffs for use by plants, animals and humans. Occurs in the chloroplasts of plant cells.
   b. Solar energy is captured in the chlorophyll of green leaves and is temporarily stored in adenosine triphosphate (ATP) and nicotinamide adenine dinucleotide phosphate (NADPH). CO_2 enters the stomata from the air and H_2O is delivered to the leaf from the soil through the xylem. Using ATP and NADPH, CO_2 and H_2O, enzymes manufacture sugars and oxygen (O_2) is released. The photosynthetic process fixes CO_2 into organic compounds. Photosynthetic formula: $6CO_2 + 6H_2O + \text{light energy} = C_6H_{12}O_6 \text{ (sugar)} + 6O_2$
   c. Plants can use sugars for energy or as structural materials for growth. They may store the sugars for future growth or store them for the next generation in the seed.

2. **Respiration:**
   a. The oxidative breakdown of organic substances. Occurs in the mitochondria of plant cells. Respiration formula: $C_6H_{12}O_6 + 6O_2 = 6CO_2 + 6H_2O + ATP$ (energy)
   b. Sugars are usually the raw material and carbon dioxide, water and energy are most often the end products.
   c. Energy is the most important product of respiration.
   d. The energy is stored in the high energy bonds of ATP and used to carry out many energy-requiring reactions in the cell.

Table 5. Photosynthesis and respiration compared

Photosynthesis	Respiration
1. Occurs in the green cells of plants.	1. Occurs in every active living cell of both plants and animals.
2. Takes place only in the presence of light.	2. Takes place at all times during the life of the cell, both in the light and in the dark.
3. Uses water and carbon dioxide.	3. Uses the products of photosynthesis.
4. Releases oxygen.	4. Releases water and carbon dioxide to the atmosphere.
5. Solar (radiant) energy is converted into chemical energy which may be used for manufacturing carbohydrates or protein.	5. Energy is released by breakdown of carbohydrates and proteins.
6. Results in an increase in weight.	6. Results in a decrease in weight.
7. Food is accumulated.	7. Food is broken down.

3. **Synthesis:**
   a. Energy released in respiration is used to synthesize more complex materials. Synthesis occurs in different cell parts, such as chloroplasts (carbohydrates), cytoplasm (fats and oils), ribosomes (proteins), and nucleus (DNA).
   b. Some of this energy is stored in complex molecules that can be subsequently respired when additional energy is needed.

4. **Net photosynthesis (Pn):**
   Energy stored in photosynthesis minus the energy released in the respiration process. May also be called net assimilation rate (NAR). Can be increased by genotype, leaf area and leaf orientation—but is limited by shading and deficiencies of water and minerals.

5. **Leaf area index (LAI):**
   The ratio of the total leaf area of crop plants to (divided by) the soil surface area occupied by the plants measured. A crop with a LAI of 3 indicates that there would be 3 ha of crop leaf surface above an hectare of ground.

6. **Canopy:**
   The space above the ground surface that is occupied by the aerial portion of plants. Canopy photosynthesis is the rate of photosynthesis of the canopy above a unit of ground area.

How does LAI affect NAR?

What is another term for CO_2 fixation?

What % of plant dry matter yield is directly due to photosynthesis?

What is the LAI of a plant with a leaf surface of 1 sq. meter occupying a space of 1/4 sq. meter?

B. Photosynthetic Efficiency

Photosynthesis is an energy conversion process. Solar energy is converted to chemical energy in the leaves of green plants. This process is not completely efficient. Leaves fail to utilize all the solar energy they intercept and not all of the CO_2 absorbed by the leaf is converted into sugar. Crop species, environment, and management practices influence the plant's photosynthetic efficiency.

1. Light quality

The quality of light refers to the wavelengths that are most effective in photosynthesis, which represent only a fraction of the total solar radiation reaching the earth's surface. Leaf pigments absorb light between 400 and 700 nm, which represents about 40% of the total solar radiation hitting the leaf. Of this 40%, some is lost as heat, some is reflected or transmitted, and some is consumed in photosynthetic and other metabolic processes. Even for a photosynthetically efficient species, only about 5% of the radiation striking the leaf is used in carbohydrate formation. The wavelength characteristics of the radiant energy spectrum emitted by the sun, ranging from cosmic and gamma rays with short wavelengths to the long radio and electric rays, are shown in Figure 5.

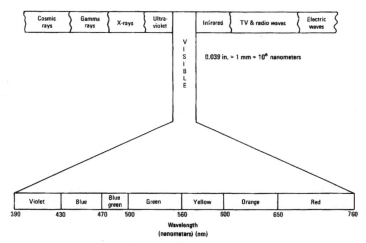

Figure 5. The Radiant Energy Spectrum

The visible portion makes up a very small part of the spectrum. Yet it is most important in terms of plant response. The absorption spectrum of a plant leaf is shown in, Figure 6. Absorption is quite efficient between 400 and 500 nanometers (nm) and also between 650 and 700 nm. Wavelengths in the green range are not effectively absorbed by chlorophyll and are reflected, thus healthy leaves appear green to the human eye.

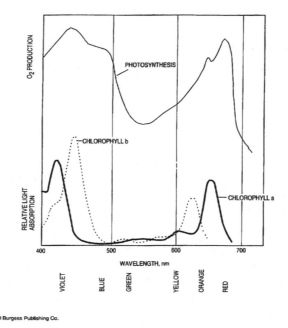

© Burgess Publishing Co.

Figure 6. Absorption spectra for leaf chlorophyll

What is the range of radiant energy wavelengths that is important in photosynthesis?

2. **Light interception**

a. **Plant spacing**

Yield can be increased by increasing photosynthesis or decreasing respiration. In the field, photosynthesis can be increased by arranging plants in a pattern that will intercept more light. This can be accomplished by adjusting the row width, plant population (LAI), or changing the shape or orientation of the plant leaves. Table 6 shows how soybean yields may be increased by using narrow rows which intercept more light.

Table 6. Light interception and soybean yields

Row width (cm)	% light intercepted	% yield index
51 (20 in)	84	115
102 (40 in)	75	100

From R. M. Shibles and C. R. Weber, "Biological Efficiencies in Soybean Production", Plant Food Review Vol. 12(4): 8-10, Winter, 1966. Reprinted with permission of The Fertilizer Institute, Washington, D.C.

In Table 7, the effect of row spacing on the yield of two soybean varieties is shown. The yield increase for 30.5 cm over 102 cm rows was 30% for Hark and 19% for Wayne. The open canopy variety (Hark) has a more erect type of growth and does not fill in the middle of the 102 cm rows (40 inch) like the closed canopy variety (Wayne). Because of this, there is considerable sunlight that reaches the ground and is not absorbed by leaves of the open canopy varieties. However, in narrow rows 51 cm (20 inches) or less the open canopy varieties are more efficient and usually give higher yields than the closed canopy varieties. The open canopy varieties, while they may not have as much total leaf area as the wide leaf, closed canopy varieties, permit more sunlight to penetrate to the lower leaves and thus increase the photosynthetic efficiency of the crop. The upright leaf pattern of the open canopy types also increases the light interception of the lower leaves.

Table 7. Yield (kg/ha) of two soybean varieties in 30.5 (12") and 102 (40") cm rows

Variety	Row spacing, cm	
	30.5 (12 in.)	102 (40 in.)
Hark	3584(53.3 bu/ac)	2757(41.0 bu/ac)
Wayne	3383(50.3 bu/ac)	2845(42.3 bu/ac)

From G. 0. Benson and J. P. Shroyer, "Soybean Row Spacing", Iowa State Univ. Extension Publication PM 864. Feb. 1980.

b.   Leaf angle

For many crops the midday intensity of full sunlight often is greater than is needed for a single leaf to reach maximum photosynthesis rate. A soybean leaf attains a maximum rate of photosynthesis at approximately one-half of full sunlight. Increasing light intensity above this level on a single leaf does not contribute as significantly to dry matter production as allowing about 50% of full sunlight to fall on several leaves down through the leaf canopy. In Figure 7, you will note the relationship between sunlight intensity and the rate of photosynthesis of several field crops and ornamentals.

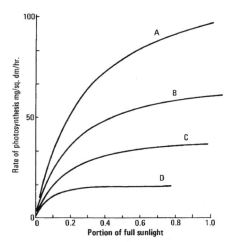

Examples of species which fit the above curves:
A. Corn, sorghum, sugarcane, bermudagrass (C4 species)
B. Soybean, alfalfa, cotton (C3 species)
C. Orchard grass, red clover, tobacco (C3 species)
D. Oak, maple, and most house plants

Figure 7. Light Utilization by Plants

For all plants, the low intensity light is utilized more efficiently than the high light intensities. This is why two leaves receiving 50 percent of full sunlight can fix more carbon dioxide than one leaf receiving full sunlight. Leaves with a more upright orientation will permit more light to penetrate further into the canopy. Figure 8 shows how leaf orientation affects light penetration.

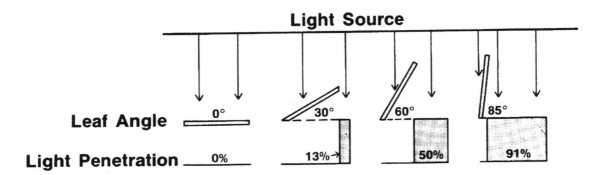

Figure 8. Leaf Angle and Light Penetration

With increasing light intensity, a unit area of a maize leaf shows an increasing photosynthetic capacity over the same area of a soybean leaf. Maize is one of the most photosynthetically efficient crop species. These relative efficiencies can be altered by such things as leaf angle and leaf shape.

The upright leaf angle of maize is used as a means of increasing yields by permitting the use of narrow rows and high plant populations that utilize more sunlight. Table 8 shows that an upright leaf can increase the yield of corn by 40 percent and reduce barrenness by 50 percent.

Table 8. Corn grain yields and barren plants with differing leaf angle*

Leaf angle	Yield kg/ha	% barren plants
Normal leaf	6,202 (99 bu/ac)	28
Upright leaf	8,769 (139 bu/ac)	14

*Population = 59,300 plants per hectare (24,000 per acre)

From ,1. W. Pendleton et al., "Field Investigations of the Relationships of Leaf Angle in Corn to Grain Yield and Apparent Photosynthesis", Agronomy Journal 60:422,1968.

3. CO_2 concentration

The efficiency of photosynthesis is also influenced by the low CO_2 concentration of the air and the plant's ability to utilize it in photosynthesis. Air contains about 0.034% (340 ppm) of CO_2, which limits the photosynthetic potential of most crops. Crops differ in their capacity to fix CO_2 into sugars depending on their photosynthetic pathway. There are two major photosynthetic pathways called C3 and C4, based on the first stable product (3-carbon or 4-carbon) of the pathway. Thus, crop plants are often referred to as "C3" or "C4" species. The C4 pathway is believed to have evolved most recently and is considerably more efficient in CO_2 fixation than the C3 pathway under the currently low atmospheric CO_2 concentrations (Table 9).

Table 9. Comparisons of C3 and C4 Plants

C3 Plants	C4 Plants
Primarily cool season crops; cooler photosynthetic maximum (15-25°C)	Primarily warm season crops; warmer photosynthetic maximum (30-47°C)
Utilizes 60% or less of maximum solar intensity; leaves light saturate (see Figure 7)	Utilizes up to 100% solar intensity; leaves do not light saturate (see Figure 7)
Inefficient leaf anatomy and enzyme that fixes CO_2; low CO_2 uptake rates; lower yield potential	Evolved a specialized leaf anatomy and enzyme that more effectively fixes CO_2; high CO_2 uptake rates; higher yield potential
Typically less efficient user of water	More efficient user of water
Crops include: Alfalfa, barley, cotton, Kentucky bluegrass, oats, potatoes, rice, rye, soybean, tall fescue, tobacco, wheat	Crops include: Bermudagrass, cassava, indiangrass, little bluestem, millet, maize, sorghum, sugarcane

The photosynthetic pathway of a crop or weed will often affect its adaptation, competitiveness or agronomic utility. Examples:

    a.   A C4 crop such as sorghum or pearl millet will use water more efficiently than a C3 crop such as soybean or perennial ryegrass, and will be better adapted and more productive in warmer and drier conditions.

    b.   A C3 crop such as oats will grow rapidly in cool temperatures, become established early and compete effectively with warm season C4 weeds such as pigweed.

    c.   Typically, C4 weeds are a greater problem in warmer climates and C3 weeds more of a problem in cooler climates.

The atmospheric CO_2 concentration in the earth's atmosphere is increasing from the burning of fossil fuels. Would you expect C3 or C4 weeds to become more competitive? Why?

V. TRANSPORT AND UPTAKE IN CROP PLANTS

A. Translocation

    1.   **Definition:** The movement of organic and inorganic solutes from one part of the plant to another.

In Figure 9, observe the following sites of synthesis and the role of translocation in the metabolism of the plant.

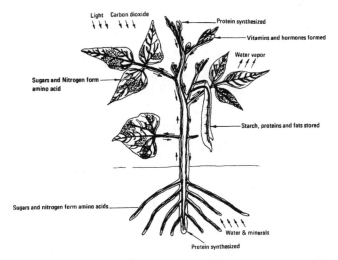

Figure 9. Plant translocation

Adapted from "The Circulatory System of Plants," Susann and Orlin Biddulph. Scientific American Reprints #53. February, 1959. Copyright © 1959 by Scientific American, Inc. All rights reserved.

    a.   When light and CO_2 are available in the atmosphere around a green leaf, sugars are formed in the leaf.
    b.   Amino acids are also formed in the leaves and roots from sugars and nitrogen.
    c.   Amino acids and carbohydrates are translocated to other parts of the plant in the phloem tissue.
    d.   Proteins are synthesized from amino acids in the growing point of the shoots and roots.
    e.   Water and minerals are absorbed by the roots and translocated upward in the xylem tissue.

In what forms may nitrogen be translocated in the plant?

What are the major storage areas for protein, starch and fats?

B.   Transpiration

    1.   **Definition:** The loss of water from plant tissues in the form of vapor.
        a.   It is an evaporative process.
        b.   It is a cooling process.

    2.   **Evapotranspiration:** A term for the total water loss in a canopy. It sums the water lost from crops by transpiration and from soil by evaporation.

    3.   In Figure 10, observe the following leaf structures and their function.
        a.   The stoma is the entrance to a large intercellular space.
        b.   The cells surrounding this space act as evaporative surfaces.
        c.   The stoma provides an easy exit for water vapor.
        d.   When the stomata are open, the amount of transpired water greatly increases.
        e.   Stomata also provide for the gaseous exchange of carbon dioxide and oxygen.
        f.   Translocation tissues are located near the evaporative surfaces.

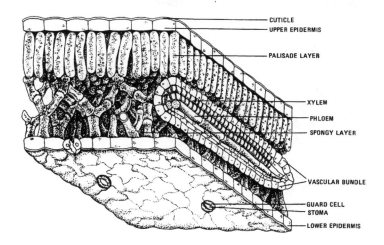

Figure 10. Diagram of leaf section

4. **Water requirement (evapotranspiration ratio)**— The units of water required to produce a unit of plant dry matter. Or, in equation form:

Water Requirement (WR) = kg H_2O evapotranspired/kg dry matter.

a. The WR varies for a given crop from one climate to another and usually decreases with increased fertility and weed control.

b. Drought tolerance is not always increased by using plants with a low evapotranspiration ratio.
   1. For instance, alfalfa with a relatively high WR of approximately 800 may be a productive crop under drought conditions because its deep root system is able to tap water supplies deep in the soil.
   2. Oats and other small grains are also grown in drier climates regardless of their higher WR because they mature early and miss much of the hot summer weather.

c. Generally the species with low WR will withstand water shortages better than species with high WR.

d. Table 10 shows the average water requirements for different climates, management, and crop species.

Table 10. Water Requirements

Climate	Evapotranspiration ratio
Hot, dry	High
Cool, humid	Low

Management	
Poor fertility	High
Good Fertility	Low
Poor weed control	High
Good Weed Control	Low

Crop Species	
Alfalfa	High (800+)
Cotton, Wheat, Soybeans	Medium (600-700)
Maize, Sorghum	Low (300-400)

Why are stomata open in the daylight and closed at night?

What causes a plant to require less moisture than another plant?

C. Mineral uptake

1. Methods of nutrient uptake by crop roots:

Roots must be in contact with soil nutrients in order for the root to absorb them. This root-nutrient contact can occur in different ways (Figure 11):
a. By root growth and interception of nutrients
b. By nutrient flow in soil water
c. By diffusion of nutrients from a high concentration zone to a low concentration zone

Once the root-nutrient contact is made, roots can "absorb" the nutrient in two ways (Figure 11):
a. Passive Uptake— nutrient ions move with the water into roots. Transpiration is the essential driving force for passive uptake of water and nutrients.
b. Active Uptake— nutrient ions are "pumped" into the root requiring ATP energy.

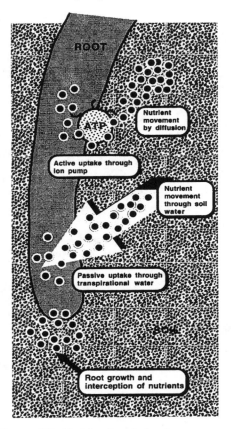

Figure 11. Nutrient uptake by crop roots
(Courtesy of Dr. Ricardo Salvador, Iowa State University)

2. Factors affecting nutrient uptake:

a. Factors that reduce root growth also reduce nutrient uptake.
b. Nutrient uptake is greater when nutrient concentrations in the root zone are high.
c. Adequate soil aeration and soil moisture improve nutrient uptake.
d. Nutrient uptake rate is generally greatest in the root hair zone and in newly formed roots than in older roots.
e. The soil and plant must maintain a balance of cation (positive) and anion (negative) nutrients to avoid a flow of electrical current. Proper soil pH improves cation-anion balance and nutrient availability.

    c.   The shaded condition increases the level of auxins (plant growth hormones), especially indoleacetic acid (IAA).

    d.   Sunlight destroys IAA. Shaded or darkened conditions increase IAA in the plants.

    e.   Too high plant population increases shading, increases IAA, increases elongation of stems and increases stalk lodging (stem breakage and falling over of plants).

C. Tillering, Branching, and Barrenness

1. Causes:

    a.   A plant will not tiller (produce secondary stems from the crown area), branch or produce seed unless the IAA level in the plant is reduced below the optimum level for vegetative elongation.

    b.   Tillering is increased by cool temperatures, adequate soil fertility and soil moisture.

    c.   None of the factors in (b) will cause tillering, branching or seed production. The IAA concentration is the critical factor and triggers the response.

    d.   Some varieties have higher optimum levels of IAA and are more population tolerant.

NOTE: Table 8 shows how barrenness (failing to produce seed) was reduced by using an upright leaf variety that permits more sunlight into the canopy to reduce the IAA level.

What is the significance of the rapid etiolation response of many weeds to shaded conditions?

What causes plants to be barren (without seed)?

D. Crop Development

1. Reproductive development

    Crop plant development proceeds from vegetative growth to reproductive growth, but this transition differs among crop species. Crop species are often categorized into determinate and indeterminate growth types, based on the nature of the vegetative-reproductive growth transition.

    a.   **Growth types:**

        1.   Determinate Growth Type— Develops most of the vegetative growth before flowering. The transition from vegetative to reproductive growth is relatively rapid and the plant terminates growth with a large reproductive structure.
Examples: wheat, oats, barley, maize, sugarcane, tobacco and most species of field crops.

        2.   Indeterminate Growth Type— Vegetative and reproductive periods overlap for a longer period. The transition period from vegetative to reproductive growth is slower and less distinct. The plant may terminate growth with a smaller reproductive structure.
Examples: alfalfa and other forage legumes, cotton, trees and many other perennials.

Soybeans are an example of an annual crop with both determinate and indeterminate growth types.

Determinate soybeans   - Used primarily in the southern U.S.A.
         - Develops most of the vegetative growth before flowering.
         - Terminal growth is a raceme usually with many pods.
         - When grown in northern areas, has shorter growth and less lodging.
         - Is more susceptible to stress.

Indeterminate soybeans
- Used primarily in the northern U.S.A.
- Vegetative and reproductive periods overlap for a longer period.
- Usually grows taller, has a thinner stem, and is more susceptible to lodging.
- More drought tolerant during the reproductive period.
- Has a small terminal raceme, has fewer pods on upper stem.

Soybeans also have a semideterminate type which is intermediate in plant height and used to avoid the lodging problems of northern indeterminate types.

2. **Time of flowering and photoperiodism**

The time that reproductive growth begins in plants is greatly influenced by growth temperature and photoperiod (the length of daylight in a 24-hour period). Reproductive development occurs when a particular growth stage is reached by crop plants; thus, moderate increases in growth temperature generally hasten the time to flowering. The flowering response may also be modified by the crop's response to photoperiod (photoperiodism). When some plants reach a certain age, reproductive growth may be induced by certain daylengths. Once these plants have been induced, warmer temperatures generally hasten the reproductive progression.

a. **Photoperiodism:** The effect of photoperiod on flowering and plant maturity.

b. **Classifications of photoperiodism:**

Long Day Plants
- plants that flower when some critical minimum period of daylength is exceeded (this critical minimum photoperiod may vary with species and environment).
- plants flower under continuous light
- includes most cool season crops

Short Day Plants
- plants that flower when daylengths are shorter than some critical maximum (this critical maximum photoperiod may vary with species and environment)
- plants will not flower under continuous light
- includes most warm season crops

Day Neutral Plants
- plants whose flowering response is insensitive to daylength
- flowering generally begins when plants reach a certain age or size

Table 13 shows some of the major crops in each daylength category.

Table 13. Plant photoperiod classification

Short day plants	Day Neutral	Long day plants
Maize	Apple	Alfalfa
Lespedeza	Buckwheat	Barley
Rice	Cotton	Bromegrass
Sorghum	K. Bluegrass	All clovers
Soybeans	Sunflower	Oats
Sugarcane	Tobacco	Rye
Peanut	Tomato	Sugar Beet
		Wheat

c. **Photoperiodic response and phytochrome**

The flowering response of plants to daylength occurs through a special plant pigment called phytochrome. Phytochrome is a single pigment that can exist in two interchangeable forms. One form (PFR or Phytochrome Far Red) is formed during the day. The other form (PR or Phytochrome Red) is formed during the night by the slow conversion of PFR to PR. Thus, the length of days and nights regulate the amounts (ratio) of PFR and PR in the leaves and consequently, the photoperiodic response. It is through this phytochrome mechanism that plants appear to "sense" the seasons and long or short days.

Photoperiod	Phytochrome Forms	Flowering response
1. Shorter days (longer nights)	less PFR; more PR	Stimulates short day plants to flower
2. Longer days (shorter nights)	More PFR; Less PR	Stimulates long day plants to flower

What effect do long days and short nights have on phytochrome?

d. **Photoperiodic response and latitude**

Figure 13 shows the effects of latitude and resulting daylength on plant growth, flowering and developmental characteristics of a soybean (short day plant) variety adapted to Central Iowa. Note the following relationships when the variety is planted at three locations.

1. The three locations are at about the same longitude.
2. The length of the longest day varies from 14.4 hours to 15.8 hours as latitude increases from 35°N to 47°N.
3. The shorter daylength and warmer temperature at Little Rock stimulates the flowering process earlier than at Ames or Duluth.
4. The plants are ready for harvest on Sept. 21 in Little Rock but are still producing leaves, stem growth and pods at Duluth.
5. This short-day plant grows taller in areas of increased daylength. The same would be true for corn, sorghum and other short-day plants when grown under longer day regimes.

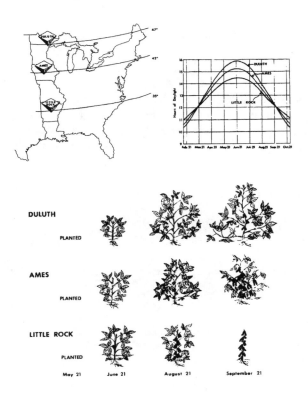

Figure 13. The Effect of Daylength on Plant Growth

Would a short day plant grow taller in Mexico than in Canada?

If the critical photoperiod is 14 hours for soybeans, would soybeans flower when daylength is 13 hours?

SELF-EVALUATION TEST

Crop Physiology

Circle letter corresponding to one best answer.

1. The ratio of the total leaf area of plants to land occupied by the plants is called the:
   a) NAR
   b) IAA
   c) LATLA
   d) LAI
   e) Auxin

2. C4 plants:
   a) have lower maximum temperatures for photosynthesis than C3 species
   b) have leaves that light saturate
   c) have lower yield potential than C3 species
   d) have higher CO_2 fixation rates
   e) include most cool season crops

3. At any light intensity the difference between line A and line B in the figure below equals:

   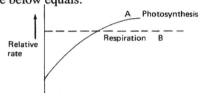

   a) PR
   b) NAR
   c) compensation point
   d) IAA
   e) assimilation rate

4. Which of the following is not true of the plant process called respiration?

   a) uses the products of photosynthesis
   b) occurs in all living cells
   c) releases energy
   d) releases water and carbon dioxide
   e) releases oxygen through stomata

5. The visible spectrum of light is indicated by the distance between which letters?

   a) A to I
   b) C to F
   c) F to H
   d) D to G
   e) B to F

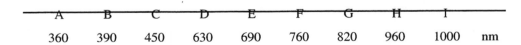

A	B	C	D	E	F	G	H	I	
360	390	450	630	690	760	820	960	1000	nm

6. High light intensity on the stalks of plants would result in:

   a) shorter plants
   b) taller plants
   c) more indole acetic acid
   d) barren plants
   e) weaker stalks

7. If a leaf respires at a rate of 14 mg CO_2 per hour and the photosynthetic rate is 27 mg CO_2 /hr, the Pn for the leaf is:

   a) 41 mg CO_2/hr.
   b) 15 mg CO_2/hr.
   c) 23 mg CO_2/hr.
   d) 13 mg CO_2/hr.
   e) 20.5 mg CO_2/hr.

8. Soybean nodulation:

   a) proceeds better at pH 4 than at pH 7
   b) provides the plant with usable nitrogen
   c) is caused by the same species of bacteria for all legumes
   d) increases the amount of nitrogen used from the soil
   e) is always adequate

9. The efficiency of photosynthesis in corn leaves is:

   a) less than that of soybeans
   b) less than that of oak trees but greater than that of soybeans
   c) less than that of soybeans but greater than that of oak trees
   d) less than that of alfalfa, but greater than that of soybeans
   e) greater than that of soybeans, alfalfa, and oak trees

10. The following statement most nearly describes transpiration:

   a) It is always helpful to the plant
   b) It causes the plant's temperature to be lower
   c) It is mostly due to water loss through the cuticle
   d) It is through the mitochondria
   e) It does not occur from the upper surface of corn plant leaves

11. Which of the following is not an important aspect of sunlight as it affects plant growth?

   a) quality
   b) intensity
   c) wavelength
   d) day length
   e) humidity

12. Pick the group of factors that will most strongly promote etiolation in corn plants.

    a) high light intensity; low fertility; low population
    b) high light intensity; high fertility; low population
    c) low light intensity; high fertility; high population
    d) low light intensity; high fertility; low population
    e) low light intensity; low fertility; low population

13. Select the correct statement concerning the flowering process.

    a) Most warm-season plants require long days for flowering.
    b) Phytochrome reversibility is regulated by temperature.
    c) Long-day plants require less PFR phytochrome than short-day plants to promote flowering.
    d) Plants exposed to daylight will have more PFR phytochrome than plants left in the dark.
    e) Rice is a day-neutral plant.

14. Translocation of amino acids:

    a) is in the phloem tissue
    b) is only from the roots to the leaves
    c) is in the xylem tissue
    d) is in the same tissue as water and minerals moving from the roots

15. The raw material for photosynthesis that enters through the stomata is:

    a) nitrogen
    b) water
    c) carbon dioxide
    d) oxygen
    e) magnesium

16. Roots absorb nutrients:

    a) through stomata
    b) by translocation
    c) by the C4 pathway
    d) by ion pumps requiring ATP
    e) in the canopy

17. Plant auxins include:

    a) gibberellic acid
    b) phosphon
    c) phytochrome
    d) NAR
    e) IAA

18. The evapotranspiration ratio of a plant is the:

    a) water transpired in 24 hours
    b) units of water required to produce a unit of dry matter
    c) water used per growing season
    d) water used per plant per day
    e) units of water required to produce one unit of seed

Chapter 4

Climate

For Nature also, cold and warm,
And moist and dry, devising long,
Thro' many agents making strong,
Matures the individual form.

(Love Thou Thy Land - A.L. Tennyson, 1809-1892)

The climate of a region describes the average weather and its variation over a long period. Weather describes the short term status of atmospheric conditions. Together, weather and climate greatly influence the selection and suitability of crops and cropping systems in a given area and influence crop management decisions on a continuous basis. The study of climate (climatology) and the processes involved in establishing weather and weather patterns (meteorology) is therefore basic to an understanding of crop production.

Three major climatic factors that determine crop distribution are temperature, humidity, and precipitation. Other important factors include weather patterns, solar radiation, wind, topographic features, as well as social and political factors. Temperature is influenced by latitude, elevation and large bodies of water. These determine the temperature extremes and the length of the growing season (number of frost-free days) available for crop growth. Temperature, precipitation, and humidity within regions determine the moisture availability and the level of heat and moisture stress crops are subjected to. The influence of climate on cropping systems is illustrated in the following data for U.S. agricultural regions.

Figure 1. Agricultural Regions and Climatic Characteristics of the United States

CROP REGION	CROP EXAMPLES
A Pacific Northwest Forest, Forage, Seed and Specialty Crop Region	Lumber Trees; Small Grains; Legume and Grass Seed Production
B California Subtropical Fruit, Truck, and Specialty Crop Region	Truck Crops, Flowers, Cotton and Grains; Alfalfa Seed Production
C Western Range and Irrigated Crop Region	Range Grasses, Forest, Forage and Irrigated Crops
D Rocky Mountain Range and Forest Region	Range Grasses and Forest
E Great Plains Range and Small Grains Region	Wheat and other Small Grains, Hay and Range Crops, Irrigated Grains, Cotton and Peanuts
F Northern Lake States Forest, Forage, Truck, and Fruit Crop Region	Forest, Forage, Vegetable and Fruit Crops; Small Grains
G Northeastern Forest and Forage Crop Region	Forest and Forage Grasses and Legumes
H Central Feed Grains Region	Corn, Soybeans, Small Grains, Forage
I Central and Eastern States General Crop, and Forest Crop Region	Corn, Soybeans, Rice, Small Grains, Tobacco, Cotton, Forage
J South Atlantic and Gulf States General Crop and Forest Region	Cotton, Peanuts, Tobacco, Feed Grains, Forages, and Forest
K South and Eastern Coastal States Forest and Truck Crop Region	Forest, Vegetables, Fruit, Forage, and General Grains
L Florida Subtropical Fruit, Truck, and Specialty Crop Region	Subtropical Fruits, Vegetables, Citrus, Sugarcane, Seed Crops, Forage

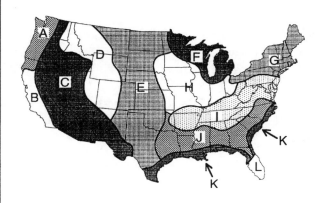

Moisture Regions and the Average Length of Frost-Free Period

Humidity Province	Annual Precipitation (cm)
Arid	0-25
Semiarid	25-50
Subhumid	50-75
Humid	75-100
Perhumid	Above 100

Less than 120 Frost-Free Days

120-200 Frost-Free Days

200+ Frost-Free Days

I. A PROFILE OF THE ATMOSPHERE

The environmental conditions immediately surrounding the aerial portion of plants is called the microclimate. The character of the microclimate is linked to the atmosphere above it. The earth's atmosphere can be divided into a vertical profile with layers of different widths and characteristics (Figure 2). The layer closest to the earth, called troposphere, directly influences crop production because most of our "weather" is caused by the reaction of forces in the troposphere. However the stratosphere plays an important role in filtering out solar radiation that would be harmful to plant and animal life on earth. Upper layers of the atmosphere are of little direct importance to plants, but are of great value in the transmission of radio waves and other technology.

A. Troposphere

1. Zone closest to the earth (0-16 km or 0-10 miles, width varies)
2. Zone of greatest climatic variability and weather events
3. Zone of cloud formation
4. Warmed by earth's radiation; air temperature decreases with height
5. Jet streams (swift flowing air currents), which can influence weather patterns, are frequently located in the upper troposphere.

B. Stratosphere

1. 16-50 km (10-31 miles) above earth's surface
2. Location of ozone layer. Ozone (O_3) absorbs the high energy, short wave ultraviolet radiation emitted by the sun. Ultraviolet radiation has enough energy to cause skin cancer and harm DNA molecules, thus ozone provides a protective shield above the earth.

C. Other Atmospheric Layers

1. Mesosphere: 50-85 km (31-53 miles), air temperature decreases with height.
2. Thermosphere: 85-500 km (53-310 miles), warmest part of the atmosphere.

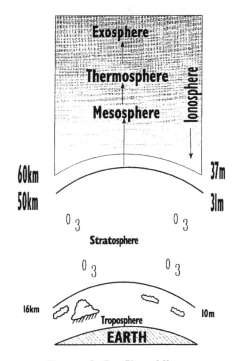

Figure 2. Profile of the Earth's Atmosphere

3. Exosphere: ≥ 500 km (≥310 miles), upper limit of our atmosphere, atoms and molecules can escape earth's gravity and enter into space.
4. Ionosphere: 60-1000 km (37-620 miles), an electrified region (largely in the thermosphere) containing ions and free electrons. Reflects radio waves back to earth.

Chlorine from chlorofluorocarbons (widely used in previous years for propellants in spray cans and in refrigerators and air conditioners) and nitrous oxides can break down ozone. What might be the agricultural consequences of ozone depletion in the stratosphere?

II. BASIC ATMOSPHERIC RELATIONSHIPS IN THE TROPOSPHERE

Many factors influence characteristics and movement of air in our atmosphere resulting in weather changes. Some of these factors are discussed below and illustrated in Figure 3.

A. Atmospheric factors that cause air to decrease in density will cause air to move upward. These factors may be:

1. increasing air temperature
2. decreasing air pressure
3. increasing water vapor

B. Rising air cools at the rate of 1°C per 100 m.

1. Precipitation requires the upward movement of air. This upward movement causes a cooling of the air mass and condensation of water vapor.
2. Generally, the more water vapor in the air, the less cooling is required to cause saturation and condensation.

C. Atmospheric factors that cause air to increase in density will cause the air to move downward. These factors may be:

1. decreasing air temperature
2. increasing air pressure
3. decreasing water vapor

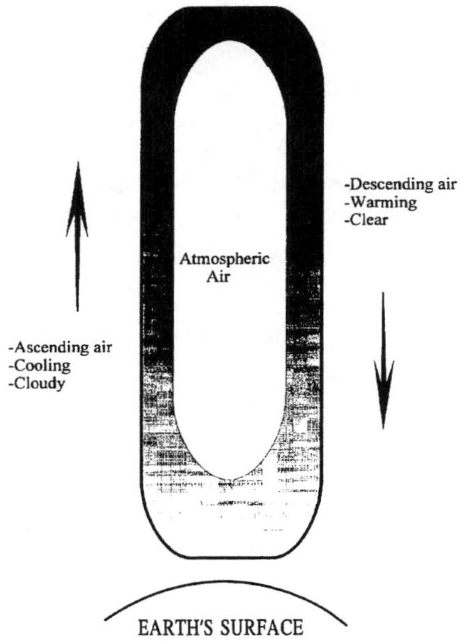

Figure 3. Atmospheric Air Movement

D. Descending air warms at the rate of 1°C per 100 m.

1. Clear skies normally occur with the downward movement of air. This downward movement causes a warming of the air mass and decreases the relative humidity.

E. Warm air has a greater capacity for moisture (water vapor) than cool air.

III. PRECIPITATION

Precipitation requires condensation of water vapor and the formation of raindrops (or snow flakes) which grow large enough to fall to the earth. This is brought about by cooling the air mass. The major mechanism to achieve this in the troposphere is by lifting air. Air may be forced to rise by adding water vapor, by heating the air mass, by forcing it to move over an elevation such as a mountain range, or by less dense air flowing up over cooler, denser air.

Why does the Pacific Northwest receive more precipitation than the Great Plains?

A. Distribution of Precipitation

1. Geographic-Cropping regions may be classified on the basis of average annual precipitation according to the designations in Table 1.

Table 1. Annual precipitation and cropping regions

Annual precipitation (cm)	Cropping region	Type of cropping
0-25	Arid	Grazing, desert vegetation
25-50	Semiarid	Small grains
50-75	Subhumid	Row and forage crops
75-100	Humid	Forest and row and forage crops
Above 100	Perhumid	All crops

2. Monthly distribution-The distribution of precipitation throughout the year is very important in determining what crops can be grown. Figure 4 shows the relationship between precipitation and crop water needs in a subhumid region.

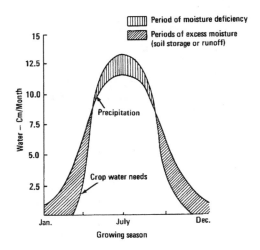

Figure 4. The annual moisture regime in a typical subhumid region

In a humid climate soil-stored moisture is usually sufficient for growing season requirements. In some years the precipitation in a subhumid region may not be sufficient to satisfy transpiration and evaporation needs.

100

Figure 5 gives the typical relationship between precipitation and crop needs in an arid or semiarid region where precipitation falls mainly in the cool season. The soil-stored moisture is usually insufficient to meet the growing season needs of the crop in these areas.

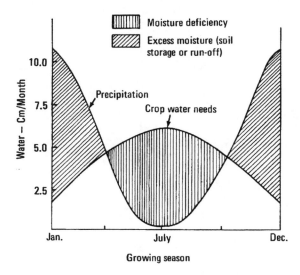

Figure 5. The Annual Moisture Regime in an Arid or Semiarid Region

The efficiency of water utilization is largely determined by the rate of transpiration from the plants and the rate of evaporation from the soil. Transpiration and evaporation are jointly called evapotranspiration. Approximately, 30 cm (12 inches) of precipitation in North Dakota is sufficient to produce a crop of wheat, while in Western Texas where temperatures are higher, this amount of precipitation is able to produce a crop of wheat only if supplemental irrigation is used. Without irrigation only sparse grazing land is supported by 30 cm of moisture. This difference in utilization efficiency shows how important temperature is in determining the rate of evapotranspiration.

Production in arid and semiarid regions can be increased by summer-fallowing. This means that two years of precipitation are utilized to produce one crop. This is accomplished by keeping the soil completely free of plant growth for one growing season in order to store up sufficient moisture to make it possible to produce a crop in the second year. However, fallowing exposes bare soil to the forces of wind and water and increases the environmental risks of soil erosion.

Why is winter precipitation in climatic regions with severe winters not as effective in crop production as the precipitation received during the growing season?

IV. TEMPERATURE

Temperature is the intensity factor of heat energy. It regulates the rate of all chemical processes in the plant; thus it plays a major role in determining the rate of crop growth and development. It also determines the length of the growing season and the kinds of plants that may be grown.

A. Air and Soil Temperature Fluctuation

Figure 6 shows the general daytime relationship between air and soil temperatures. At night the relationship would tend to follow the dotted lines near the soil surface. Whenever the temperature of the air near the ground level is lower than the temperature of the air above it, it is called an inversion (See dotted line Figure 6).

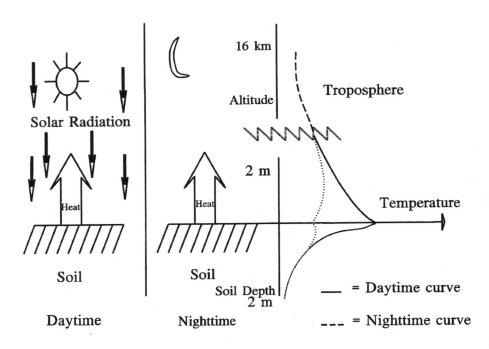

Figure 6. The Temperature Profile of the Atmosphere and the Soil in Summer

Do soil temperatures fluctuate as much as air temperature? Why?

What is the name of the condition when air temperature increases with height?

B. Temperature and Crop Growth

Plants differ in their temperature requirements for growth (Figure 7). The cardinal temperatures (minimum, optimum, and maximum) for crops can be defined as:

1. Minimum Cardinal Temperature-lowest temperature required for growth or process.
2. Optimum Cardinal Temperature-temperature required for maximum growth or process.
3. Maximum Cardinal Temperature-highest temperature limit for growth or process

Short-term temperatures beyond the minimum or maximum cardinal temperatures do not necessarily kill the plant but the activity of growth or the process ceases. Within the normal temperature range for plant growth, the growth rate is approximately doubled for each 10°C increase in temperature.

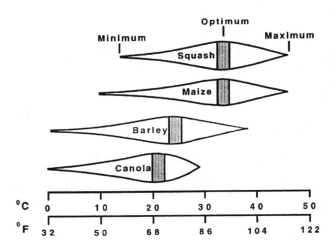

Figure 7: Cardinal Temperatures for Crop Growth

Crops are planted at different times in different regions across the U.S. According to Hopkins Bioclimatic law, events such as planting, harvesting and specific morphological developments in plants are delayed 4 days for one degree of latitude north, 5 degrees of longitude east and for every 400 feet of altitude (122 m). For example, planting is later as one moves northward, eastward, and upward in the United States.

Temperature also determines the length of the growing season. Crops vary in the number of days required to complete their life cycles. Increased temperatures during crop growth generally decrease the number of days required to maturity for a particular crop. Table 2 shows the growing season required for some major crops.

Table 2. Crop growing season requirements

Crop	Approx. days required for life cycle
Corn	120
Oats	90
Barley	80
Sugarcane	450
Cotton	180

Temperature is used to quantify the amount of plant growth that occurs. This correlation between temperature and growth is used to predict the harvest dates for crops, as well as determine the adaptability of species and varieties to a given area. Plant development can be measured in *Heat Units*.

A Heat Unit is Defined as: The number of °F that the mean daily temperature exceeds a base minimum growth temperature.

H.U. = $\dfrac{\text{Daily Minimum Temperature} + \text{Daily Maximum Temperature}}{2}$ - Base temperature (°F)

The base temperature varies with the species under consideration:

Table 3. Base growth temperatures for calculating heat units

Crop	Temperature °F (C°)
Small grains	40 (4)
Corn	50 (10)
Soybeans	50 (10)
Sorghum	60 (16)
Cotton	60 (16)

When limits are placed on the daily minimum and maximum temperatures, the heat units may be called Growing Degree Days (GDD). When GDD are summed over the growing season, it provides an index of varietal adaptation. In determining GDD, the minimum daily temperatures below the base temperature and maximum daily temperatures above a critical level are not used. The base temperature and the optimum maximum temperature are used instead. Note the following examples of calculating GDD and assume the critical maximum and minimum temperatures for maize are 86°F (30°C) and 50°F (10°C):

Example—Day 1
Max. Temp. = 84°F
Min. Temp. = 60°F
$GDD = \left(\dfrac{60 + 84}{2}\right) - 50 = 22$

Example—Day 2
Max. Temp. = 90°F
Min. Temp. = 45°F
$GDD = \left(\dfrac{50 + 86}{2}\right) - 50 = 18$

This system of logging a crop's development by measuring temperature has many variations and applications. It has found its greatest application in vegetable crops where harvest at the peak of quality has great economic significance. It is also used in determining the staggered planting dates of the male and female parents in hybrid seed production fields to guarantee successful cross pollination.

V. HUMIDITY-WATER CONTENT OF THE AIR

The amount of water that a plant must have to maintain normal growth is related very directly to the water content of the air. If the air is moist, there is relatively little evapotranspiration. In dry air, evapotranspiration is much more rapid.

Relative humidity, expressed as a percent, is the ratio of the amount of water vapor in the air to the total amount the air could hold at a given temperature. Expressing humidity values in units of relative humidity (measured with a psychrometer), while a common practice, is unsatisfactory in describing the moisture environment of crop plants. This is because relative humidity depends on both the concentration of water vapor in the air (vapor pressure) and on the temperature. An increase in temperature without any change in the amount of water vapor results in a decrease in relative humidity. As seen in Figure 8, the same relative humidity may refer to widely different water vapor contents depending on air temperature. The rate of transpiration, evaporation, and diffusion are affected directly by the vapor pressure of the atmosphere.

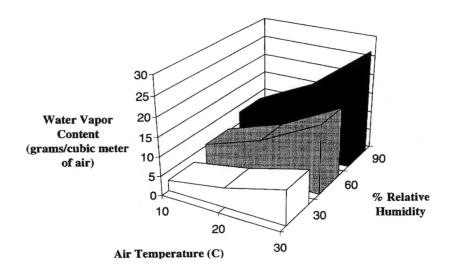

Figure 8. The relationship between temperature, water vapor, and relative humidity

Vapor pressure is that part of the total air pressure caused by the presence of water vapor molecules in the air. Vapor pressure deficit (V.P.D.), sometimes referred to as the drying power of the air, is the difference between the vapor pressure needed to saturate the air and the actual vapor pressure. In other words, the lower the water content of the air, the greater the vapor pressure deficit and the greater the drying power of the air. Figure 9 shows the relationship between V.P.D., temperature, relative humidity, and the drying power of the air. It is obvious that V.P.D. is a better indicator of drying power than relative humidity. Winds tend to increase the drying power of the air by removing saturated air or by importing dry air.

R.H. = 50% for both Air Masses

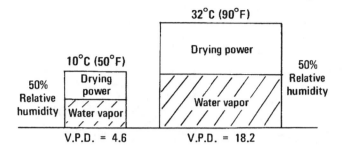

Figure 9. The Drying Power of Two Air Masses (at the same relative humidity but at different temperatures)

The relationship between relative humidity, temperature, and vapor pressure deficit is shown in Table 4. It shows the wide range of drying conditions that exist at the same relative humidity. Note the difference in temperature and relative humidity in Table 6 which produce nearly the same vapor pressure deficit of ~6.4.

Table 4. The relationship between relative humidity, temperature, and vapor pressure deficit

Temperature °C (°F)	Actual vapor pressure deficit (mm Hg.) at indicated relative humidity		
	80%	50%	30%
0 (32)	0.92	2.29	3.21
5 (41)	1.31	3.27	4.58
10 (50)	1.84	4.60	**6.45**
15 (59)	2.56	**6.40**	8.95
20 (68)	3.51	8.77	12.28
25 (77)	4.75	11.88	16.63
30 (86)	**6.36**	15.91	22.27
35 (95)	8.44	21.09	29.53

What is the drying power of the air today? Using Table 6 and the temperature and relative humidity determine today's V.P.D.

VI. WEATHER PATTERNS

In many climatic regions, weather is constantly changing on a seasonal, weekly, and even on a daily basis. What makes the weather change? Our temperature, wind, humidity, cloud and precipitation patterns are determined by changes in air pressure and air masses.

A. Characteristics of pressure cells

High pressure	**Low pressure**
1. High pressure	Low pressure
2. Anticyclonic	Cyclonic
3. Clockwise air circulation (Northern Hemisphere)	Counterclockwise air circulation (Northern Hemisphere)
4. Sinking air	Rising air
5. Very few clouds	Many clouds
6. Very little precipitation	Much precipitation
7. Air moves outward from cell center	Air moves inward to cell center

From which direction is the wind over your area today? In Figure 10 the wind would be generally from the south. The low pressure would be on the left and the high pressure on the right. This is an easy way to determine the location of pressure cells relative to a given location: stand with your back to the wind and the high pressure will be on your right hand and the low pressure on your left hand.

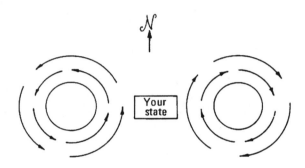

Figure 10. Air Circulation Around Pressure Cells in the Northern Hemisphere

B. Air masses

An air mass is a large body of air which is essentially uniform in horizontal directions. There are many kinds and descriptions of air masses. However, there are four major ones that greatly influence the weather of North America. These air masses are described by their origin. Air masses originating over land (continental) are dry and those originating over water (maritime) are moist. Continental and maritime air masses can be further described as polar (cool, cold) or tropical (warm, hot), depending on the latitude of the source region. Abbreviations are commonly used to denote these characteristics of origin.

cP- *Continental Polar*
1. Originates over polar land masses
2. Dominates the winter weather in northern climates
3. Produces cold and clear weather in winter
4. Causes cool periods in the summer
5. Cold, dry, stable air mass

mP- *Maritime Polar*
1. Originates over polar marine areas
2. Contains considerable moisture
3. Is usually modified to cP air by moving over mountains and land
4. Cool, moist, unstable air mass

cT- *Continental Tropical*
   1.   Originates over superheated land masses, e.g., Southwest U.S.A.
   2.   Produces clear, hot and dry summer weather
   3.   Permits wide range of diurnal temperatures
   4.   Hot, dry stable air mass

mT- *Maritime Tropical*
   1.   Originates over large bodies of water in the tropics
   2.   Dominates the summer weather of central and eastern U.S.A.
   3.   Produces hot, humid summer weather
   4.   Brings moisture for summer rains to central U.S.A.
   5.   Warm, moist, unstable air mass

C. Weather fronts

When two or more air masses with different properties come together, they create an area of instability at their interface. This boundary zone of unstable weather is called a "front". The following three figures show the three principle types of weather fronts.

A cold front occurs when a cold air mass replaces warm air. The cold heavier air mass can rapidly force the lighter, warmer air aloft where condensation occurs. Thunderstorms and local, heavy showers frequently result.

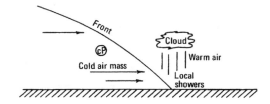

Figure 11. A Cold Front Profile

A warm front occurs when a warm air mass replaces cold air. The warm, less dense air rides up over the top of the cooler, more dense air, and if the warm air is moist, it may cause widespread precipitation.

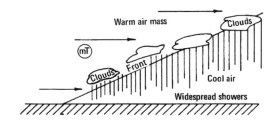

Figure 12. A Warm Front Profile

An occluded front occurs when one front moves another front aloft. In the figure shown here, a cold front has overtaken a warm front (this is usually the case with occluded fronts because cold fronts generally travel faster than warm fronts). The warm air has been forced aloft. Occluded fronts have weather characteristics of both warm and cold fronts, resulting in cool "drizzly" weather.

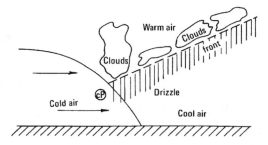

Figure 13. An Occluded Front Profile

Why does an advancing warm front produce more widespread rain than an advancing cold front?

D. Surface features

The surface features of the earth and associated bodies of water have great effects on the regional weather patterns. The direction of the prevailing winds and storm tracks play a major role in determining the magnitude and specifics of surface feature effects.

Figure 14 shows the role of a mountain range in bringing about wide differences in climate. The leeward (downwind) side of mountains is usually drier than the windward (upwind) side. Whenever air is forced to rise, it cools, condenses, and falls as rain. When air descends a mountain slope, it is warmed and, having lost its moisture, is a very dry air mass. Because of this and the prevailing westerly winds, states on the eastern side of the Rocky Mountains frequently require irrigation for crop production.

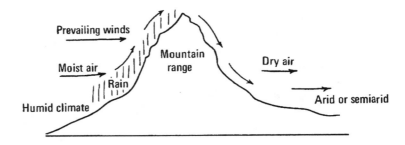

Figure 14. The role of mountain ranges in altering the climate

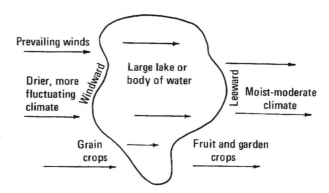

Figure 15. The role of bodies of water in altering the climate

Figure 15 shows how a body of water can affect the climate and the crops grown around its shores. The air moving across the large body of water becomes modified by the water. Bodies of water warm and cool more slowly than surrounding land. Because of this, the climate on the leeward shore is more moderate, subject to less temperature fluctuation, and more moist than the windward shore. Hardy crops such as cereal grains are predominant on the windward shore, while more delicate crops such as vegetables and fruits are grown on the leeward shore.

Cold air runs downhill much like water. In hilly areas, the coldest air is usually found at the valley floor especially in evening hours after sunset. Slopes which are exposed to the direct rays of the sun are usually warmer, drier, and support drought-tolerant species such as grasses. Slopes which are not subjected to direct sunshine for long periods of time are cooler and support more lush vegetation such as deciduous and coniferous trees.

Which state would likely produce the most cold sensitive fruits, Michigan or Wisconsin? Why?

VII. CLIMATIC CHANGE

There are many agricultural practices that change the microclimate surrounding a growing crop. Using wind breaks, different tillage and planting practices, irrigation, and soil drainage are examples of how temperature, moisture, wind speed, and/or relative humidity can be altered by human activity.

An important and increasing concern, however, is how human activity can affect climate on a macro scale. Most scientists agree that human activity is increasing factors that can cause macroclimatic changes. However, the difficulty and debate are in estimating the extent and the consequences of climatic change due to human activity from the normal trends and variation of global climates over time. Acid rain from industrial sulfur emissions, deforestation, desertification (expansion of desert regions) from misuse or overuse of semi-arid lands, and increased emissions of certain atmospheric gasses from human activity are examples of factors that can force changes in macroclimates.

Much concern lies with factors that influence the "atmospheric greenhouse effect" and its role in global warming. The greenhouse effect refers to temperature buildup in greenhouses due to the trapping of infared (heat) radiation. Direct solar radiation passes through glass but the infared radiation emitted by heated objects is absorbed and re-emitted by glass allowing temperatures to increase inside the greenhouse. This phenomenon, when applied to our atmosphere, is termed the atmospheric greenhouse effect. Solar radiation passes relatively freely through our atmosphere but infared radiation emitted from the earth as heat energy is partly blocked, absorbed, and re-emitted by atmospheric gases, such as nitrogen, oxygen, carbon dioxide, and water vapor (Figure 16). Clouds also help trap heat thus, the risk of frost injury to crops during cloudless nights is greater than on cloudy nights.

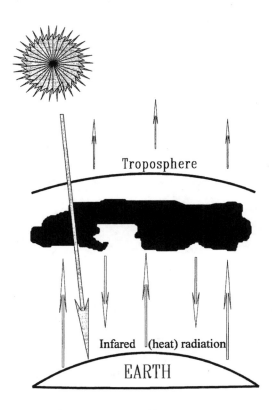

Figure 16: Atmospheric Greenhouse Effect

Of the atmospheric gases that influence infared absorption (also called "greenhouse gases"), scientists have identified four that have been measurably increased due to human activity:

1. Carbon Dioxide-CO_2 is the major potential greenhouse gas contributing to global warming from human activity. There has been a 25% increase in atmospheric CO_2 concentration (280 to 350 ppm) in the last 150 years. If the present trend continues, estimates of global warming by 2050 vary from 2 to 9°C (3.6 to 16.2°F). The global surface temperatures have not been more than 1 to 2° C warmer during modern history. Major causes of CO_2 emissions from human activity:
    a. burning of fossil fuels (coal, oil, and petroleum fuels)
    b. deforestation (burning)

2. Methane-constituent of natural gas and product of anaerobic decay in wetlands and the digestive system of ruminant animals. There has been a 100% increase in methane in the last 100 years. Wetland rice production is considered one of the primary contributors of methane from human activity.

3. Nitrous Oxide-product of oxidation and reduction of nitrogen in the soil. Natural microbial activity in the soil, burning of forests and fossil fuels, spread of agriculture, and increased fertilizer usage are sources of nitrous oxides.

4. Chlorofluorocarbons (CFCs)-historically used as cooling fluids in refrigeration, as propellants in aerosols, as solvents, and in plastic manufacturing. CFCs, unlike other greenhouse gases, are not naturally produced and are a direct result of industrial production. The estimated atmospheric lifetime of CFCs is 60-100 years.

Agriculture in the U.S. contributes an estimated 5% of the total U.S. warming potential of carbon dioxide, methane, and nitrous oxide emissions, and 1% on a global basis (Figure 17).

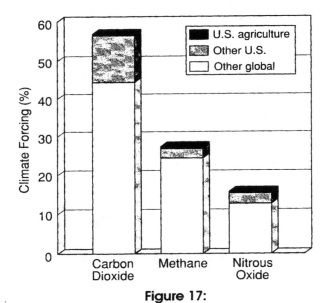

Figure 17:

The climate forcing by U.S. agriculture related to that by other activities on the globe. Climate forcing combines estimates of emissions of the various greenhouse gases by each activity with the absorption of long-wave radiation from the earth and the estimated lifetime in the atmosphere of each gas. It is expressed as the percentage of the forcing during the next 100 years by the 1990 global emission of three gases. For example, emissions of methane from the globe are 27% of all forcing, and methane from U.S. farming is 0.4% of all forcing. U.S. agriculture's emissions of all three gases is 0.8% of the global forcing from the three gases.

From: Preparing U.S. Agriculture for Global Climate Change by Paul E. Waggoner, Science of Food and Agriculture, July, 1992.

Individuals and industries like agriculture can and should strive to reduce factors that can cause global climate change. Increased minimum tillage, reduced fossil fuel consumption, improved water and fertilizer usage, more efficient crop and animal production, and proper land management are practices that sustain agricultural productivity and at the same time, reduce the impact on global climates.

SELF-EVALUATION TEST

Climate

Circle letter corresponding to one best answer.

1. On the leeward side of a large body of water you would expect climate to be:

    a) drier and fluctuating
    b) drier and moderate
    c) more fluctuating and moist
    d) moderate and moist
    e) rainy and cold year-round

2. Condensation occurs when:

    a) warm dry air is forced to move over a mountain range
    b) warm moist air contacts a warmer surface
    c) a cool moist air mass is heated in the ionosphere
    d) warm moist air is forced to move over a mountain range
    e) a warm dry air mass receives considerable water vapor

3. Which greenhouse gases have been measurably increased due to human activity?

    a. O_2, CO_2, methane, nitrous oxide
    b. O_2, CO_2, methane, water vapor
    c. CO_2, methane, chlorofluorocarbons, water vapor
    d. CO_2, methane, chlorofluorocarbons, nitrous oxide
    e. CO_2, water vapor, methane, ozone

4. Relative humidity is:

    a) always higher at 30°C than at 20°C
    b) always higher at 20°C than at 30°C
    c) the ratio of the water content at a given temperature to what the air can possibly hold at that temperature
    d) equal vapor pressure

5. Which of the following would most likely increase the drying capacity of the air?

    a) increase temperature and water vapor
    b) increase relative humidity
    c) decrease relative humidity but increase temperature
    d) decrease vapor pressure deficit
    e) decrease temperature but increase relative humidity

6. Which of the following statements does not generally apply to a high pressure air mass?

    a) It is anticyclonic.
    b) Air movement is clockwise.
    c) There is much precipitation.
    d) There are few clouds.
    e) Air moves away from pressure center.

7. If the wind is blowing from south to north, a low pressure system is most likely located:

    a) to the north
    b) to the west
    c) to the east
    d) to the south

8. When the temperature near ground level is lower than the temperature of air above it, the situation is called:

    a) a profile
    b) a greenhouse effect
    c) an inversion
    d) a dry power
    e) a horizon

9. A low pressure air cell:

    a) is anticyclonic
    b) has counterclockwise circulation
    c) has a downdraft
    d) causes very few clouds
    e) has air moving away from its cell center

10. During the growing season, the day temperature at:

    a) 2 meters in the air should be cooler than the soil surface
    b) 1/2 meter below the soil surface should be warmer than the surface
    c) 2 meters in the air should be warmer than the soil surface
    d) 1/2 meter below the soil surface should be the same as the surface
    e) 2 meters in the air should be the same as the soil surface

11. Select the air mass that dominates the winter weather in central U.S.A.:

    a) mP
    b) mT
    c) cP
    d) cT
    e) pH

12. A warm air mass overtaking a cooler air mass causes:

    a) stable weather conditions
    b) widespread shower activity
    c) local shower activity
    d) sunny weather
    e) high air pressure

13. The earth's atmosphere up to 16 kilometers above the earth's surface:

    a) includes the ionosphere
    b) is heated mainly by the earth
    c) excludes the troposphere
    d) is warmer than the thermosphere
    e) reflects radio waves back to earth

Chapter 5

Soils

The soil is important in crop production because it gives support and nutrition to the plants. It also provides the foundation for our homes and highways, food for our nutrition, antibiotics for our health, a depository for our wastes, beauty for our viewing, and financial security. Soils affect directly or indirectly the standard of living of everyone on the earth. Soil is a dynamic body that is ever changing according to physical, chemical and biotic influences and the way we use and misuse soil. Soil is a natural resource that must be protected and managed with the utmost care.

I. SOIL-FORMING FACTORS

The kinds of soil that evolve and develop in a region are mainly determined by 5 soil-forming factors: climate, vegetation, topography, parent material, time

A. Climate

The basic features of climate are discussed in a separate unit. This factor plays a primary role in determining not only the rate of soil formation but also the type of soil that is formed. The amount of moisture, humidity, frost, heat, wind, and sunlight all play a role in determining the rate of weathering of the basic minerals from which our soils are formed.

The climate also determines the type of soil produced by influencing the vegetation that is able to grow on a particular soil. The type of vegetation affects the amount and distribution of the organic matter, and also influences the rate and amount of leaching. Figure 1 shows how climate affects soil formation and characteristics over time. The Alfisols are a broad category (order) of soils that are usually formed under forest vegetation and are more highly weathered, acidic, and lighter in color (reddish or yellowish) than Mollisols. Mollisols are formed under tall grass vegetation and are dark soils higher in natural fertility and organic matter than Alfisols. Aridisols are formed under desert grasses and shrubs. They are usually light in color, low in organic matter content, and require irrigation for crop production.

B. Vegetation and Other Living Organisms

Figure 1 also shows the direct effect that vegetation has on soil formation. The organic matter in a short grass soil is limited to the few inches at the surface. As the climate is able to support larger grass species, the organic matter is distributed to greater depths in the soil. Soils formed under forests have a mantle of organic matter on the surface. Thus, cultivation usually improves the productivity of forest soils to a greater extent than grassland soils by mixing the organic matter into the plow layer.

Microorganisms and soil animals such as earthworms, help breakdown and mix organic matter in the soil and influence decomposition and soil chemical reactions. Human activity, such as removing natural vegetation, tilling and irrigating soil can influence soil formation.

C. Topography

The topography of the land refers to its slope characteristics. Slope affects the process of soil formation in two ways:
1. By determining the rate of erosion and thus the depth of the soil.
2. By determining the patterns and rates of drainage and thus affecting the availability of moisture in the weathering process.

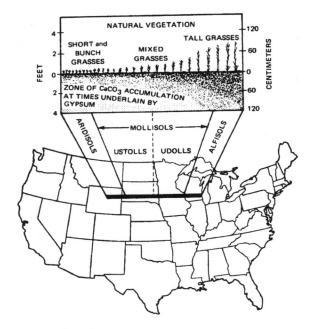

Reprinted with permission of The Macmillan Company from The Nature and Properties of Soils by Nyle C. Brady, 10th Edition, p. 68. Figure 3.12. Copyright by the Macmillan Publishing Company, 1990.

Figure 1. Correlation Between Climate, Natural Vegetation and Soil Formation in North Central U.S.

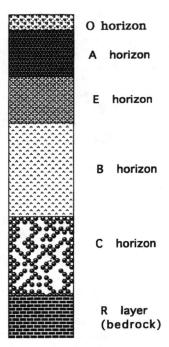

Soil Profile

Figure 2 shows the relationship between slope and the type of soil formed. Note the differences in the features of the various soil profiles. A soil profile is a vertical cross section of the soil showing the horizontal layers which are called horizons. Every well-developed, undisturbed soil has its own distinctive profile characteristics. These characteristics are used in classifying soils and in determining their uses and management practices.

The upper layers of a soil profile are usually higher in organic matter and are thus darker in color than the lower layers. The subsoil layers are areas of transition and accumulation. Clays, mineral oxides, and calcium carbonates gradually concentrate in the subsoil due to the percolation of water through the profile. The substratum or parent material is found below the subsoil. It is in the process of becoming a part of the soil through the activity of the various soil-forming factors.

In mineral soils, the upper, darker layer is typically called the "A" horizon. The "E" horizon is just below the "A" horizon and is generally lighter in color and is a zone of maximum leaching of clays, organic matter and some minerals, depending on how the soil was formed. The "B" horizon is found below the E horizon and is an accumulation zone of clays and mineral oxides. The C horizon is the unconsolidated material lying beneath the B horizon and is little affected by soil forming processes that influence the solum (A through B horizons collectively).

Some soils, such as forest soils, have an unusually high content of organic matter in various stages of decomposition in a layer above the A horizon and is called an O horizon. In shallow soils the underlying consolidated bedrock (R horizon) may be evident.

Is organic matter higher in the `A' or `B' horizon?

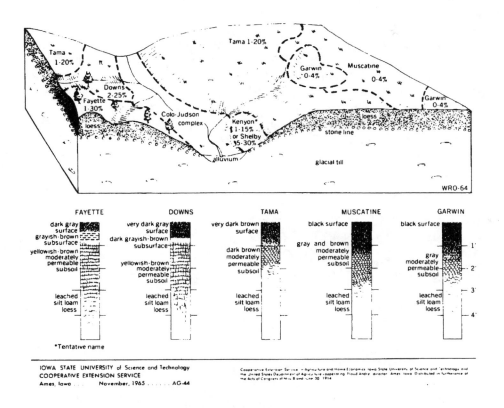

IOWA STATE UNIVERSITY of Science and Technology
COOPERATIVE EXTENSION SERVICE
Ames, Iowa . . . . November, 1965 . . . . . . AG-44

Figure 2. Topography and Soil Formation

D. Parent material

Parent material is the unconsolidated mineral matter lying underneath the 'B' horizon and is the material from which the soil has been formed. The chemical and mineralogical characteristics of the parent material have a great deal to do with the type of soil formed and the rate of its formation.

The relationship between parent material, the agencies of deposition and the soils produced are shown in Table 1.

Table 1

Type of parent material	Cause of movement	Type of soil produced
Sedentary	No movement	Residual
Transported	Gravity	Colluvial
	Water	Alluvial Lacustrine Marine
	Ice	Glacial
	Wind	Eolian

1. **Residual** soils are formed from parent material without movement away from the original bedrock.
2. **Colluvial** soils are produced from fragments detached from higher elevations and carried to lower elevations by gravity.
3. **Alluvial** soils are produced from parent material deposited by moving water.
4. **Marine** soils are developed from marine sediments with the subsequent recession of the sea and the exposure of these sediments to weathering and soil-building processes.
5. **Lacustrine** soils are developed from parent material deposited in glacial lakes during the ice age.
6. **Glacial** soils are developed from parent material deposited by the action of glaciers.
7. **Eolian** soils are developed from material deposited through the action of wind. A major eolian deposit of agricultural importance is loess (pronounced "luss") which is primarily composed of windblown silt from floodplains of rivers and glacial meltwaters.

What is the difference between colluvial and alluvial soils?

Figure 3 shows the soils of the U.S.A. which were affected by the glacial ice sheets. Note that loess deposits overlay vast areas of glacial deposits in the central part of the United States. Most of the U.S.A. is not affected by glacial deposits of parent material.

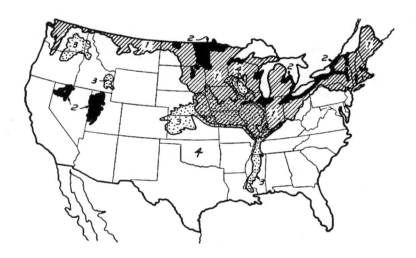

Figure 3. Origin of Soils in the U.S.

1. Glacial till deposits
2. Glacial-lacustrine deposits
3. Loess deposits
4. Non-glaciated area

E. Time

This factor is obviously important in all natural processes. Soil formation is a slow but continuous process. Some soils may take thousands of years to form, others may be formed in a relatively short time, depending on the nature of the parent material and the intensity of the weathering process.

Soils are referred to as young or mature according to the amount of profile development they exhibit. Young soils usually have poor surface drainage and are in the process of adjusting to their environment. Mature soils have definite profile development and usually have well developed external drainage.

II. PROPERTIES OF SOIL

What is soil? There are many kinds of soil ranging from organic peat bogs to sandy desert soils. A surface sample of a typical mineral soil contains four major constituents: mineral matter, organic matter, water, and air. Figure 4 shows the percent composition of a loam soil with optimum conditions for plant growth.

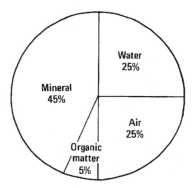

Figure 4. Composition of Loam Soil

Physical, chemical, and biological properties are three major areas of interest that affect soil productivity and suitability for crop production and non-agricultural uses of land.

A. Physical properties

The two major physical features of the soil are texture and structure. These physical properties are extremely important in determining the characteristics and suitability of a particular soil for different purposes and the manner in which it is managed.

1. Texture

The mineral fraction of a soil consists of a wide range of particle sizes from large rock to microscopic sized clay particles. Soil texture refers to the percentages (by weight) of the soil separates: sand, silt, and clay in a given soil. The relative amounts of sand-, silt- and clay-sized particles in the soil influences soil management properties such as erodibility, stability, fertility, and soil drainage. Table 2 shows the relationship between soil particle size and soil separates based on the U.S. Department of Agriculture classification system.

Table 2. Particle Size of Soil Fractions*

Particle size (diameter mm)	Soil separates
Less than 0.002	Clay
0.002 - 0.02	Silt
0.02 -0.2	Fine sand
0.2 - 2.0	Coarse sand

*USDA Classification System

Most soils are composed of varying amounts of the different soil separates. Agricultural soils are seldom made up of only one soil separate. The textural class (textural name) of a soil indicates the relative proportions of sand, silt and clay, and is not readily changed or altered. Once the percentages of sand, silt and clay in a soil are known, then the soil textural class can be determined using a textural triangle (Fig. 5).

U.S. DEPARTMENT OF AGRICULTURE SOIL CONSERVATION SERVICE
GUIDE FOR TEXTURAL CLASSIFICATION

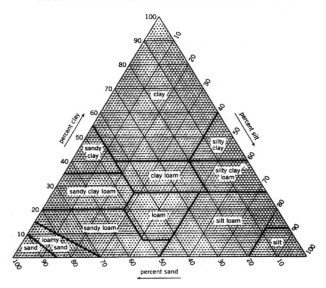

Figure 5. Soil Textural Triangle for Determining Textural Class

What is the soil textural class of a sample that contains 30% silt and 20% clay?

If the clay percent is reduced to 5%, what is the soil textural class?

2. Structure

Soil structure refers to the manner in which the individual particles are arranged. These structural units, called aggregates or peds, bear the same relationship to each other as bricks in a brick wall.

The type of structural aggregates in a soil affects:

    a. Soil pore size
    b. Water-holding capacity
    c. Water-infiltration rate
    d. Soil permeability to water and air

Two soils with the same texture may have completely different physical qualities because of differences in soil structure. The fine soil particles like clay and humus stick together creating various types of soil structure. Types of structural units ranked in order of size are:

1. Prismlike-Particles arranged in a vertical plane. Usually found in the subsoil.

2. Blocklike-Arranged in rectangular shape, well integrated with adjacent units. Usually found in the subsoil.

3. Platelike-Particles arranged in a horizontal plane. Occurs in any part of the profile.

4. Granular (spheroidal)-Arranged in circular fashion not well integrated with adjacent units. Characteristic of the topsoil.

Note the difference in aggregate size between continuous corn and continuous alfalfa or bluegrass.

Table 3. Aggregate analysis of a silt loam soil under different cropping treatments

Crop	% proportion of desirable soil aggregates*
Continuous corn	33
Corn in C-O-Cl rotation	42
Oats in C-O-Cl rotation	51
Clover in C-O-CI rotation	57
Continuous alfalfa	60
Continuous bluegrass	62

*aggregates > 0.25 mm in diameter

Adapted from Browning et al., United States Department of Agricultural Technical Bulletin 959; 41.

Soil Structure and Management - Improving or maintaining good soil structure enhances soil productivity. Unlike soil texture, soil structure can be readily changed through use and misuse of the soil. The following statements can apply to soil structure:

1. Granular and crumb structure types are spheroidal units found in many productive soils.
2. Granular and crumb structure types are greatly influenced by soil management.
3. Soil structure deteriorates with cultivation.
4. Soil structure deteriorates with compaction.
5. Applications of organic matter improve soil structure.
6. In some cases, there may not be a clear-cut relationship between crop yields and the amount of aggregation (structural units) in a soil.
7. Crop production becomes more expensive and the results more uncertain as soil aggregation decreases.
8. Soil crusting, impervious layers, low water permeability, poor water-holding capacity, all may be due in part or in total to poor aggregation.
9. Good soil structure makes it easier to till and prepare a good seedbed, increases water infiltration and improves soil aeration.
10. Reduced tillage systems promote better soil structure.

Influence of organic material on aggregate stability- Organic matter in the soil helps promote the formation of desirable granular structure in the topsoil and makes the aggregates more water stable. Products of organic matter decomposition help bind soil particles together and prevent the aggregates from disintegrating from tillage and beating action of rainfall. The result is better soil drainage and aeration for crop growth.

B. Chemical properties

Soil chemistry is a dynamic and complex phenomena. The soil constantly undergoes many chemical reactions ranging from breakdown of mineral and organic substances, changes in soil pH and nutrient solubility, to pesticide chemical reactions. The major chemical properties that have a direct effect on crop production include:

1. Soil fertility and mineral nutrition
2. Soil acidity and alkalinity (soil pH)

1. Soil Fertility and Mineral Nutrition

a. Organic Matter

In a productive soil, plants obtain some of their mineral nutrient requirements and much of their nitrogen from the decomposition of organic materials such as plant roots, stems, leaves, and animal manure. Decaying organic matter also supports bacteria and fungi, aids in bringing insoluble soil minerals into solution, and improves the physical condition of the soil. Practices that help in maintaining soil organic matter include:

a. Growing sod-forming crops
b. Using green manure crops
c. Conserving and applying animal manures
d. Using proper tillage and crop residue management. Conservation tillage practices improve soil tilth and reduce soil erosion and rapid crop residue decomposition in the topsoil.
e. Controlling erosion

How does organic matter affect soil fertility and soil structure?

Figure 6 shows the effect of management practices on soil organic matter as measured by organic carbon content. Crop rotation and additions of manure, lime, and fertilizer can improve the level of soil organic matter. Typically, virgin forest or prairie soils have the highest level of soil organic matter compared with similar soils that are cultivated. In cultivated soils less organic residue is returned to the soil.

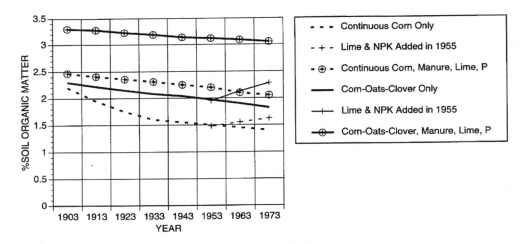

Figure 6. The Effects of Crop Management on Soil Organic Matter

Adapted from Odell, R.T., S.W. Melsted, and V.M. Walker, 1984. Changes in organic carbon and nitrogen of Morrow plot soils under different treatments, 1904-1973. Soil Science, 137:1060-171.

b. Mineral Nutrition

Some of the nutrients required by plants are obtained from the air and water. Over 90 percent of all plant substance is composed of these elements such as hydrogen, oxygen, and carbon. The relative concentrations and amounts of nutrients found in crop dry matter are shown in Table 4. These concentrations and total amounts vary with many factors, such as soil, climate, crop species, plant part, and growth stage. These values allow one to compare the relative nutrient amounts found in crops but do not indicate a ranking of importance to crop growth (they are all important). Also, these values indicate the amount of nutrients taken up by the plant but not the amounts actually needed in fertilizer applications because types and amounts of fertilzer nutrients vary with environmental and management factors.

Table 4. Relative concentrations and amounts of nutrients found in crops.

Nutrient	Symbol	Common % in Crops*	Amount in Unit Area of Maize Crop**		Source
			kg/ha	lbs/a	
Hydrogen	H	6	na	na	Water
Oxygen	O	45	na	na	Air and Water
Carbon	C	45	na	na	Air
Nitrogen	N	1.5	386	345	Air and Soil
Potassium	K	1	370	330	Soil
Calcium	Ca	0.5	59	53	Soil
Magnesium	Mg	0.02	44	39	Soil
Phosphorus	P	0.2	70	63	Soil
Sulfur	S	0.1	40	36	Soil
Chlorine	Cl	0.01	na	na	Soil
Iron	Fe	0.005	1.9	1.7	Soil
Manganese	Mn	0.002	0.9	0.8	Soil
Boron	B	0.002	0.13	0.1	Soil
Zinc	Zn	0.002	0.8	0.7	Soil
Copper	Cu	0.0006	0.14	0.1	Soil
Molybdenum	Mo	0.00001	na	na	Soil

*Percentages by weight based on plant dry matter weight

**Expressed as kg/ha (lbs/a) based on the aerial portion of maize plants producing 31.8 Mg/ha (14 ton/a) of total dry weight, which included 16.3 Mg/ha (260 bu/a) of grain dry weight at physiological maturity. Data adapted from Karlen, D.L., R.L. Flannery and E.J. Sadler. 1988. Aerial Accumulation and Partitioning of Nutrients by Corn. Agron. J. 80:232-242.

na = not analyzed

Soil elements essential for the growth of most plants may be divided into four groups.

Macronutrients		Micronutrients
Primary nutrients	**Secondary nutrients**	
Nitrogen (N)	Calcium (Ca)	Molybdenum (Mo)
Phosphorus (P)	Magnesium (Mg)	Boron (B)
Potassium (K)	Sulfur (S)	Copper (Cu)
		Iron (Fe)
		Manganese (Mn)
		Zinc (Zn)
		Chorine (Cl)

N, P, and K are called primary nutrients because they are the essential elements most frequently found deficient in the soil. Even though they may or may not be used by plants in quantities as great as Ca, Mg, and S, which are called the secondary nutrients, they are, nevertheless, more universally deficient and added to mixed fertilizers. The percentages by weight of N, P, and K in fertilizers are normally given as %N, %P_2O_5, and %K_2O (for analytical purposes in fertilizer manufacturing). However, none of these forms are actually taken up by plants.

Nitrogen and the Plant

1. Nitrogen in plants occurs mainly in protein.
2. Nitrogen is a component of chlorophyll.
3. Lack of nitrogen causes yellowing of leaves.
4. Deficiency symptoms occur first on older leaves.
5. Nitrogen deficiency also causes reduced growth and stunting of plants.
6. At maturity, there is more nitrogen in the seed than in any other plant part.
7. Nitrogen promotes vegetative growth and may delay maturity.
8. Plants take up nitrogen in the forms of NO_3^- and NH_4^{++}.

Phosphorus and the Plant

1. Phosphorus is a major component of chromosomes in each cell nucleus.
2. Phosphorus is a part of the DNA (deoxyribonucleic acid) and RNA (ribonucleic acid) molecules in the chromosomes.
3. Phosphorus is important in energy transfer and storage in the cell.
4. Phosphorus stores cell energy for use in tissue synthesis, and absorption of nutrients and water.
5. Younger leaves of some plants (grasses) turn reddish-purple when deficient.
6. Legume plants may be darker green or have a bluish cast when deficient.
7. Stunted growth is a common deficiency symptom.
8. At maturity, more phosphorus is in the seed than in any other plant part.
9. Phosphorus promotes plant maturing processes.
10. Plants take up phosphorus in the forms of HPO_4^{-2} and H_2PO_4.

Potassium and the Plant

1. Potassium is important in the synthesis of protein, carbohydrates and chlorophyll.
2. Potassium is important in energy transfer related to the absorption of N and P by plant roots.
3. Potassium is important in the translocation and storage of carbohydrates.
4. Potassium helps plants regulate water uptake by roots and the internal water and ionic balance of plant cells.
5. Deficiency symptoms occur on older leaves.
6. Deficiency symptoms vary among plant families-yellowing of leaf tip and margins in grasses, black leaf in many dicots and speckled leaf in most legumes.
7. Deficiencies also cause weak stems and increased lodging.
8. At maturity, most of the potassium is in the leaves and stem rather than in the seed.
9. Plants take up potassium in the form of K^+.

Why do deficiency symptoms of N, and K occur in the older leaves?

Micronutrients

The elements required by plants in the smallest amounts are called micronutrients. Although they are required by plants in small or trace amounts, they may have to be added to the soil or sprayed on the plants. Deficiencies of micronutrients most likely occur:

1. After many years of intensive cropping
2. In soils of high pH and low pH, depending on the nutrients (see Fig. 7).
3. In droughty soils (sandy soils)
4. In years of excessively high or low precipitation
5. In soils deficient in and also extremely high in organic matter.

Are micronutrients essential for plant growth?

The degree of availability of all soil nutrients for plant growth is conditioned by:

1. The amount of the nutrient present in the soil
2. The amount of moisture present in the soil
3. The amount of organic matter in the soil
4. The texture of the soil
5. The temperature of the soil
6. The pH of the soil

A good soil fertility program is necessary to optimize crop yields, minimize production costs, and protect the environment from excessive fertilizer usage. Good soil fertility programs begin with soil testing and require regular and accurate field sampling of soils. Fertility needs vary among crop species, growth stage, and according to soil type within and among fields. Thus, soil testing and laboratory analysis provides the necessary information on soil pH, soil fertility level, and crop nutrient needs to maximize fertilizer efficiency.

2. Soil Acidity and Alkalinity (soil pH)

Soil reaction, or soil pH, is one of the most important factors that influences soil chemical properties. The degree of acidity or alkalinity of a soil is expressed in terms of pH values. The pH scale is divided into fourteen units numbered from 1 to 14. Soils with a pH value of 7.0 are neutral. Soils with pH values above 7.0 are called alkaline, while those below 7.0 are acid. A soil with a pH of 7 is ten times more acid than a soil with a pH of 8. And a soil with a pH of 6 is 100 times more acid than one with a pH of 8. The pH of most agricultural soils falls between 4.0 and 8.0.

Figure 7 shows how the availability of several of the essential nutrients are affected by the pH of the soil. Some nutrients are so completely absent from the soil that the pH has very little to do with the availability of the nutrient.

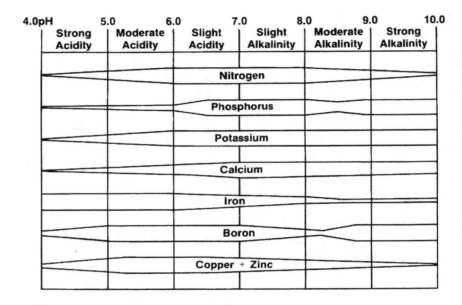

Figure 7. Soil pH and Availability of Some Soil Nutrients

In many cases, the raising of the pH through the application of lime makes the nutrient available at less cost than applying the nutrient. Strongly acid soils result in low availability of all nutrients except Fe, Mn, Zn, and Cu.

Most bacteria are more active in the pH range from 6.0 to 8.0. Actinomycetes (mold bacteria) prefer a very narrow pH range between 6.0 and 7.5. Fungi are active over a wide pH range, but predominate, in most soils, in acid conditions and some may prefer conditions as low as a pH of 4.0 to 5.0. The two main groups of nitrogen fixing organisms fail to function in strongly acid soils. The nonsymbiotic nitrogen fixers are not active at pH levels below 6.0. The symbiotic nitrogen-fixing bacteria show strong preference for soil pH in the range of 6.0 to 8.0. The microorganisms that change the ammonia to nitrite and then to nitrate do not function in strongly acid soils. These factors explain why nitrogen availability is greatest at a pH of 6.0 to 8.0. Earthworms generally are most active in moist, aerated soils in a pH range of 5.0-8.4.

Figure 8 shows the suitable pH ranges for several crops. The optimum pH for a given crop may be a direct response of the plant or it may be an indirect relationship between the pH and the availability of a particular nutrient or the effect of pH on a disease to which the plant is susceptible. Potatoes thrive in soils high in lime, but the actinomycetes that cause potato scab also prefer high lime soils. Potatoes will grow in acid soils, but the scab organism will not. Therefore, an acid soil is preferred for growing potatoes because it controls a serious disease of the potato.

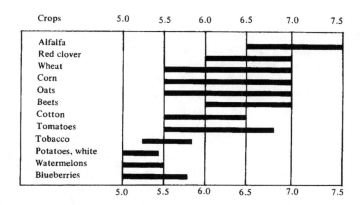

Figure 8. Suitable pH Range For Various Crops

Name three crops that prefer acid soils.

Factors That Affect Soil pH:

Lowers the pH (increases acidity)	**Raises the pH** (increases alkalinity)
1. Adding sulfur compounds	1. Adding lime ($CaCO_3$)
2. Adding nitrogen fertilizer	2. Poor drainage
3. Good soil drainage	3. Low rainfall
4. High rainfall	4. Parent material high in alkaline base elements
5. Parent material high in acid elements	

Organic matter has a buffering effect on soils (neutralizes both acid and alkaline conditions) so additions of organic materials tend to prevent rapid changes in soil pH. Some organic matter, such as pine needles and sawdust, can decompose releasing organic and inorganic acids which lower soil pH. Other organic matter, such as farm manure, has higher base content, which tends to increase soil alkalinity.

Would forest soils more likely be acid or alkaline in reaction?

Liming Acidic Soils:

In many cases soils are often too acidic for optimum crop growth. The most common method of increasing soil pH in acidic soils is to apply agricultural limes, which are carbonates, oxides, or hydroxides of calcium and magnesium. The most common liming material is ground limestone which contains calcium and magnesium carbonates. Advantages of liming acidic soils include:

1. Reduces soil acidity
2. Adds calcium and magnesium as nutrients
3. Increases the availability of many soil nutrients such as phosphorus and potassium
4. Favors many soil organisms that decompose organic material
5. Improves soil structure
6. Reduces solubility of potentially toxic amounts of elements such as aluminum and iron

Soil pH and Iron Chlorosis:

Iron is required by plants in very small amounts. Iron is necessary in the formation of chlorophyll and in many of the metabolic enzymes. An iron deficiency causes the younger leaves to lose their green color (chlorosis). Iron is relatively immobile once incorporated in the plant, thus the older leaves are not usually adversely affected by this chlorotic condition. Plants differ in their susceptibility to iron chlorosis. Soybeans, citrus trees and bluegrass will become chlorotic on high lime soils where corn, cotton, clover, and oats will show no ill effects.

The permanent solution of the iron chlorosis problem is to lower the pH of the soil and thus increase the availability of iron. This may take several years to accomplish, so the immediate needs of the crop may be met by applying iron sulfate as a spray to the affected plant leaves, or by applying a buffered form of iron to the soil in the problem areas.

3. Crop Rotations and Soil Fertility

Crop rotation (the order or yearly sequence of growing different crops on a field - see Chapter 2) greatly influences soil fertility and productivity. The types of crops used in rotations influence the amount and kind of residual nutrients left in the soil after crop removal. Legumes in a rotation (especially perennial legumes) may increase the nitrogen available to non-legume crops that follow. Crop rotation also influences soil characteristics that affect nutrient uptake, such as soil structure and the moisture and nutrient holding capacity of the soil. The advantages of using crop rotations as part of a good soil fertility program include:

1. Soil building crops may be used
2. Reduces soil erosion
3. Increases organic matter and improves soil tilth
4. More complete use of soil profile (nutrients and water)
5. May reduce the amount of inorganic fertilizers needed for the next crop.
6. More flexibility in weed control
7. Better distribution of labor and income
8. Crop diversification reduces production risks

Even though crop rotation is a desirable farming practice, continuous cropping with the same crop (monoculture) is often used for a variety of reasons: 1) suitability of climate and soil, and 2) ease and ability to specialize management, production, facilities, and marketing. In some cases continuous cropping of sod crops or forest is highly desirable for soils that have high erosion potential. However, abusive use of monocultures using row crops can increase soil erosion and reduce soil tilth and productivity. Selective use and strong land stewardship are needed to sustain long-term productivity of soils under monocultures or other intensive farming practices.

General statements on rotations involving maize, soybeans, oats, and meadow

1. A healthy legume meadow, such as alfalfa or clover, can increase yields of the following cereal crop as much as the equivalent of 112-168 kg/ha (100-150 lbs/a) of fertilizer nitrogen.
2. Two or more years of meadow provides more benefit to soil health than one year of meadow.
3. Highly productive legumes provide more benefit to soil productivity and residual soil nitrogen than less productive legumes stands.
4. The yields of first year maize after meadow usually are greater than yields of continuous maize regardless of the amount of fertilizer N applied.
5. A greater frequency of high maize yields is produced by maize following a legume than by continuous maize.
6. Rotations have little effect on oat yields, because oats usually do not follow a legume. Therefore, oats do not benefit from residual soil nitrogen resulting from nitrogen fixation.
7. Rotations have little effect on meadow yields.
8. Fertilizer treatments have little effect on soybean yields in well-managed soils.
9. Of the crops grown in the rotation, oat yields vary the most (due to weather sensitivity) and soybean yields vary the least among years.

C. Biological properties

The biology of the soil refers to the living organisms (including plant parts) that inhabit the soil. There are many forms of life in the soil from obscure molds which produce some of our medicinal drugs to large animals that use their homes in the soil for retreat and protection. Organisms contribute to the soil-building and nutrient-releasing processes in various ways:

Macroorganisms - range in size from gophers, moles, and mice, to ants, millipedes, and earthworms. Large animals help breakdown crop residues and mix soil but can leave large, undesirable mounds and burrows in the ground. Smaller animals, such as earthworms, are very important in building soil tilth and fertility. Earthworms ingest and breakdown crop residues, release nutrients, aerate, mix, and granulate soil, and improve soil structure and drainage.

Microorganisms - include many kinds of nematodes, protozoa, algae, fungi, actinomycetes, and bacteria. Fungi, actinomycetes, and bacteria are major decay organisms in soil.

> Bacteria and Actinomycetes - Most soil bacteria live on the bodies of dead plants and animals (saprophytes). Actinomycetes are filamentous, like molds, but are similar to bacteria in size and having unicellular bodies. Bacteria and actinomycetes generally compete better with other microorganisms, and are the dominant decay organisms, in neutral or slightly alkaline soils.

> Fungi - occur in water, soil, and air. Most fungi are large enough to be seen with the naked eye. Parasitic fungi such as smuts, rusts, and mildews that live on living tissue are harmful. Most saprophytic fungi cause decomposition of dead plant matter and are beneficial to man. Fungi are generally more competitive with other microorganisms in a slightly acid soil.

> Mycorrhizae-Mycorrhizae (MY-core-rye-zee) are a special group of soil fungal organisms that form a symbiotic (mutually beneficial) relationship with plant roots of most crops. Mycorrhizae colonate on root surfaces feeding on metabolic products of the plant and the fungal hyphae extend into the soil helping the plant to absorb water and nutrients. Crop yields have been significantly improved, especially in infertile soils, from the greater surface area and absorption capacity of mycorrhizal infested roots.

Soil microorganisms decompose the plant and animal residues added to the soil. Thus, they liberate the nitrogen and minerals necessary for the growth of higher plants and also produce considerable quantities of CO_2, which is essential for plant growth. Microorganisms synthesize a variety of organic substances such as protein from the inorganic compounds in the soil, and thus compete with higher plants for available nutrients, notably nitrogen.

Plant residues are made up of three groups of constituents: 1) water, 2) organic materials, and 3) inorganic compounds. The water content of plant residues varies from 50 to 95% depending on the type and degree of maturity of the plant. The water-free plant matter contains 88 to 99% organic matter and 1 to 12% mineral or inorganic matter. Soil humus, the dark, relatively stable fraction of soil organic matter, is produced from the decomposition of organic matter (Fig. 9). The chemical and physical properties of soils are largely controlled by humus and clay. They act as centers for chemical reactions and as sites where nutrient exchanges occur. By attracting ions to their surface, they reduce the loss by leaching of essential nutrients. Humus also acts as a "binder" between soil particles to maintain a stable granular structure and improve soil aggregation.

How do microorganisms increase crop yields?

What soil organic fraction helps give soil a black, rich color?

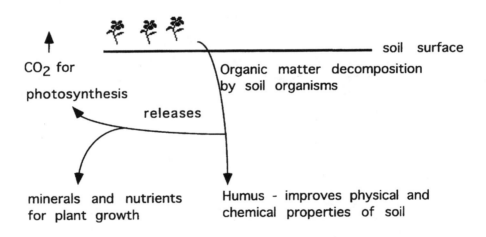

Figure 9. Decomposition of Crop Residues

Although soil organisms include both agriculturally desirable and injurious types, soil conditions that favor a large, diverse population of organisms generally indicate a healthy, productive soil. The soil environment, and therefore management practices, greatly influence the type and population of soil organisms. One gram of living soil is estimated to contain up to 100,000 algae, 1-4 million bacteria, and 8,000-1 million fungi. A square meter of soil is estimated to have 60-300 earthworms or approximately 220-1100 kilograms of earthworms per hectare (200-1000 lb/a).

Pesticides, soil erosion, excessive tillage, and the use of monocultures are examples of factors that can reduce or change the diversity of soil organisms. Keeping the soil in fertile condition using manure applications, green manure crops, fertilizers, and lime, avoiding excessive tillage, controlling erosion, and properly draining and aerating the soil are examples of practices that increase and diversify soil organisms. Thus, good soil stewardship imposes proper management for productive yields of above and below ground plant and animal life.

SELF-EVALUATION TEST

Soils

Circle letter corresponding to one best answer.

1. Deficiency of micronutrients most likely occurs on:

    a) soils of very high pH
    b) soils of fine texture
    c) soils of neutral pH
    d) clay loam soils
    e) grain crops

2. Which type of soil is moved by wind during the soil-forming process?

    a) residual
    b) loess
    c) alluvial
    d) marine
    e) lacustrine

3. A soil pH of 9 would indicate:

    a) conditions 20 times more alkaline than pH 7
    b) conditions 10 times more acid than pH 8
    c) conditions 1000 times more alkaline than pH 6
    d) less acidity than pH 10
    e) lime is needed

4. A soil profile:

    a) always has highest clay content in the upper horizon
    b) is divided into horizons A, B, and C
    c) has most organic matter in the C horizon
    d) has subsoil in the A horizon
    e) has most organic matter in the B horizon

5. The following is a micronutrient:

    a) phosphorus
    b) calcium
    c) sulfur
    d) magnesium
    e) manganese

6. The upper layers of a soil profile are usually darker in color than the lower layers because of:

    a) higher moisture content
    b) higher clay content
    c) type of parent material
    d) more organic matter
    e) more microorganisms present

7. Which of the following terms is most closely related to soil structure?

   a) sand
   b) particle size
   c) silt
   d) aggregate size
   e) potassium content

8. Which of the following is considered to be a primary soil-forming factor?

   a) time
   b) cultivation
   c) runoff
   d) erosion
   e) civilization

9. The following is a primary nutrient:

   a) calcium
   b) boron
   c) potassium
   d) sulfur
   e) magnesium

10. In the relationship between soils, climate, and natural vegetation:

    a) the zone of lime accumulation is very close to the surface in Alfisol soils
    b) bunch grasses predominate in acid soils
    c) increasing precipitation increases the depth of lime accumulation
    d) tall grasses predominate in the Aridisol soils
    e) acid soils are usually found in low rainfall areas

11. The availability of soil nutrients for plant growth is *least* affected by which of the following?

    a) soil moisture
    b) concentration of nutrient
    c) soil temperature
    d) soil texture
    e) soil structure

12. Select the statement which best describes the role of fungi.

    a) They are parasitic, attacking only dead plant matter.
    b) They are saprophytic, attacking only living plants.
    c) They are both parasitic and saprophytic.
    d) They are more competitive in an alkaline soil.
    e) They occur only in the soil.

Chapter 6

Soil Water

I. WATER AND LIFE

Water is basic to all forms of life. Plants, animals, and humans cannot exist without it. The earth has plentiful supplies of water, which cover about 70% of the earth's surface. However, agriculture and humans depend on useable fresh water, which is scarce on a global basis. Salty ocean water makes up 97% of the earth's water. The remaining 3% is fresh water, but most of it is locked up in glaciers, polar ice caps and the atmosphere. Only about 0.5% is available in rivers, lakes, and underground aquifers. Excluding fresh water that is highly polluted and too expensive or difficult to extract, the remaining supply is lowered to 0.003% of our earth's water. Thus, for every 100 liters (26 gallons) of water on earth, about 3 ml (0.1 oz.) is directly useable. Because of the relative scarcity, fresh water has been the source of many disputes throughout history. Issues concerning the equal distribution and the contamination of water are important to agriculture.

An 80 hectare (200 acre) farm in the Central United States that supports a family of 4 in addition to 75 cattle and 200 hogs will require the following amounts of water annually:

Crops (evapotranspiration)	450,000,000 liters (120,000,000 gallons)
Livestock	2,600,000 liters (700,000 gallons)
Family	400,000 liters (100,000 gallons)
Total	453,000,000 liters (120,800,000 gallons)

Over 99 % of the total water needs of this farm is related to the production of crops. In arid regions, the quantity as well as the relative percentage of water required to produce the crops would increase.

Soil is a complex system made up of varying proportions of mineral matter, organic matter, water, and air. The mineral and organic fractions do not fluctuate greatly in a given soil, however the water content varies widely and the amount of air fluctuates inversely with the water content.

What percentage of the water used on a farm is used by the crops?

II. WATER IN THE SOIL

Soil water is extremely important for many reasons: it is the primary source of water for crop growth, plants absorb essential nutrients through soil water, soil moisture influences soil aeration and soil temperature, and excessive soil water can contribute to erosion. Soil structure and texture greatly influence the amount and usefulness of soil water for crop growth.

A. Influence of Soil Structure

Good soil structure improves the effectiveness of a given amount of soil moisture by improving water infiltration, movement, and retention. A well granulated soil has more macropores (large pores) for proper aeration than the same soil where the granulation has been destroyed. A compacted soil with poor structure will have more micropores (small pores) that can limit drainage, reduce soil aeration, and lower the amount of soil water available to plants.

How does soil structure affect the availability of soil water to plants?

B. Influence of Soil Texture

Soil-texture has two important effects on soil moisture availability:

1. The size of the pores
2. The size of the soil particle surface area

The total pore space is not as important as the size of the pores. Macropores from which water drains by gravity are normally filled with air and are called noncapillary pores. Sandy soils with large noncapillary pores are better drained and aerated but have lower water-holding capacity than soils containing silt and clay. The latter soils have a larger proportion of small capillary pores (micropores).

Table 1. Soil Texture, Pore Size and Soil Water Properties

Soil Texture	Soil Porosity	Pore Size	Internal Drainage	Water Holding Capacity	Water Available For Plants
Sandy	Macropores	Large	Excellent	Poor	Very little
Loam	Micro and Macropores	Small and Large	Excellent	Excellent	Excellent
Clay	Micropores	Small	Poor	Excellent	Good

Soil texture plays an important role in determining the effectiveness of soil moisture because of its effect on pore size. Except in very coarse textured soils, most pores in the soil are able to support capillary action. These pores retain water for use by plants and for evaporation.

A wet soil loses water first from the largest size pores and then from the progressively smaller size pores. As the soil becomes dry, the remaining water will be mostly in thin films on the surface of the soil particles. This water is held by strong forces of adhesion.

Fine textured soils containing silt and clay are composed of small soil particles having a large total particle surface area. The larger this surface area, the greater the adsorption and adhesive powers of the soil. The large differences in suface area among soil separates are shown in Table 2.

Table 2. Total Surface Area of 1 kg of Soil

Soil Type	Total Surface Area Equivalent	Compared to Fine Sand
Fine Sand	0.002 ha (200 ft^2)	1X
Fine Silt	0.2 ha (1/2 acre)	100X
Fine Clay	100.0 ha (247 acres)	50,000X

How does soil texture affect moisture availability?

How does pore size affect drainage and water holding capacity?

C. Surface Forces

Two forces account for the retention of water by soil particles. First, there is the attraction of the soil particles for water molecules. This is called adhesion. Second is the attraction of water molecules for one another. This is called cohesion. Soil particles firmly hold water molecules at their soil-water interfaces by adhesion. By cohesion these water molecules hold other water molecules. Together these forces make it possible for soil particles to build water films around themselves and to control the movement of this water. As the film of water around a soil particle increases, the forces holding the water diminish. Figure 1 shows the relationship between the size of the water films and the forces with which the films are held by the soil particle.

Water held by adhesive and cohesive forces can keep the capillary pores completely charged with water. As the films thicken, they become more subject to movement in response to the forces of gravity or to the attraction of adjacent soil particles with thinner films of water.

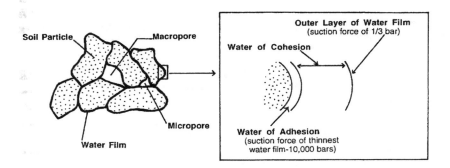

Figure 1. Water retention by a soil particle

What is the difference between cohesive and adhesive forces?

As plant roots absorb soil moisture, the thickness of water films surrounding soil particles decreases. This will continue until removal of water by the plants is too slow to maintain cell turgor, and wilting occurs. At this point, the moisture tension or suction at the outer surface of the water film is about 15 atmospheres or 15 bars (see Figure 2).

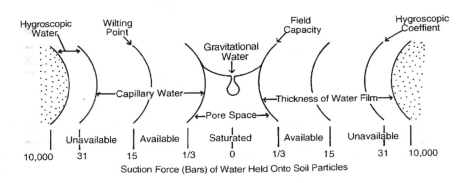

Figure 2. Suction Force of Soil Moisture

III. SOIL WATER CONCEPTS AND TERMINOLOGY

A. Forms of Soil Water

Because of the noticeable variation in the behavior of soil water of different film thicknesses, it has been classified according to its properties at different degrees of soil wetness. On this basis, three forms of soil water are recognized and illustrated in Figure 2:

1. *Gravitational water*-Any water in the soil in excess of the retentive power of the soil particles. It occupies the larger pore spaces and drains away under the influence of gravity. This form of soil water is often injurious to plants if drainage is too slow. It is relatively unavailable for plant growth.
2. *Capillary water*-Water held by the surface forces of the soil particles and water molecules as films around the soil particles. It moves from thicker to thinner films or along moisture gradients. Capillary water is the only important source of water for our cultivated plants.
3. *Hygroscopic water*-Water held as very thin films on the soil particles. It is retained by the soil after air drying and is unavailable to plants. It can be removed from the soil by drying at 1100C or above.

B. Soil Moisture and Plants

There are numerous terms used to describe soil moisture and its relationship to plants. Some of the commonly used terms are described below.

1. *Moisture suction or tension*-The energy, suction, or tension with which the soil holds moisture. Does not include osmotic forces.
2. *Moisture stress*-The total moisture stress on the plant. It includes both groups of forces; soil moisture suction plus the osmotic potential (caused by dissolved salts that attract water away from plants) of the soil solution.
3. *Saturated soil*-When all the pores of the soil are filled with water, the soil is said to be saturated.
4. *Field capacity*-The moisture content of the soil after a thorough wetting and subsequent draining away of the gravitational water.
5. *Plant available water*-The soil water that can be used by plants in growth. It is the moisture held by the soil between field capacity and the permanent wilting point.
6. *Permanent wilting point*-The moisture content of the soil at which plants can no longer absorb water at a rate necessary to live and do not recover after wilting. Most agricultural plants reach permanent wilting point when the soil water is held at 15 bars. Crop plants frequently undergo wilting and recovery cycles long before permanent wilting point is reached. Crop species vary in factors, such as rooting depth and water use efficiency, which influence their ability to grow as soil water moves toward the permanent wilting point.
7. *Wilting range*-The range of soil moisture from the permanent wilting of the first leaves to the complete permanent wilting of the entire plant. Little or no growth is made and most plants die unless water is added to the soil.

C. The Energy of Soil Moisture and its Units

Several different units are used to express differences in the energy levels of soil water. The energy potential with which water is free to move in the soil is always less than that of pure water and thus is a negative value. The osmotic potential of the soil solution is also a negative value. Consequently, these negative potentials are referred to as suctions or tensions, indicating the soil's ability to attract and adsorb water. The terms "suction" and "tension" permit the use of positive rather than negative units.

The common units for expressing suction and tension are bars and atmospheres, respectively. An atmosphere of tension will support a 1033 cm column of water. A bar (10^6 dynes/cm^2) will support a 1020 cm column of water. Thus, a bar of suction and an atmosphere of tension are essentially the same. The bar units of suction are more commonly used.

Soils vary widely in their ability to hold moisture. There is no direct relationship between plant response and the percent of moisture in the soil because of the variability in soils. This is due mainly to textural differences and related surface adhesion qualities. If the moisture content of the soil is expressed in terms of the energy status of the moisture, we can easily compare the availability of the soil moisture in soils of different textures. When most soils are at field capacity, the soil moisture has an energy level of about 0.3 bars. At the wilting percentage, the soil moisture has an energy level of about 15 bars.

What is the difference between a bar and an atmosphere?

What plant characteristics influence the wilting range?

D. The Availability of Soil Moisture to Plants

As a plant transpires and loses water, a water suction develops in the cells of the plant. This suction is transmitted from cell to cell into the roots of the plant. Water moves into the plant whenever the water suction in the plant is greater than the suction of the water in the soil. The rate of water movement from the soil into the plant depends on the suction difference between the plant and the soil. Most plants can withdraw water from soils until the soil moisture suctions reaches about 15 bars.

Many soil, plant, and atmospheric factors affect the movement of soil moisture to plant roots and the rate of water movement in the soil and the plant. These factors are:

1. Soil factors
    a.   soil texture (see Figure 3)
    b.   soil structure - high organic matter improves soil structure and soil tilth which improve soil water holding capacity. Soils with good tilth and earthworm activity provide macropores which help drain excess gravitational water and improve soil aeration necessary for roots to grow and proliferate into greater soil depths.
    c.   soil moisture suction

2. Plant factors
    a.   leaf and stomatal anatomy - regulate the rate of water loss from the plant and the rate of water uptake by roots
    b.   rooting characteristics - length and density of the root system influence the ability of the plant to extract soil water

3. Atmospheric factors
    a.   humidity - higher humidity lowers evapotranspiration rates
    b.   wind velocity and air and soil temperature - higher temperatures with greater wind velocities increase evapotranspiration rates

Figure 3a shows the effect of soil texture on the retention of soil moisture and particularly its effect on the amount of moisture available for plant growth. Coarse sandy soils do not hold a lot of water at the permanent wilting point, but they also do not hold a lot of water at field capacity. Fine textured clay soils hold a lot of water at field capacity, but they also retain a lot of water at the permanenet wilting point. In both cases the result is a lower amount of plant available water than is possible with some other soils of different texture.

E. Soil Moisture Retention and Soil Texture

Soil moisture for crop production can come from rainfall during the growing season or from stored soil moisture. The roots of most cultivated plants function effectively in absorbing water and nutrients from within the upper 1.5 meter (5 ft.) of the soil profile. In most parts of the country, rainfall during the growing season is not sufficient to produce a crop, and stored moisture must be utilized. The extent of the subsoil moisture reserve is an important factor in making decisions on planting rates, fertilizer rates, and market futures.

A sandy loam and a clay loam soil can have the same moisture content when oven dried, but their ability to provide moisture for growing plants differs considerably. The total amount of plant water available in the sandy loam soil is about 10% of the dry weight of the soil. In contrast, the amount in a clay loam soil is about 30% of the dry weight of the soil. Note in Figure 3b, that less than 8 cm of moisture per meter of sandy soil is available to the plant while a silt loam soil has over 16 cm of available moisture per meter of soil. A clay soil has less available moisture than a silt loam soil because of the larger surface area of the clay particles which exerts a larger adhesive suction force on the moisture.

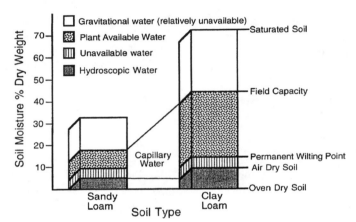
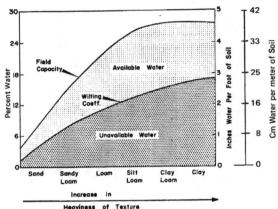

Reprinted with permission of The Macmillan Company from The Nature and Properties of Soils by Nyle C. Brady, 10th Edition, p. 147, Figure 5-22. Copyright the Macmillan Publishing Company, 1990.

Figure 3a and 3b. Relationship Between Soil Texture and Soil Moisture

IV. SOIL MOISTURE AND CROP MANAGEMENT

Moisture characteristics vary among different soil types, which influence crop management decisions. In turn, crop management practices influence the soil moisture status for a given soil. Crop selection, planting management, and tillage practices are examples of factors that affect the amount and rate of water use and loss from soil.

A. Crop Selection

Some crops such as small grains can mature before severe drought occurs in a region. These crops are called drought avoiding crops. Other crops tolerate drought conditions better than others and are called drought tolerant crops. For example, some crops extract more water from the soil than others. Alfalfa because of its deep root system is able to extract water from deeper levels than most crops. Sorghum plants because of their extensive root system and drought tolerance can remove more water from the soil than most grass family species. Table 4 shows the difference in soil moisture following a continuous corn system (C-C) and a meadow-corn (M-C) rotation.

Table 4. April 15 Soil Moisture After Continuous Corn (CC) and Meadow-Corn (M-C)

Crop System	Years of Comparison	Number of Sites	Number of Yrs. System Higher by 2.54 cm (1 in.) or More
C-C	13-17	15	9 years
M-C	13-17	15	2 years

Iowa State University Cooperative Extension Service, Ames, Iowa. November, Special Report No. 70.

In most of the years (up to 9) the soil moisture after continuous corn was at least 2.54 cm above the level following Meadow-Corn. In only 2 years was the soil moisture following a Meadow-Corn rotation higher than the C-C rotation.

B. Plant Population and Evapotranspiration

Table 5 shows the effect of corn population and row spacing on the evapotranspiration and efficiency of water use. Note that in 53 cm (21 inch) equidistant rows, a population of 28,000 plants uses less water (15 in. or 38 cm) in evapotranspiration than 14,000 plants in 81 or 107 cm rows. Also note that doubling the population does not double the amount of evapotranspiration but only increases water use about 10%. Water use efficiency is greatest with the narrower row spacings and the higher population. Yields follow the same pattern. The corn was irrigated as needed.

Table 5. Corn Row Spacing-Population Regimes and Evapotranspiration (irrigated)

Row Spacing Plant Spacing (at 14,000)	53 cm (21 in.) 53 cm (21 in.)		81 cm (32 in.) 35 cm (13.8 in.)		107 cm (42 in.) 27 cm (10.5 in.)	
Plant Population/ac*	14,000	28,000	14,000	28,000	14,000	28,000
Yield kg/ha (bu/ac)	3353 (132)	3886 (153)	3124 (123)	3785 (149)	3150 (124)	3632 (143)
Evapotranspiration cm (May-Sept.) (in.)	33.5 (13.2)	38.1 (15.0)	39.4 (15.5)	42.2 (16.6)	40.6 (16.0)	42.7 (16.8)
Water-Use Efficiency (kg/cm) (bu/in)	100 (10.0)	102 (10.2)	80 (8.0)	89 (8.9)	74 (7.4)	83 (9.3)

*14,000/ac = 34,594/ha
 28,000/ac = 69,188/ha

From A.Y.M. Yao and R. H. Shaw. Agron. Jour. 56:147-152,1964.

C. Other Management Factors

Many management factors influence water evaporation, runoff and infiltration rates, thus influencing soil moisture. The degree of ground cover by residue greatly influences soil water loss and retention. The following are brief examples of practices used to decrease evaporation and/or runoff and increase infiltration rates:
1. Use of plastic or residue mulches
2. Selecting tillage implements and tillage systems that conserve soil water and leave more residue on the soil surface (discussed in the following chapter)
3. Controlling weedy growth to prevent unnecessary transpirational loss of soil water
4. Establishing contour farming and terracing to control water runoff

V. IRRIGATION

A. General Considerations

Irrigation is the artificial application of water to soil to enhance crop growth. Irrigation is used in many areas of the world to supplement the amount and/or distribution of rainfall needed for crop production. Irrigation is usually practiced during the dry months in cropping regions that have wet-dry seasons and in arid regions where evapotranspiration exceeds precipitation for most of the growing season. The term "dryland farming" is used to indicate crop production without irrigation in arid or semiarid regions. Irrigation is also used in regions with adequate rainfall where soils do not have adequate water holding capacity to sustain crop growth between rainfall occurrences or where high evapotranspiration rates exceed precipitation and deplete soil water during critical stages of crop growth. In the United States, most of the irrigated land is west of the Mississippi River and totals about 18 million hectares (45 m. acres). Irrigation in the more humid eastern areas of the U.S. is usually directed toward high value crops.

Advantages of irrigation:
1. Crop yields and quality can be improved.
2. Timing, location, and quantity of water can be controlled.
3. Water application rates can be adjusted to the runoff, erosion, infiltration, and drainage characteristics of different soils.
4. Food production potential of arid and semiarid regions can be drastically improved.

Disadvantages/concerns of irrigation:
1. Irrigation costs are high and increase economic risk.
2. Some forms of irrigation can increase erosion rates and sediment deposition.
3. Excessive salt accumulation at or near the soil surface from irrigation in arid lands can inhibit crop growth and reduce or destroy land productivity.
4. Irrigation is the major consumptive use of the world's fresh water supply. On a global basis, almost 75% of the fresh water withdrawn is used for irrigation. Excessive withdrawal severely lowers fresh water levels in rivers, lakes, and underground aquifers and has contributed to saltwater intrusion and groundwater contamination.

Because of the economic, ecological, and sociological significance of fresh water utilization, sound water conservation and management practices are important in agricultural and non-agricultural water use. Practices to improve water use efficiency and reduce water loss in irrigated areas include:
1. Improving the timing, control, and quantity of irrigation to avoid excessive amounts and frequency of application
2. Encouraging deeper root development through proper irrigation practices
3. Matching proper irrigation methods with different soil types to prevent excessive runoff and percolation
4. Using low-application irrigation methods, such as drip or trickle systems to reduce evaporative loss of soil water
5. Reducing evapotranspiration rates by selecting more water efficient species/varieties and tillage practices, utilizing surface mulches, and controlling weed growth

B. Methods of Irrigation

The major irrigation methods can be categorized into surface (gravity), subsurface, sprinkler, and trickle (drip) systems. Different irrigation methods are used depending on soil type, topography, climate, cropping system, and other factors. A brief description and examples of the major irrigation methods are given.

1. **Surface (also called Gravity) Irrigation systems** have been used for centuries throughout the world and are still the most popular method. It is used on nearly 75% of the irrigated lands. Water is applied to the field by gravity flow and land leveling is usually required for adequate field coverage. Irrigation water may be brought to the field by open ditches or by above or below ground pipes. Two major methods of surface irrigation systems are flood and furrow irrigation.

   a. **Flood irrigation**-water is applied over the entire surface area of the field. Fields or sections of fields may be diked or divided into strips bordered by levees to control water flow.

   b. **Furrow irrigation**-water is applied to the field in furrows previously created by some type of ridge-furrow operation.

2. **Subsurface irrigation systems** supply water to growing plants from beneath the soil surface through underground pipes or tile lines or by some means of controlling the depth of the underground water table. Subsurface irrigation is not widely used because it requires relatively flat soils with uniform subsoil characteristics or where a shallow water table can be maintained.

3. **Sprinkler irrigation systems** utilize pumps to move and distribute water through sprinkler units. Pipelines and/or sprinkling units may be movable or permanently fixed in the field. Various types of sprinkler irrigation include:

   a. **Permanently fixed**-underground pipes supply water to sprinkling units.
      Examples: -orchard sprinkler systems
                       -pop-up sprinklers used in lawns and golf courses.

   b. **Portable**-pipelines/hoses and sprinkling units that are moved by hand or tractor.
      Examples: -hand moved pipe
                       -tractor pulled gun units (extremely large sprinkler units on wheels)

   c. **Self-propelled units**-
      Examples: -rolling line (self-propelled lateral lines on wheels that move horizontally across the field)
                       -self-propelled traveling gun units
                       -Center pivot (self propelled sprinkler line that rotates from a center pivot and irrigates the field in a circular pattern)

   Sprinkler irrigation requires a large investment in equipment and well development. Because of the large amounts of water used in sprinkler methods, many states have restricted the drilling of wells to support sprinkler systems in order to protect their shrinking ground water supplies for domestic use.

4. **Trickle (also called Drip) irrigation systems** were developed in Israel and are increasingly used in U.S. irrigated areas, especially in orchards and vineyards where plants are widely spaced. Small tubing is used to carry water to the base of plants or trees where water, under low pressure, drips or trickles out of small orifices at a very slow but constant rate. Trickle systems are becoming more popular because comparable yields are obtained using only a fraction of the water used in other irrigation methods. This method has wide application in sandy soils and has also proved beneficial in clays of low permeability. It has decreased soil crusting and has permitted production on erodable soils without the expense of terracing.

VI. SALT ACCUMULATION

Salt accumulation is a frequent problem in arid or semi-arid regions where evaporation rates are high and rainfall and irrigation are insufficient to flush salts out of the soil profile. Salts (compounds formed from the reaction of an acid and base, such as chlorides and sulfates of calcium, magnesium, sodium and potassium) naturally occur in soils and they can be added from rainfall, ground water, or irrigation water. Soluble salts are brought to the soil surface through the evapotranspirational loss of water. As water leaves the soil surface through roots and evaporation, salts are left behind to accumulate (Figure 4). Salts in the soil solution can accumulate to the point where existing soil water becomes less available to plant roots. Salts increase the osmotic concentration of the soil solution and decrease, and in severe cases reverse, the normal flow of soil water into the root, Thus, salt accumulation increases the amount of water held in the soil at wilting point. Wilting is a common symptom of salt injury in plants.

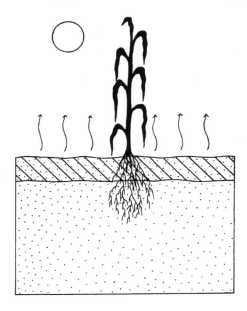

Figure 4. Surface salt accumulation

Salt affected soils are characterized according to their pH and salt and sodium contents. Soils that contain high enough levels of soluble salts to impair plant growth and have a pH<8.5 are called saline soils if the sodium content is low or saline-sodic soils if the sodium content is high. Both soils are sometimes referred to as "white alkali" soils because of the white salt crust that forms on the soil surface. Sodic soils do not have excessive amounts of soluble salts, have a pH>8.5, and have excessive sodium levels that can interfere with plant growth and soil conditions. Sodic soils frequently have a dark soil surface and are sometimes referred to as "black alkali" soils.

Various methods have been used to maintain or improve the productivity of salt affected soils. Some of the soluble salts may be temporarily leached from the surface by a combination of flooding and drainage. On saline-sodic soils special management is usually required that involves large amounts of leaching water and special soil amendments of gypsum or sulfur to neutralize the sodium. Other methods include proper timing and use of irrigation water and selecting crops with greater salt tolerance. Table 6 shows the relative tolerance of certain crops to salty conditions. Note the low tolerance of most clovers and the moderate to high tolerance of most grass species.

Table 6. Relative Tolerance of Crop Plants to Saline Soil Conditions

Sensitive	Moderately Tolerant	Tolerant
Alsike clover	Alfalfa	Barley
Ladino clover	Corn	Bermudagrass
Potatoes	Oats	Cotton
Red clover	Sorghum	Rye
White clover	Soybean	Sugar Beets
Field bean	Wheat	Western Wheat grass

What effect does salinity have on soil moisture availability?

VII.   SOIL DRAINAGE

The removal of excess water from soils is just as important for plant growth as the availability of water when soil moisture is low. Draining excess moisture from the land promotes the following conditions that are favorable to plant growth:

1. Increases granulation
2. Provides a deeper rooting zone
3. Warms the soil
4. Permits better seedbed preparation
5. Permits better weed control
6. Improves soil aeration
7. Reduces iron and manganese toxicity
8. Reduces heaving and thawing damage

Perhaps the greatest benefit of drainage is its effect on soil aeration. Good aeration:

1. Promotes the diffusion of oxygen to plant roots
2. Promotes the removal of CO_2 from plant roots
3. Increases activity of aerobic microorganisms
4. Increases the availability of soil nutrients
5. Oxidizes many toxic elements to a less soluble state

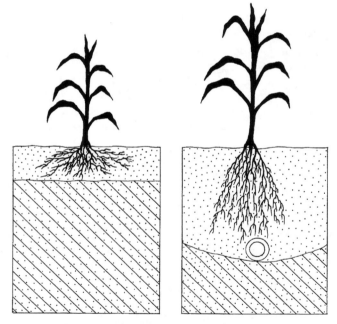

Figure 5. Subsurface drainage by tiling

Surface and subsurface drainage methods can be used to remove excessive water from poorly drained soils. Excessive water can be diverted off the field using surface ditches or terraces. Subsurface drainage is accomplished by tiling (using porous subsurface tile to remove gravitational water and lower the water table) (Figure 5).

Artificial soil drainage has improved the productivity of many lands that were too wet for crop production. However, its widespread use has been extremely detrimental to wetland habitats. Wetland habitats have more than intrinsic value. Wetlands:

1. Collect excess water from runoff. By holding water, they allow increased infiltration, which helps recharge groundwater supply and regulate stream flow.
2. Serve as environmental filters for soil water contaminants. Wetland soils filter out sediments, pollutants, and chemical contaminants in water that would otherwise enter fresh water supplies that humans and wildlife depend upon.
3. Provide important habitats for plants and wildlife. Blueberries, cranberries, and wild rice are produced on wetlands. Migratory water fowl are especially dependant on wetland habitats.

Thus, wetlands have functional value in our environment and should be a meaningful part of a sound water management program.

Explain why most crop plants grow poorly in saturated soils.

How do sediments and pollutants enter fresh water supplies?

VIII. SOIL WATER UTILIZATION AND CONSERVATION

Climate greatly influences the goals, management, and conservation practices of soil water (Figure 6). For example, in humid temperate areas, precipitation often exceeds evapotranspirational use during much of the year . Management goals focus on controlling excess water to minimize runoff and erosion, to maximize infiltration of water and to provide adequate soil moisture for deficit periods when crop water use exceeds precipitation.

In irrigated arid regions, high temperatures and low humidity result in rapid evapotranspirational rates which exceed precipitation during all or most of the year. Water deficits during the growing season are so great that stored soil moisture cannot supply crop water needs and irrigation is required. Management goals focus on conserving soil moisture, minimizing evapotranspirational loss, and supplying crop water needs through irrigation.

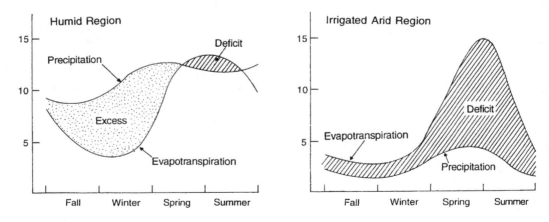

Adapted from The Nature and Properties of Soils by N. C. Brady 10th Edition., p. 417. Copyright by Macmillan Publishing Company. 1990.

Figure 6. Climate and Soil Water Management

Effective water management programs, although vastly different in different climates, are essential in maintaining agricultural productivity. The control, supply, and quality of fresh water are key factors in the success of long-term crop productivity in any climatic region.

SELF-EVALUATION TEST

Soil Water

Circle letter corresponding to one best answer.

1. A soil at field capacity

   a) contains gravitational water
   b) contains no capillary water
   c) contains hygroscopic water
   d) is air-dry soil
   e) contains water, all of which is available to plants

2. Increasing salinity of soil water

   a) decreases the osmotic potential of the soil solution
   b) reduces the range of available water in the soil
   c) increases as environmental conditions become more humid
   d) decreases the amount of water in the soil at the wilting percentage
   e) increases the organic matter of soils

3. Gravitational water is often injurious to plants because

   a) the force of gravity moving the water physically damages the root tissue
   b) it is relatively unavailable to plants
   c) of lack of oxygen for the plant if drainage is too slow
   d) it is the only important source of water for most crop plants
   e) it is retained by the soil after air drying

4. The following statement about water of cohesion is true.

   a) None is available to plants.
   b) Some is available to plants.
   c) All is available to plants.
   d) Water of cohesion is held with greater force than water of adhesion.
   e) All water of cohesion is held at the same suction.

5. The amount of capillary water in the soil is usually

   a) greater in sandy than in loam soil
   b) greater in soil which is low in organic matter
   c) greater in loam than in clay loam soil
   d) greater in loam than in sandy soil
   e) not related to the texture

6. Soil porosity

   a) is the portion of the soil volume occupied by air and water
   b) amounts to about 30% in loam soils
   c) is greater in sandy soils than in clay soils
   d) is not affected by soil structure
   e) is not affected by soil texture

7. An example of a drought avoiding crop is

   a) sorghum
   b) corn
   c) alfalfa
   d) wheat
   e) field beans

8. The irrigation method with the greatest water conservation efficiency is

   a) furrow
   b) flood
   c) center pivot
   d) traveling gun
   e) trickle

9. Salt accumulation

   a) is a common problem in humid areas
   b) occurs less often in areas with low evapotranspiration rates
   c) decreases the amount of soil water held at wilting point
   d) helps plant roots absorb soil water
   e) improves potato yields

10. Artificial drainage of natural wetlands

   a) improves their ability to act as environmental filters for soil water contaminants
   b) improves water quality entering fresh water streams and rivers
   c) improves soil conditions for growth of most row crops
   d) improves habitat for migratory water fowl
   e) is not usually done in humid agricultural regions

Chapter 7

Tillage and Seeding

TILLAGE

"Tillage" is a general term referring to manual or mechanical soil stirring actions. "Tillage systems" refer to the type and sequence of tillage operations used for the proper establishment and growth of crops. Types and forms of tillage vary widely among different farmers, environments and geographical areas. Even though technology has changed the nature of tillage operations in recent years, the goals and purposes of tillage have essentially remained the same.

I. GOALS AND PURPOSES OF TILLAGE SYSTEMS

A. *Seed bed preparation*

The goal of tillage for seedbed preparation is to provide an optimum environment for seed germination and subsequent growth of crops while preventing or minimizing soil erosion. Seedbed preparation must be suitable for the crop being planted and must provide a soil in which the seed can be placed at the proper depth. Adequate soil temperature, soil moisture, seed aeration and seed-soil contact must also be provided for rapid seed germination and seedling growth.

B. *Incorporation and mixing*

Tillage operations may be used to incorporate and mix crop residues, lime, fertilizers or pesticides into the soil. Crop residues can be managed through tillage operations to help control soil erosion, to improve soil organic matter, and to improve the seedbed for planting. The effectiveness of lime and certain types or forms of fertilizers and pesticides can be reduced when left on the soil surface. Therefore, proper mixing and distribution of these materials in the soil are necessary to maximize their efficiency.

C. *Weed control*

Tillage for weed control includes tillage operations before planting, between planting and crop emergence, and following crop emergence.

D. *Conservation of soil and water*

Conserving soil and water resources is an important goal for any tillage system. Tillage methods greatly differ in the amount of erosion that can occur, with the degree of erosion depending on the situation in which the tillage methods are used. Some methods can leave the soil surface very vulnerable to erosive forces. Other methods leave crop residues on the soil surface which help prevent water and wind erosion, conserves precipitation in the form of rain and snow, and improves water infiltration rates.

II. TILLAGE VOCABULARY

A. Primary and secondary tillage

Primary and secondary tillage are two general categories of tillage referring to the depth of tillage, type of implement (machine) and goals in preparing a seedbed.

1. Primary tillage - Tillage which inverts, cuts or shatters the soil to a depth of 15-36 cm (6-14 in) and usually leaves the soil rough. The goals of primary tillage may include loosening and aerating the surface layer of the soil, incorporating fertilizer, and covering plant residue from the previous crop or mixing the residue into the surface layer of the soil. Primary tillage is usually deeper so implements are usually heavier and more strongly constructed than are secondary tillage implements.

2. Secondary tillage - Refers to tillage operations that follow primary tillage and are for the purpose of preparing a final seedbed suitable for planting, seed germination, seedling establishment and weed control. The goals of secondary tillage include leveling and firming the soil, further pulverizing of the soil to ensure good seed-soil contact and to control weeds. Depth of tillage is usually 5-15 cm (2-6 in.). Excessive secondary tillage may increase the evaporation of water from the surface layers of soil resulting in sub-optimum soil moisture for proper germination.

B. Tillage Implements

Tillage implement terminology varies widely among engineers, agronomists, machinery manufacturers, and farmers. Local nicknames are often given to different implements that may describe the implement, operation, or the manufacturer's name of the equipment. For example, "plowing" many mean moldboard plowing or chisel plowing, depending on the equipment used. "Disking" is a shortened term that usually means disk harrowing or using a disk harrow to "disk" land. "Harrowing" is a frequently used, shortened version of the final seedbed preparation using a spring-, spike-, or tine-toothed harrow. In some areas, "ripping" land refers to a subsoiling operation. The following terminology used in this section is based on the American Society of Agricultural Engineers Standard S414, "Terminology and Definitions for Agricultural Tillage Implements".

1. Primary tillage implements commonly used in the U.S. are: moldboard plows, disk plows, chisel plows, sweep plows, combination chisel plows, powered rotary tillers, listers/bedders, and heavy and offset disk harrows.

   a. Moldboard plow-Cuts slices of the soil and inverts or partially inverts them, depending on the implement used and its adjustment and operation. Note Figure 1.

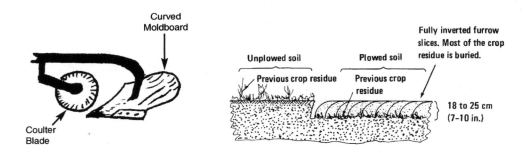

Figure 1. Moldboard plow

b. Disk plow-The resulting action is similar to the moldboard plow, except heavy disk blades are used instead of moldboards and a disk plow only partially inverts the furrow slice. Disk plows have been used in hard, dry soils, sticky soils, highly abrasive soils, hardpan soils, and in "new-ground" soils with remaining stumps and logs where moldboard plows may not function properly (Figure 2).

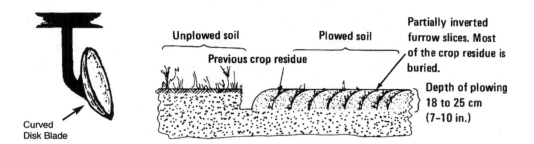

Figure 2. Disk plow

c. Chisel plow-This implement is heavily constructed for primary tillage operations and consists of chisels attached to curved shanks arranged in staggered rows (Figure 3). Different chisel sizes and shapes are available depending on soil conditions and the amount of residue coverage desired. The desired action of the chisel plow is to break and shatter the soil while leaving enough residue on the surface to help control soil erosion. Chisel plows are also used to break up plow pans caused by moldboard plowing at the same depth for many years.

1. Combination chisel plow (disk chisel, mulch tiller)-Frequently, before a chisel plow operation, a pre-liminary disking of stalk residue is done to facilitate the chiseling operation. To combine the operations of chiseling and disking, a combination chisel plow is used. This implement consists of disk blades in front to cut and loosen crop residue and a chisel plow in the rear section to break and shatter the soil (Figure 4). Because of the dual action of the disk blades and chisels, more residue is incorporated into the soil. Combination chisel plows are commonly used in fields where heavy crop residue may interfere with chisel plow operation.

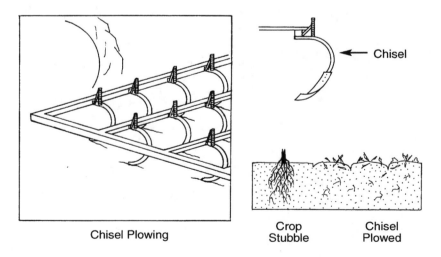

Figure 3. Chisel plow

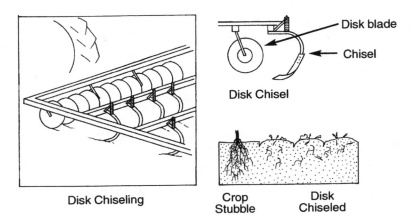

Figure 4. Combination chisel plow

d. Sweep plow (Stubble-mulch plow)-These plows have sweeps [30 to more than 152 cm wide (12-60 in.] that can be operated at shallow depths [8-10 cm (3-4 in.)] to cut the roots of the old crop residue and weeds or at deeper depths to lift and loosen the soil (Figure 5). The crop residue is left intact on the soil surface, thus providing for good erosion control (especially for wind erosion) and rapid water infiltration. The implement is mostly used in areas with limited precipitation. The residue on the soil surface depresses the soil temperature and thus, in some instances, may cause some difficulty in achieving field stands.

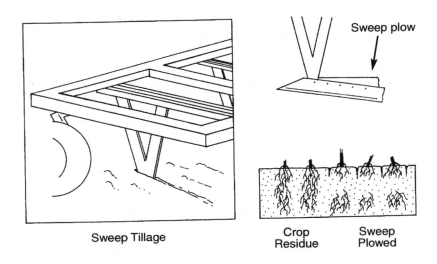

Figure 5. Sweep plow

e. Powered rotary tiller-This implement requires engine power to rotate blades for cutting, lifting and loosening the soil rather than relying solely on the forward motion for tilling action as in the previously described primary tillage implements (Figure 6). Powered rotary tillers are effective in chopping and incorporating residue into the soil and preparing a fine seedbed. They are often used at shallower depths for secondary tillage. Excessive rotary tillage may pulverize the soil, thereby limiting water infiltration and increasing the erosion hazard.

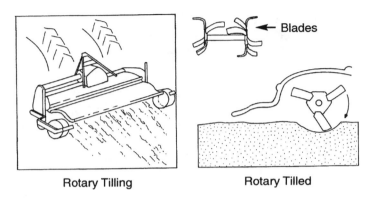

Figure 6. Powered rotary tiller

f. Lister/Bedder-Listers utilize either disk blades or V-shaped moldboards to "throw" soil into ridges and thus leaving a ridge (bed)-furrow situation (Figure 7). The seed may be planted on the ridge or in the furrow depending on the farming area, crop planted and soil moisture conditions.

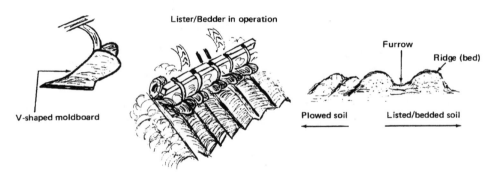

Figure 7. Lister/Bedder

Some factors to consider in a primary tillage operation are:

Depth of primary tillage-The depth of primary tillage varies considerably depending on several factors, including the amount of plant residue to be covered, soil type, and personal preference of the farmer. Experimental results have generally indicated no yield differences due to moldboard plowing deeper than 10 to 18 cm (4-7 in.), or chisel plowing deeper than 20-25 cm (8-10 in.), as long as previous plant residue is managed adequately for seedbed preparation. Deeper tillage requires more power, more fuel and has not generally "paid off" in increased profits.

Time of primary tillage-The proper time of primary tillage is usually determined by the optimum seeding time for the crop, soil type, the moisture situation of the soil, the climate, and the susceptibility of the soil to erosion. An example of the importance of soil type in determining the time of primary tillage is that, in some cases in the Midwest Corn Belt, farmers till level, heavier soils in the fall under a continuous corn cropping system where large amounts of surface crop residue can slow spring soil warm up. In this situation, soils in the fall are typically drier than in spring and tillage can be done with minimum soil compaction and soil structural damage. In addition, winter freezing and thawing of soils reduces harmful effects of tillage compaction. Fall tillage, however, exposes soil to erosive forces for longer periods of time than spring tillage so extreme care should be used in selecting the proper crop rotation, soil type and topography, and tillage system for fall tillage operations. Many farmers have switched to different tillage and crop residue management systems to avoid fall tillage. In general, spring tillage is recommended whenever possible and especially for erosive soils.

2. Secondary tillage implements commonly used in the U.S. are: disk harrows, field cultivators, powered rotary tillers (previously discussed in primary tillage), spring-, spike-, and tine-tooth harrows, roller packers, bed shaping equipment (ridgers, levelers, shapers), and various weed control equipment (discussed in section V).

a. Disk harrow-This implement (commonly referred to as "disk" and the operation as "disking") consists of rows of disk blades designed to pulverize soil clods, and to level and firm the soil. Disk harrows, depending on their size, may be used for secondary and/or primary tillage. A commonly used disk harrow is the tandem disk (Figure 8a). Heavily constructed disk harrows, such as the offset disk, are frequently used but their design is for primary tillage rather than secondary tillage (Figure 8b).

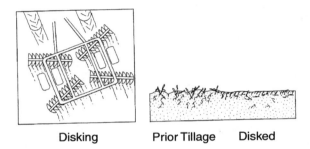

Figure 8a. Disk harrow for secondary tillage

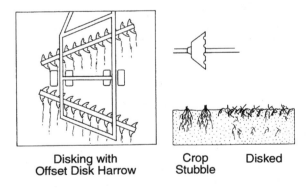

Figure 8b. Offset disk harrow for primary tillage

b. Field cultivator-This implement resembles the chisel plow except it is lighter constructed and designed for shallower tillage (Figure 9). Various sizes and shapes of shovels and sweeps can be attached to the shanks. Field cultivators are widely used for seedbed preparation and weed control. Field cultivators leave more residue on the soil surface than disk harrows but their roles in seedbed preparation are similar.

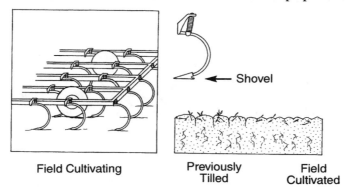

Field Cultivating   Previously   Field
                            Tilled   Cultivated

Figure 9. Field cultivator

c. Spring-, spike-, and tine-tooth harrows-Although these harrows vary in design, their purpose and operation (commonly referred to as "harrowing") are similar (Figure 10). Their use results in additional leveling, pulverizing, and firming of the soil, and possibly in weed control. These implements are lightly constructed and may be operated separately or pulled behind or directly attached to plows, disk harrows, or field cultivators.

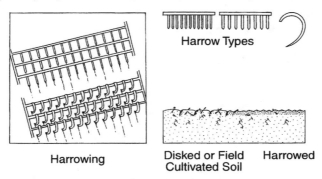

Harrow Types

Harrowing   Disked or Field   Harrowed
                   Cultivated Soil

Figure 10. Finishing harrows (eg. spike-, spring-toothed harrows)

d. Roller packer-This implement consists of heavy rollers and is especially designed to crush soil clods and to firm the soil surface (Figure 11). This implement is often used to prepare the fine, firm seedbed that is especially important for good seed-soil contact for small-seeded grasses and legumes. Proper soil conditions are necessary when using this implement. Operating the packer on wet soils can result in severe crusting of the soil surface.

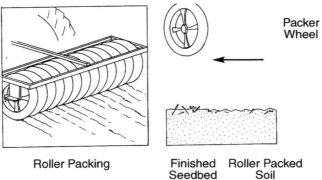

Packer
Wheel

Roller Packing   Finished   Roller Packed
                        Seedbed   Soil

Figure 11. Roller packer

It is important to realize that primary and secondary tillage may be conducted with separate tillage implements in separate operations or they may be combined into one operation either by specially designed equipment or by attaching the secondary tillage implement behind the primary implement. Some tillage implements, such as the disk harrow, chisel plow or field cultivator can be used for both primary and secondary tillage by adjusting the depth of tillage. In some situations, secondary tillage implements such as the disk harrow may be used to reduce surface residues in order to facilitate a primary tillage operation.

C. Tillage Systems

"Tillage systems" usually refer to the nature and sequence of tillage operations used in preparing a seedbed for planting. The terminology used to describe tillage methods is not well defined and may vary in meaning in different areas. The following definitions are used to describe general tillage systems:

Conventional Tillage: The primary and secondary tillage operations normally performed in preparing a seedbed for a given crop grown in a given geographical area. Conventional tillage varies with time and region.

Clean Tillage: Tillage systems that leave little or no crop residue on the soil surface at planting time.

Mulch Tillage: Tillage systems that leave crop residues on or near the soil surface to reduce soil and water loss. Sometimes used interchangeably with conservation tillage.

Conservation Tillage: Tillage systems that leave 30% or more of the soil surface covered with crop residue at planting time to reduce soil and water loss.

Minimum Tillage: Tillage systems that employ the least amount of tillage required to create the proper soil condition for seed germination and plant establishment under existing conditions.

Reduced Tillage: Tillage systems that utilize fewer or less energy intensive operations compared to conventional tillage.

Full Width Tillage: Tillage systems that use implements to till the entire surface area of the field.

Strip Tillage: Tillage systems that use implements designed to till the soil surface in narrow strips leaving undisturbed soil in the non-tilled portion.

No-Till (also referred to as slot-planting or zero till): A tillage system that utilizes specially designed planters to plant seed directly into previously undisturbed soil. The soil is not tilled except for the immediate row zone where the seed is planted. This term usually applies to seedbed preparation and not to post-plant operations, such as mechanical cultivation for weed control or ridging operations.

Ridge Tillage: Tillage systems in which ridges/furrows are formed and maintained during the year. Crops are usually planted on the ridges, or in the furrows in some cases where moisture may be limited. Ridging operations may also be referred to as bedding or listing.

III. TILLAGE METHODS

The following section describes some specific tillage systems used in the U.S. and has been divided into categories based on the amount of crop residue left on the soil surface at planting time (clean or conservation tillage systems) and the amount of soil surface that is tilled (full width, strip, and no-till tillage systems):

A. *Clean, Full Width Tillage Systems*

By definition, clean tillage systems utilize only full width tillage and implements that bury all or most of the surface crop residues (strip tillage and no-till are usually classified as conservation tillage systems).

The following systems frequently use a moldboard plow, disk plow or other implements that invert or partially invert a 10-30 cm (4-12 in.) layer of soil and thus leaves a clean (residue-free) soil surface. The tillage systems differ only in the amount or type of secondary tillage operations.

1. Conventional Tillage

Steps:
-Primary tillage: moldboard plowing (or similar plowing operation in fall or spring). A preliminary operation of disking or stalk shredding on soils with heavy crop residue may precede the plowing operation.
-Secondary tillage: disking or field cultivating 2-4 times followed by harrowing 1-2 times with a spike-, spring-, or tine-toothed harrow.

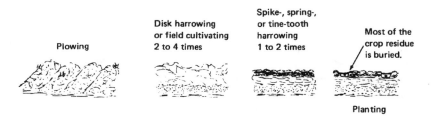

Figure 12. Conventional tillage

The number of required trips through the field including planting is frequently 4 to 8. This system is frequently referred to as "conventional tillage" because it was the predominate tillage system up to the 1980s, particularly for the cornbelt region in the midwestern United States. This system is still used throughout the U.S. but its popularity is declining. This system buries almost all crop residue that might interfere with older, conventional planters and leaves the soil very vulnerable to erosive forces. It is used as a base to compare other tillage systems in controlling soil erosion.

2. Plow and Combined Secondary Tillage

Steps:
-Primary tillage: similar to conventional tillage.
-Secondary tillage: various secondary tillage implements may be hooked together or specially designed implements that combine several secondary tillage operations can be used in conjunction with a planter.

This system is used to reduce the number of secondary tillage operations. A harrow attached to a field cultivator or a planter pulled behind a field cultivator are examples. Combined tillage is primarily used to reduce soil compaction, fuel consumption, and seedbed preparation time. The soil condition for planting is similar to conventional tillage.

3. Plow and Strip-till Planting

Steps:
-Primary tillage: similar to conventional tillage.
-Secondary tillage: the row zone is tilled with implements such as cultivator shovels or rotary tillers attached in front of the planting unit. The interrow zone receives no secondary tillage.

This system is similar to the combined tillage concept, however, the interrow zone is left rough (from primary tillage) for better water infiltration and less weed emergence. Because of the initial plowing operation, this system is classified as a clean, full width tillage system.

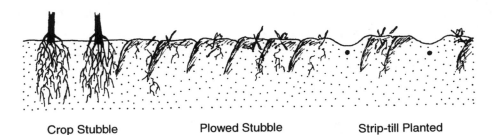

Crop Stubble   Plowed Stubble   Strip-till Planted

Figure 13. Plow and Strip-till Planting

4. Plow, Listing and Planting

Steps:
>   -Primary tillage: similar to conventional tillage.
>   -Secondary tillage: listing (also referred to as "bedding" or "ridging") uses listers/bedders/ridgers to throw soil into ridges leaving a ridge-furrow situation.

The seed is often planted in the furrow (lister planting) in areas with less than optimum rainfall. In farming areas where soils have limited internal and surface drainage, the seed is planted on the bed (bed planting). The primary tillage operation in this full width system results in a clean tillage classification. The seed placement for these two situations is shown in Figure 14.

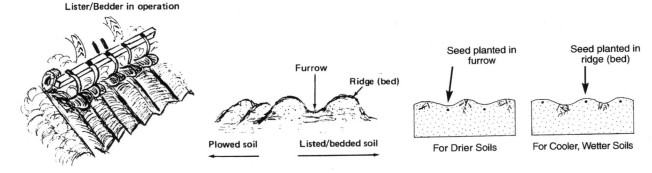

Figure 14. Soil condition and seed placement after plowing, listing and planting in the furrow or ridge

5. Other Clean, Full Width Tillage Systems

There are other tillage implements that can be used for clean tillage systems depending on the amount of initial crop residue after harvest and the amount buried during tillage operations. For example, using an offset disk or chisel plow for primary tillage, followed by 1-3 secondary tillage operations (disking/field cultivating and/or harrowing) will probably bury all or most soybean residue by planting time and thus is a clean tillage system for soybean ground. However, this same tillage system may be classified as conservation tillage on corn ground which has much more initial, post-harvest crop residue and if significant amounts of residue remain on the soil surface at planting time.

A summary of clean-tillage systems is shown in Table 1.

Table 1. Clean Tillage Systems

Tillage System	Steps in Tillage Operations*			
Conventional	Plowing →	Disking → →	Harrowing → →	Planting →
Plow, Combined Secondary Tillage	Plowing →	Disking-planting →		
Plow, Strip-till Planting	Plowing →	Strip-till Planting →		
Plow, Listing, Planting	Plowing →	Listing →	Planting →	

*Arrows indicate number of trips through the field (may vary widely depending on many factors).

B. Conservation Tillage Systems

Tillage systems in this category can be full width, strip, or no-till that leave 30% or more of the soil surface covered with crop residues at planting time. It should be noted that excessive tillage in any of the following tillage systems can bury all or most of the surface residues similar to the clean-tillage systems, thus losing the benefit of surface residues in controlling soil and water loss.

B1. Full Width, Conservation Tillage

1. Chisel Plow Systems

    Steps:
    -Primary tillage: chisel plowing in fall or spring usually at a 20-25 cm (8-10 in.) depth. A preliminary disking or stalk shredding may be used to cut and reduce heavy surface residues prior to chiseling.
    -Secondary tillage: one or more passes with a disk, field cultivator or chisel plow with sweeps operating at 10-15 cm (4-6 in.), and harrowing.

    This system substitutes the chisel plow for the moldboard plow or disk plow in primary tillage operations and has gained wide popularity since more crop residue remains on the soil surface after chiseling to prevent soil erosion. Chisel plow systems work well on rolling, well drained land and where the potential for wind and water erosion of soil is high. Chiseling flat soils with poor internal or surface drainage may lower spring soil warm-up due to the insulating effect of more surface residues compared with conventional tillage using fall plowing. Many variations of the chisel plow system are used and the number of trips through the field prior to planting (and percent bare soil) may be as high as the conventional tillage system using the moldboard or disk plow.

    a) Combined Tillage in Chisel Plow Systems-tillage operations may be combined to reduce the number of field passes in chisel plow systems by using:

        1) Chisel plows equipped with curved disk blades or straight coulter blades attached in front of the chisel shanks (combination chisel plow) to cut residue and eliminate the need for disking or stalk shredding prior to chiseling.

        2) Chisel plows, field cultivators or disk harrows with a spring-, spike-, or tine-tooth harrow attached in the rear for leveling the soil and reducing the number of separate secondary tillage operations.

3) Chisel plows with sweeps and equipped with planting units for a one-pass, chisel plow-plant operation in the spring on soil previously fall chiseled.

Figure 15 illustrates the soil condition and seed placement following a chisel plow system.

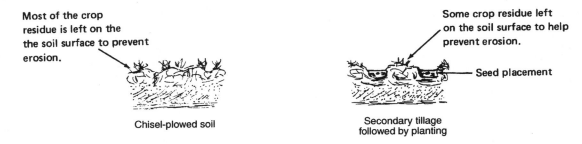

Figure 15. Chisel plow system

2. Disk (and/or field cultivating) and plant

Steps:
-Primary tillage: large-bladed, heavier constructed disk harrows or offset disks can be used for primary tillage (if needed) in the fall or spring.
-Secondary tillage: 1-2 passes with lighter disk harrows or field cultivators and harrowing.

This widely used system utilizes the disk harrow as a primary and/or secondary tillage implement. Tillage operations on heavy residue soils (e.g. corn ground) may involve fall disking and/or one or two spring diskings (or field cultivatings), harrowing, and planting. On light residue soils (e.g. soybeans ground), primary tillage is often omitted and a disk or field cultivator is used for secondary tillage in order to leave enough surface residues at planting time for conservation tillage objectives.

3. Sweep tillage

Steps:
-Primary tillage: none
-Subsurface and secondary tillage: this system utilizes subsurface implements, such as wide sweep-blade implements (implements that have wide, horizontally V-shaped sweeps) and rod-weeders (implements that use horizontal, rotating rods rather than sweeps). These subsurface implements cut beneath the soil surface without inverting and mixing the topsoil, thus leaving the surface crop stubble relatively undisturbed. Subsurface implements are recommended in areas that do not have heavy residue cover so that maximum surface residue cover can be maintained. Disks, field cultivators, or rod-weeders may be used for secondary tillage prior to planting.

This tillage system is widely used in dry land wheat areas such as in the Great Plains and Pacific Northwest states and in Canada. Because of the low rainfall, crop rotations in these areas may include a year of fallow (preventing crop and weed growth on land during a growing season) so that soil moisture can accumulate in the root zone for next year's crop. Tillage operations during fallowing are primarily aimed at weed control and soil moisture conservation. Sweep tillage has two main objectives in addition to seedbed preparation:

1. To conserve soil moisture
2. To protect the soil from wind and water erosion by leaving crop residue on the soil surface and by creating a better physical condition of the soil surface to resist erosion

An example of a sweep tillage system is shown in Figure 16.

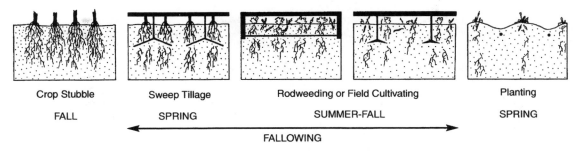

Crop Stubble	Sweep Tillage	Rodweeding or Field Cultivating		Planting
FALL	SPRING	SUMMER-FALL		SPRING

FALLOWING

Figure 16. Sweep tillage system

B2. Strip Till, Conservation Tillage

Some strip till systems may be used on ridged or non-ridged soil. Ridge tillage transforms a flat soil surface into a ridge-furrow condition and can be imposed on full-width, strip till, and no-till systems. In strip and no-till systems, the ridging operation is usually conducted in the previous year during row cultivation for weed control. In this section, lister-planting and strip rotary tillage are usually used on non-ridged soil while till-plant can be used on ridged or non-ridged soil.

Ridge tillage is an increasingly popular term in tillage system terminology and probably originated from the older concepts and earlier use of listing and bedding for cotton, potatoes, and other row crops. The terms, listing, bedding, and ridging are used interchangeably in many areas to denote the action of creating a ridge-furrow condition. However, "bed" traditionally implies an elevated and level ridge top wide enough for 2 or more rows while "ridge", in popular usage, implies a narrower ridge top suitable for 1 row. Ridging soil provides faster soil warming on the ridges and utilizes crop residues to improve water infiltration, weed control, and erosion control in the interrow zone.

1. Lister-planting (non-ridged soil)

Steps:
-Primary tillage: none
-Secondary tillage: no separate secondary tillage operations are used. Seedbed preparation for the row zone is provided by listing tools attached to the planter ahead of the planting unit.

This method has been used for many years, especially in areas that are somewhat deficient in rainfall and soil moisture. The listing and planting is done in one operation on non-plowed soil. The listing tool forms a furrow where the seed is planted (lister planting). The furrows range from deep (10 to 15 cm) to very shallow (approximately 5 cm). The shallow listing cuts the crop residue and pushes it into the interrow zone, thus providing an acceptable row zone for the crop seed to germinate and grow. Deeper listing incorporates more of the residue into the soil. Figure 17 illustrates the soil condition following both shallow and deep lister-planting.

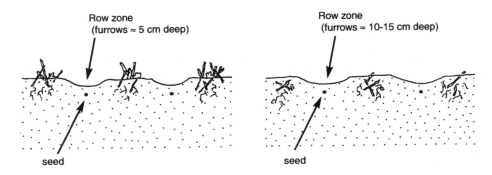

Figure 17. Left: Shallow lister-planting. The crop residue is pushed into the interrow zone. The seed is usually planted in the row of the previous crop.

Right: Deeper lister-planting. The crop residue is turned into the interrow zone and partially covered with soil.

2. Strip Rotary Tillage (non-ridged soil)

Steps:
-Primary tillage: none
-Secondary tillage: no separate secondary tillage operations are used. Seedbed preparation for the row zone is provided by strip rotary tillers attached on the planting implement (strip rotary tiller-planter).

Rotary tillage implements employ power-driven, rotating blades that cut and mix soil and residues. Rotary tillage implements can be designed for full width or strip tillage (strip rotary tiller) at depths deep enough for primary tillage or at shallower depths for secondary tillage . The seedbed is usually good for germination and plant emergence. However, if full width rotary tillage is used, soil conditions for water infiltration and erosion control are somewhat limiting since the soil is finely pulverized and surface crop residues are incorporated into the soil. To avoid these problems, strip rotary tillers with attached planting units can be used in a one-pass tillage and planting operation. Figure 18 illustrates the soil condition and seed placement following strip rotary tillage.

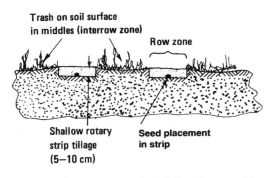

Figure 18. Soil condition and seed placement following a strip rotary tiller-planter

3. Till-Plant (on ridged or non-ridged soil)

Steps:
-Primary tillage: none
-Secondary tillage: no separate secondary tillage operations are used. Seedbed preparation for the row zone is provided by sweeps, 25-36 cm (10-14 in.) wide, attached to the planting implement (till planter).

162

In this method the sweeps and trash bars clear crop residues and stubble from a 25-36 cm strip and the seed is placed and firmed in the cleared zone by planting units attached behind the sweeps. Other planting units designed for strip tillage on ridged or non-ridged soil may use disk row cleaners or other tools to clear and till a strip of soil ahead of the planting unit.

If till-plant is used on ridged soil, the ridging operation is usually done during row cultivation for weed control of the previous crop. This method provides a good seedbed and good conditions for water infiltration and erosion control since the residue remains on the soil surface in the interrow zone. Figure 19 illustrates the soil condition and seed placement following the till-plant method.

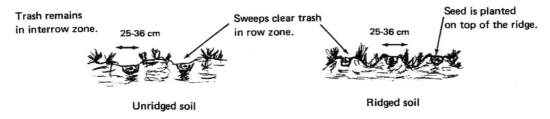

Figure 19. Soil condition and seed placement following the till-plant method.

B3. No-till (slot planting or zero till), Conservation Tillage (for ridged or non-ridged soil)

Steps:
-Primary tillage: none
-Secondary tillage: no separate secondary tillage operations are used. Seedbed preparation for the row zone is provided by attachments, such as coulter blades (vertical, rolling blades), that are part of the no-till planter.

This system uses a specially designed no-till planting implement that cuts through surface residues and plants in a narrow seed zone (slot) 5-8 cm (2-3 in.) wide in untilled soil. If no-till is used on ridged soil, the ridging operation is usually done during row cultivation for weed control of the previous crop.

No-till planting systems offer several advantages over conventional tillage systems:
a. Maximum crop residue is left on the soil surface to increase water infiltration and conserve soil moisture.
b. Soil erosion from wind and water is minimized.
c. Less fuel is required because of the one-pass operation.
d. Double-cropping can be more feasible in marginal areas where time for seedbed preparation is limited.
e. Row crops can be planted in sod and on slopes too steep and erodible for clean tillage.

Disadvantages associated with no-till systems include lower soil temperatures that may delay or hinder seed germination, greater dependence on chemical weed control, and a greater risk of insect or disease problems associated with surface residues. Figure 20 illustrates the soil condition and seed placement following no-till planting.

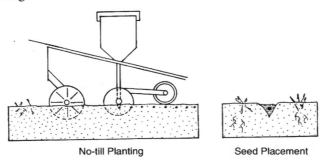

No-till Planting   Seed Placement

Figure 20. Soil condition and seed placement following no-till planting

A summary of conservation tillage systems is shown in Table 2.

Table 2. Conservation tillage systems

Tillage System	Steps in Tillage Operations*
Full Width	
1. Chisel Plow	Chiseling (Fall or Spring) → Disking → Harrowing → Planting →
a. Chisel Plow-Plant	Chiseling (Fall) → Chisel plow-plant →
2. Disk (and/or field cultivating) and Plant	Disking (Field Cultivating) → Harrowing → Planting →
3. Sweep Tillage	Stubble-mulch Plowing → Rodweeding →→→ Field Cultivating → Planting → ←Fallowing→
Strip Till	
1. Lister-planting (non-ridged soil)	Lister-Planting →
2. Strip Rotary Tillage (non-ridged soil)	Strip rotary tiller-planting →
3. a. Till-Plant (non-ridged soil)	Till-planting →
b. Till-Plant (ridged soil)	Ridging (summer) → Till-planting (spring) →
No-till	
1. a. No-till Planting (non-ridged soil)	No-till planting →
b. No-till Planting (ridged soil)	Ridging (summer) → No-till planting (spring) →

*Arrows indicate number of trips through the field (may vary widely depending on many factors).

IV. TILLAGE OPERATIONS FOR SPECIAL SITUATIONS

Some crop, soil, climate and weather situations require the consideration of special tillage techniques not included in the previous discussion. A description of two of those techniques follows.

A. *Subsoiling*

Subsoiling is sometimes used to break up relatively impervious layers either naturally formed in the soil or caused by compaction from tillage operations. These impervious layers can limit root growth and nutrient and water-holding capacities of soil. The term subsoiling generally refers to pulling a chisel type implement through the soil at a depth greater than 35 cm (13-14 in.) resulting in the disruption of the relatively impervious layers. Figure 21 illustrates the subsoiling operation. Reports vary as to the benefits (increased crop yields) resulting from subsoiling, depending on geographical location. If soil has a dense hardpan that restricts water movement, such as frequently found in the Coastal Plain soils in the Southeast, subsoiling has resulted in better root growth and higher yields in most years. The use of specially designed subsoil-planting implements that subsoil in the row zone directly ahead of the planting unit is increasing in these areas. In many soil types, especially in the Midwest and other areas that receive freezing temperatures in winter, the value of regular subsoiling is questionable. The expansion and contraction from the freezing and thawing of soil water break up impervious layers in the soil. Also, subsoiling is not effective when subsequent tillage operations recompact the soil or if internal drainage beneath the impervious layer is poor.

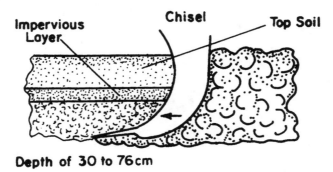

Depth of 30 to 76 cm

Figure 21

B. *Extremely deep primary tillage*

Very deep primary tillage [down to 120 cm (4 ft.) deep] is sometimes used to salvage land that could not be used for growing crops by utilizing ordinary tillage methods. Extremely large "plows" are used for operations such as "turning up" topsoil that has been buried by sand from floods or wind.

V. TILLAGE FOR WEED CONTROL

A. *Tillage before planting*

Most tillage operations prior to planting provide some measure of weed control. This is especially true of secondary tillage operations immediately before planting since weeds are often germinating and beginning growth at that time. One such method of tillage is known as delayed seedbed preparation. In this method, secondary tillage is used on the previously tilled soil, providing favorable conditions for the weed seed to germinate. After weed seedlings have started to grow, another shallow secondary tillage operation is performed to kill the weeds and to prepare a seedbed for the crop. Shallow tillage just before planting is necessary to prevent bringing new weed seeds to the surface where they could germinate.

B. *Tillage after planting and before crop emergence is completed*

Tillage of large seeded crops such as corn and soybeans may be done between planting and crop emergence and shortly after crop emergence. This tillage is usually done with a harrow or rotary hoe. When used, it may serve two purposes-weed control and breaking soil crusts for better crop emergence. Care must be taken not to destroy the crop stand if cultivation is done at this time. Frequently, 10% of the crop stand is destroyed by the hoeing operation during seedling emergence but the loss in stand due to hoeing is usually less severe than the loss of stand resulting from soil crusting. Hoeing during mid-day, when the seedlings are less turgid (less brittle), helps minimize seedling breakage. The rotary hoe is most often used following crop emergence and when the weeds are still very small (Figure 22).

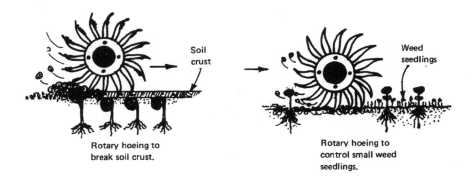

Rotary hoeing to break soil crust.

Rotary hoeing to control small weed seedlings.

Figure 22

C. *Cultivation after crop emergence*

Although chemicals have provided some measure of weed control, cultivation of row crops often provides the most economical and surest method for controlling troublesome weeds. Some research data indicate other benefits, but in most instances the major benefit of cultivation is killing weeds by uprooting the weed seedlings, clipping the weeds below the soil surface, or by covering them with soil (Figure 23). Cultivation should be shallow to minimize root injury of the crop plants. Cultivation, as compared to other methods of weed control, can cause lower yields if the crop roots are severely pruned.

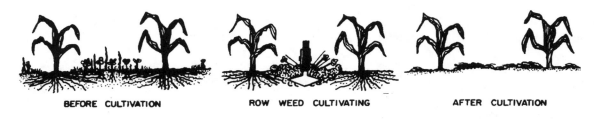

BEFORE CULTIVATION   ROW WEED CULTIVATING   AFTER CULTIVATION

Figure 23

VI. GENERAL CONSIDERATIONS IN ADOPTING TILLAGE TECHNIQUES

Any reduced tillage or special tillage technique must be compared to existing tillage operations before being adopted. The methods must be compared from the standpoints of proper seed placement, pest control, water infiltration, soil erosion, planting dates possible with each method, machinery costs, and crop yields.

A. *Agronomic Aspects in Adopting Tillage Systems*

1. Soil and climatic factors-Tillage systems influence soil factors, which in turn, can influence crop response. Reduced tillage systems that leave more crop residues on the soil surface generally lower soil temperatures and increase moisture content of soils in spring. Soil tilth and organic matter content of topsoils are usually improved by conservation tillage systems that concentrate crop residues near the surface, which also improve the activity of microorganisms and earthworms. Precipitation and length of growing season are also considerations in adopting tillage systems. Conservation tillage systems conserve soil moisture and have been more readily adopted in drier agricultural regions and in regions that have longer growing seasons.

2. Seed and fertilizer placement-Surface crop residues, although desirable for preventing soil erosion, can present problems in seed and fertilizer placement. Heavy residues can interfere with proper seed placement, covering of seed with soil, and seed-to-soil contact. Specially designed planters are overcoming these problems. Fertilizer placement and nutrient availability problems can result from no-till systems. Surface applications

166

of fertilizer, especially in one-pass tillage systems, tend to concentrate nutrients and lime in the top 5 or 8 cm of soil which may be a problem in low fertility soils in dry weather. Cooler soil temperatures under the residue mulch and the relative immobility of phosphorus, potassium, and micronutrients in soils can reduce nutrient uptake efficiency of plants growing in low fertility soils.

3. Pest Control-Weed seeds accumulate near the soil surface in reduced tillage systems and greater problems with weeds can occur, especially with perennial weed species. Crop residues on the surface interfere with conventional weed cultivation equipment such as the rotary hoe and the sweep-type weed cultivator. However, surface residues can help lower weed seed germination and establishment. Disk-type cultivators, crop residue management, and chemical weed control are used to overcome this difficulty. Surface residue may necessitate changes in methods and strategies of weed control.

Tillage may also influence the type and severity of diseases, nematodes and insects. Surface residues harbor some pest organisms which can become more serious problems in conservation tillage systems compared to clean tillage where residues are buried by tilling. Therefore, effective and timely pest management programs are essential for successful crop production using conservation tillage systems.

4. Soil conservation-Soil erosion is directly linked to the amount of residue remaining on the soil surface after tillage (Table 3). Clean tillage using the moldboard plow in the fall leaves the soil unprotected during most of the year. A 63 quintal/hectare (100 bu/A) corn crop leaves about 6720 kg/ha (6,000 lbs/A) of post harvest residue. As a general rule, soil erosion can be reduced one-half by leaving 2240-3360 kg/ha (2000-3000 lbs/A) of the post-harvest corn stalk residue in the field after planting. The amount of residue buried is affected by the type of tillage implement and frequency of use (Table 4).

Table 3. Runoff and soil loss on a sloping (9%) silt loam soil (previously grown to corn) from one-hour artificial rainstorms*

Tillage System	Runoff Water centimeters (inches).		Soil Loss Metric T/ha (T/A)	
	1st Hour	2nd Hour	1st Hour	2nd Hour
Spring plow, disk, plant	4.6 (1.8)	5.6 (2.2)	23.3 (10.4)	27.1 (12.1)
Spring chisel, field cultivate, plant	1.0 (0.4)	3.8 (1.5)	0.7 (0.3)	2.5 (1.1)
Till-plant	3.8 (1.5)	5.1 (2.0)	7.4 (3.3)	8.5 (3.8)
No-till	2.5 (1.0)	3.8 (1.5)	3.6 (1.6)	3.8 (1.7)

*Storms of 6.4 cm (2.5 in.) per hour were applied within 4 weeks after planting. Rows were across slope.

Adapted from Mannering, J. V., D. R. Griffith, and C. B. Richey. 1975. Tillage for moisture conservation. Paper No. 75-2523. Am. Soc. Agr. Eng., St. Joseph, MO.

Table 4. **Percent residue and percent soil cover remaining after various tillage operations and tillage systems**

Tillage Operation	Percent Residue Remaining[a]
Moldboard plow	0-10
Offset disk (24" blades, 6" deep)	25
Full-width rotary tillage (6" deep)	25
Chisel plow (twisted shanks)	25
Full-width rotary tillage (3" deep)	50
Tandem disk	50
Field cultivator (with sweeps)	70
Chisel plow (straight shanks)	80
Sweep plows (30" or greater V sweeps)	90
Rodweeder	90-95

Tillage System	Percent Soil Cover Remaining[b]
Conventional, fall plow	1.0
Till-plant	8.4
Disk (twice) and plant	12.9
Chisel and plant	19.0
Strip rotary	62.0
No-till	76.0

[a] Estimated residue remaining after the first trip across a field.

[b] Estimated immediately after planting corn in a field previously grown in corn. Adapted from the USDA Soil Conservation Service. July, 1978. The facts about conservation tillage. Des Moines, IA; Mannering, J. ,.., D. R. Griffith, and C. B. Richey. 1975. Tillage for moisture conservation. Paper No. 75-2523. Am. Soc. Agr. Eng., St. Joseph, MO; and Fenster, C. R. 1970. Conservation tillage in the Northern Plains in Conservation Tillage: Problems and Potentials. Special Publication No. 20: Soil Conservation Society of America, Ankeny, 1A.

B. *Economic Aspects in Adopting Tillage Systems*

A primary consideration is net profit over a long period. When a farmer adopts a new tillage system, initial yields may drop from the conventional tillage system previously used. However, yields often improve as management experience is gained with the new tillage system. Using crop yields, solely as an estimate of potential profits without considering factors such as soil erosion and fuel energy costs, is misleading in judging the long-range economic potential of a tillage system. Profits and losses from reduced tillage systems can be influenced by soil type, effectiveness of weed, insect and disease control, crop yields and costs of altering or buying tillage implements in changing tillage systems. Soils must be recognized as a priceless resource, but the above uncertainties and risks hinder farmers from adopting different tillage systems. Additional research and innovative farming are making reduced tillage systems more successful and their adoption should be encouraged.

1. What are two ways in which the number of tillage operations in conventional tillage can be reduced using the existing machinery?

2. Which of the following implements is normally used for primary tillage? Secondary tillage? Which implement could be used for both primary and secondary tillage?

    a. Spike-toothed harrow
    b. Chisel plow
    c. Disk harrow

3. Describe a reduced tillage system that would not be classified as conservation tillage.

4. What tillage system when used on corn stalk residue would leave enough residue after planting to cut soil erosion in half?

SEEDING

VII. OBJECTIVES

There are several objectives that must be satisfied if a planting is to result in an adequate field stand.

A. *Proper Depth Placement*

Crop seeds must be planted at the proper depth if an adequate stand is to be achieved. Seed size is generally related to the optimum planting depth. Seedlings from large seeds will usually emerge from greater depths than seedlings from small seeds for the following reasons:

1. Large seeds have a larger food reserve that can be utilized in the emergence process.
2. The elongation potential of seedlings from large seeds is usually greater, i.e., the hypocotyl (epigeal emergence) or mesocotyl (hypogeal emergence) has a greater possibility for elongation. Table 5 illustrates the general relationship of depth of seeding to seed size.

Table 5. Relationship between seed size and planting depth for several crops

Crops	Approximate seed size no./kg (no./lb.)	Normal planting depth cm (in.)
Kentucky bluegrass	4.8 million (2.2 million)	0.64 (0.25)
Birdsfoot trefoil	770,000 (350,000)	0.64 (0.25)
Orchardgrass	1.3 million (600,000)	1.30 (0.50)
Red clover	550,000 (250,000)	1.30 (0.50)
Alfalfa	440,000 (200,000)	1.30 (0.50)
Smooth bromegrass	308,000 (140,000)	1.30 (0.50)
Sudangrass	121,000 (55,000)	2.50 (1.00)
Wheat	33,000 (115,000)	3.80 (1.50)
Oats	31,000 (14,000)	3.80 (1.50)
Soybeans	5,500 (2,500)	3.80 (1.50)
Pea	8,800 (4,000)	5.10 (2.00)
Corn	2,640 (1,200)	5.10 (2.00)

Adapted with permission of The Macmillan Company from Principles of Field Crop Production by John H. Martin and Warren H. Leonard, 2nd Edition. Copyright by The Macmillan Company, 1967.

The type of emergence exhibited by a species also influences the optimum depth of planting. Crops of a given seed size with epigeal emergence should generally not be planted as deeply as crops with hypogeal emergence because of the difficulty of pushing the cotyledons through the soil.

The depth of planting is also influenced by soil type. Deeper plantings are usually possible in lighter soil types and in soils with better structure than in heavier soil types. In sandy soils, the soil surface is frequently dry and therefore deeper plantings may be necessary to place seed in moist soil. In heavier soils or soils with poor drainage, soil temperatures and oxygen concentrations may be too low for proper germination at deeper planting depths and may require seed placement closer to the soil surface.

B. Good Seed-Soil Contact

Good seed-soil contact depends on proper planting equipment and procedure and also on proper tillage prior to planting.

1. Proper tillage prior to planting should prepare a seedbed free of clods and firm enough so the seed, regardless of size, can have a large part of its surface in contact with soil.
2. The planting equipment used should provide for good seed-soil contact without "packing" the surface layer of the soil. Such packing of the surface layer often results in formation of "crusts" that may inhibit seedling emergence.

C. Proper Rate and Distribution

The rate of planting (number of plants per unit land area) and the distribution of plants (arrangement of plants within the area) are very important in determining the crop yield. Some of the factors affecting planting rate and distribution are the following:

1. Percent germination and percent purity of the seedlot-A combination of purity and germination determines the pure live seed percentage. The number of live seeds of the crop being planted is very important in determining the final stand of desired plants per unit area.

2. Competitive ability of the plant or the ability of the plant to utilize space:

   a. Plant size and canopy characteristics-Larger plants should usually be planted at lower populations and with wider distribution. Plant size varies among species and also among varieties within species. An example of varietal differences in recommended rates of planting is presented in Table 6. Soybean varieties that are short in height with narrow canopies generally require higher seeding rates and narrower rows to maximize yield than taller, larger varieties. This illustrates the importance of plant size in determining plant distribution.

   b. Tillering or branching-In general, species or varieties that have a greater tendency to tiller or branch are planted at lower populations. Tillering and branching provide a method for the plant to take advantage of the surrounding space.

Table 6. Proposed planting rate of two varieties of soybeans related to canopy type for the Midwest

| Variety | Description | Recommended Seeding Rates (Seeds/30.5 cm (Seeds/ft.) Row Width | | |
		76 cm (30 in.)	38 cm (15 in.)	18 cm (7 in.)
Williams 79	large plant (indeterminate)	8	5	3
Gnome	small plant (determinate)	12	7	4

Personal communication from R. L. Cooper, Ohio State University, ARS, USDA.

    c.   Competitive ability of a plant in mixtures of species or varieties-The overall competitive ability of a plant becomes very important in determining the seeding rate in mixtures, such as those used with many of the forages. This is especially true when there are differences in seedling vigor within the mixture. Seeding recommendations for birdsfoot trefoil reflect concern for its lack of competitive ability, especially as a seedling. Birdsfoot trefoil should be planted as a pure stand or with a grass of low seedling competitive ability. It should not be planted in a mixture of other legumes because it would be "crowded out" before it could become established.

3.   Environmental factors affecting rate and distribution:

    a.   Soil type-It would seem logical that more fertile soils and soils with greater water-holding capacity or irrigated soils should support a higher plant population and thus should have higher seeding rates. This is generally true, but there are some exceptions. Plants with the characteristic of tillering may sometimes be planted at a lower rate on fertile, moist or irrigated soils because tillering will "fill in" the stand. There may not be much tillering in infertile, drier soils, so a higher rate of planting may be needed to insure adequate ground cover for high yields.

    b.   Planting date-The date of planting, with its effects on the temperature and moisture environment of the plant, may also affect the rate of planting. Spring-planted crops which tiller may be planted at a lower rate of planting. Spring-planted crops which tiller may be planted at a lower rate at early dates because lower temperatures cause increased tillering. Figure 24 illustrates this principle.

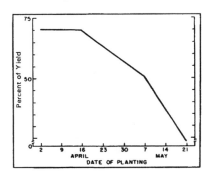 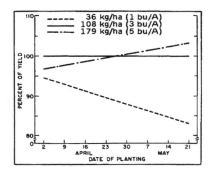

Figure 24

Left: Shows that oat yields in central Iowa decreased as planting was delayed from April 16 to May 21.

Right: Illustrates that if 108 kg/ha (3 bu/A) was considered to give 100% yield from each date of planting, a heavier rate of seeding gives a higher yield in later dates of planting. This is because tillering is not sufficient to provide an adequate number of seed-bearing stems at the 108 kg/ha rate in the later dates of planting.

Adapted from S. C. Wiggans and K. J. Frey, *Your Oat Seeding-How Early-What Rate?*, FS-704, Iowa Farm Science, Iowa State University.

It has also been observed that corn planted early and seeded at high rates produces higher yields with fewer barren stalks than corn planted at later dates. Planting a high population of corn late in the season may result in taller plants, greater shading, more barren stalks (stalks without ears), and lower yields.

c. Climate-Climate can have an effect on planting rate and plant distribution. One of the primary climatic factors affecting planting rate is precipitation, especially rainfall during the growing season. The seeding rate for maximum grain yield in corn may be around 40,000 to 44,500 seeds per hectare (16,000 to 18,000 seeds/A) in an area with limited rainfall during the growing season. However, the optimum rate may be above 64,000 seeds per hectare (26,000 seeds/A), properly distributed, with adequate rainfall.

D. Time of Planting

With most crops, any delay in planting after an optimum date results in decreased yields. The crop plant needs time to build a factory (vegetative growth resulting in maximum sunlight interception) and then have all the time possible for this factory (plant leaves) to conduct photosynthesis and produce total dry matter or grain yield. Therefore early dates of planting usually give higher production, other factors being equal.

E. Row Fertilizer Placement

Although row fertilizer placement is not actually a seeding operation, it is often done in the same operation and thus could be considered an integral part of seeding. With row crops such as maize and soybeans, there are three methods of applying row fertilizer (Figure 25). The most common method is the side-band method, which allows a soil barrier between the fertilizer and seed. Soluble salts from fertilizer placed too close to the seed can dehydrate the seed causing "fertilizer salt injury" and interfere with germination.

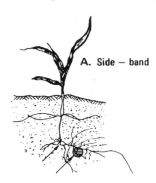
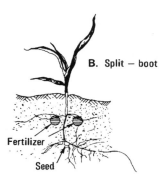
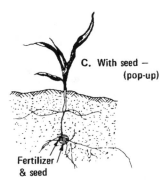

| Fertilizer is placed 5 cm to the side and slightly below the seed. The primary root system absorbs fertilizer first. This is a relatively safe placement of fertilizer since it is at least 5 cm from the seed. | Fertilizer is placed in bands on both sides of and above the seed. The secondary root system will probably be the first to absorb the fertilizer. There is some danger of having fertilizer too close to the seed if more than 33.6 kg/ha (30 lbs/A) of nitrogen plus potassium are used on corn or 22.4 kg/ha (20 lbs/A) on soybeans. | Fertilizer is placed in the seed furrow. The primary root system would be the first to absorb this material. No more than 11.2 kg/ha (10 lbs/A) of nitrogen plus potassium should be used. |

Figure 25. Three methods of applying row fertilizer

From Regis D. Voss and J. Clayton Herman, Three Ways to Place Row Fertilizer. Pm-361, Cooperative Extension Service, Iowa State University.

VIII. PLANTING METHODS

The basic steps in manual or completely mechanized planting operations are 1) opening a furrow in the soil 2) proper spacing of seed 3) placement of seed 4) firming the soil around the seed and 5) covering the seed with soil. The value of any planting method or of planting equipment will be judged by the accuracy and efficiency with which the above steps can be completed.

A. Manual Planting

In countries where mechanized planters are not available, partial or complete manual planting operations are performed. Small hand tools may be used to open a furrow and place seed in the soil. Covering the seed and firming the soil is often done by the human foot. It would be a mistake to assume that manual planting would always ensure optimum planting conditions. Consider the following problems associated with manual planting:

1) Uneven depth of placement from variable furrow depths made with a hoe.
2) Uneven spacing of seed caused by human errors in judgment.
3) Uneven covering of seed and excessive soil compaction above the seed by covering and firming with the human foot.
4) Non-uniform planting operations caused by fatigue.

B. Mechanized Planting

Equipment for planting is generally divided into four categories as shown in Table 7.

Table 7

Planting Equipment	Examples
1. Row-crop Planters	Corn, cotton, peanuts, sorghum, soybeans, sunflowers
2. Grain Drills	Barley, oats, rice, rye, wheat, soybeans, forage grasses and legumes
3. Broadcast Seeders	Barley, oats, rice, rye, wheat, soybeans, forage grasses and legumes
4. Specialized Planters	Potato planter, tobacco transplanters, vegetable-seed planters

1. *Row-crop Planters*-These planters are designed for crops that require accurate spacing between rows and between plants within the rows. Rows are spaced far enough apart to allow proper mechanical cultivation for control of weeds and mechanized harvesting of crops. Planting rate, seeding depth, and row and seed spacing can be adjusted on row-crop planters so that various row crops can be planted with the same planter. Row-crop planters can be used in *three different planting patterns based on how seeds are placed in the row:*

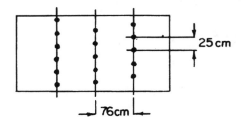

Drill Pattern-Seeds are individually dropped in the row at a uniform distance apart based on the desired population per acre. Drill pattern using a row-crop planter is the most popular and widely used planting method for most row crops.

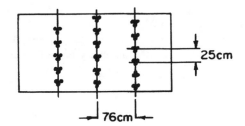

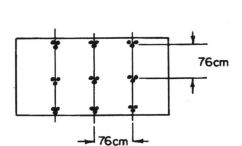

Hill-drop Pattern-Seeds are placed in soil in groups of 2 or more. The location of the grouped seeds is called a hill. Hill-drop planting decreases the chances of skips within the row and uneven stands. However, inter-plant competition between grouped seedlings can be severe enough to reduce growth and yields. This method was once popular for planting corn but generally has been replaced by the drill pattern. Indigenous farmers in some countries continue to use this method.

Checkrow Pattern-Three or more seeds are planted in hills. Hills within the row are spaced at the same distance as row width resulting in a cross-hatched planting pattern. Notched wire, stretched across the length of the field, triggers the planter release of seed in hills at the desired spacing. Checkrow planting was popular before the development of herbicides since the field could be cross-cultivated for weed control. Because of the high labor and time requirement, and the availability of herbicides, this method is now rarely used except for some specialty crops and in some countries.

Row-crop planters vary widely in design. They may be equipped so that fertilizer, insecticide, and herbicide can be applied during the planting operation. The basic components of a row-crop planter are illustrated in Figure 26.

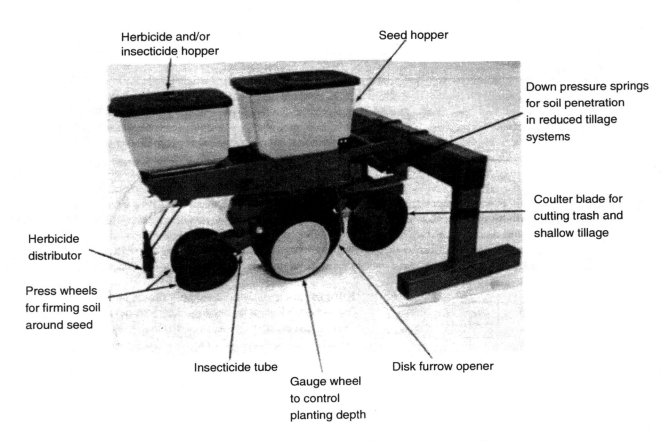

Figure 26. Basic components of a row-crop planter

A popular type of furrow opener generally used in row-crop planters is the disk opener:

Disk openers-Double disks cut through residue and open a V-shaped furrow in the soil where seed is deposited.

Press wheels are used to firm the seedbed for good seed-to-soil contact and may also serve as the soil covering mechanism. Press wheels are slightly V-shaped to provide more soil firming action to the side of the seed and to reduce the compaction of soil directly over the seed (Figure 27). Soil crusting resulting from press wheel compaction in moist soil can lower germination and emergence.

Figure 27

2. Grain Drills-Grain drills are widely used to plant crops such as small grains and soybeans that require high population rates and/or are solid seeded (grown in rows too narrow for mechanical cultivation or other cultural practices requiring interrow driving). Seeds are planted in rows varying from 13 to 50 cm (5-20 in.) apart. For larger-seeded crops such as soybeans, grain drills can be adjusted to approach equidistant planting (seeds are essentially a uniform distance from each other within and among rows). Grain drills can be equipped with press wheels or drag chains for covering and firming the soil, fertilizer hoppers and special grass and legume seed hoppers for seeding small seeded crops or crops that have light, chafy seeds. Grain drills are commonly used to seed companion crops, such as small grains, and small-seeded forage legumes. "Drilling" crops with a grain drill should not be confused with "drill pattern" using a row-crop planter. Figure 28 illustrates the basic components of a grain drill.

Figure 28. Basic components of a grain drill

Courtesy of Deer and Company. Moline, IL.

3. Broadcast Seeders-Broadcast seeders have no furrow openers or seed covering devices and distribute seed in a random uniform manner on the soil surface. Thus, the seedbed must be totally prepared prior to broadcast seeding and a separate shallow tillage operation, such as spike-toothed harrowing, is required after seeding to cover the seed with soil. Broadcast seeding is another method for solid seeding of crops. Ideally, broadcasting seed should result in equidistant spacing of seeds but this is rarely achieved in field situations due to the lack of control in seed distribution and seed coverage with this planting method. Methods of broadcasting seed are shown in Figure 29.

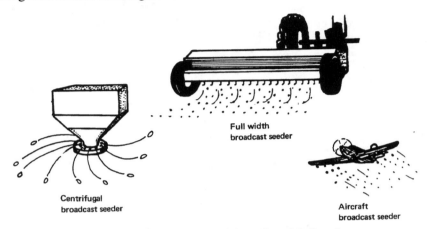

Centrifugal broadcast seeder

Full width broadcast seeder

Aircraft broadcast seeder

Figure 29. Broadcast Seeding Methods

Broadcast seeding is a rapid seeding operation and can be used to sow companion crops and small-seeded forage legumes. However, this method has several disadvantages compared to row seeding using grain drills:

1) Seeding rates cannot be controlled as accurately.
2) Uneven terrain, poor soil conditions and windy weather during seeding results in non-uniform seed distribution.
3) A subsequent tillage operation is needed to cover the seed with soil and usually results in uneven depth of seed. Due to the lack of control in planting depth, small-seeded legumes, when sown with companion crops, may be placed too deeply in the soil resulting in poor germination and seedling establishment.
4) Higher seeding rates are usually required to overcome poorer germination and seedling establishment associated with broadcast seeding.

4. Specialized Planters-Specialized planters are similar in principle to row-crop planters but are designed for specific crops and unique planting operations.

a) Potato planters-These planters are designed to plant small potatoes or seed pieces cut from whole potatoes. Furrow openers open a 8 to 10 cm (3-4 in.) wide furrow in the seedbed and covering disks "hill" the soil over the seed and fertilizer.

b) Vegetable seed planters-These planters are similar to the row-crop planter but are designed to plant a wide variety of shapes and sizes of vegetable seeds. More accurate planting depth adjustments can be made since planting depth is a critical factor for small seeded vegetable crops.

c) Tobacco transplanters-Normally tobacco plants are started from seeds and then transplanted to the field. Several models are available. Tobacco plants are hand-fed into the planting unit which sets the plant in a furrow. Water (which may or may not contain a starter fertilizer) is released into the furrow at the transplant site and packing wheels firm the soil around the plant. Figure 30 illustrates the operation of a tobacco transplanter.

Figure 30

What are four major objectives to be considered when seeding a crop?

What is the relationship of seed size and type of emergence to the optimum depth of planting for crops?

How does the following factors affect optimum planting rates in general?

Large versus small-sized plants?
Tillering vs. non-tillering crops?
Fertile versus non-fertile soils?

What is the difference between drilling wheat with a grain drill and drill planting with a row-crop planter?

How might broadcast seeding be responsible for poor emergence of alfalfa when sown with oats?

IX. DEMONSTRATION EXERCISES IN SEEDING

The following demonstration exercises provide an opportunity to observe the effects of planting depth, fertilizer placement and soil aeration on seedling emergence and rooting patterns.

A. *Methods and Materials*

On day 0, seeds and fertilizer were placed in paper cups (Figure 31) according to instructions in Table 8-The treatments were conducted in cups in a sandbench and labeled according to the identification scheme in the table. Treatments were observed at two-day intervals until the completion of the experiment on day 14.

Table 8. Seeding Demonstration Exercise

Treatment Identification	Crop (Number of seeds)	Planting depth[1]	Fertilizer[2] placement	Aeration[3] treatment
Depth of planting experiment:				
A-1	Maize (10)	5 cm	-	holes
A-2	Maize (10)	15 cm	-	holes
B-1	Soybeans (10)	5 cm	-	holes
B-2	Soybeans (10)	15 cm	-	holes
C-1	Alfalfa (25)	1.2 cm	-	holes
C-2	Alfalfa (25)	2.5 cm	-	holes
C-3	Alfalfa (25)	7.5 cm	-	holes
Fertilizer placement experiment:				
D-1	Maize (10)	5 cm	with seed	holes
D-2	Maize (10)	5 cm	10 cm	holes
E-1	Soybeans (10)	5 cm	with seed	holes
E-2	Soybeans (10)	5 cm	10 cm	holes
Aeration experiment:				
F-1	Maize (10)	5 cm	-	holes
F-2	Maize (10)	5 cm	-	no holes
G-1	Soybeans (10)	5 cm	-	holes
G-2	Soybeans (10)	5 cm	-	no holes

[1] Planting depth was achieved by placing part of the soil (sand) in the cup, packing lightly, placing seed evenly on surface of soil, and then filling the cup with soil to within 1.2 cm of top of cup and again packing lightly. (Example-For 5 cm planting depth, cup was filled to within 6 cm of top of cup and packed lightly. Seeds were placed on soil surface and cup was filled with soil to within 1.2 cm of top of cup.)

[2] Fertilizer placement-

- = no fertilizer
With seed = 2.5 cc (1/2 teaspoon) of granular fertilizer (12-12-12) placed with each seed.

10 cm = fertilizer [25 cc (5 teaspoons)] placed 5 cm below seed and only on one side of cup per following drawing.

[3] Aeration treatment-
Holes = 5 holes (size of pencil) punched in side of each cup 1.2 cm from bottom.

No Holes = no holes for improper soil aeration treatment.

Note: The aeration treatments were liberally watered in order to keep the soil somewhat "waterlogged."

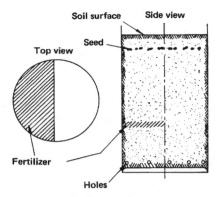

Figure 31. Diagram showing seed, fertilizer, and aeration hole placement in paper cups. Cups are approximately 18 cm tall and 7.5 cm in diameter.

B. Results-

1. **Depth of planting - Maize:** The results of A-1 and A-2 treatments are shown in Figure 32.

Figure 32

Note the following:

a: There was a higher percent emergence at the 5 cm depth (A-1).

b. The mesocotyls were extremely elongated at the 15 cm depth (A-2). Some mesocotyls and coleoptiles could not elongate enough to effect emergence. The endosperm energy may have been exhausted or the mesocotyls may have reached their maximum elongation potential.

c. There is a danger in planting maize too deeply, especially in early dates of planting because the elongation potential of plants is generally decreased by lower temperatures.

2. **Depth of planting-Soybeans:** The results of B-1 and B-2 treatments are illustrated in Figure 33.

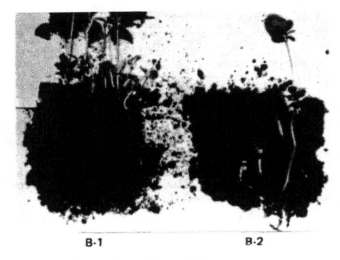

B-1   B-2

Figure 33

a. Soybeans were more adversely affected by deep planting than maize.

b. Most of the hypocotyls in the deep planting elongated, but not enough to cause emergence (B-2). The reasons for poor emergence from deep plantings may be lack of energy supply in the cotyledons, lack of hypocotyl elongation potential, or too much soil resistance to the cotyledons as they were pushed toward the surface.

3. **Depth of planting-Alfalfa:** The results of C-1, C-2, and C-3 treatments are shown in Figure 34. Note that better stands and more vigorous plants resulted from shallow planting depths (C-1 and C-2 treatments).

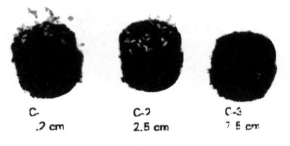

C-   C-2   C-3
.2 cm   2.5 cm   7.5 cm

Figure 34

a. The 1.2 cm depth of planting (C-1) resulted in better stands than deeper plantings.

b. Alfalfa is a small seed with a small food reserve and the hypocotyl of a small seedling has a limited potential for elongation. Thus, shallower planting depths are necessary.

4. **Fertilizer placement with maize and soybeans:** The results of fertilizer placement with maize (D-1 and D-2) and with soybeans (E-1 and E-2) are shown in Figure 35.

a. The adverse effect of placing large amounts of fertilizer with the seed (D-1 and E-1) can be seen in lower germination and emergence and in smaller or abnormal seedlings.

   b. Soybeans (E-1) were more adversely affected than maize (D-1) by high fertilizer concentrations placed with the seed.

   c. The primary root system of corn shows better development where fertilizer was placed 5 cm below and to one side of the seed (D-2).

5. **Soil aeration and seedling development:** Figure 36 shows the results of lack of aeration on germination and emergence of corn (F-1 and F-2) and soybeans (G-1 and G-2).

   a. Poor aeration (F-2 and G-2), caused by a "waterlogged" situation, resulted in lower germination and emergence and an increase in abnormal seedlings than proper aeration (F-1 and G-1).

   b. Soybeans (G-2) appeared to be affected more than corn (F-2) by lack of aeration.

   c. In order for respiration to occur, oxygen must be present. Respiration is essential for the energy release necessary for proper germination and seedling growth.

Figure 35

SELF-EVALUATION TEST

Tillage and Seeding

Circle letter corresponding to one best answer.

1. Alfalfa planted at which of the following depths in sand emerged best (Section IX)?

   a) 0 cm
   b) 1.2 cm
   c) 2.5 cm
   d) 7.5 cm

2. Of the following list, which is the most important purpose of tillage before seeding?

   a) To provide good drainage so the seedlings do not "drown"
   b) To provide a situation in which the seeding depth and the seed-soil contact is optimum
   c) To control soil insects that would otherwise feed on the planted seed
   d) To incorporate fertilizer in the proper position for seedling use
   e) To provide a rooting zone for the plant

3. The following factor would usually not be related to the depth of planting of crop seed:

   a) elongation potential of a seedling
   b) type of emergence
   c) general soil fertility
   d) seed size
   e) date of planting

4. The following is characteristic of conservation tillage as compared to clean tillage:

   a) It is used in areas with more erosion potential.
   b) It results in less reflected radiation.
   c) It results in more absorbed radiation.
   d) It results in warmer soil temperatures.
   e) It results in better soil drainage.

5. The following statement about the best time for doing primary tillage is true:

   a) Time is not influenced by soil type.
   b) Fall tillage is usually better than spring tillage whenever possible.
   c) It is probably better to till "heavier" soils when the risk of compaction is lower.
   d) It is probably better to till "sandy" soils in the fall.
   e) Fall tillage is best on fields with "rolling" topography.

6. The following clean tillage system involves reduced secondary tillage following an initial moldboard plowing operation:

   a) conventional tillage
   b) chisel plow-plant
   c) one-pass, lister-planting
   d) plow and strip-till planting
   e) disk and plant

7. In fertilizing maize, it is best to put fertilizer below and to the side of seed because:

   a) roots seek out fertilizer
   b) fertilizer develops strong attraction for roots
   c) fertilizer can injure germinating seeds
   d) fertilizer sends out messenger ions to tell roots where to grow
   e) roots attract fertilizer

8. What is the greatest advantage of no-till systems?

   a) greater yields
   b) lower erosion and operational costs
   c) less fertilizer required
   d) stimulates the economy through increased purchase of new, modern equipment
   e) less pesticides required

9. An alfalfa-smooth bromegrass mixture was seeded in soil with "clods" from .6 to 2.5 cm in diameter. Which of the following was probably responsible for an inadequate field stand?

   a) depth of planting
   b) seed-soil contact
   c) rate of planting
   d) distribution of seeds
   e) time of planting

10. Till-planting on ridged soil as compared to conventional tillage results in which of the following?

    a) more weed seeds germinating in the row zone
    b) fewer weed seeds germinating in the interrow zone
    c) less water infiltration in the interrow zone
    d) cooler soil in the row zone
    e) less residue in the interrow zone

11. A farmer plans to plant a forage mixture of alfalfa and smooth bromegrass by broadcasting the mixture about April 1. How should seed be worked into the soil?

    a) with a moldboard plow
    b) with a subsoiler
    c) chisel plow
    d) harrow
    e) with a disk plow

12. When seeding oats early (cool, moist conditions) little difference is observed between yields when a seeding rate of either 14.5 or 72.5 kg/ha (1 or 5 bu/A) is used. This is, most likely, because of:

    a) a reduction of stand in the 72.5 kg/ha seeding rate
    b) germination differences
    c) increased tillering in early dates of planting
    d) decreased branching at the 14.5 kg/ha rate
    e) decreased branching at the 72.5 kg/ha rate

13. "Delayed seedbed preparation" in soybeans

    a) is minimum tillage
    b) is used to provide a better seedbed for the crop
    c) reduces the number of tillage operations in seedbed preparation
    d) eliminates the need for a herbicide
    e) is a method of weed control

14. Conventional seedbed preparation for soybeans on corn ground (fall plow, disk twice, harrow, plant), as compared to spring chisel plow system, would result in

    a) higher grain yields
    b) lower grain yields
    c) lower tillage costs
    d) later dates of planting
    e) more erosion

Chapter 8

Plant Breeding

I. IMPORTANCE

In order for farmers to achieve optimum yields of high quality crop products, the appropriate management practices must be combined with the correct varieties (cultivars). The improvement of genetically controlled traits of plants and the production of improved varieties of crops are included in the art and science of plant breeding.

Although great benefits have been obtained from plant breeding in the modern era of world agriculture, we should not overlook the efforts of ancestral peoples in the improvement of crops. Crop breeding has been practiced since humans first selected seeds from wild plants and grew them under controlled conditions. The centuries of crop selection and improvement efforts by native peoples have undoubtedly been an integral part of our current genetic makeup in the major world food crops. Outstanding achievements have also been made from modern crop breeding efforts. One of the most noteworthy was the development of hybrid corn varieties. Another was the development of high-yielding, stiff-stalked, white wheat varieties to specifically fit into the environment and production practices of the Pacific Northwest. Achievements such as these have greatly increased the food production and income of farmers throughout the world.

II. PLANT INHERITANCE

In order to understand applied concepts and methods of plant breeding, it is necessary to review the basic concepts of plant inheritance.

A. Phenotypic Variation

Plant performance and/or appearance (phenotype) of a plant or plant trait is regulated by the genotype (heritable portion) and environment as shown in the following equation:

$$P \text{ (phenotype)} = G \text{ (genotype)} + E \text{ (environment)}$$

The genotype is not changed by environment, but the phenotypic expression of heritable traits can be, and frequently is, changed by environment and management practices. Therefore, the phenotypic variation of an individual plant or trait can be extremely great. Selecting crop plants for desired traits is often difficult because one must distinguish the portion of variation due to genotype from environment. This difficulty is illustrated in Figure 1.

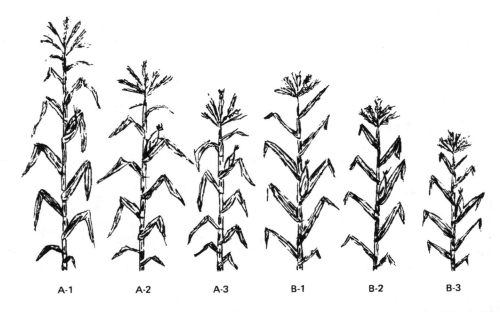

A-1   A-2   A-3   B-1   B-2   B-3

Figure 1. An example of the effects of genotype and environment on plant height. Plants A-1, A-2, and A-3 have the same genotype for height and differences are due to environment. Plants B-I, B-2, and B-3 also have the same genotype for height.

Assume that the height of A-2 and B-2 represent the true genotypes of A and B, respectively. Further suppose that B-2 has the correct plant height for a given management situation. If you selected plants on the basis of the correct phenotype, you would select plants B-2 and A-3. However, only plant B-2 would have the correct genotype. Therefore, selection for plant height would not be completely successful. The selected A-3 plants would produce progeny that were genetically too tall.

What two general factors are responsible for differences in crop plants?

B. GENETIC STORAGE IN PLANT CELLS

Each cell carries a genetic blueprint of the plant. The cell nucleus contains chromosomes which are linear strands containing hundreds of genes (Figure 2). Normal cells of most crop plants contain two sets of chromosomes (one set from each parent) and are termed diploid (2N). Reproductive cells, called gametes, contain one set of chromosomes and are termed haploid (lN). When male and female gametes unite during fertilization, the normal diploid number of chromosomes is restored in the zygote cell (fertilized egg cell). Plant species vary in the number of chromosomes. For example, barley, maize, and wheat contain 14, 20, and 42 chromosomes in each diploid cell, respectively.

Genes are the basic unit of inheritance and consist of DNA segments. Because the nucleus of a diploid cell contains 2 sets of chromosomes, there are 2 copies of each gene (gene pair) for each character. The location of a particular gene on the chromosome is called the locus. Plant traits may be controlled by one or many genes. For instance, flower color may be controlled by one gene but yield is controlled by many genes.

Each gene can express itself in various forms, called alleles, such as tall, normal, or dwarf for the character of height. Most genes have many alleles but a diploid individual has only one pair. A population of individuals, however, may express many different forms of the same gene. Alleles or characters can be dominant or recessive.

186

Dominant alleles express themselves with or without the presence of a recessive allele. Recessive alleles are masked in the presence of a dominant allele and thus, are only expressed when paired with another recessive allele on the locus of homologous chromosomes (pairs of identical chromosomes). When the gene pair at the locus of homologous chromosomes has identical alleles (TT or tt), the condition is termed homozygous. When the gene pair has different alleles (Tt), the condition is termed heterozygous. Realizing that some characters are controlled by more than one gene and that each gene can have different alleles, it is not surprising that a crop species can have a wide variation of genetic expression.

C. GENETIC DUPLICATION AND EXCHANGE IN PLANTS

1. Cellular level

Normal, non-reproductive cells (somatic cells) - An individual plant is made up of millions of cells that originated from a single zygote cell. Meristematic cells continually produce new cells that allow the plant to grow and function. The mechanism for somatic cells to reproduce an exact copy of the genetic information contained in the chromosomes is through mitosis. During mitosis, the nucleus is divided into 2 nuclei, each having identical chromosome numbers and content. Thus, the genetic content of each new cell is identical to the original cell.

Gene For	Gene Pair	Condition
Height	Tt	Heterozygous dominant
Color	RR	Homozygous dominant
Leaf shape	ll	Homozygous recessive

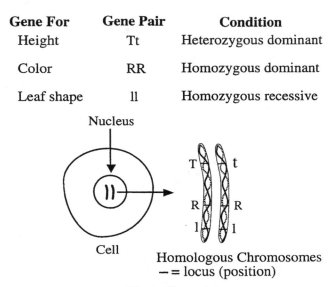

Figure 2.

Reproductive cells (gametic cells) - Most crop plants are sexually reproduced (via seed production) meaning that male and female gametes (sperm and egg cells) unite during fertilization to produce a new zygote. Thus, the new zygote cell has a chromosome set (genome) from each parent. Meiosis is a process of cell division occurring in male and female reproductive organs of plants where the chromosome number in normal diploid cells is reduced by one-half to form the haploid egg and sperm cells. When the egg and sperm cells are united, the normal diploid number of chromosomes is restored. In this way the normal chromosomal number is maintained throughout generations.

2. Whole-Plant Level

The transfer of genetic material among crop plants can occur through vegetative propagation (asexual reproduction) and/or by seed formation (sexual reproduction).

Asexual Reproduction - Vegetative tissue, such as tubers, rhizomes, bulbs, and various root and stem cuttings that have meristematic cells can give rise to new plants. New growth is achieved simply by mitotically reproducing cells which pass on the entire chromosome complement of the individual to each new cell. Thus, all cells are genetically identical to the original. Crops such as sugarcane, potato, bermudagrass and cassava can reproduce sexually but are normally propagated and established by asexual means. The genetic variation among a group of asexually propagated plants would be extremely limited due to the lack of sexual genetic exchange.

Sexual Reproduction - Sexual reproduction in crop plants occurs through the formation of seed. Genetic information is exchanged among parents through the union of male and female gametes to form the 2n zygote. The zygote, with a new genetic makeup, mitotically divides passing on its combinaton of genes to new cells as the embryonic plant grows and develops. Crops such as maize, alfalfa, wheat, rice, and soybeans are normally sexually reproduced and are propagated and established by seeds.

D. SEED FORMATION

1. Steps:

Sexual reproduction in crop plants is achieved through gametogenesis (formation of male and female gametes), pollination (the transfer of male gametes to female gametes), and fertilization (fusion of male and female gametes). On a practical basis, improvement of a species through plant breeding requires a thorough understanding of these processes. The steps in the formation of a seed of sexually reproducing plants are illustrated and described in Figure 3.

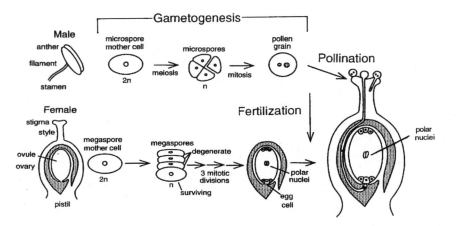

Figure 3. Steps in Seed Formation

Several important aspects of seed formation are as follows:

1. During gametogenesis, meiosis reduces the chromosome number from diploid (2n) to haploid (n).
2. All nuclei developed by mitosis from each haploid product of meiosis, are identical. Therefore, the two polar nuclei and the egg nucleus are genetically identical and the sperm nuclei and the tube nucleus are genetically identical.
3. The development of the fertilized egg cell restores the diploid situation in the embryo that will develop into the new diploid plant.
4. The development and divisions of the cell containing the fertilized polar nuclei (triple fusion) results in triploid (3N) endosperm cells.
5. A newly formed pollen grain has one sperm nucleus and one tube nucleus. During pollination the sperm (generative) nucleus mitotically divides, forming two sperm nuclei.
6. Double fertilization refers to the fertilization of the sperm and egg to form the zygote and the fertilization of the second sperm and the two polar nuclei to form the endosperm.

The diploid number of chromosomes in corn is 2N = 20. What will be the number of chromosomes in:

1. an egg cell?
2. a pollen grain?
3. a sperm cell?
4. a tube nucleus?
5. an embryo cell?
6. an endosperm cell?

2. SEGREGATION AND RECOMBINATION OF ALLELES

One of the advantages of sexual reproduction in plants is the segregation and recombination of alleles. Segregation is the separation of allelic pairs and the distribution of the single alleles to new gametes through meiosis. Recombination is the formation of new combinations of genes and alleles from fertilization of parents differing in genotype. If a plant produces offspring that are genotypically different from each other, then segregation and recombination of alleles occurred and genetic variation was expressed.

In order for the plant breeder to select superior plants, whose progeny can be used for the production of superior varieties, genetic variation must exist. If all of the individuals in a population of plants are genotypically identical for the traits of interest, then the population is homogeneous and genetic variation is minimal. If the population consists of individuals with different genotypes, then the population is heterogeneous and genetic variation is expressed. From this variation, a plant breeder can begin to select improved plants.

One way the plant breeder can create heritable variation is the hybridization (cross pollination) of plants that differ in alleles at one or more loci to produce F_1 (first generation offspring) hybrid plants. When the F_1 plants are either self- or cross-pollinated to produce F_2 (second generation offspring), the F_2 progeny and later generations will show variation. The segregation that occurs among the F_2 and later generation progeny of the F_1 hybrid plants would provide the variability from which the plant breeder may be able to select improved plants. The segregation may be at a single locus or it may be at many loci, as in practical plant breeding situations.

What is the difference in meaning of the terms: homozygous/heterozygous and homogeneous/heterogeneous?

a. Segregation at one locus for one independently inherited trait

An example of segregation from a monohybrid cross (parents differing in their alleles at one locus on a chromosome pair) is shown in the following steps:

1. Hybridization of Two Parents (TT=tall; tt=short)
   Male parent: tt   Possible gametes: t
   Female parent: TT   Possible gametes: T

Parental Cross F_1 Generation

	t	t
T	Tt	Tt
T	Tt	Tt

4/4 or 100% of the individual genotypes are heterozygous. Population is homogeneous (becase all individuals have the same genotype). No segregation in the F_1.

2. Selfing the F_1
   Male parent: Tt   Possible gametes: T and t
   Female parent: Tt   Possible gametes: T and t

F_1 Cross F_2 Generation

	T	t
T	TT	Tt
t	Tt	tt

Genotypic ratio: 1:2:1 (TT:Tt:tt)
Phenotypic ratio: 3:1 (Tall:short)
1/4 (25%) of the individuals are homozygous dominant, 1/2 (50%) are heterozygous, and 1/4 (25%) are homozygous recessive. Population is heterogeneous. Segregation is evident in the F_2.

3. Segregation of Traits From Successive Generations of Selfing

Cross	Progeny	Genotypes	% of Offspring Genotypes Heterozygous	Homozygous Dominant	Recessive
Parental Lines (TT x tt)	F_1	Tt	100	0	0
F_1 selfed	F_2	1/4TT 1/2Tt 1/4tt	50	25	25
F_2 selfed	F_3	3/8TT 1/4Tt 3/8tt	25	37.5	37.5
F_3 selfed	F_4	7/16TT 1/8Tt 7/16tt	12.5	43.75	43.75
F_4 selfed	F_5	15/32TT 1/16Tt 15/32tt	6.25	46.87	46.87

Note: For each successive generation of selfing, the heterozygosity of the offspring decreases by half and the homozygosity increases by half (split evenly between homozygous dominant and homozygous recessive). If selfing the progeny continues, the population will essentially reach 100% homozygosity with 50% being homozygous dominant and 50% homozygous recessive.

Crop Science: Principles and Practice

Work through the following practice problem in Figure 4. Assume that a cross of normally self-pollinating soybean lines were made between a normal green colored line (GG) and a yellow line (gg). The F_1 plants were light green color (Gg). Indicate the expected kinds of eggs, kinds of sperms, genotypes, and phenotypes in Figure 4.

Crop: Soybean (self-pollinating)
Genotype of F_1 parent: Gg

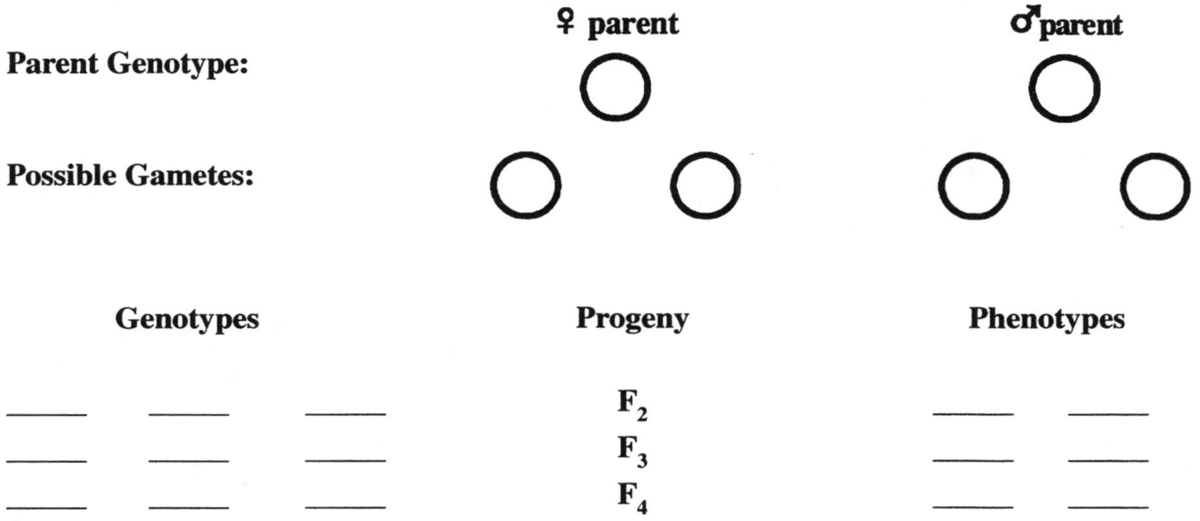

♀ parent   ♂ parent

Parent Genotype:

Possible Gametes:

Genotypes			Progeny	Phenotypes	
___	___	___	F_2	___	___
___	___	___	F_3	___	___
___	___	___	F_4	___	___

Figure 4

b. **Segregation at two loci for two independently inherited traits**

Plant breeders often desire to combine the desirable characters, determined by genes from the two parental plants, into one progeny. This can be done by allowing the recombination of characters following hybridization. Assume that high yield is caused by a dominant allele (Y) at one locus and low yield is caused by a recessive (y) at the same locus. Assume also that tallness is caused by a dominant allele (T) at a locus on another chromosome and shortness (t) is caused by a recessive allele at the same locus. Figure 5 illustrates the segregation and recombination of alleles for these characters.

Answer the following questions relative to the information given in Figure 5.

1. What proportion of the F2 plants would be homozygous (breed true) for high yield?

2. What proportion of the F2 plants would breed true for tallness?

3. What proportion of the F2 plants would breed true for high yield and tallness?

4. What proportion of the F2 plants would breed true for the recombinant type desired (high yield and shortness)?

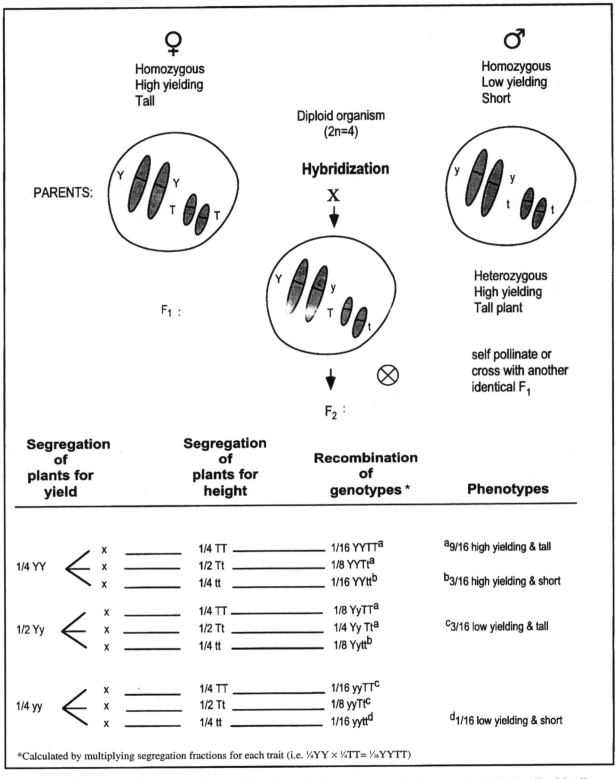

Figure 5. Segregation and recombination of alleles for two independently inherited traits

III. IMPROVING CROPS THROUGH PLANT BREEDING

After reviewing the basic concepts of plant inheritance in Section II, it is appropriate to discuss the objectives and methods plant breeders use to improve yield and quality of agronomic crops.

A. Objectives in plant breeding

1. Increased capacity or efficiency to produce- usually achieved through breeding for:

    a. greater economic yield (e.g., grain, forage, or fiber) under near optimum conditions
    b. greater production efficiency under lower inputs of fertilizer, water, energy and other resources

2. Greater stability of yield (the ability of a variety to give a good yield under varying environmental conditions)-usually achieved through breeding for improved:

    a. resistance or tolerance to diseases, insects, unfavorable soil and weather conditions
    b. quality of planting seed and improved seedling emergence

3. Improved adaptability to harvesting-usually achieved through breeding for plant characters such as:

    a. more erect stalks
    b. shorter or taller stalks
    c. non-shattering of seed
    d. lack of chaff or fuzz

4. Improved product quality-usually achieved through breeding for:

    a. higher content of protein or specific amino acids
    b. higher starch content or improvement in specific kinds of carbohydrates
    c. improved product odor, taste, or color
    d. better fiber qualities

B. General methods

Once the goal for varietal improvement has been established, the plant breeder must determine the nature of the inherited trait, such as dominance, recessiveness, single or multiple gene controlled, and the degree of environmental influence on the phenotypic variation. Then, the proper breeding methods must be used to identify improved genotypes and to create an improved cultivar.

All plant breeding methods depend upon the presence of genetic variability for the characters desired and the successful identification of and selection for the plant characteristics desired (e.g., high seed yield, plant standability, high quality product, etc.). Because yield capacity is extremely important to producers, yield tests of lines are almost always a prerequisite for new cultivar release in the final stages of the breeding program. Three general methods of plant breeding are introduction, selection and hybridization.

1. **Introduction**

    This principal method of plant breeding may introduce genetic variability or diversity by bringing a collection of plants of a species from one area into another. These plants could have characteristics previously not available in the given area. Plant introductions could be used as varieties without change, or additional breeding methods may be later applied to make them more suitable to local conditions. An example of the introduction method is the early introductions of European wheat cultivars into the U. S. during colonial times.

2. **Selection**

A second principal method of plant breeding is selection. Selection is the process by which the desirable genetic variation is retained by sorting and saving desirable plants or groups of plants from a population of plants.

Historically, selection was frequently the next step after introduction to further help identify the best genotypes. Two of the most common methods of selection used in developing new varieties of crops are mass selection and pure line selection.

a. *Mass selection-* A group of plants possessing the same desired traits are selected, the seed from all plants is composited, and the mixture is planted to produce a "mass selected line" that could become a variety if it is superior in its performance. Mass selection has been widely used for many crops particularly in the earlier stages of the breeding program. It has given way to pure line selection in many crops.

b. *Pure line selection-* involves selection of individual homozygous plants and growing the progenies of each selected plant. The progeny of a homozygous plant is known as a "pure line". The performance of the progenies of each selected plant can be observed. The best progeny could become a variety if it is truly superior in performance. Pure line selection is widely used in breeding programs for self- pollinated crops like barley, oats, peanuts, soybeans, wheat, and in many other crops.

3. **Hybridization**

Hybridization, followed by selection, is the third principal method of plant breeding and is the mating of genetically different individuals to obtain genetic recombination. Genetic diversity can be exposed through hybridization by the recombination of alleles and genes for character(s), which will be visible in the segregating populations after the initial hybridization step. Then, individuals can be selected with genotypes that are superior to either parent. Hybridization is widely used to achieve various objectives in crop breeding programs for many crops. Three examples are shown where hybridization can be used to identify superior genotypes:

a. **Hybridization of two parents to recombine alleles for a single character-**

Selection in the segregating progeny of the F_2 may result in a variety with improvement for that character. A hypothetical example is presented on the next page.

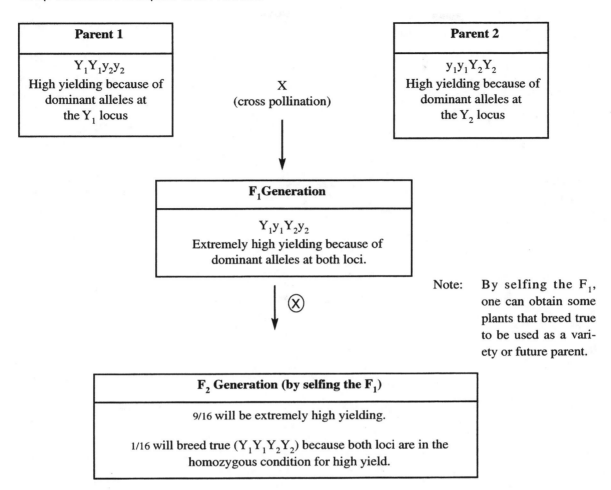

The extremely high yielding plants (higher yielding than either parent) would be selected by the breeder for their high yielding ability.

b. **Hybridization to recombine two or more desirable characters from the parents into one individual.**

Selection in the segregating progeny of the F_2 may result in the production of an improved variety. A hypothetical example is presented below.

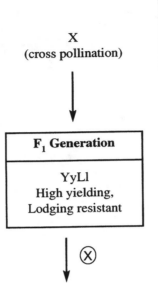

Parent 1
YYll High yielding dominant alleles Lodging susceptible recessive alelles

X
(cross pollination)

Parent 2
yyLL Low yielding recessive alleles Lodging resistant dominant alleles

F₁ Generation
YyLl High yielding, Lodging resistant

Ⓧ

F₂ Generation (by selfing the F₁)
9/16 will be high yielding, lodging resistant
1/16 YYLL - The two desired characters have been recombined into a plant that will breed true for high yield and lodging resistance.

c. Hybridization to produce an F_1 hybrid

This is used to produce a superior variety when the F_1 hybrid expresses heterosis (hybrid vigor). Heterosis is a condition in which the F_1 hybrid performs better than the average of the two parents for the characters in question. A hypothetical example is presented below.

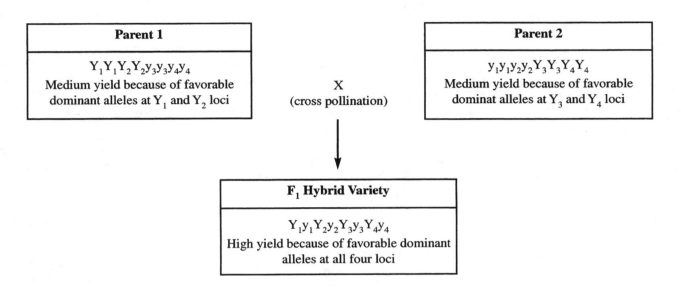

Parent 1
$Y_1Y_1Y_2Y_2y_3y_3y_4y_4$ Medium yield because of favorable dominant alleles at Y_1 and Y_2 loci

X
(cross pollination)

Parent 2
$y_1y_1y_2y_2Y_3Y_3Y_4Y_4$ Medium yield because of favorable dominat alleles at Y_3 and Y_4 loci

F_1 Hybrid Variety
$Y_1y_1Y_2y_2Y_3y_3Y_4y_4$ High yield because of favorable dominant alleles at all four loci

List three ways in which an improved variety may result from hybridization.

1.

2.

3.

IV. BREEDING METHODS USED IN SELF- AND CROSS-POLLINATED SPECIES

A. GENETIC CONSIDERATIONS OF SELF- AND CROSS-POLLINATED CROPS

Knowing whether crops are naturally self- or cross-pollinated is extremely important to plant breeders because the method of pollination will produce different genetic populations, which in turn will determine the type of breeding approach for developing new cultivars.

1. Self-Pollinated Crops

Self-pollinated crops naturally produce homozygous genotypes. Even if two plants with different, but homozygous, genotypes happen to cross with each other (this hybridization occasionally happens), succeeding generations of selfing will move the genes within the population to a homozygous state (see section II.D.2.a.3). Once homozygosity is reached for one or more traits, then those traits will breed true (offspring remain genetically identical to parents). This is why farmers can save seed from the harvest of a self-pollinated crop for planting next year's crop (using proper procedures) and be relatively certain that genotypic performance of the offspring will be similar to that of the originally purchased seed.

Natural inbreeding occurs from breeding closely related plants by self-pollination. One might wonder how self-pollinated crops avoid the harmful effects of inbreeding associated with some crops and animals. Natural selection over time undoubtedly has promoted the development of beneficial alleles and eliminated the negative or lethal alleles. The homozygous dominant and homozygous recessive traits that contribute to the survival and strength of a species have been naturally selected for and predominate the genomes of a self-pollinated species.

The homozygosity of genotypes developed from self-pollination leads to genetic uniformity of individuals from one generation to another. Thus, one might assume that self-pollination would limit genetic diversity. Although self-pollination tends to produce homozygous individuals, a broad population of plants within a species can contain great variation among individual genotypes. This genetic diversity across a population of plants of a self-pollinated species is the source of genetic diversity needed for the species to survive and for plant breeders to manipulate in crop improvement programs.

Therefore, the goal for breeding self-pollinated crops is to identify and select superior genotypes, develop homozygosity in the population (pure line), and release the resulting pure line as a new cultivar or as part of a mixture with other pure lines to form a varietal blend.

2. Cross-Pollinated Crops

Unlike self-pollinated crops, populations of cross-pollinated crops contain many heterozygous genotypes. This is due to the random mating of parents in normally cross-pollinated (open-pollinated) species that give rise to countless gene combinations and mixing of alleles. Therefore, the genetic composition of the population changes for each succeeding generation and is not stable like pure lines of self-pollinating crops. When a plant breeder identifies and selects desirable plants in a cross-pollinated species, there is no guarantee that their offspring will also be desirable. This is because of the random mating from cross-pollination.

Because of the many heterozygous genotypes present in a population of cross-pollinated species, undesirable recessive alleles may be present but masked by the dominance of the beneficial alleles. When inbreeding occurs, these negative alleles may express themselves in a homozygous state and result in a less vigorous progeny than the parents (inbreeding depression). The degree of inbreeding depression will vary among cross-pollinated crops and will influence the breeding methods used for these species.

To approach these challenges in cross-pollinated crops, plant breeders have (1) used vegetative propagation of some species to continue advancing desirable genotypes in successive generations, (2) controlled pollination of male and female parents to produce F_1 hybrids (for crops like maize and sorghum in which one can control the mating of parents), and (3) selected plants that, when randomly cross-pollinated, produce desirable progeny (for crops like alfalfa which are insect pollinated and pollination can not be feasibly controlled).

B. Breeding Methods for Self-pollinated Crops

1. Objectives:

To identify and select genotypes with desirable traits and incorporate those traits into a pure line that is used as a variety or is mixed with other pure lines to form a variety (or blend).

Of the general breeding methods discussed earlier in section III.B., hybridization and pure line selection are the most common components of modern breeding programs for self-pollinated species. Artificial hybridization between lines or cultivars is used as the initial step in recombining genes or characters and creating variability for the subsequent step, selection. Selection is conducted on the segregating generations. The combined use of hybridization and selection is an attempt to recombine the good traits of two or more parents and to select progenies from a cross that are superior to either parent in economically important characters. Any resulting new cultivars will be lines that are homozygous and homogeneous and genetically stable in succeeding generations (pure lines).

2. Methods:

Four common breeding methods used in self pollinated crops are 1) pedigree selection, 2) bulk method of selection, 3) single seed descent method of selection, and 4) backcross method of hybridization.

a. Pedigree Method of Selection

Steps:

1) Hybridization of selected pure line parents

2) Selection of desired plants begins in the F2 generation and in succeeding generations of selfing.

3) Yield trials of remaining selected plants begins at about F7 .

4) F11 -F12: increase seed supplies for new cultivar release. By this time new cultivars are homozygous pure lines.

Comments: Used for improvement of traits that are readily observable. Selection and culling begins early but this method requires extensive labor and note taking.

b. Bulk Method of Selection

Steps:

1) Hybridization of selected pure-line parents.

2) Selection of desired plants does not begin until F6. From F1 to F5, seed from all plants in each generation is harvested in bulk and a sample of seed is grown to produce the succeeding generation.

3) Yield trials of remaining selected plants begins at about F7.

4) F11-F12: increase seed supplies for new cultivar release.

Comments: Used for improvement of traits not readily observable or costly to identify. Because selection doesn't begin until the F6, the method is less expensive and less labor intensive than the pedigree method of selection.

c. Single-Seed Descent Method of Selection

Steps:

Similar to the bulk method of selection except that instead of harvesting all seed of a generation and growing a sample from the bulk for the next generation, a single seed from each plant in the generation is saved and grown to produce the next generation.

Comments: Allows for rapid inbreeding of populations before actual selection begins. Inbreeding is faster because the plant needs to produce only one seed to grow the next generation. Thus, one can use a greenhouse or growth chamber to rapidly grow a small sized plant that produces a few seeds and to grow two or more generations per year until actual selection of desired plants begins. This method shortens the number of years required to develop and release a new cultivar. It is especially suited for rapidly maturing self-pollinating species like soybeans and spring cereals (wheat, barley and oats) that do not require vernalization for flowering.

d. Backcross Method of Hybridization

This method is used to add gene(s) for superior character(s) from another line or variety (donor parent) to an otherwise productive adapted variety (recurrent parent).

Steps:

1) Hybridization of a donor parent and the recurrent parent. This will allow the superior genes from the donor parent to move into the F_1 progeny.

2) The F_1 progeny is mated back to the recurrent parent (backcrossing) to produce the first backcross progeny (BC_1 progeny). The BC_1 progeny is backcrossed to the recurrent parent to produce the BC_2 and so on until the BC_4 progeny is obtained.

3) Desirable plants in the BC_4 progeny are self-pollinated to obtain plants from the segregating population that are homozygous for the desired genes so that a pure-line can be obtained for release to producers.

Comments: This method is widely used to transfer desirable gene(s) from other lines into adapted varieties. For example, backcrossing might be used to transfer resistance to a new disease into a previously productive, but now susceptible, variety. By backcrossing to the recurrent parent and proper selection, the new cultivar will have the gene(s) needed from the donor parent and be essentially identical to the original productive, adapted variety (Figure 6).

Figure 6. An example of the backcross method of hybridization in which disease resistance, caused by a dominant allele (R), is being transferred from a donor parent to an adapted variety (used as the recurrent parent)

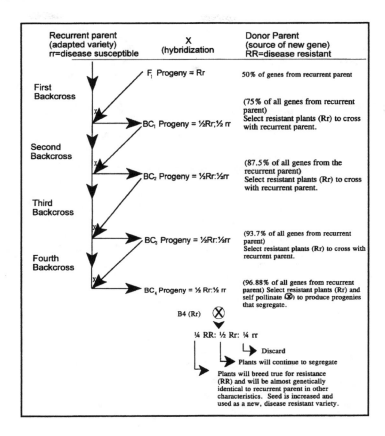

In the backcross method of hybridization, why is an adapted variety used as a recurrent parent?

A variety of a self-pollinated species that is produced by hybridization, followed by either the pedigree, bulk, single seed descent, or backcross methods is a "pure line". What is a pure line?

C.   BREEDING METHODS FOR CROSS-POLLINATED SPECIES

The overall objective in breeding cross-pollinated species is to find lines that, when cross-pollinated, will produce progeny that are superior in their performance. The hybridization method of breeding is often used to take advantage of the hybrid vigor (heterosis) of the F_1 hybrid plants. This has especially been true in species that have a high degree of natural cross-pollination such as maize. However, it is not feasible to produce F_1 hybrids for all cross-pollinated species. Plant mechanisms for producing a large volume of hybrid seed may not be available or the increase in economic yield may not pay for the extra cost of hybrid seed.

1.   Species In Which Cross-Pollination Can Be Controlled On A Commercial Scale

Objective: To produce an F_1 hybrid that expresses superior hybrid vigor (heterosis) over the parents.

For some species, like maize and sorghum, cross-pollination can be controlled on a commercial scale by artificial or manual means, so that pollen from selected male parents is directed to selected female parents. This controlled pollination assures that the resulting F_1 hybrid progeny is a true hybrid cross of the desired parents. Otherwise, female parents could be pollinated by stray pollen or be self-pollinated. To avoid these problems, proper isolation distance from unwanted pollen sources and emasculation of male flowers or male sterility of female plants are used.

Steps to produce single cross hybrid maize (Figure 7):

1) Superior homozygous inbred lines are developed through self-pollination and inbreeding programs. Inbred lines are selected as parents based on agronomic traits and superior combining ability (the ability to produce superior F_1 hybrid progeny when crossed together)

2) To produce seed on a commercial basis, male and female inbred parents are grown in the field and allowed to cross-pollinate by wind pollination. Female plants are detasseled so that pollen from the female plant will not pollinate female ears (this would be self-pollination, if allowed to occur).

3) Ears on the female plants are harvested and represent the F_1 hybrid seed. Seed is cleaned, sorted and bagged to be sold to farmers as single cross hybrid corn seed.

Comments: Because a single cross F_1 hybrid is the progeny of a cross between two different, but homozygous, inbred lines, the F_1 plants are genetically identical and heterozygous (see section III.B.3.). Thus, the population is homogenous and uniform in appearance, which is desired by farmers. Farmers do not save harvested seed of a single cross for next year's planting because the F_1 plants would pollinate each other (self-pollination) and the resulting F_2 plants would segregate into undesirable genotypes. Therefore, farmers must buy hybrid corn seed each year.

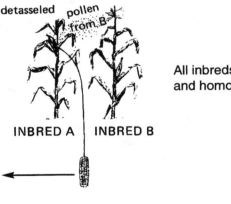

All inbreds are homozygous and homogeneous.

INBRED A | INBRED B

Single cross seed (A X B) produced in an isolated field. Plants are heterozygous and the population is homogeneous.

This single cross seed may be sold to the farmer and planted as a high yielding single cross corn variety.

Figure 7. A method of producing single cross hybrid corn, utilizing detasseling

Historical Note: Before the discovery of hybrid corn, corn was open-pollinated by wind. Native peoples and early farmers saved the best seed for next year's planting (an example of mass selection). However, this random mating of parents from open-pollination did not take full advantage of the heterosis possible with controlled hybridization. Early adoption of hybrid corn by farmers was slow because inbred lines were weak and the female inbred did not produce much seed resulting in high seed costs to farmers. To improve seed yields of the parents used in the hybrid cross and to lower the hybrid seed costs to farmers, double crosses were developed. Double crosses are a hybrid cross between two single crosses. In this way double cross hybrid corn seed could be produced from parents that were higher yielding hybrids rather than lower yielding inbreds. Double cross plants were less uniform (more heterogenous) in the field but seed costs were much lower and more affordable to farmers. Much of the hybrid corn in the U.S. is now produced as single cross seed. Breeders have developed much stronger, higher yielding inbreds that have resulted in more affordable seed costs of single cross hybrid corn seed.

a. Male Sterility:

The possibility of inducing male sterility (either through genetic or chemical means) to force hybridization is of interest to breeders. In hybrid corn production, hand or machine detasseling of female plants in seed production fields could be avoided if male sterility were imposed on the female parent (pollen produced from anthers on female plants would be sterile and self-pollination would be prevented). In fact, most hybrid corn in the 1960s was produced using male sterility until male-sterile plants became susceptible to a race of Southern Corn Leaf Blight disease.

Male sterility also makes commercial hybridization possible for crops that have a high degree of natural self-pollination or where hand or mechanical emasculation of male flowers is not feasible. Male sterility makes hybridization possible in crops like millet, rice, sorghum, sunflower and wheat in which female and male reproductive structures are located in the same flower or on the same inflorescence. Male sterility is widely used to produce hybrid sorghum, hybrid millet and hybrid sunflower varieties.

Which of the following terms would describe a single cross hybrid? A double cross hybrid?

homogeneous

heterozygous

heterogeneous

homozygous

2. **Species in Which Cross-Pollination Can Not Be Controlled on a Commercial Scale**

Objective: To select agronomically superior parents that when randomly cross-pollinated with each other, produce superior progeny.

For many cross-pollinated forage grass and legume species, production of F₁ hybrid varieties is not feasible. Possible reasons include: 1) lack of male sterility mechanisms or other methods to force hybridization on a commercial scale and 2) severe inbreeding depression and/or self sterility (failure of self-pollinated flowers to produce viable seed) that might occur when homozygous inbred lines are being developed as parents in the hybrid cross. When production of hybrid varieties is not feasible for cross-pollinated species, synthetic varieties have been used. A synthetic variety consists of a mixture of selected lines, clones, or hybrids among them which, when cross-pollinated, will produce agronomically superior progenies. The commercial seed of a synthetic variety is obtained (and maintained for a limited number of generations) by open pollination. A brief summary of steps used in the development of a synthetic variety of alfalfa is shown.

Steps in the development of a synthetic variety of alfalfa:

1) Selection of 200-400 superior looking plants from a source nursery that contains several thousand plants. Clones (from vegetative cuttings) are made from the selected mother plants in the source nursery for further evaluation.

2) The selected clones are allowed to randomly cross-pollinate with each other, seed is collected from each clone, and the progeny evaluated for agronomic performance (polycross test). This step tests the combining ability of the selected clones (some may not produce much seed or the progeny is inferior).

3) The selected clones are narrowed to as few as 4 to as many as 50 which will be used in the new synthetic variety. These clones will be moved to a new location and allowed to randomly cross-pollinate with each other. The seed from these clones will be harvested in bulk, mixed together and sold to farmers as a synthetic variety.

Comments: A synthetic variety is actually a heterogeneous population of heterozygous individuals because the parents are 4-50 clones with different genotypes that hybridize (cross-pollinate) with each other. This form of hybridization does produce an important, but limited, amount of heterosis (hybrid vigor). The synthetic variety method is a way to combine desirable genotypes selected on the basis of agronomic appearance/performance and their ability to cross together to produce superior progeny.

A summary of the main breeding methods discussed in this section is shown in Table 1.

Table 1. Summary of Main Breeding Methods Used in Crop Varietal Development

Main Breeding Methods   **Crop Examples**

Introduction ➞ All crops

Selection
- Mass ➞ All crops
- Pure line
  - pedigree
  - bulk
  - single seed
  - backcrossing

Self pollinated crops: (Wheat, Oats, Barley, Rice, etc.)

Used to develop inbred lines in cross-pollinated crops

Hybridization
- Producing F1 Hybrids → Cross-Pollinated Crops: (Corn, Sorghum, Sunflowers)
- Producing Synthetic Varieties → Forage Grasses: (Orchardgrass, smooth bromegrass, etc.)
  Forage Legumes: (Alfalfa, clovers, etc.)
  Turfgrasses: (Kentucky bluegrass, fescues, etc.)
  Also used to recombine traits in self pollinated lines as a step before selection

V. CELLULAR AND MOLECULAR GENETICS

Traditional plant breeding methods previously discussed rely on sexual reproduction of whole plants for genetic improvement in crops. Because of this, genetic transfer among whole plants is relatively slow and limited by the lack of sexual compatibility among species. In fact, crosses between two different crop species (interspecific hybrids) are rare. Thus, gene transfer and recombination and the potential for genetic improvement is restricted by the sexual reproduction system in crop plants.

Advancement in knowledge and techniques of cellular and molecular genetics is making it possible to manipulate and transfer genetic information without the need for sexual reproduction in crop plants. The following are some key tools that geneticists use to transfer genetic information at the molecular or cellular level:

1) *Plant Cell and Tissue Culture* - Using plant cells or tissues to regenerate a new plant. Advantages include shortening the time between generations, rapid screening for variation, and by-passing the problems of self-sterility.

2) *Somatic Cell Hybridization* - Fusion of cell protoplasts from somatic cells (normal 2n cells) that differ genetically. May allow genetic exchange at the cellular level that results in new individuals when whole plants are cultured from fused cells. This method by-passes sexual reproduction.

3) *Genetic Engineering (also referred to as gene transfer, gene splicing, recombinant DNA technology)* -Involves the identification, isolation, duplication and insertion of genes or pieces of DNA from one genome into another. Potentially, any gene from any species can be used and inserted into another species thus avoiding limitations of sexual incompatibility among crop species.

VI. CONCERNS AND CONSIDERATIONS IN MOLECULAR GENETICS AND PLANT BREEDING

Technological advances in plant breeding, genetics, and mechanized agriculture have been successful in improving crop yields and productivity; however, new issues associated with these developments have also been raised. These issues include the following:

1. **Germplasm Base and Diversity**

The ability of conventional and advanced plant breeding techniques to improve crop species and the ability of crop species to adapt and survive to changing environments greatly depends on genetic diversity. Native peoples, often women, took great care in identifying, saving and storing diverse genotypes for planting crops in unpredictable growing conditions. These farmer-breeders preserved genetic diversity throughout hundreds of years of agriculture. Genetic diversity and survival were closely linked concepts; genetic diversity in the field meant some insurance against total loss of production from a particular disease, insect or other calamity. In areas where subsistence farming moved to commercial agriculture (selling agricultural products for profit), genetic diversity in the field became undesirable. Intensive, mechanized farming of monocultures encouraged the adoption of mainly the highest yielding, most uniform genotypes. For some staple crops grown in developed countries, much of the production is from a relatively small number of varieties with a rather narrow and similar genetic base. The loss of genetically diverse genotypes from modern farming practices and land use from other commercial industries raises concern for preserving genetic diversity among crop species before landraces (early cultivated forms of a crop species) and wild relatives become extinct. Plant breeders and governments throughout the world have established programs to collect, store, and preserve the great variety of germplasm among crop species. But, more world understanding, effort, and support are needed to protect germplasm from extinction and to preserve it for possible future use.

2.   Intellectual property rights

In commercialized agriculture in recent years, there has been a trend to patent varieties, molecular breeding techniques, and even genes of potential economic importance that have been isolated and purified. Protecting the unauthorized sale of intellectual discoveries through patents that give exclusive rights to the owner or discoverer helps provide a financial return for research and development costs through exclusive sales and/or licensing agreements with others. Protecting genetic advances through patenting offers financial incentives for breeding and genetic research, which can, and has, stimulated genetic diversity from private enterprises searching for unique markets and competitive traits among crop species. However, the trend has also raised ethical questions concerning: 1) the impact on free germplasm exchange among public and private institutions and among countries, 2) whether genetic material found in nature or what type of genetic material should be patentable, 3) the impact on distribution of genetic wealth among developed and developing countries, and 4) whether economic incentives from patenting genetic advances will enhance or hamper humanistic goals of society and long-term food production efforts. Ethical and sociological considerations of plant breeding and genetic research are increasingly important for determining the appropriate use and availability of new discoveries.

3.   Goals of Modern Breeding Programs

The flexibility and effectiveness of modern breeding programs to meet changing needs and goals are important for the sustained success of crop agriculture. Potential changes in the environment, awareness of environmental problems, changing production systems, and new technology are examples of forces that may change the traditional needs and goals of breeding programs. Breeding crops for highest yield under highest inputs may be appropriate for some agricultural systems, but breeding crops for optimum yields under existing natural resources may be more appropriate for other agricultural systems. Breeding crops for long-term sustainability of natural resources might include a greater emphasis on crops bred for less tillage, more efficient use of water, fertilizer, and other inputs, less dependence on pesticides or petroleum based products, or for crops better suited to multiple cropping systems than to monocultures. Plant breeding and genetics can be extremely important tools to meet the needs of a productive and sustainable agriculture, if guided by the proper blend of short- and long-term goals.

SELF-EVALUATION TEST

Circle letter corresponding to one best answer.

1. Study the diagram below. What genotype should be placed in the blank space to make the scheme reasonable?
    AABB X aaBB = AaBB

    $\downarrow$

    AaBB X _____ = 1AaBB:1AABB

    a) AaBb
    b) aaBB
    c) aabb
    d) AABB
    e) aAbB

2. A normal plant cell (not a reproductive cell) is usually:

    a) 1n
    b) 2n
    c) 3n
    d) 4n
    e) 5n

3. If a variety of maize, homozygous for high lysine caused by the opaque gene $(o_2 o_2)$, is pollinated by a variety homozygous for low lysine content $(0_2 0_2)$ and the low lysine allele is completely dominant, the resulting endosperm will be:

    a) high in lysine
    b) similar to popcorn
    c) similar to sweet corn
    d) no different
    e) low in lysine

4. Which of the following must exist in order for the plant breeder to select superior plants?
    a) an Fl generation
    b) an artificial hybridization
    c) a homogeneous population
    d) genetic variation
    e) a changing environment

5. Plant A is of the genotype TTRr. Plant B is TtRR. TT or Tt = tall, tt = short, RR or Rr = red, rr = white. If A is crossed with B, what proportion of the progeny will be short and white?

    a) 100%
    b) 75%
    c) 50%
    d) 25%
    e) 0%

6. The following would have heterozygous plants in it:

    a) a soybean variety
    b) an oats variety
    c) a single cross hybrid corn variety
    d) a wheat variety
    e) an inbred corn line

7.   Phenotype refers to:

   a)   the breeding potential of a plant
   b)   the physical appearance of a plant
   c)   the genetic makeup of a plant
   d)   the chromosome content of a nucleus
   e)   the concentration of phenol in the cytoplasm

8.   If pure line selection is used as a breeding method,

   a)   the variety originates from a single plant
   b)   the variety originates from bulking seed of several similar plants
   c)   two inbreds were used as parents
   d)   two single crosses were used as parents
   e)   selection was made from a pure line rather than from a heterogeneous group

9.   In which generation is a plant breeder least likely to practice selection in the pedigree method?

   a) F_1
   b) F_2
   c) F_3
   d) F_4
   e) F_5

10.   A double cross corn hybrid has as its immediate parents:

   a)   three inbreds
   b)   three single crosses
   c)   two single crosses
   d)   one single cross and one inbred
   e)   one double cross and one inbred

11.   A synthetic variety of a cross-pollinated crop would have the following characteristic:

   a)   all plants would be homozygous
   b)   some plants would express hybrid vigor
   c)   the variety would be homogeneous
   d)   no plants would express hybrid vigor
   e)   it would yield less than an inbred line

12.   The breeding method involving cross fertilization of two or more lines, varieties, or species is called:

   a)   hybridization
   b)   bulk method
   c)   pedigree method
   d)   pure line method
   e)   mass method

13. Inbreeding leads to:

    a) heterosis
    b) homozygosity
    c) allelism
    d) increased productivity
    e) sterility

14. How many different combinations of genes could be found in egg cells produced by a plant with genotype AaBbCc?

    a) 1
    b) 2
    c) 4
    d) 8
    e) 16

15. Gene recombinations occur as a result of:

    a) vegetative propagation
    b) clonal propagation
    c) self-pollination of a pure line
    d) sexual reproduction
    e) asexual reproduction

16. In maize, if you wanted to make a cross between male A and female B, you should remove the tassel from:

    a) A
    b) B
    c) both
    d) either
    e) neither

17. A breeding method often used to contribute a superior characteristic of one unadapted variety to an otherwise desirable variety is:

    a) mass selection
    b) pedigree selection
    c) the backcross method
    d) introduction
    e) bulk selection

18. From which of the following would plants be more uniform in appearance?

    a) an open pollinated variety
    b) a single cross hybrid variety
    c) a double cross hybrid variety
    d) a cross-pollinated variety
    e) a synthetic variety

19. Which of the following methods would help overcome the limitation of sexual compatibility among species?

    a) F$_1$ hybridization
    b) backcrossing
    c) introduction
    d) somatic cell hybridization
    e) male sterility

20. The breeding method which may involve bringing a species or variety into an area and using it without change or additional breeding methods is called:

    a) hybridization
    b) introduction
    c) pedigree selection
    d) pure line selection
    e) mass selection

Chapter 9

Seed and Grain Quality

The quality of seed produced by agricultural crops is extremely important from several aspects. The quality and volume of products produced by processing crop seed are quite closely related to the initial quality of seed being used. The number of emerged normal seedlings in a field is related to the number of seeds planted per unit area and also to the viability and purity of the seed sample. In addition, the feeding and food value of cereal, protein, or oil crop seeds are related to seed quality. Thus, there is expanding interest in the quality of agricultural seed used for processing, feed, food, and for planting purposes.

In general, seed quality can be used to describe the various physical and chemical characteristics of seed. The relative importance of seed characteristics depends on the end use. In this chapter characteristics, such as protein and oil content, that are important to feeders or food processors will be referred to as grain quality. Characteristics that are important for planting seed will be referred to as seed quality. In many instances, desirable characteristics are often similar for high seed or grain quality, such as proper moisture for storage and freedom from disease, damage or physical defects.

SEED QUALITY

I. IMPORTANCE

Two important aspects of seed quality are seed viability (the ability of the seed to germinate) and seed vigor (the ability of the seed to produce strong, rapidly emerging seedlings). Seed quality involves many other aspects including varietal purity and freedom from weed seeds, other crop seed and foreign material. In most instances, seed germination and establishment account for only 5-10% of the growing period of a crop and seed costs generally are only 5-10% of the total cost of producing and harvesting the crop. Nevertheless, poor stands, low yields and crop failure can result from underestimating the importance of high seed quality during the critical time of germination and establishment of seedlings. The importance of the quality of seed for planting purposes is shown in Table 1.

Table 1.   Laboratory and field performance of corn of different vigor levels, averaged across six single crosses, grown in Iowa.

	Performance						
	Laboratory				Field		
Vigor Level	Shoot Wt. mg/seedling	Root Wt. mg/seedling	Germ %	Cold Test %	Ht. June 1 cm	Ht. June 23 cm	Leaf area June 1 cm^2
High	58.2	20.9	97	97	19.2	111.4	30.2
Medium	49.5	16.5	98	95	18.5	107.4	26.4
Low	43.3	13.9	97	96	16.8	98.5	22.9

From J. S. Burris, "Seedling Vigor and Its Effect on Field Production of Corn," Iowa Certified Seed News, Vo. 30(6): 2-4. Iowa Crop Improvement Assoc., Ames, IA.

The data in Table 1 relate seedling vigor of corn to germination and growth characteristics in laboratory and field conditions. In general:

1. High vigor seeds resulted in greatest shoot and root weights of seedlings in the laboratory and greatest height and leaf area of seedlings in the field.
2. The standard laboratory germination test did not necessarily predict seedling vigor and seedling performance and stand establishment.
3. Seed quality affected seedling performance and stand establishment.

Seed quality can be lowered due to natural aging of the seed or poor handling and storage conditions. Frequently, estimates of quality based solely on a warm germination test does not adequately predict field performance. Note Table 2.

Table 2. Effect of age of wheat seeds (*Triticum vulgare*, cv. 'Elmar') on their performance.

Seed age, years	Warm germination %	Emergence from soil, %	Shoot dry weight per plant/mg	'Speed' of emergence (higher figures mean greater speed)
1	97	77	108	21.9
3	96	55	107	14.5
6	98	39	103	8.1

Adapted from Kittock, D. L. and A. G. Law. Relationship of Seedling Vigor to Respiration and Tetrazolium Chloride Reduction by Germinating Wheat Seeds, (*Agronomy Journal* 60(3): 286-288. American Society of Agronomy, Madison, WI.

From Table 2:

1. How did seed age affect seed quality based only on the warm germination test? Field emergence?

2. Even if you doubled the planting rate of 6 year-old wheat seed used in this study, what additional risks might there be in stand establishment (compared to using one year-old seed)?

Visual inspection of seed is a weak indicator of seed quality. Obvious defects, diseases, and contamination can be visually detected, but seeds often lose viability and vigor without any visual changes. Thus, proper care, handling, storage, and laboratory tests are necessary to ensure high quality seeds. The multi-billion dollar seed industry in the U.S. was established on the need to provide high quality seed to farmers. Many growers buy seed every year from reputable seed companies to obtain the highest possible seed quality.

II. SEED GERMINATION

There are several requirements if a seed is going to germinate. One of the first requirements is that seeds are viable. Viable seeds, however, may not germinate because of seed dormancy factors or the absence of one or more external conditions necessary for germination.

A. Seed Dormancy

Seed dormancy refers to the physical or physiological condition of a viable seed that prevents germination even under favorable germination conditions.

1. **Physical dormancy**-occurs when physical characteristics of the seed prevent germination. Some crops, like alfalfa or other forage legumes, may have seed with varying amounts of hard seed (seed with seed coats that are impervious to water or oxygen). The seed remains viable but does not imbibe water, and remains hard or firm. Scarification (abrasion of the seed coat) is sometimes used to reduce seed coat impermeability.

2. **Physiological dormancy**-occurs when some internal physiological characteristic(s) of the seed prevent(s) germination. Examples include hormonal inhibition or immature embryos.

   a. Hormonal inhibition - Seeds may have germination inhibitors or an imbalance of chemical promoters/inhibitors that prevent germination. Some of the important cereals like wheat and barley have short-term dormancy due to imbalances of germination hormones and require an after-ripening (storage) period for maximum germination.

   b. Immature embryos - Seeds of some species may initially have immature embryos that lack the critical size and/or cell differentiation necessary for germination. An after-ripening period may be necessary for the embryo to develop full germination capability.

Dormancy in seed used for planting crops can be either beneficial or detrimental. In annual crops, seed dormancy would usually be considered detrimental. Annuals generally should emerge readily and produce seedlings of a uniform size. However, seed dormancy in perennial crops, is thought to be beneficial in some situations. One such situation is when the environmental conditions following planting are favorable for fast germination and emergence of seedlings from nondormant seeds; and, before these seedlings become fully established, an adversity such as a severe drought may occur and kill the germinating and emerged seedlings. If dormant seed are present, they may eventually germinate and produce an adequate stand of the perennial crop. Generally speaking, however, seeds which imbibe water readily, germinate rapidly, and produce healthy seedlings in a minimum length of time are preferred for crop species.

B. External Requirements

External requirements for germination include correct temperature, moisture, oxygen, and, in some cases, light. One of the initial steps in the germination process is the imbibition of water. Water and oxygen are required if respiration and germination are to take place. Species and varieties may differ in the minimum, maximum, and optimum temperatures for germination and growth.

Most agricultural crops do not require light for germination. Examples of plants which do require light for optimum germination are:

tobacco
some lettuce varieties
bentgrass
bermudagrass
Kentucky bluegrass
many weed species

The light requirement for the germination of some species can be directly related to crop management practices such as weed control. For example, weed seeds that require light for germination will not germinate when covered deeply by soil. However, seeds near the soil surface can receive light and germinate. In some crops "delayed seedbed preparation" is recommended for weed control. This method involves the following steps:

1. Conduct tillage operations to prepare the soil for planting.
2. Wait until the weed seed has germinated.
3. Perform a shallow secondary tillage operation to kill the weed seedlings without moving additional weed seed to the soil surface where they would be subjected to light and would germinate.

C. Seed Treatments and Coatings

1. **Seed Treatments** - Seeds planted in soil are subjected to microbial attack from seed- and/or soil-borne diseases. Seed and environmental conditions that promote rapid germination and seedling establishment reduce the risk of pathological reductions in germination and stand establishment. Crops with hypogeal germination and those that are planted in cool, wet soil conditions are particularly vulnerable to pathogens. Seed treatments are fungicides and/or insecticides that are adhered to seeds and designed to improve germination and establishment success of crops that are particularly susceptible. Such seed treatments can be effective and widely used for some crops. However, treated seeds can be toxic to animals and humans and should be handled with care.

2. **Seed Coatings** - Seed coatings refer to general substances that coat the seed. Research is being conducted to utilize pill coating technology commonly used in the medicinal field to seed coatings. Proper application procedures to prevent seed injury, proper polymer characteristics, and controlling proper breakdown rates are some of the research challenges. Seed coatings offer the possibility of meeting a variety of objectives:

   a. To coat small or irregular shaped seed to a uniform size for planting accuracy.

   b. To impregnate seed treatment chemicals into the coating to reduce environmental hazards of toxic dust and leaching of pesticides used in seed treatments.

   c. To artificially program seed germination for a specific interval after planting or when environmental conditions favor germination. This may reduce the need for potentially hazardous seed treatment chemicals.

   d. To improve injury resistance and storability of seed.

---

1. What would be the limiting factor for germination of seeds in warm, waterlogged soils?

2. Would a 15 cm tilling depth be desirable for the last secondary tillage operation in a "delayed seed bed" method for weed control?

III. SEED TESTS

Most states have a seed law that outlines the seed tests required when seed is offered for sale. The following tests are commonly available through recognized seed testing laboratories in each state.

A. Germination Test

This test is one of the most widely used laboratory tests to estimate seed germinability. This test is usually conducted on germination paper, sand, or in other mediums in warm, moist conditions. Thus, it estimates the maximum percentage of seed capable of developing healthy seedlings. Normal and abnormal seedlings and hard seeds are recorded. The germination procedures vary for different crops and are standardized by the Association of

Official Seed Analysts and the International Seed Testing Association. These standards also outline germination procedures for crop seeds that commonly have seed dormancy.

B. Vigor Test

The germination test often overestimates the germination obtained in the field because field conditions for germination are usually more stressful than those used for the laboratory germination test. Several vigor tests have been developed to further describe the quality of a seed lot for field planting. The cold test and accelerated aging test are two common vigor tests:

1. **Cold test** - Seeds are usually placed in moist soil or sand and subjected to a period of cool temperatures (approximately 10°C/50°F) and then allowed to germinate under warm conditions. Cold tests are used to estimate seed germination and seedling growth under cold, wet field conditions. Cold testing has been largely limited to hybrid seed corn. However, cold tests may also be used for other kinds of seeds.

2. **Accelerated Aging test** - Seeds are exposed to high temperature (approximately 41°C/106°F) and nearly 100% relative humidity for 3 to 4 days and then allowed to germinate under optimum conditions. Like the cold test, the accelerated aging test is used to estimate germination potential under more stressful conditions. It can be used for many species and is often used to estimate vigor of soybean seeds.

C. Tetrazolium Test (TZ test)

Tetrazolium (TZ) tests are based on color changes in the embryo of the seed produced by a chemical (tetrazolium chloride). This is a quick test of seed viability, requiring only one to two days to complete. However, it is not recognized as official for seed sales purposes.

D. Purity Analysis

Purity analysis is a physical examination and separation of different components of the seed sample. Different fractions of the seed sample are reported in percentages based on weight and include the following:

1. **Pure seed**- The percentage by weight of the sample that is seed of the kind submitted for testing.

2. **Other crop seed**- The percentage by weight of other crop seed present in the sample. An example would be barley seed in a wheat sample.

3. **Weed seed**- The percentage by weight of all weed seed present in a sample. The names and number of secondary noxious weeds seeds (from the state's noxious weed list) per unit weight are reported. The presence of any primary noxious weeds render the seed lot unsalable.

4. **Inert matter**- The percentage by weight of chaff, stones, stems and other materials which are not seeds.

In the U.S., federal and state seed laws regulate the sale of seed within the country. These laws require that certain information from seed tests be printed on a seed label and attached or printed on the seed package. The seed label meets the seed industry's truth-in-labeling requirements for the consumer. The kinds of information usually

Figure 1

SEED LABEL

American Seed Co.
RR 4, Heartland, IA

Variety & Kind:	Vigor
	Alfalfa
Lot No.:	114-44
Pure Seed:	98.75%
Inert Matter:	00.75%
Other Crop Seed:	00.05%
Weed Seed:	00.45%
Noxious Weeds:	00.00%
Germination:	92.00%
Hard Seed:	04.00%
Date Tested:	Feb. 20, 199_
Net Weight:	60 lbs.

---

found on a seed label are shown in Figure 1:

IV. THE TETRAZOLIUM (TZ) TEST FOR SEED VIABILITY

It is often desirable to determine the amount of germinable seed in a lot so that the seeding rates may be adjusted. Standard laboratory germination tests may require two weeks or more to obtain results. Tetrazolium testing has been developed to furnish quick estimates of seed viability. In addition, tetrazolium tests may add to the information from standard germination tests by indicating dead or weak embryo tissue (unstained tissue). Viable seeds respire and change colorless tetrazolium dyes (tetrazolium chloride) into highly colored compounds by a chemical reduction reaction. Dead seeds (dead tissue) do not respire and therefore are not stained.

A. Quick Laboratory T.Z. Test (unofficial):

1. Select ten maize seeds from each of the lots.
2. Soak seeds in water for twenty-four hours to facilitate cutting and to permit completion of the test in the shortest possible period.
3. Dissect the seed longitudinally through the embryo.
4. Place one of the halves in open petri dishes containing 0.1 percent solution of tetrazolium chloride.
5. Keep the two lots separate and allow the seeds to soak for approximately one hour.
6. Examine and record the number of seeds in each lot in which the complete embryos are stained red. Use Figure 2 as an example to help you interpret the tetrazolium tests.
7. Calculate the percent germination based on the TZ test results.
8. Compare with percent germination in the standard germination test results in the laboratory.

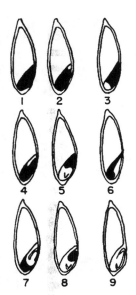

No. 1   GERMINABLE. Embryo completely stained.
No. 2-4 GERMINABLE. Extremities of scutellum unstained.
No. 5   NON-GERMINABLE. Lower half of embryo unstained.
No. 6   NON-GERMINABLE. Embryonic axis unstained.
No. 7   NON-GERMINABLE. Upper half of embryo unstained.
No. 8   NON-GERMINABLE. Scutellum and radicle unstained.
No. 9   NON-GERMINABLE. Embryo completely unstained or only stained very light pink.

(From Tetrazolium Testing Handbook for Agricultural Seeds (AOSA Handbook No. 29), 1970, Don F. Grabe, editor p. 19.

Figure 2 Interpretations for Tetrazolium staining patterns for grass seeds. Black areas represent stained, living tissue; white areas represent unstained, dead tissue.

Figure 2. Interpretations for Tetrazolium staining patterns for grass seeds. Black areas represent stained, living tissue; white areas represent unstained, dead tissue.

B. Seed Viability and Storage

The tetrazolium test has sometimes been used to estimate viability of seed from various storage conditions. Improper temperature and relative humidity during storage can reduce seed viability and thus lower seed quality. Note the results (Figure 3) of various storage conditions on corn seed viability from a study conducted in Mississippi.

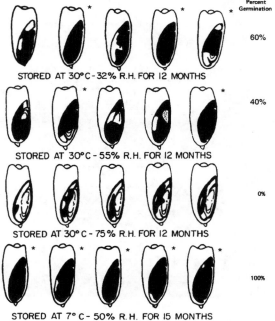

STORED AT 30°C - 32% R.H. FOR 12 MONTHS — 60%
STORED AT 30°C - 55% R.H. FOR 12 MONTHS — 40%
STORED AT 30°C - 75% R.H. FOR 12 MONTHS — 0%
STORED AT 7°C - 50% R.H. FOR 15 MONTHS — 100%

*Germination expected.

Figure 3

From N. 8. Gill, "Patterns of Deterioration in Corn Seed Embryo as Revealed by Tetrazolium Test" Newsletter of the Assoc. of Official Seed Analysts. Vol. 42(4).

From the results of Gill's study shown in Figure 3, what would you conclude about the effect of relative humidity (R.H.) during storage on seed viability? Effect of temperature?

V. MECHANICAL DAMAGE IN SEEDS

Mechanical damage refers to seed injury caused by harvesting, conditioning and handling of seed. Severe mechanical damage can reduce otherwise good seed to poor seed. Large and fragile seeds are especially vulnerable. Splits and large cracks in the testa are readily visible to the naked eye and may indicate damage to the embryo that is not readily apparent. Smaller cracks in the testa are not as easy to see but may be quite important as an indicator of mechanical damage to the embryo. A sodium hypochlorite test can be used for a quick analysis of cracked seed-coats in soybeans as an indicator of mechanical damage.

Sodium Hypochlorite Test for Cracked Seedcoats in Soybeans

Lab Procedure:

1. Select twenty soybean seeds at random from each of the seed lots.

2. Place the seed from each lot in separate containers filled with 1% solution of sodium hypochlorite. Household bleach contains about 5% sodium hypochlorite so one can mix 1 part bleach with 4 parts water to form the testing solution.

3. Allow the beans to soak for a few minutes and then observe the cracked seeds in each lot. The seed coat of the cracked soybeans will be swollen and separated from the cotyledons.

4. Check again at 10-15 minutes and record the percent cracked seed coats.

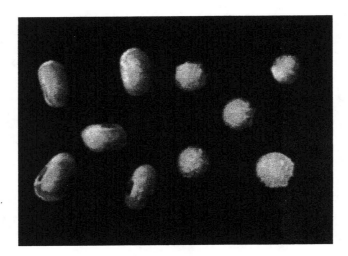

Sodium hypochlorite test for cracked seedcoats in soybeans: Note seed coats have swollen and separated from cotyledons in soybeans with cracked seed coats (5 soybeans on left side).

Table 3 indicates the importance of using mechanical damage in estimating potential loss in seed quality from rough handling.

Table 3. Effect of initial and subsequent drop on soybean seed quality.

Initial Drop (Meters)	Subsequent Drop (Meters)	Germination %	Mechanical Damage %*
0	0	90	12.4
	2	89	13.7
	3	88	13.4
	4	88	16.9
3	0	87	13.1
	2	88	19.8
	3	86	16.4
	4	85	19.2

*Determined by the hypochlorite soak procedure.
From J. S. Burris, "Bulk Handling of Soybeans", Proc. Second Annual. Seed Tech. Conf., 1979. Iowa State University

Data from this study indicated that:

1. Soybeans without an initial drop withstood subsequent drops up to 3 meters in height without appreciable difference in percent mechanical damage.
2. Soybeans with an initial drop of 3 meters in height did not withstand subsequent drops of 2, 3, or 4 meters without sharp increases in percent mechanical damage.
3. These data indicate that soybean seed quality can be improved by minimizing frequency and height of drops during handling.

Do visual rankings likely agree with the laboratory evaluation of seed quality? Why?

VI. DETERMINATION OF PURE-LIVE SEED

The definition of pure-live seed (PLS) is the percent of the *desired* variety that *will* germinate. Therefore, PLS is a function of the percent purity and germination of a seed sample:

Percent (%) PLS = (% Germination x % Purity) ÷ 100

PLS is very useful because the real cost of seed and actual seeding rates based on percent PLS can be determined. In this way seed costs and seeding rates can be based exclusively on the amount and germination ability of the desired seed:

Real Cost (of PLS) = Quoted Price of Seed Per Unit ÷ (% PLS ÷ 100)

Actual Seeding Rate = Recommended Seeding Rate of PLS ÷ (% PLS ÷ 100)

Suppose the following data were recorded after conducting several seed tests (Table 4):

Table 4

Seedlot

	1	2	3	4
% Germination	73	80	89	92
% Pure seed	98	91	99	94
% Other crop seed	0.7	7.5	0.1	0.5
% Inert	1.1	1.3	0.8	5.4
% Weed	0.2	0.2	0.1	0.1

Calculate the following for each seed lot and enter in Table 5:
1. Percent pure-live seed
2. Real cost per kilogram of pure-live seed
3. Actual seeding rate needed to achieve a recommended seeding rate of 20 kg/ha

Table 5

Seedlot	% PLS	Quoted Price/Kg	Real Cost of PLS	Actual Seeding Rate (to achieve 20 kg of PLS/ha)
Lot 1	71.5	25 cents	35 cents	28 kg/ha
Lot 2		25 cents		
Lot 3		28 cents		
Lot 4		30 cents		

From Table 5: Which seed lot is the best buy? Which seed lot requires more seed to achieve the recommended seeding rate?

VII. INCREASING SEED SUPPLIES

Once a plant breeder has developed a superior variety, several questions become extremely important:

1. How can the supply of seed be increased for use by farmers and ranchers?
2. How can the genetic purity be maintained for the newly-developed variety?
3. How can high quality, weed-free seed be obtained in continuous supply?

In past years promising varieties have been lost or adulterated with other varieties, weed seed or other crop seed. To prevent these problems, federal and state seed laws and seed certification program have been developed.

A. Legal Seed

States, in conjunction with the federal seed regulations, have seed laws that regulate the sale of seed to be used for planting purposes in that state. Everyone selling seed in that state must abide by those laws. Some typical regulations in these seed laws are as follows:

1. Any seed offered for sale must have a valid seed label according to the laws of the state in which the seed is sold.

2. The seed must be tested for germination and purity. Germination results must be current (germination tests are valid only for a specified period).

3. No primary noxious weed seed can be present.

4. The name and number of secondary noxious weed seed per unit sample weight must be printed on the seed label according to labeling requirements.

5. The seed must contain less than 1.5% total weed seed.

B. Seed Certification

1. Certification Agency-The organization certifying seed is usually the State Crop Improvement Association. The membership is made up of persons engaged in agricultural work and participation in one or more functions of the association. Seed producers and seed dealers usually make up the major portion of the membership.

    The primary purpose of the certification program is to encourage the availability of high quality seed of superior varieties. A field producing certified seed is inspected for weeds and "off-type plants" by an official of the Crop Improvement Association. The seed is sampled after harvest and tested in a state approved laboratory.

2. Requirements for certification-All states have strict standards for varietal purity but additional requirements may vary among states. Some of the common requirements for seed certification may include:
    a. The germination percentage must be high for that particular group.
    b. No primary noxious weed seeds in the sample.
    c. Limited number of secondary noxious weed seeds in the sample.
    d. Limited amount of total weed seed.
    e. Limited amount of inert matter.
    f. Limited number of other crop seeds.

    State certification of seed is purely voluntary and the grower must contact the state certification officials if certification is desired. Private individuals or seed companies may choose to not certify their seed through the state certification program. Thus, the buyer must rely on the reputation of the seller to obtain pure, high quality seed.

3. Classes and sources of certified seed-Four classes of seed are usually recognized in seed certification programs. These are as follows:

    a. Breeder seed
    b. Foundation seed
    c. Registered seed
    d. Certified seed

4. Limitation of generations-The number of generations through which a variety may be multiplied is usually limited to that specified by the originating breeder or owner of a variety. The limit is often two generations beyond foundation seed. This restriction helps ensure that the variety will not lose its genetic identity through unchecked and unlimited generations of seed multiplication.

C. Seed Increase of New Varieties

Varieties developed by plant breeders in colleges, universities, and other public or government supported institutions will usually be increased through the seed certification programs in the originating state. The pathway of seed as it leaves the breeder's hands is shown in Figure 4. Assume the new variety is wheat and for each hectare sown, 2800 kilograms of seed can be harvested. Seeding rate is 70 kg/ha and enough certified seed for 200,000 hectares is desired to meet the farmer's or rancher's needs.

Commercial seed companies may have their own unique program to increase seed supplies while maintaining genetic purity. However, most seed increase programs follow similar programs described previously. Commercial companies may offer seed for public sale at the foundation level if enough seed is available.

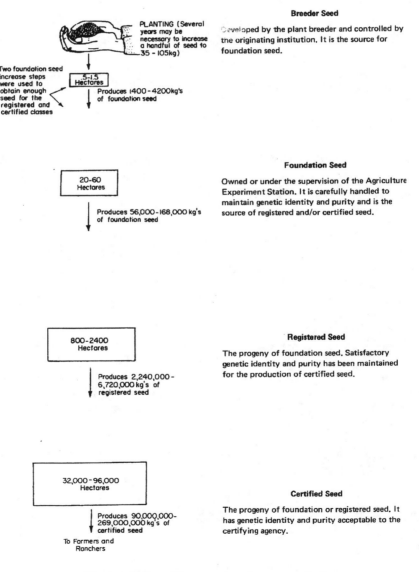

PLANTING (Several years may be necessary to increase a handful of seed to 35 - 105kg)

Two foundation seed increase steps were used to obtain enough seed for the registered and certified classes

.5-1.5 Hectares
Produces 1400 - 4200kg's of foundation seed

Breeder Seed
Developed by the plant breeder and controlled by the originating institution. It is the source for foundation seed.

20-60 Hectares
Produces 56,000-168,000 kg's of foundation seed

Foundation Seed
Owned or under the supervision of the Agriculture Experiment Station. It is carefully handled to maintain genetic identity and purity and is the source of registered and/or certified seed.

800-2400 Hectares
Produces 2,240,000 - 6,720,000 kg's of registered seed

Registered Seed
The progeny of foundation seed. Satisfactory genetic identity and purity has been maintained for the production of certified seed.

32,000 - 96,000 Hectares
Produces 90,000,000 - 269,000,000 kg's of certified seed
To Farmers and Ranchers

Certified Seed
The progeny of foundation or registered seed. It has genetic identity and purity acceptable to the certifying agency.

Figure 4. Seed increase of new varieties

D. Plant Variety Protection Act

This Act was originally passed in 1970 and modified in 1994 for sexually propagated crops to enable the developers of a new variety to protect the variety from unauthorized sale by others and thus ensure a return on an investment in research. Asexually propagated crops can be protected through regular patenting procedures established since 1930. Therefore, the Plant Variety Protection Act (PVP act) is a means to "patent" a new sexually propagated variety. Such varieties are called "protected" varieties. People illegally selling protected varieties can be prosecuted. Varietal protection through the Plant Variety Protection Act lasts for 17 years.

Sexually propagated varieties may be protected under the Plant Variety Protection Act *with* or *without* certification.

1. Plant Variety Protection With Certification-Permission to use or sell the variety must be obtained from the breeder or owner of the variety and the variety <u>must be sold</u> by variety name as a class of certified seed. This option, identified as "Title V" of the PVP act, provides the breeder or owner of the variety (and buyer) added insurance that genetically pure high quality seed is being offered for sale.

2. Plant Variety Protection Without Certification-Permission to use or sell the variety must be granted by the breeder or owner of the variety but certification is <u>optional</u>. Protected varieties by this method may be sold with or without certification according to the demands or needs of a specific market.

Private varieties are developed by private individuals or companies and patented or protected through the Plant Variety Protection Act. Permission to sell and conditions for sale must be obtained from the owner of the variety. *Public* varieties are developed by university or government supported institutions and may also be protected through the Plant Variety Protection Act. *Common* varieties is a term used to identify varieties that are not protected and thus can be grown and sold to the public without approval of the originating institution. It should be remembered that the requirements for legal seed must be met before selling the seed of any variety.

1. How would cold tests benefit the grower?

2. If legal seed and certified seed of a variety are both available at the same price, why would certified seed be a better buy?

3. Certification requirements are usually more stringent at the foundation level than at the registered or certified level. Why is this?

GRAIN QUALITY

The term "grain quality" has different meanings to different people depending on their interest and end purpose of the crop. To a livestock producer grain quality might refer to feeding value of the grain. Moisture percentage as a quality factor of barley grain might be more important to an elevator manager. The miller is more interested in flour yields of wheat while the baker might be more interested in protein and gluten content. In each case grain quality has a different meaning. Before the early 1900's no official grain standards were established to reflect the quality of grain. As a result, "quality" and price were determined by the buyer and were unknown to the seller until the sale was transacted.

I. GRAIN STANDARDS

Terms to describe grain quality as "good - fair - poor" were very ambiguous and buyers were reluctant to pay top prices for grain so poorly described. However, certain interests in the market channels benefitted from a lack of grain standards. After much debate among producers, middlemen, processors and consumers of grain, Congress passed the U.S. Grain Standards Act in 1916. For the first time in U.S. history this act provided grain quality standards which were uniform throughout the nation:

SIXTY-FOURTH CONGRESS Sess 1 Chapter 313.1916

Part B

"That this Act shall be known by the short title of the "United States grain standards Act.' Sec. 2. That the Secretary of Agriculture is hereby authorized to investigate the handling, grading, and transportation of grain and to fix and establish as soon as it may be after the enactment hereof standards of quality and condition for corn (maize), wheat, rye, oats, barley, flaxseed, and such other grains as in his judgment the usages of the trade may warrant and permit, and the Secretary of Agriculture shall have power to alter or modify such standards whenever the necessities of the trade may require. Sec. 3 That the standards so fixed and established shall be known as the official grain standards of the United States."

This Act (since amended) established: (1) official grain standards and grading procedures, (2) the Federal Grain Inspection Service to license and supervise grain inspectors and to regulate grain inspection and weighing; (3) an appeal procedure if grain grades are challenged. Most of the grain is shipped by grade to other states in the U.S. or to different countries and therefore is inspected and graded under the requirements of the Act.

Some benefits of uniform grain grading:

1. Provides an easier and more honest transaction between buyer and seller.
2. Provides a means of financing and trading grain of known quality and value (for local and foreign transactions).
3. Allows bulk storage of grain with known quality and facilitates transportation of grain.
4. Provides a basis for premiums and discounts with regard to quality.
5. Allows market quotations from major grain markets in the U.S. (major market quotations of grain are based on a U.S. No. 2 grade basis).

II. GRAIN GRADING

A. Procedure

Step 1-Sampling

The most important factor is to obtain a correct and representative sample of the lot to be graded. Certain guidelines and procedures are established by the Federal Grain Inspection Service. Grain probes and other samplers may be used in collecting representative samples (Figure 5).

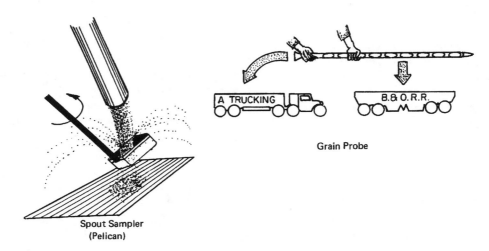

Spout Sampler
(Pelican)

Grain Probe

Figure 5

Step 2-Preliminary Examination

- The sampler's report is examined and verified regarding uniformity of grain, evidence of heating of grain, and presence of weevils or odors such as musty, sour, insect refuse, or pesticide odors.

- Determines (usually by visual observation) what class of grain it is (i.e.: type of wheat, barley, corn, mixed grain, etc.).

Step 3-Preparation of Sample Portions

To allow further analysis and a file sample (for record and appeal purposes) the original sample must be divided into smaller samples without bias and each sample must be a true representation of the grain as a whole. This is done with a Boerner Divider or similar dividing device (Figure 6).

A generalized procedure for dividing the original sample is shown in Figure 7.

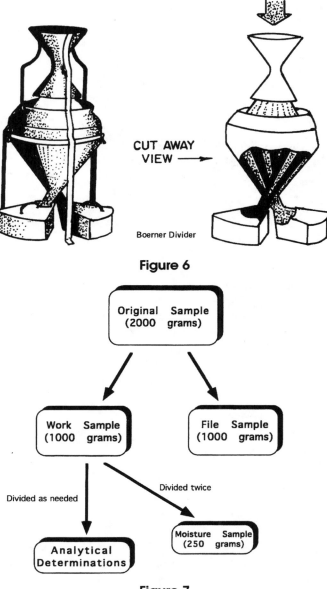

CUT AWAY VIEW ⟶

Boerner Divider

Figure 6

Original Sample (2000 grams)

Work Sample (1000 grams)

File Sample (1000 grams)

Divided as needed

Divided twice

Analytical Determinations

Moisture Sample (250 grams)

Figure 7

225

Step 4-Inspecting the Work Sample

Grain from the work sample is inspected and the final grade is determined. The work sample may be further divided into analytical portions for appropriate determinations of various factors necessary for finalizing the grade.

B. Various Determinations in Grain Grading

1. Class and Subclass

Frequently, the type or variety of grain greatly influences the value and suitability of the grain for a particular purpose. "Classes" have been established in grading standards to distinguish groups, varieties, or types within a crop that differ in suitability and/or utilization. "Subclass" is a more specific subdivision of class.

Kernel characteristics and color are frequently used to identify classes and subclasses. Note the following examples:

- a. Crop (wheat), Class (Durum wheat), and subclasses (Hard Amber Durum Wheat and Amber Durum Wheat).
- b. Crop (Corn), Class (Yellow corn), and no subclasses.

2. Special Grade Designations

Numerical grades alone may not reflect the true commercial value or suitability of the grain. Therefore, special grade designations (if applicable) may be used to characterize grain quality in addition to the numerical grade. Special grade designations can indicate desirable or undesirable properties of the grain as shown in the following examples:

a. U.S. No. 2 Corn, Infested* (infested with greater than a specified number of live grain weevils and/or other injurious grain insects in the sample)

b. U.S. No. 4 Soft Red Winter Wheat, Ergoty* (presence of greater than a specified number of potentially poisonous ergot bodies in the sample)

c. U.S. No. 1 Barley, Garlicky*, Smutty* (presence of greater than a specified number of smut balls and garlic bulblets and/or a strong garlic or smutty ordor)

d. U.S. No. 1 Extra Heavy* Oats (an exceptionally good test weight of oats that exceeded a specified weight)
*Special Grade Designations

3. Dockage

Generally refers to foreign material such as hulls, weed seeds, and dust that can be readily removed by appropriate sieves (hand sieves and dockage machines are used). Not all grains (i.e. corn and soybeans) require dockage determinations.

4. Moisture

Grain moisture of each sample is determined by approved and regularly inspected moisture meters. Although grain moisture does not influence the numerical grade of the sample, it is extremely important and noted on the grain grading ticket. Grain moisture indicates the suitability for transporting, storing, or processing grain.

5. Grade Factors

Grade factors are items that will determine the numerical grade of the grain sample. Some factors are determined by machine and/or by manual determination. Each factor is graded separately. The overall grade of the sample is the lowest numerical grade of the individual factors. Examples of grade factors are test weight, heat damaged kernels, total damaged kernels, and foreign material. Grade factors will vary for different crops and are specified by official grain standards.

6. Test Weight

Measured in kilograms per hectoliter (hl) or pounds of grain per Winchester bushel [2,150.42 cubic inch (.35 hl) capacity] on an approved test weight apparatus. Test weight is an indicator of grain quality because the weight of grain that fills a standard volume is measured. Higher test weights indicate plumper kernels and higher flour and starch yields.

7. Analytical Determinations

Analytical determinations are used to help determine the numerical grades of some factors. Analytical determinations vary with different crops and may involve hand screening, sorting, and visual separation of different grain damages. Percentages are calculated on a weight basis. (Sample size varies with different determinations from 25 to 1000 grams.) Examples:

Wheat: Heat damaged kernels, total damaged kernels, foreign material, shrunken and broken kernels, total defects and contrasting classes of wheat.

Corn: Broken corn and foreign material, heat damaged kernels, and total damaged kernels.

Rye: Foreign matter other than wheat, total foreign material, heat damaged kernels, and total damaged kernels.

It should be noted that "heat-damage" is an especially important quality factor in grading and requires a separate analysis. Heat-damage usually results in kernel discoloration due to high temperatures from respiration of improperly stored grain. Heat damaged kernels are poor in feeding and processing value.

The factor "total damage" includes many damages and the kinds of damage will vary for different crops. Total damage may include: weather and ground damaged, insect damaged, sprout damaged, heat damaged or otherwise materially discolored grain.

C. Placing the Final Grade

1. Procedure:

Prior to determining the final grade, each factor must be calculated and graded separately according to grade requirements published in the *Official United States Standards For Grain*. Grades and grade requirements are summarized in tables. Note the example using soybeans shown in Table 6.

Table 6. Grades and grade requirements for Soybeans.
(From the Grain Inspection Handbook II, Soybeans, 1997. Federal Grain Inspection Service).

Grade	Minimum test weight per bushel (pounds)	Maximum limits of --				
		Damaged kernels		Foreign material	Splits	Soybeans of other colors[1]
		Heat (part of total) (percent)	Total (percent)	(percent)	(percent)	(percent)
U.S. No. 1	56.0	0.2	2.0	1.0	10.0	1.0
U.S. No. 2	54.0	0.5	3.0	2.0	20.0	2.0
U.S. No. 3	52.0	1.0	5.0	3.0	30.0	5.0
U.S. No. 4	49.0	3.0	8.0	5.0	40.0	10.0

U.S. Sample grade:
  U.S. Sample grade is soybeans that:
    (a) Do not meet the requirements for the grades U.S. Nos. 1, 2, 3, or 4; or
    (b) Contain 4 or more stones which have an aggregate weight in excess of 0.1 percent of the sample weight, 1 or more pieces of glass, 3 or more crotalaria seeds (*Crotalaria* spp.), 2 or more castor beans (*Ricinus communis* L.), 4 or more particles of an unknown foreign substance(s) or a commonly recognized harmful or toxic substance(s), 10 or more rodent pellets, bird droppings, or an equivalent quantity of other animal filth per 1,000 grams of soybeans; or
    (c) Contain 11 or more animal filth, castor beans, crotalaria seeds, glass, stones, or unknown foreign substance(s) in any combination; or
    (d) Have a musty, sour, or commercially objectionable foreign odor (except garlic odor); or
    (e) Are heating or otherwise of distinctly low quality.

[1] Disregard for Mixed soybeans.

Grades can vary from U.S. No. 1 (best quality) to U.S. Sample Grade (poorest quality). Note that test weight is the only factor based on minimum limits while the remaining factors are based on maximum limits.

2. Hypothetical example:

Soybeans - Lot No. 114

Factor	Determination	Grade for the Factor
Test weight	55.6 lbs.	U.S. No. 2 (Note: minimum limit for No. 1 is 56 lbs.)
Heat damage	3.8%	U.S. Sample Grade
Total damage	8.2%	U.S. Sample Grade
Foreign material	1.0%	U.S. No. 1
Splits	15%	U.S. No. 2
Soybeans of other colors	1.9%	U.S. No. 2

The individual factor which is graded the lowest also determines the final grade for the entire lot. For example if all factors of a sample graded U.S. No. 1 or 2 except for splits which graded U.S. No. 4, then the final overall grade would be U.S. No. 4. In the example shown above, the final grade would be U.S. Sample Grade. In this case there were two determining factors which caused the lot to be graded sample grade: heat damage and total damage.

3. Writing the Grade:

It is generally recommended that the grade should be written in the following order:

"U.S. No. _____"(numerical grade) or "U.S. Sample Grade" (if applicable)
Class of grain or subclass (if applicable)
Special grade designations (i.e.: weevily, ergoty, etc. - if applicable)
Factors which determined the grade

Examples: U.S. No. 1 - Yellow Corn (no factors)
U.S. No. 3. - Sorghum, Smutty, determining factor: Test Weight Per Bushel (54 lbs/bu)
U.S. No. 4 - Dark Northern Spring Wheat, Infested, determining factors: Foreign Material (2.4%); contrasting classes (4%).

1. How would grain standards benefit a buyer of soybeans in Japan?

2. How many times must a grain sample (2000 grams) be divided through a Boerner divider to obtain a representative 60 gram sample?

3. Determine and write the proper grade for the following hypothetical sample of sunflower seed:

GRADES AND GRADE REQUIREMENTS FOR SUNFLOWER SEED

(From the Grain Inspection Handbook II, Soybeans, 1997. Federal Grain Inspection Service).

Grade	Minimum test weight per bushel (pounds)	Maximum limits of —		
		Damaged Sunflower Seed		Dehulled seed (percent)
		Heat Damaged (percent)	Total (percent)	
U.S. No. 1	25.0	0.5	5.0	5.0
U.S. No. 2	25.0	1.0	10.0	5.0

U.S. Sample grade:

    U.S. Sample grade is sunflower seed that:

        (a) Does not meet the requirements for the grades U.S. Nos. 1 or 2; or

        (b) Contains 8 or more stones which have an aggregate weight in excess of 0.20 percent of the sample weight, 2 or more pieces of glass, 3 or more crotalaria seeds (*Crotalaria* spp.), 2 or more castor beans (*Ricinus communis* L.), 4 or more particles of an unknown foreign substance(s) or a commonly recognized harmful or toxic foreign substance(s), 10 or more rodent pellets, bird droppings, or an equivalent quantity of other animal filth per 600 grams of sunflower seed; or

        (c) Has a musty, sour, or commercially objectionable foreign odor; or

        (d) Is heating or otherwise of distinctly low quality.

Sample Data for Sunflowers, Lot 220

Factor   *Grade*

Test wt. = 23 lbs./bu.

Heat-damage = .21%

Total damage = 9%

Dehulled Seed = 3%

FINAL GRADE:

Crop Science: Principles and Practice

2/6 - 8

SELF-EVALUATION TEST

Seed and Grain Quality

Circle letter corresponding to one best answer.

1. A farmer bought a seedlot for $9.80 per 50 kilograms. Laboratory tests indicate that the pure-live seed content is 70%. What was the cost per 50 kilograms of P.L.S.?

   a) $6.86
   b) $9.80
   c) $12.40
   d) $14.00
   e) $14.80

2. The following statement about the membership of most state crop improvement associations is true?

   a) They are made up primarily of crop breeders.
   b) They are made up primarily of state university officials.
   c) They are made up primarily of state government officials.
   d) They are made up primarily of Department of Agriculture officials.
   e) They are made up primarily of seed producers and seed dealers.

3. A farmer buys a seedlot that tests 80% P.L.S. and desires to plant 64 kilograms of P.L.S. per hectare. What should the actual seeding rate be to achieve this desired planting rate?

   a) 5.12 kg/ha
   b) 8.0 kg/ha
   c) 51.2 kg/ha
   d) 80 kg\ha
   e) 92 kg/ha

4. Registered seed is produced from

   a) foundation seed
   b) certified seed I
   c) breeders seed
   d) previous registered seed
   e) certified seed II

5. A laboratory germination test using the standard wet towel germination technique measures

   a) only normal seedlings
   b) normal seedlings and hard seed
   c) normal seedlings under cool, moist conditions
   d) field emergence
   e) seedling vigor

6. You wish to check soybean seed for cracked seed coats. One unofficial method is to use

   a) a tetrazolium solution
   b) a 1% sodium hypochlorite solution
   c) water
   d) a cold test
   e) a sandbench test

7. A trained seed analyst in an official seed-testing laboratory normally makes the following tests:

   a) germination and cracked seed coats
   b) seed purity and seedling vigor
   c) protein and oil
   d) germination and purity
   e) germination and reserve carbohydrates

8. Tetrazolium tests

   a) are based on color changes in the endosperm of the seed
   b) are recognized as official for seed sales purposes
   c) indicate cracked seed coats in soybeans
   d) indicate pure-live seed
   e) are "quick" tests

9. The term "Infested" in grain grading refers to:

   a) class
   b) subclass
   c) grade factor
   d) special grade designation
   e) dockage

10. Consider the seedlot described below:

% primary noxious seeds	=	0.8
% total weed seed	=	3.8
% purity	=	90.0
% foreign material	=	5.0
% germination	=	80.0
% cracked seed coats	=	10.0

    The pure-live seed percentage of this seedlot is which of the following?
    a) 89%
    b) 8.9%
    c) 72%
    d) 95%
    e) 80%

11. The market grade for a sample of yellow soybeans is indicated as No. 1 for test weight, No. 5 for heat damage, No. 2 for splits, No. 1 for damaged kernels, and No. 2 for foreign material. The overall market grade of the sample would be:

    a) No. 1
    b) No. 2
    c) No. 3
    d) No. 4
    e) No. 5

12. The term "hard seed" refers to:

    a) seed that is filled with SiO_2 instead of an embryo, which makes them physically hard.
    b) seed in which the seed coat remains hard and does not imbibe water
    c) seed that is hard to plant because they are very small in size
    d) seed that is hard to harvest due to its large size
    e) seed that is hard and unpalatable to livestock

Chapter 10

Weed Management

I. DEFINITION OF WEED

A common definition of a weed is "a plant out of place" or simply "an unwanted plant." It is a definition determined by humans not nature.

> Once in a golden hour,
> I cast to earth a seed.
> Upon there came a flower
> The people said, a weed...
>
> *(The Flower - A.L. Tennyson, 1809-1892)*

In crop production, a weed is a plant that reduces yield, product desirability, production efficiency, or results in some other undesirable effect. Thus, any plant species can be a weed, even those normally considered to be desirable crop plants. For example, crop plants can be called "weeds" in the following situations, 1) volunteer maize plants growing in a soybean field, 2) bermudagrass, usually a valuable forage or lawn species, growing in a cotton field, 3) smooth bromegrass growing in a seed production field of orchardgrass.

II IMPACT OF WEEDS

A. Beneficial Effects

Plant species designated as "weeds" because they interfere with a specific human activity should not imply that the species has no inherent value. Weedy species can be very valuable to our ecosystem in the following ways:
1. Erosion control-provides ground cover and mulch for the soil.
2. Wildlife habitat-provides food and habitat for many types of wildlife.
3. Germplasm source-much of the genetic wealth and potential improvement in plants is concealed in the genomes of wild and weedy species.
4. Nitrogen fixation-weedy legumes fix nitrogen for use by other plant species.
5. Host for desirable and undesirable biological organisms-helps maintain populations of desirable organisms that control undesirable pests and can attract pest organisms away from the crop.
6. Food and feed source-many of our weeds are edible and marketable in different regions and have been used for animal grazing and forage.

B. Losses Due to Weeds

Weeds cost millions of dollars each year. Costs can be incurred, not only in weed control, but in the variety of direct and indirect losses associated with weeds. Examples of different types of losses from weeds are as follows:

1. Reduced Crop Yields
    The amount of crop yield loss is directly related to weed population in the field. Low weed infestations usually have little impact on crop yields; however, yield losses increase at an increasing rate as weed population exceeds a critical threshold level. Yield losses can range from 0-100%.

2. Reduced Quality or Value
    a. Agricultural Products
        -Crop planting seed that is contaminated with weed seed.
        -Hay containing weeds that are low in nutritive value or that are unpalatable or poisonous.
        -Cotton fibers stained by chlorophyll present in actively growing weeds at cotton harvest time.
        -Foreign material in grain such as seeds, stem, and leaves of weeds.

    b. Land Values
        Severe weed infestations can significantly reduce land values. Weeds can cause added costs in utilizing the land for production of crops, or in some cases, render agricultural land essentially useless.

3. Added Costs
    a. Control Practices
        -Expense of removing weed seed from crop seed.
        -Mechanical cultivation and other tillage practices.
        -Purchase of weed control chemicals (herbicides) and herbicide application equipment.
        -Hand weeding and other labor costs.

    b. Human and Animal Health Problems
        -Posion ivy can cause a severe skin irritation.
        -Ragweed pollen aggravates hay fever.
        -Locoweed (Jimsonweeed) causes "blind staggers" in animals.
        -Squirrel-tail grass and sandbur can cause wounds around the mouth of grazing animals.

    c. Harboring of Other Pests
        -Weeds may serve as the host for insects or diseases that move to the crop and lower yield or product quality.

Why do insects and diseases often cause a greater amount of crop injury in weedy fields?

Give two ways in which weeds may lower the value of forage crops.

In what scenario would weeds be desirable to an area?

III. COMPETITIVE CHARACTERISTICS OF WEEDS

Weed species differ in their competitive growth habits and ability to survive and reproduce in different environments. Some weeds may have outstanding growth characteristics that provide a competitive advantage over other plant species. Other less aggressive weeds may have morphological or reproductive characteristics that enable them to survive and persist. Knowing the characteristics of each weed species will help shape crop management and control strategies for effective weed control.

A. Competitve Growth Characteristics

Weedy species often have one or more growth characteristics that enable them to quickly establish dominance for sunlight, moisture and nutrients in plant communities. Some examples of these characteristics are:

1. Rapid development of a tall canopy
2. Large leaves and/or rapid leaf development
3. Rapid stem elongation in response to competition from other plants
4. Early and rapid development of the root system and high nutrient uptake potential
5. Efficient photosynthetic system
6. Root secretion of allelopathic substances (compounds that restrict the growth of neighboring competitor plants) - a phenomenon referred to as allelopathy.

B. Competitive Reproductive Characteristics

Many weed species produce an enormous number of seeds per plant and produce seed under stressful and competitive conditions. Many perennial weeds may also propagate themselves vegetatively through vegetative organs, such as rhizomes, stolons, or other tissues.

C. Other Competitive Survival Characteristics

In addition to their competitive growth and reproductive characteristics, weeds also exhibit other excellent survival characteristics. Examples include:

1. Seed and plant dormancy - seeds of some weed species can remain dormant and survive in the soil for many months or years. Seed from one plant can cause a continuing problem for many years because of varying levels of seed dormancy. Many biennial and perennial plants have large roots or other storage organs that allow them to survive in a dormant state during the winter or other unfavorable growth periods.

2. Resistance to injury - plant characteristics, such as spines, thorns, or unpalatable leaves, may enable the plant to survive animal grazing. Some weed species may be resistant to different types of herbicides because of morphological or biochemical characteristics.

3. Adaptive growth - some weed species can be very adaptive in growth and seed production characteristics in response to unfavorable conditions. For example, some weed species can produce seed under frequent clipping and mowing in pastures and lawns because they can adapt a low growth habit and produce seed on plants that avoid the clipping or mowing process.

What are three characteristics of a weedy species that may increase its ability to compete with a crop species?

How might seed and plant dormancy of weeds influence weed infestation characteristics?

IV. WEED MANAGEMENT STRATEGIES

Weed management has been an integral and challenging component of crop production over the ages. Mechanized, commercial agriculture in the last century has moved cropping practices toward monocultures and the maintenance of weed-free crop stands. Weed pressure did not decrease, and in some ways increased, because of the ease of weed invasion in open, uncolonized areas in monocultural crops grown in rows. Soil tillage increased to help control weeds, but intensive tillage increased soil erosion rates to intolerable levels. Thus, the discovery of herbicides (chemicals that kill or control weeds) in the 1940s gave farmers an attractive tool to manage weed control and reduce tillage. Many believed that total weed control could be achieved with herbicides; and, herbicide technology and use has steadily increased. However, intensive herbicide use has created new problems:

1. Herbicides can be toxic to humans and wildlife. Excessive or prolonged exposure over time or improper handling of herbicides without protective equipment pose health risks.

2. Some herbicides have been detected in minute amounts in surface and ground waters. The presence of contamination even at very low levels, is an early warning sign that urban and agricultural herbicide use can move herbicide chemicals into non-targeted water sources.

3. Species that survive or adapt to current herbicides may produce more aggressive and herbicide-resistant offspring; thus, encouraging the dependence and use of more potent herbicides.

Chemical herbicides are powerful tools, but they are an expensive input cost and carry human and environmental risks. A more complete weed management program that utilizes a variety of methods, maintains effective weed control, minimizes herbicide use and protects our environment is essential. To accomplish this, one must look at different weed management strategies that include preventative control, maximizing crop competitiveness to weeds, and controlling or destroying existing weed growth. The goal of an effective weed management program is to prevent weed problems as well as to control existing problems; thus, enabling one to aim corrective weed control measures at the cause and not just the symptom. The following section discusses many different control strategies, some that embrace preventive control and at the same time, correct an existing problem. Therefore, classifying weed control measures according to purpose is inappropriate; instead, examples have been classified into general categories of cultural, biological, and chemical methods.

A. Cultural Methods

Cultural methods generally include the various crop management decisions and practices that can influence pest infestation and growth. Examples of cultural methods of weed control are:

1. Crop Management Methods
Crop management for weed control is largely aimed at prevention and providing a competitive growth advantage for crop plants over weedy plants. Examples include:

   a. Varietal selection - Vigorous, adapted varieties and hybrids will help give the crop an advantage over weed seedlings. A vigorous plant that develops a large LAI early in the season will usually compete well with weedy plants.

   b. Crop rotation - A general rule is that summer annual weeds are a greater problem in summer annual crops, winter annual weeds in a winter annual crop, and biennial and perennial weeds in biennial and perennial crops. Disrupting the life cycle of the weed by rotating crops with differing life cycles is a good method of weed control.

   c. Selection of weed-free crop seed - Weed-free crop seed is a must. Because of the relatively small size of many weed seeds, a given weight of planting seed may contain as many weed seeds as it does crop seed. Analyzing the weed seed content of crop seed and using weed-free seed are good methods of preventative control.

d. Manipulation of planting and harvest dates - Planting dates should be timed to give the crop species the best advantage over the weedy species. Planting at optimum soil temperatures for the crop species, not the weedy species, can be used. For example, early planting dates of oats (minimum soil temperature for emergence ≈ 3°C or 37 to 40°F)) can be used to help control infestations of giant foxtail (minimum soil temperature for emergence ≈ 15°C or 58 to 60°F). Timely harvest may allow fall weed control measures that weaken and destroy overwintering biennial and perennial weeds.

e. Row spacing and population management - Narrow rows and/or higher populations of the crop species can provide greater crop competition to the weedy species. Narrow-row soybeans [18-25 cm (7-10 inch rows)] have total light interception 10 days to two weeks earlier than 76-102 cm (30-40 inch) rows.

f. Soil fertility and pH management - Proper soil fertility and pH can help in controlling weeds. For example, ironweed (a plant that tolerates acid soil) often causes problems in pastures with low soil pH. Correcting the soil pH by liming will help ironweed control by giving the pasture species a better competitive advantage. Weeds, because of their competitive growth characteristics, often utilize fertilizer better than crop plants. Thus, timing, application methods, and amounts of fertilizer should be designed to favor crop, not weed, growth.

2. Mechanical Methods
Mechanical methods, such as tillage practices, row cultivation, and mowing, are those that physically injure or destroy existing weed vegetation. They can also be used to lower weed populations and prevent weed seed production.

a. Tillage practices - One of the primary purposes of tillage during seedbed preparation is to destroy existing weeds prior to crop planting. Primary and secondary tillage implements can destroy growing weeds and bury weed seed beyond the germinating zone. Unfortunately, tillage can also bring buried weed seeds to the soil surface enabling them to germinate. Because many weed seeds may remain alive in the soil for many years (up to 40 years in some cases), there is a vast reservoir of viable weed seeds in the soil. Therefore, tillage practices will influence weed seed movement in the soil and the type and severity of weed problems. No-till systems may favor the spread of some types of perennial weeds because overwintering roots are not disturbed with tillage.

A general example of using tillage management to help control weeds is the use of the two-zone tillage concept. A good seedbed is prepared in the crop row zone for crop emergence while the middle zone between rows (interrow zone) is left rough or covered with crop residues to provide a poor seedbed for weed germination and emergence. Another example is a tillage practice that employs "delayed planting" (also called "delayed seedbed preparation"). The soil is tilled for seedbed preparation but planting is delayed allowing weed seeds to germinate followed by a shallow tillage operation (to kill young weed seedlings) and crop planting. Another version of delayed planting is the "stale seedbed" which substitutes a herbicide for the shallow tillage operation immediately prior to planting.

b. Row cultivation - Cultivation with a harrow, rotary hoe, or a conventional row cultivator has been used for years in controlling weeds. Proper tillage and cultivation are often the most economical methods of weed control and aid in reducing herbicide use.

c. Mowing or clipping weeds - Cutting weeds is often aimed at depleting the reserve carbohydrates in the storage organs of weedy plants and preventing seed production. With low amounts of carbohydrates, weed regrowth is slow or absent, allowing the crop plant to outcompete the weeds and possibly causing winter killing or death of the weeds under stress conditions.

B. Biological Methods

Biological control refers to the use of biological organisms to control pests. Examples of biological methods of weed control are:

1. **Disease organisms**
   In the Western U.S., a rust fungus has been used to help control rush skeletonweed.

2. **Insect organisms**
   A head-infesting weevil has been used on musk thistle in the Midwest to help control seed production of this biennial weed. In Australia, a moth borer was used to help control prickly pear.

3. **Animal organisms**
   Cattle, goats, sheep and other grazing animals have been used to selectively control weeds in crop land, pastures, and non-crop land areas. Geese have been used for weed control in cotton fields and special breeds of fish have been used for aquatic weed control.

4. **Plant organisms**
   Allelopathic crop plants, which secrete substances that restrict the growth of neighboring competitor plants, can be used in weed control. Sorghum has been grown for one year prior to the establishment of switchgrass because sorghum is allelopathic to weeds that may be troublesome to switchgrass. Wheat, rye, and other crops have shown allelopathic growth suppression of weeds.

C. Chemical Methods

Chemicals developed to control weeds (herbicides) are widely used in weed management programs. They can be used to destroy existing weeds, prevent or delay weed emergence or growth to give the crop plants an earlier competitive growth advantage, and to prevent seed production and the buildup of weed populations. There are many different classifications of herbicides based on specificity, mode of action, chemical characteristics, method and timing of application, and other factors. The following are examples of major types and classifications of herbicides:

1. **Based on Selectivity**
   -Selective vs. Non-selective herbicides - Selective herbicides kill or damage unwanted plant species (weed) without significantly injuring the desired plant species (crop). A non-selective herbicide kills or damages all plant species on which it is applied.

   Selectivity often depends on the rate and time of application. A normally selective herbicide, applied at an incorrect rate or time, may kill or stunt the crop plant or fail to control the weeds. Using soil sterilants, that can kill all organisms in the soil including plants and seeds, is an extreme example of using a chemical as a non-selective herbicide.

2. **Based on Method of Application**
   - Broadcast vs. Banded herbicides - Broadcast herbicides are those applied over the entire area of the soil or crop. Banded herbicides are those applied in a restricted band or area of the soil or crop. Banded herbicides, in conjunction with other control measures, can help reduce the total amount of herbicide needed.

   - Directed vs. Non-directed Spray herbicides - Directed spray herbicides are used to reduce the amount of herbicide applied and are applied to a directed area within the crop canopy. Non-directed spray herbicides are applied over the whole area of the crop canopy.

   - Foliar- vs. Soil-Applied herbicides - Foliar herbicides are applied to the plant foliage and require direct plant contact for effectiveness. Soil applied herbicides are applied and/or incorporated into the soil and disrupt the germination and establishment of weed seedlings.

- Other designations- Wick or wipe-on application treatments apply the herbicides to weedy plants by brushing or rubbing the herbicide on weed foliage using special applicators. Spot application treatments apply herbicides to small localized areas of weed infestation.

3. **Based on Formulation**
   Herbicide formulation refers to the form or carrier characteristics that contain the active ingredient of the herbicide. Examples of a few different herbicide formulations are liquid, granular, and wettable powder herbicides.

4. **Based on Movement Within the Plant**
   - Contact vs. Systemic (Translocated) - Contact herbicides kill all parts of plants receiving the application. Contact herbicides can be used as a selective herbicide by directing the spray on the weedy plants while minimizing contact with crop plant tissue. Systemic (translocated) herbicides are absorbed into the plant and translocated to other tissues within the plant. Thus, remote parts of the plant, such as rhizomes and stolons, can be killed from applications to the weed foliage.

5. **Based on Timing of Application**
   - Preplant herbicides - applied prior to planting. They are usually incorporated and mixed into the soil at shallow depths of 2.5 to 7.5 cm (1 to 3 inches).

   - Preemergence herbicides - applied following the planting operation and before the crop and weeds emerge. Usually applied to the soil surface and requires rainfall or irrigation to move the herbicide into the soil.

   - Postemergence herbicides -applied after emergence of the crop and/or weed species. Usually applied to foliage and is not strongly influenced by soil characteristics, unlike preplant and preemergence herbicides.

   Postemergence, non-directed applications of some selective herbicides are used in an "over-the-top" or broadcast method. Both crop and weedy plants are sprayed, with the herbicide selectively killing or damaging the weedy species. Postemergence, directed applications of some non-selective herbicides are used to selectively control weeds without severely damaging the crop plants. An example would be spraying the herbicide on smaller weed plants at the base of larger crop plants, without allowing the herbicide to contact much of the crop's foliage. Another example would be using a "wick-type" applicator that contacts the taller weeds without contacting the shorter crop plants.

   Herbicide-tolerant crops/varieties are also being genetically developed. A crop or variety that is genetically tolerant to specific herbicides may reduce crop injury risk and increase flexibility in chemical weed control. However, in order to minimize herbicide use and protect our environment, one must not abandon other non-chemical weed control measures.

6. **Based on Mode of Action**
   Herbicides are classified into general and specific modes of action based on how the chemical interferes with normal plant growth processes. Selectivity of a herbicide often depends on its mode of action and whether the weed is resistant or susceptible to the affected growth process. Rotating herbicides with different modes of action is recommended to help prevent weeds from developing genetic resistance to herbicides. The following are a few of the many different types of herbicide modes of action:

   - Plant growth regulators - work at multiple sites in a plant . Often disrupts hormone balance within the plant causing a variety of growth abnormalities.

   - Enzyme inhibitors - usually inhibit a specific enzyme necessary for the synthesis of key compounds required for normal growth and development (i.e., amino acid synthesis inhibitor, fatty acid synthesis inhibitor, etc.)

- Photosynthetic inhibitors - inhibit some phase of the normal photosynthetic pathway of susceptible plants.

D. Weed Management Programs

A sound weed management program employs the concepts of integrated pest management involving the use of environmentally acceptable control methods in a production system. A well planned pest management program should be based on:

1) Identification of pests and an accurate estimation of pest populations - Scouting weeds in the field and using weed maps help determine location, severity, and population and species changes in different fields and over time. Weed mapping can help reduce herbicide use by tailoring weed control to specific problems rather than treating broad areas for control of localized infestations.

2) An assessment of damage levels to help make intelligent decisions about control such as economic justification and selection of control method- Rarely should one employ an eradication ("weed-free") mentality in weed control programs, except for special situations, because of high input and environmental costs. A more environmentally sound program employs a "weed management" concept that is based on economic returns rather than eradicating all weeds.

3) Instituting an integrated approach to control - Integrated weed management programs utilize many different weed control strategies and tactics for short- and long-term weed management. Weed control tools include cultural, biological, and chemical methods, not just a single technique.

Weed management programs will vary with different cropping systems and practices. For example, weed management in a perennial hay crop such as alfalfa, may employ proper hay cutting management to maintain vigorous, healthy alfalfa plants. For grazing crops such as pasture species, proper animal grazing management is needed for effective weed control. In annual row crops, tillage, crop residues, and planting management may be used to help control early and mid-season weeds. Thus, there is no one best weed management program for crop production. Instead, it is a combination of tactics, strategies, and flexible approaches depending on many crop production factors.

> What are three different strategies to control weeds in weed management programs?
>
> What would be examples of cultural control methods for controlling a persistent weed in alfalfa grown for hay?

V. IDENTIFICATION AND PROPERTIES OF WEEDS

Control methods are often dictated by the type of weed species and their method of spreading and propagation. In general:

1) Summer annual and winter annual weeds are propagated by seeds. Therefore, control measures are directed toward the prevention of the production and spread of seeds. Biennial weeds establish vegetative growth during the first year usually in a rosette stage (low growing, circular pattern of leaf growth) and then flower and produce seed the second year. Control can be directed toward eliminating first year growth in addition to preventing seed production in the second year.

2) Perennial weeds may be propagated primarily by seeds (simple perennials) and, in addition, vegetative organs (creeping perennials). Therefore, control may include the prevention of vegetative propagation as well as seed production. Using practices such as timely mowing and herbicide application are frequently used to exhaust storage carbohydrates in weedy plants with large taproots or vegetative organs.

Crop Science: Principles and Practice

Translocated herbicides are often used to control creeping perennials, with the herbicide being translocated and destroying vegetative organs such as rhizomes and stolons.

Therefore, the proper identification of the problem weeds and an understanding of their anatomical and reproductive properties and other habits are integral parts of a weed management program. Depending upon the situation, it may be important to identify the weed as a seed, shortly after emergence, or in a more advanced stage of growth. Identification in any stage of the life cycle entails careful examination. The following section is a description of some of the troublesome weeds in crop production. They are grouped into the following categories:

A. Identification and control characteristics of grassy weeds

1. **Annual grassy weeds with dense panicles and non-spreading habit**
   Giant foxtail, Green foxtail, Yellow foxtail
2. **Annual grassy weeds with raceme or spike inflorescence and spreading habit**
   Large crabgrass, Smooth crabgrass
3. **Annual grassy weeds with bunch type growth**
   Fall panicum, Barnyardgrass
4. **Winter annual grassy weeds with bunch type growth**
   Downy brome
5. **Perennial grassy weeds**
   Quackgrass, Johnsongrass
6. **Grass-like weeds**
   Yellow nutsedge

B. Identification and control characteristics of broadleaf weeds

1. **Broadleaf weeds with prickles**
   Horsenettle, Canada thistle, Bull thistle
2. **Broadleaf twining weeds**
   Hedge bindweed, Field bindweed, Wild buckwheat
3. **Broadleaf weeds with large, non-lobed leaves**
   Velvetleaf, Common cocklebur, Wild sunflower
4. **Broadleaf weeds with deeply lobed leaves**
   Common ragweed, Giant ragweed, Dandelion
5. **Broadleaf weeds with medium sized leaves having serrations**
   Common lambsquarters, Redroot pigweed
6. **Broadleaf weeds with slender leaves**
   Curly dock, Pennsylvania smartweed, Swamp smartweed
7. **Broadleaf weeds with milky sap**
   Common milkweed, Hemp dogbane

The figures on pp. 216-245 in Chapter 10 are from: Agriculture Handbook No. 366. 1970,1976. Selected Weeds of the United States. Agricultural Research Service, United States Department of Agriculture. Descriptions and distribution maps by Clyde F. Reed, research botanish and plant explorer, ARS. Drawings by Regina A. Hughes, scientific illustrator, ARS.

Refer to Crop Plant Classification and Identification chapter if you do not understand the identification terms used in this section.

A. IDENTIFICATION AND CONTROL CHARACTERISTICS OF GRASSY WEEDS
A1. ANNUAL GRASSY WEEDS WITH DENSE PANICLES AND NON-SPREADING HABIT.

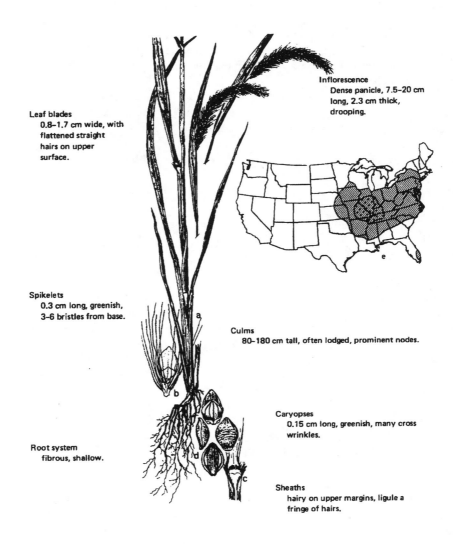

Inflorescence
Dense panicle, 7.5–20 cm long, 2.3 cm thick, drooping.

Leaf blades
0.8–1.7 cm wide, with flattened straight hairs on upper surface.

Spikelets
0.3 cm long, greenish, 3–6 bristles from base.

Culms
80–180 cm tall, often lodged, prominent nodes.

Caryopses
0.15 cm long, greenish, many cross wrinkles.

Root system
fibrous, shallow.

Sheaths
hairy on upper margins, ligule a fringe of hairs.

Giant Foxtail, *Setaria faberi Herrm.* a, habit; b, spikelet showing subtending bristles; c, ligule; d, caryopses; e, distribution.

Life Cycle-annual, reproducing by seed.

Habitat-Cultivated fields and waste places, especially lowland. Introduced from China, probably in seed of Chinese millet in 1931.

Control-prevent the production and dispersal of seed.

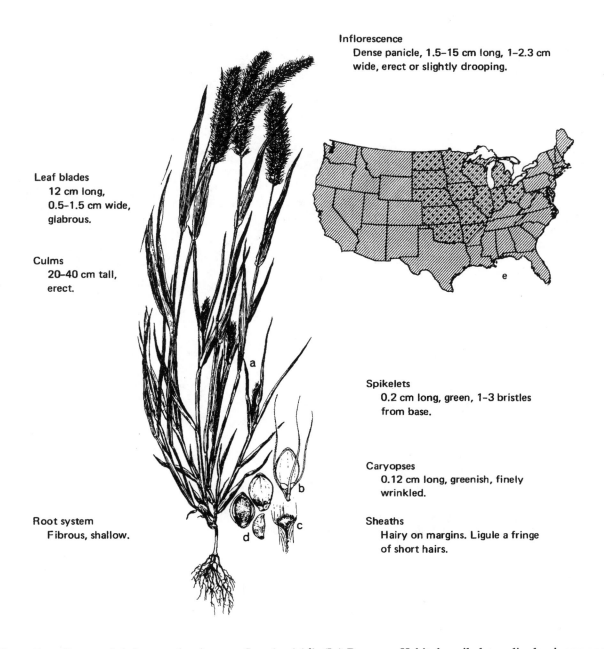

Inflorescence
Dense panicle, 1.5–15 cm long, 1–2.3 cm wide, erect or slightly drooping.

Leaf blades
12 cm long,
0.5–1.5 cm wide,
glabrous.

Culms
20–40 cm tall,
erect.

Spikelets
0.2 cm long, green, 1–3 bristles from base.

Caryopses
0.12 cm long, greenish, finely wrinkled.

Root system
Fibrous, shallow.

Sheaths
Hairy on margins. Ligule a fringe of short hairs.

Green Foxtail, green bristlegrass, bottlegrass, *Setaria viridis* (L.) Beauv. a, Habit; b, spikelet; c, ligule; d, caryopses; e, distribution.
Life Cycle-annual, reproducing by seed.
Habitat-cultivated fields, pastures, hay fields, and waste areas. Introduced from Europe.
Control-prevent the production and dispersal of seed.

Inflorescence
Dense panicle, 1.5–12 cm long, 0.9–1.4 cm wide, cylindrical, yellow.

Culms
50–120 cm tall, erect, flattened.

Leaf blades
20 cm long, 0.3–1.0 cm wide, often spiraled.

Spikelets
0.3 cm long, yellowish, 5 to 20 bristles from base.

Caryopses
0.2 cm long, yellowish, strongly wrinkled.

Root system
fibrous, shallow.

Long hair at base of blade. Sheath open.

Yellow Foxtail, yellow bristlegrass, pigeon grass, *Setaria glauca* (L.) Beauv. a, Habit; b, spikelet; c, ligule; d, caryopses; e, distribution.
Life Cycle-annual, reproducing by seed. Habitat-cultivated fields, pastures, hay fields, waste areas. Control-prevent the production and dispersal of seed.

A2. ANNUAL GRASSY WEEDS WITH RACEME OR SPIKE INFLORESCENCE AND SPREADING HABIT.

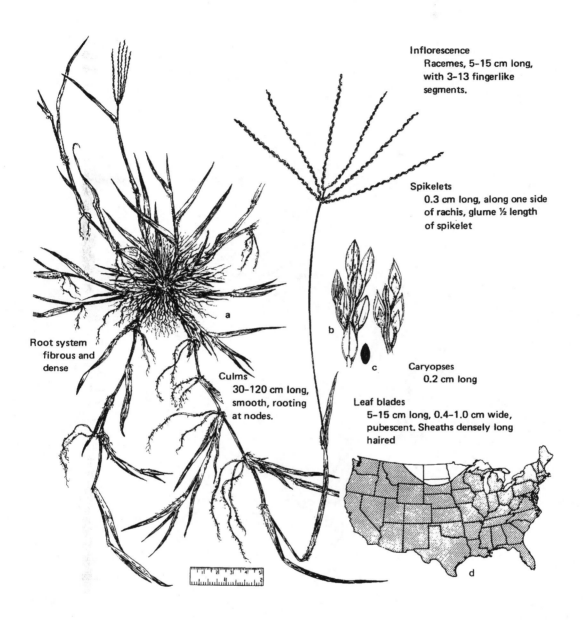

Inflorescence
Racemes, 5–15 cm long, with 3–13 fingerlike segments.

Spikelets
0.3 cm long, along one side of rachis, glume ½ length of spikelet

Caryopses
0.2 cm long

Leaf blades
5–15 cm long, 0.4–1.0 cm wide, pubescent. Sheaths densely long haired

Root system fibrous and dense

Culms
30–120 cm long, smooth, rooting at nodes.

Large Crabgrass, *Digitaria sanguinalis* (L.) Scop. a, Habit; b, florets, front and back view; c, caryopsis; d, distribution.
Life Cycle-annual reproducing by seed.
Habitat-cultivated fields, lawns, waste areas. Introduced from Europe.
Control-prevent production and dispersal of seed and spread of "rooting" stems. Mechanical cultivation may spread this species.

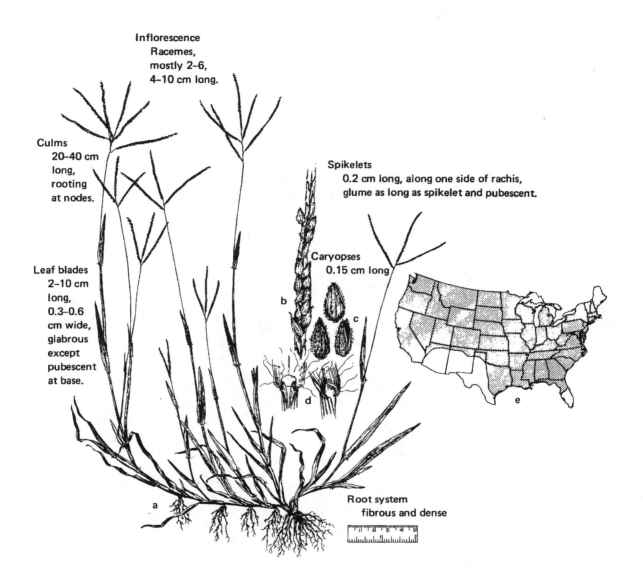

Inflorescence
Racemes,
mostly 2–6,
4–10 cm long.

Culms
20–40 cm
long,
rooting
at nodes.

Spikelets
0.2 cm long, along one side of rachis,
glume as long as spikelet and pubescent.

Leaf blades
2–10 cm
long,
0.3–0.6
cm wide,
glabrous
except
pubescent
at base.

Caryopses
0.15 cm long

Root system
fibrous and dense

Smooth Crabgrass, *Digitaria ischaemum* (Schreb.) Schreb. ex Muhl. a, Habit; b, raceme detail; c, florets; d, ligules; e, distribution.
Life Cycle-annual, reproducing by seed.
Habitat-cultivated fields, lawns, waste areas. Introduced from Europe.
Control-prevent production and dispersal of seed and spread of "rooting" stems. Mechanical cultivation may spread this species.

246

A3. ANNUAL GRASSY WEEDS WITH BUNCH TYPE GROWTH.

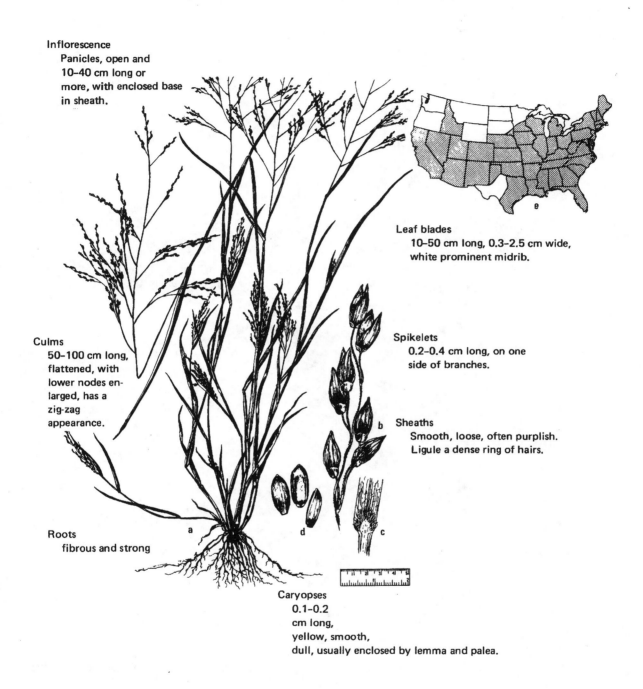

Inflorescence
Panicles, open and
10–40 cm long or
more, with enclosed base
in sheath.

Leaf blades
10–50 cm long, 0.3–2.5 cm wide,
white prominent midrib.

Culms
50–100 cm long,
flattened, with
lower nodes en-
larged, has a
zig-zag
appearance.

Spikelets
0.2–0.4 cm long, on one
side of branches.

Sheaths
Smooth, loose, often purplish.
Ligule a dense ring of hairs.

Roots
fibrous and strong

Caryopses
0.1–0.2
cm long,
yellow, smooth,
dull, usually enclosed by lemma and palea.

Fall panicum, *Panicum dichotomiflorum* Michx. a, Habit; b, spikelet; c, ligule; d, caryopses; e, distribution.
Life Cycle-annual, reproducing by seed, sometimes rooting from lower nodes.
Habitat-cultivated fields and waste areas, especially moist ground.
Control-prevent production and dispersal of seed.

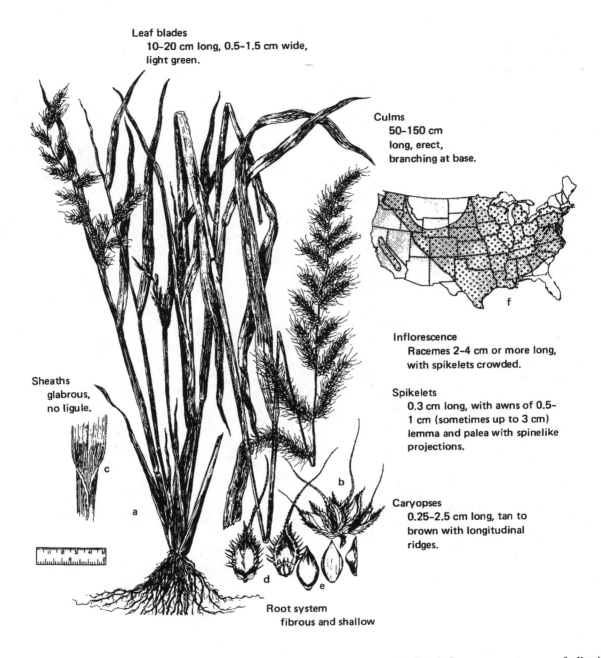

Leaf blades
10–20 cm long, 0.5–1.5 cm wide,
light green.

Culms
50–150 cm
long, erect,
branching at base.

Inflorescence
Racemes 2–4 cm or more long,
with spikelets crowded.

Spikelets
0.3 cm long, with awns of 0.5–
1 cm (sometimes up to 3 cm)
lemma and palea with spinelike
projections.

Sheaths
glabrous,
no ligule.

Caryopses
0.25–2.5 cm long, tan to
brown with longitudinal
ridges.

Root system
fibrous and shallow

Barnyardgrass, *Echinochloa crus-galli* (L.) Beauv. a, Habit; b, spikelet; c, ligule; d, florets; e, caryopses; f, distribution.
Life Cycle-annual, reproducing by seed, bunchgrass.
Habitat-cultivated fields, waste areas, pastures, prefers moist ground, a problem in rice fields. Introduced from Europe.
Control-prevent production and dispersal of seed.

A4. WINTER ANNUAL WEEDS WITH BUNCH TYPE GROWTH.

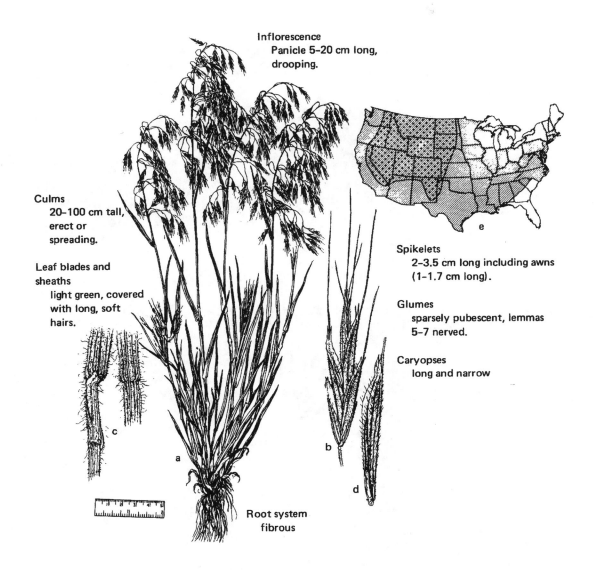

Inflorescence
Panicle 5–20 cm long, drooping.

Culms
20–100 cm tall, erect or spreading.

Leaf blades and sheaths
light green, covered with long, soft hairs.

Spikelets
2–3.5 cm long including awns (1–1.7 cm long).

Glumes
sparsely pubescent, lemmas 5–7 nerved.

Caryopses
long and narrow

Root system
fibrous

Downy brome, downy chess, cheatgrass, *Bromus tectorum* L. a, Habit; b, spikelet; c, ligules; d, floret; e, distribution.
Life Cycle-winter annual, reproducing by seed, bunch type habit.
Habitat-small grain fields, hay fields, pastures, waste areas.
Control-prevent production and dispersal of seed.

A5. PERENNIAL GRASSY WEEDS.

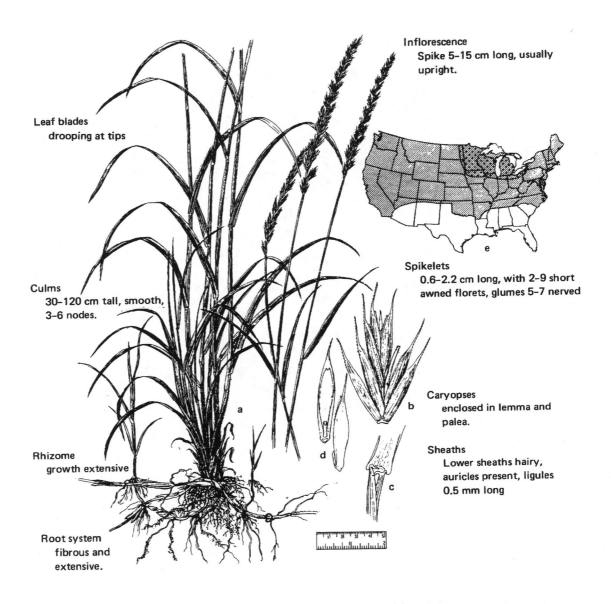

Inflorescence
Spike 5–15 cm long, usually upright.

Leaf blades
drooping at tips

Culms
30–120 cm tall, smooth, 3–6 nodes.

Rhizome
growth extensive

Root system
fibrous and extensive.

Spikelets
0.6–2.2 cm long, with 2–9 short awned florets, glumes 5–7 nerved

Caryopses
enclosed in lemma and palea.

Sheaths
Lower sheaths hairy, auricles present, ligules 0.5 mm long

Quackgrass, couchgrass, *Elytrigia repens* (L.) Beauv. a, Habit; b, spikelet; c, ligule; d, florets; e, distribution. Life Cycle-perennial, reproducing by seed and rhizomes 4–20 cm deep.
Habitat-Most cropped areas, pastures, waste areas. Introduced from Europe.
Control-prevent production of seed and dispersal of seed and rhizomes.

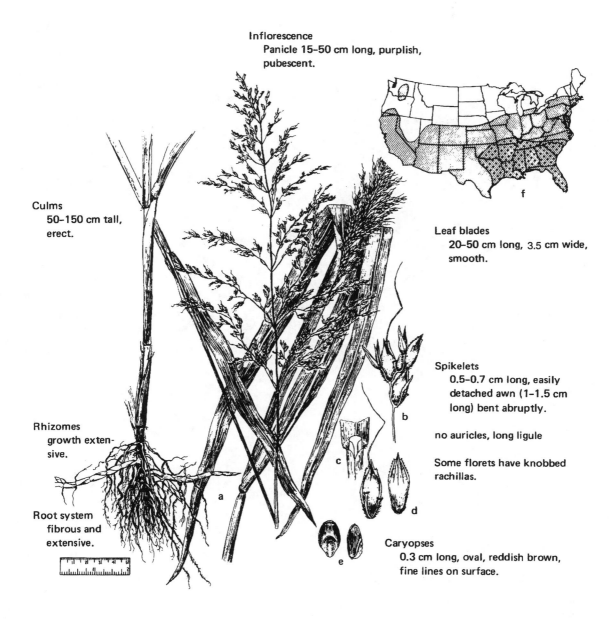

Inflorescence
  Panicle 15–50 cm long, purplish, pubescent.

Culms
  50–150 cm tall, erect.

Leaf blades
  20–50 cm long, 3.5 cm wide, smooth.

Spikelets
  0.5–0.7 cm long, easily detached awn (1–1.5 cm long) bent abruptly.

no auricles, long ligule

Some florets have knobbed rachillas.

Rhizomes
  growth extensive.

Root system
  fibrous and extensive.

Caryopses
  0.3 cm long, oval, reddish brown, fine lines on surface.

Johnsongrass-*Sorghum halepense* (L.) Pers., a, Habit; b, spikelet; c, ligule; d, florets; e, caryopses; f, distribution.
Life Cycle-perennial, reproducing by seed and rhizomes.
Habitat-most cropped and waste areas. Introduced from the Mediterranean area as a forage grass.
Control-prevent production and dispersal of seed and rhizomes.

A6. YELLOW NUTSEDGE-A GRASS-LIKE WEED.

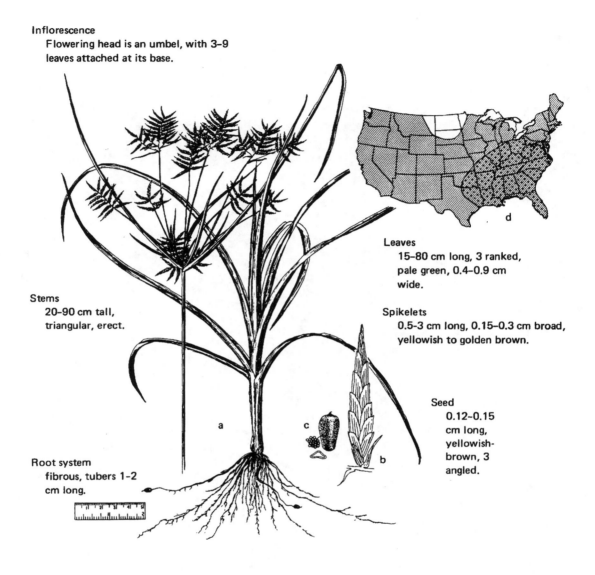

Inflorescence
Flowering head is an umbel, with 3–9 leaves attached at its base.

Stems
20–90 cm tall, triangular, erect.

Root system
fibrous, tubers 1–2 cm long.

Leaves
15–80 cm long, 3 ranked, pale green, 0.4–0.9 cm wide.

Spikelets
0.5–3 cm long, 0.15–0.3 cm broad, yellowish to golden brown.

Seed
0.12–0.15 cm long, yellowish-brown, 3 angled.

Yellow nutsedge, yellow sedge, yellow nutgrass, *Cyperus esculentus* L. a, Habit; b, spikelet; c, seed; d, distribution.
Life Cycle-perennial, reproducing by seed and stolons terminated by hard tubers.
Habitat-cultivated fields, gardens, and grain fields; often limited to low, poorly drained areas. Native of North America.
Control-prevent production and dispersal of seeds, stolons, and tubers.

B. IDENTIFICATION AND CONTROL CHARACTERISTICS OF BROADLEAF WEEDS
B1. BROADLEAF WEEDS WITH PRICKLES.

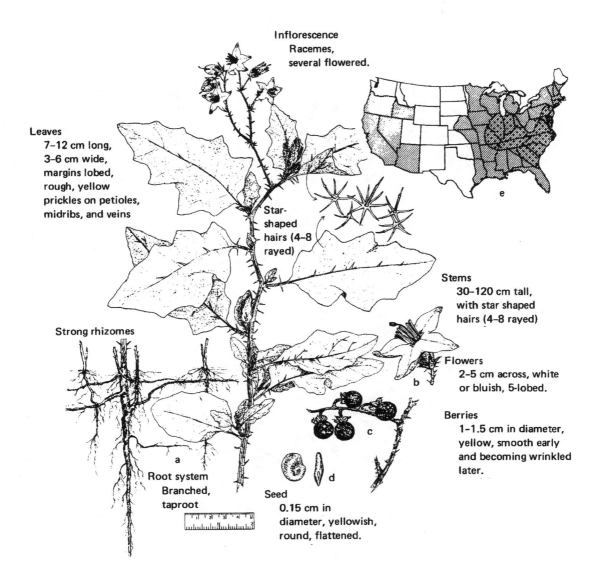

Inflorescence Racemes, several flowered.

Leaves
7–12 cm long,
3–6 cm wide,
margins lobed,
rough, yellow
prickles on petioles,
midribs, and veins

Star-shaped hairs (4–8 rayed)

Strong rhizomes

Stems
30–120 cm tall,
with star shaped
hairs (4–8 rayed)

Flowers
2–5 cm across, white
or bluish, 5-lobed.

Berries
1–1.5 cm in diameter,
yellow, smooth early
and becoming wrinkled
later.

Root system
Branched,
taproot

Seed
0.15 cm in
diameter, yellowish,
round, flattened.

Horsenettle, sand brier, Carolina nettle, *Solanum carolinense* L. a, Habit; b, flower; c, berries; d, seed; e, distribution.
Life Cycle-perennial, reproducing by seed and rhizomes.
Habitat-cultivated fields, waste areas, often a problem in sandy soils.
Control-prevent production and dispersal of seed and rhizomes.

Inflorescence
Dioecious plants, 2–2.5 cm in diameter, with lavender, rose-purple or white disk flowers

Seed
0.25–0.35 cm long, flattened, ridge around blossom end and with tannish down sometimes on tip.

Stems
40–120 cm tall, erect, grooved, branching only at top, slightly hairy when young and increasingly hairy with maturity.

Leaves
Crinkled edges, spiny margins, lobed, not extending down stem.

Strong, spreading rhizomes.

Root system
Deep branched roots.

Canada thistle, *Cirsium arvense* (L.) Scop. a, Habit; b, head; c, flower; d, seed; e, distribution.
Life Cycle-perennial, reproducing by seed and rhizomes.
Habitat-cultivated fields, pastures, hay crops and waste areas. Introduced from Eurasia.
Control-prevent production and dispersal of seed and rhizomes.

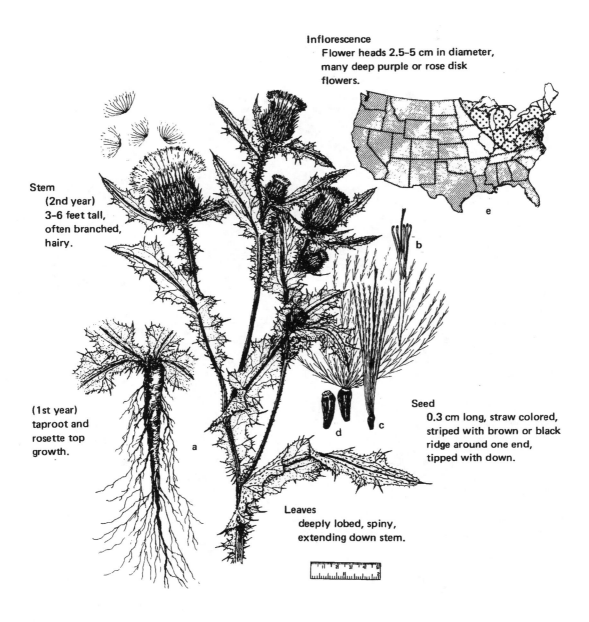

Inflorescence
Flower heads 2.5–5 cm in diameter,
many deep purple or rose disk
flowers.

Stem
(2nd year)
3–6 feet tall,
often branched,
hairy.

(1st year)
taproot and
rosette top
growth.

Seed
0.3 cm long, straw colored,
striped with brown or black
ridge around one end,
tipped with down.

Leaves
deeply lobed, spiny,
extending down stem.

Bull thistle, *Cirsium vulgare* (Savi) Tenore. a, Habit; b, flower; c, immature fruit; d, seed; e, distribution.
Life Cycle-biennial, reproducing by seed. First year plants form a rosette of leaves and a large, fleshy
taproot.
Habitat-pastures, first year hay fields, waste areas. Introduced from Eurasia.
Control-prevent seed production and dispersal.

B2. BROADLEAF TWINING WEEDS.

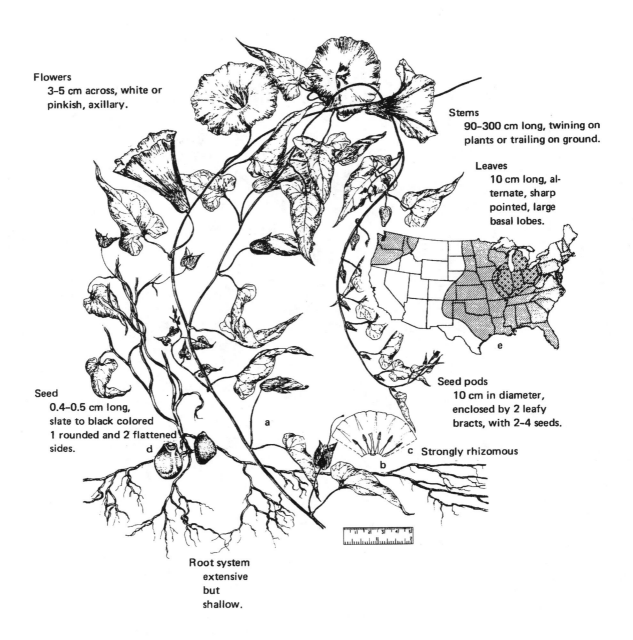

Flowers
3–5 cm across, white or pinkish, axillary.

Stems
90–300 cm long, twining on plants or trailing on ground.

Leaves
10 cm long, alternate, sharp pointed, large basal lobes.

Seed
0.4–0.5 cm long, slate to black colored 1 rounded and 2 flattened sides.

Seed pods
10 cm in diameter, enclosed by 2 leafy bracts, with 2–4 seeds.

Strongly rhizomous

Root system extensive but shallow.

Hedge bindweed, *Convolvulus sepium* L. a, Habit; b, rootstock; c, diagram of flower, showing structure; d, seeds; e, distribution.

Life Cycle-perennial, reproducing by seed and rhizomes.

Habitat-cultivated fields, waste areas, especially bottomlands, less drought tolerant than field bindweed. Introduced from Eurasia.

Control-prevent production and dispersal of seed and rhizomes.

Crop Science: Principles and Practice

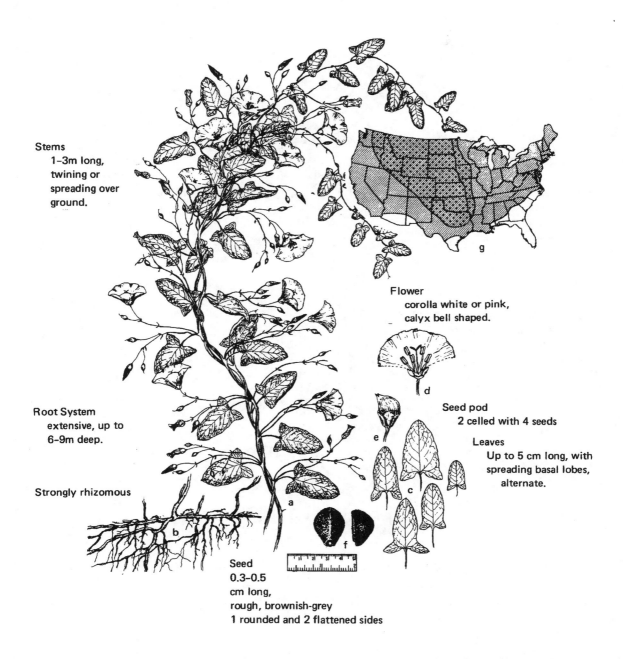

Stems
1–3m long, twining or spreading over ground.

Root System
extensive, up to 6-9m deep.

Strongly rhizomous

Flower
corolla white or pink, calyx bell shaped.

Seed pod
2 celled with 4 seeds

Leaves
Up to 5 cm long, with spreading basal lobes, alternate.

Seed
0.3-0.5 cm long, rough, brownish-grey 1 rounded and 2 flattened sides

Field bindweed, *Convolvulus arvensis* L. a, Habit; b, rootstock; c, leaf variation; d, flower showing 5 stamens of unequal length; e, capsule; f, seed; g, distribution.
Life Cycle-perennial, reproducing by seed and rhizomes.
Habitat-cultivated fields, grain fields, waste areas.
Control-prevent the production and dispersal of seed and rhizomes.

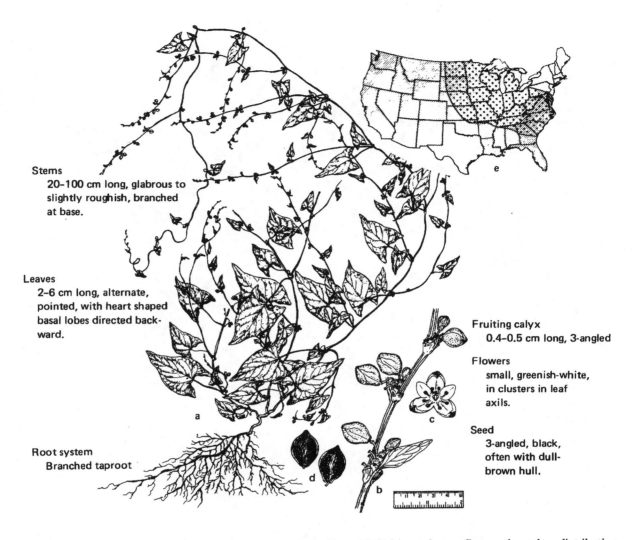

Stems
20-100 cm long, glabrous to slightly roughish, branched at base.

Leaves
2-6 cm long, alternate, pointed, with heart shaped basal lobes directed backward.

Root system
Branched taproot

Fruiting calyx
0.4-0.5 cm long, 3-angled

Flowers
small, greenish-white, in clusters in leaf axils.

Seed
3-angled, black, often with dull-brown hull.

Wild buckwheat, *Polygonum convolvulus* L. a, Habit; b, branchlet with fruiting calyx; c, flower; d, seed; e, distribution.
Life Cycle-annual, reproducing by seed.
Habitat-cultivated fields, grain fields, and waste areas. Introduced from Eurasia.
Control-prevent production and dispersal of seed.

B3. BROADLEAF WEEDS WITH LARGE, NON-LOBED LEAVES.

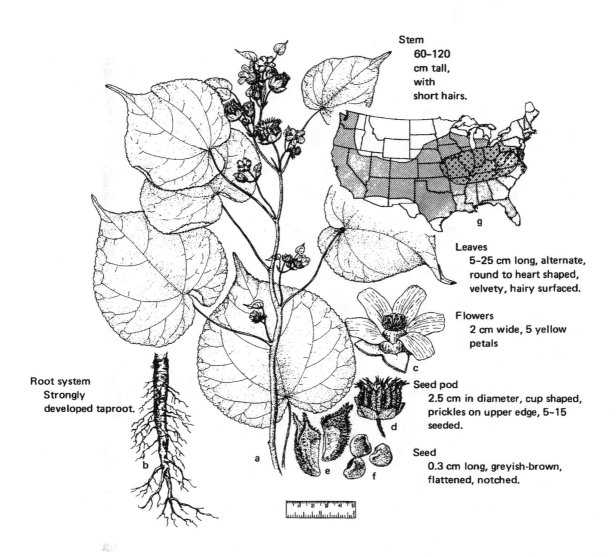

Stem
60–120 cm tall, with short hairs.

Leaves
5–25 cm long, alternate, round to heart shaped, velvety, hairy surfaced.

Flowers
2 cm wide, 5 yellow petals

Seed pod
2.5 cm in diameter, cup shaped, prickles on upper edge, 5–15 seeded.

Seed
0.3 cm long, greyish-brown, flattened, notched.

Root system
Strongly developed taproot.

Velvetleaf, Buttonweed, Butterprint, Indian Mallow, *Abutilon theophrasti Medic.* a, Habit; b, root; c, flower; d, capsule; e, carpels; f, seed; g, distribution.
Life Cycle-annual, reproducing by seed.
Habitat-cultivated fields-especially corn and soybean fields, waste areas. Introduced from India.
Control-prevent production and dispersal of seed.

Stems
20–90 cm tall, erect, ridged, rough, hairy, often spotted.

Leaves
Alternate triangular, toothed, rough.

Root system
Strong, branched taproot.

Monoecious
Male and female flowers separate in clusters. Male flowers shed soon after pollination.

Bur
1–2 cm long, prickles 0.3–0.6 cm long, light brown.

Seed
1–1.5 cm long, 2 in each bur, dark brown, flattened, with pointed apex.

Common cocklebur, Clotbur, *Xanthium pensylvanicum* Wallr.
a, Habit; b, seedling; c, bur; d, seed; e, distribution.
Life Cycle-annual, reproducing by seed. Habitat-cultivated fields, poor pastures, waste areas. Introduced from Eurasia. Control-prevent production and dispersal of seed.

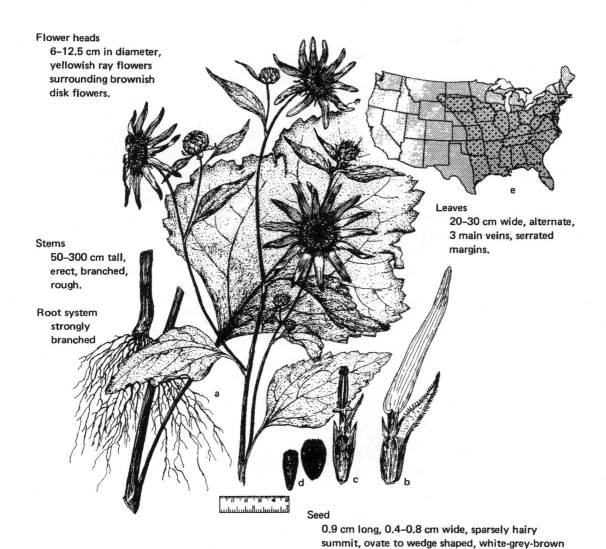

Flower heads
6–12.5 cm in diameter, yellowish ray flowers surrounding brownish disk flowers.

Leaves
20–30 cm wide, alternate, 3 main veins, serrated margins.

Stems
50–300 cm tall, erect, branched, rough.

Root system
strongly branched

Seed
0.9 cm long, 0.4–0.8 cm wide, sparsely hairy summit, ovate to wedge shaped, white-grey-brown with lighter spots or stripes.

Wild Sunflower, *Helianthus annuus* L. a, Habit; b, ray flower; c, disk flower; d, seed, 2 views; e, distribution.
Life Cycle-annual, reproducing by seed.
Habitat-cultivated fields, grain fields, pastures, waste areas.
Control-prevent production and dispersal of seed.

261

B4. BROADLEAF WEEDS WITH DEEPLY LOBED LEAVES.

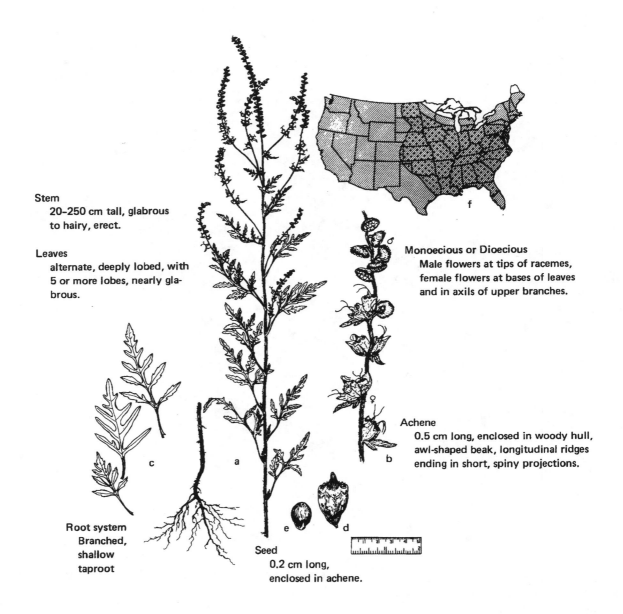

Stem
20–250 cm tall, glabrous to hairy, erect.

Leaves
alternate, deeply lobed, with 5 or more lobes, nearly glabrous.

Monoecious or Dioecious
Male flowers at tips of racemes, female flowers at bases of leaves and in axils of upper branches.

Achene
0.5 cm long, enclosed in woody hull, awl-shaped beak, longitudinal ridges ending in short, spiny projections.

Root system
Branched, shallow taproot

Seed
0.2 cm long, enclosed in achene.

Common ragweed, *Ambrosia artemisiifolia* L. a, Habit; b, raceme with male heads (above) and female involucres (below); c, leaf variations; d, achene; e, seed; f, distribution.
Life Cycle-annual, reproducing by seed.
Habitat-cultivated fields, poor pastures, grain fields, waste areas.
Control-prevent production and dispersal of seed. Note-abundant pollen is a hazard to hay fever sufferers.

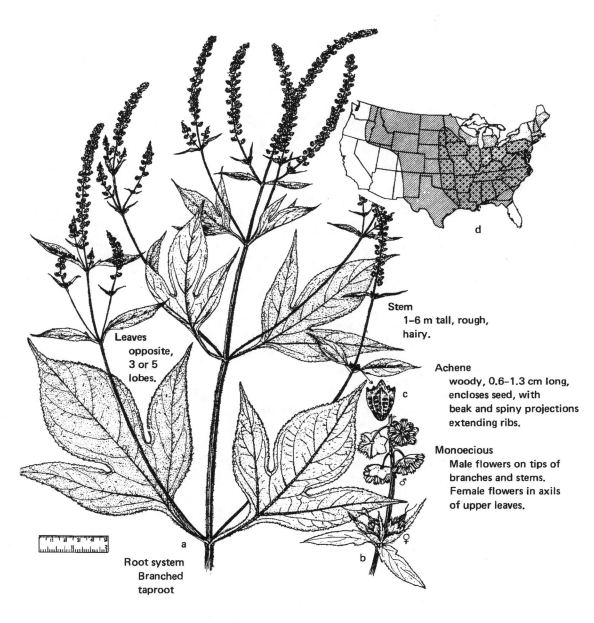

Stem
1–6 m tall, rough,
hairy.

Leaves
opposite,
3 or 5
lobes.

Achene
woody, 0.6–1.3 cm long,
encloses seed, with
beak and spiny projections
extending ribs.

Monoecious
Male flowers on tips of
branches and stems.
Female flowers in axils
of upper leaves.

Root system
Branched
taproot

Giant ragweed, Horseweed, Buffaloweed, (*Ambrosia trifida* L.). a, Habit, upper portion; b, portion of flowering raceme; c, achene enclosing seed; d, distribution.
Life Cycle-annual, reproducing by seed.
Habitat-cultivated crops, waste areas, especially fertile bottomlands. Introduced from Europe.
Control-prevent production and dispersal of seed.
Note: abundant pollen is a hazard to hay fever sufferers

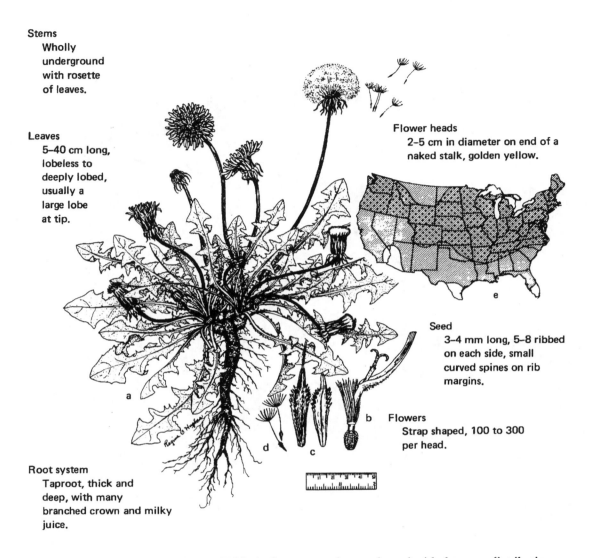

Stems
Wholly underground with rosette of leaves.

Leaves
5–40 cm long, lobeless to deeply lobed, usually a large lobe at tip.

Flower heads
2–5 cm in diameter on end of a naked stalk, golden yellow.

Seed
3–4 mm long, 5–8 ribbed on each side, small curved spines on rib margins.

Flowers
Strap shaped, 100 to 300 per head.

Root system
Taproot, thick and deep, with many branched crown and milky juice.

Dandelion, *Taraxacum officinale* Weber. a, Habit; b, flower; c, achenes; d, seed with down; e, distribution.
Life Cycle-perennial, reproducing by new growth from the branched crown of a thick, deep taproot.
Habitat-lawns, overgrazed pastures and meadows, and waste areas. Introduced and naturalized from Eurasia.
Control-prevent production and dispersal of seed and use translocated herbicides to destroy taproot. Good soil fertility and management allows pasture or lawn species to compete with dandelion.

264

B5. BROADLEAF WEEDS WITH MEDIUM SIZED LEAVES HAVING SERRATIONS.

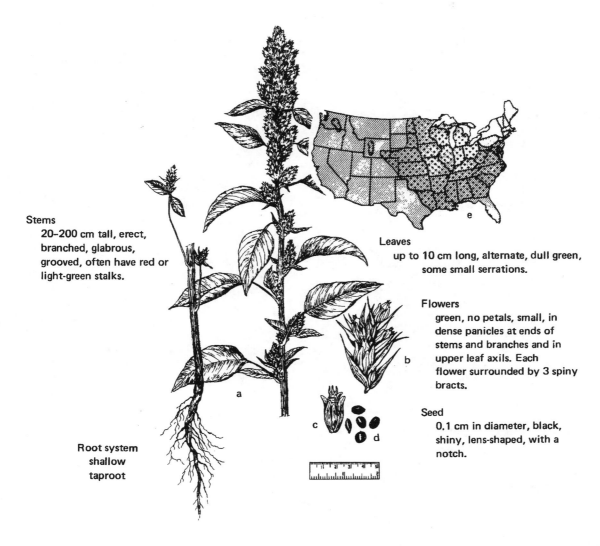

Stems
20–200 cm tall, erect, branched, glabrous, grooved, often have red or light-green stalks.

Leaves
up to 10 cm long, alternate, dull green, some small serrations.

Flowers
green, no petals, small, in dense panicles at ends of stems and branches and in upper leaf axils. Each flower surrounded by 3 spiny bracts.

Seed
0.1 cm in diameter, black, shiny, lens-shaped, with a notch.

Root system shallow taproot

Redroot pigweed, Rough pigweed, *Amaranthus retroflexus* L. a, Habit; b, pistillate spikelet; c, utricle; d, seed; e, distribution.
Life Cycle-annual, reproducing by seed.
Habitat-cultivated fields, grain fields, waste areas. Introduced from tropical America.
Control-prevent production and dispersal of seed.

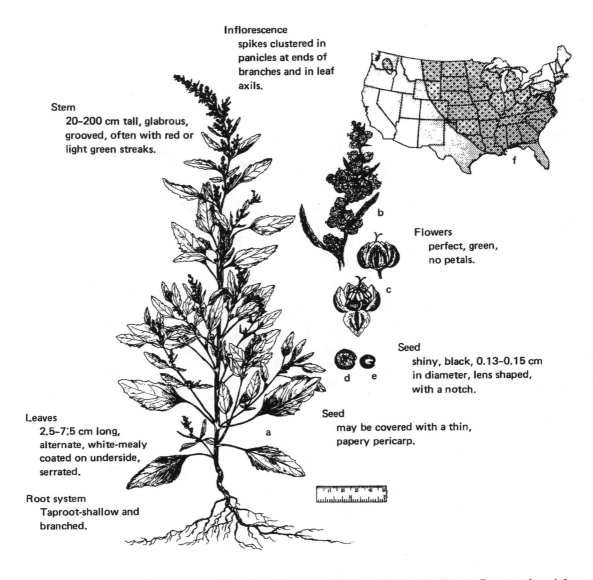

Inflorescence
spikes clustered in panicles at ends of branches and in leaf axils.

Stem
20–200 cm tall, glabrous, grooved, often with red or light green streaks.

Flowers
perfect, green, no petals.

Seed
shiny, black, 0.13–0.15 cm in diameter, lens shaped, with a notch.

Leaves
2.5–7.5 cm long, alternate, white-mealy coated on underside, serrated.

Seed
may be covered with a thin, papery pericarp.

Root system
Taproot-shallow and branched.

Common lambsquarters, *Chenopodium album* L. a, Habit, small plant; b, floral spike; c, flowers; d, utricle; e, seed; f, distribution.
Life Cycle-annual, reproducing by seed.
Habitat-cultivated fields, grain fields, waste areas. Introduced from Eurasia.
Control-prevent production and dispersal of seed.

B6. BROADLEAF WEEDS WITH SLENDER LEAVES.

Stems
up to 1 m tall,
glabrous, erect.

Leaves
15–30 cm long, wavy-
curled margins, papery
sheath surrounding stem.

Root system
Taproot, large,
yellow, branched.

Inflorescence
many branched, with small
leaves intermingled.

Seed
0.2 cm long, brown, shiny,
triangular, surrounded by
3 heart-shaped valves.

Curly dock, sour dock, *Rumex crispus* L. a, Habit; b, fruit; c, surrounded by persistent calyx; d, showing 3 valves; e, seed; f, distribution.
Life Cycle-perennial, reproducing by seed and regrowth from crown of the taproot.
Habitat-pastures, hay fields, waste areas. Introduced from Eurasia.
Control-prevent production and dispersal of seed and killing of the taproot.

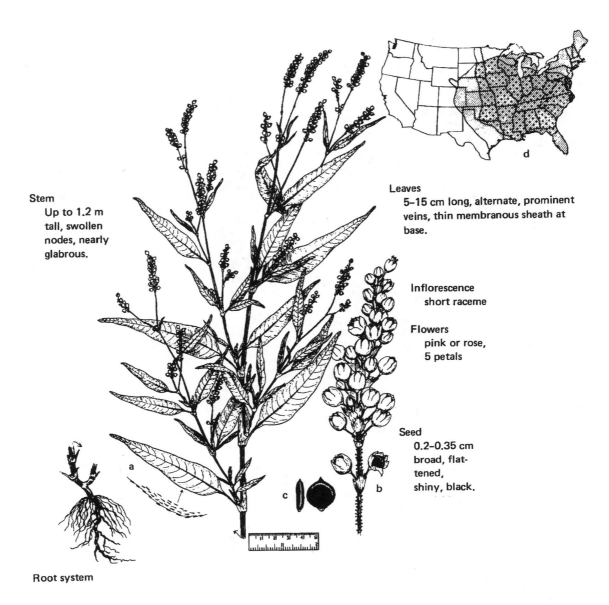

Stem
Up to 1.2 m tall, swollen nodes, nearly glabrous.

Leaves
5–15 cm long, alternate, prominent veins, thin membranous sheath at base.

Inflorescence
short raceme

Flowers
pink or rose, 5 petals

Seed
0.2–0.35 cm broad, flattened, shiny, black.

Root system

Pennsylvania smartweed, *Polygonum pensylvanicum* L. a, Habit; b, raceme; c, seed; d, distribution.
Life Cycle-annual, reproducing by seed.
Habitat-cultivated fields, waste areas, especially damp soil.
Control-prevent production and dispersal of seed.

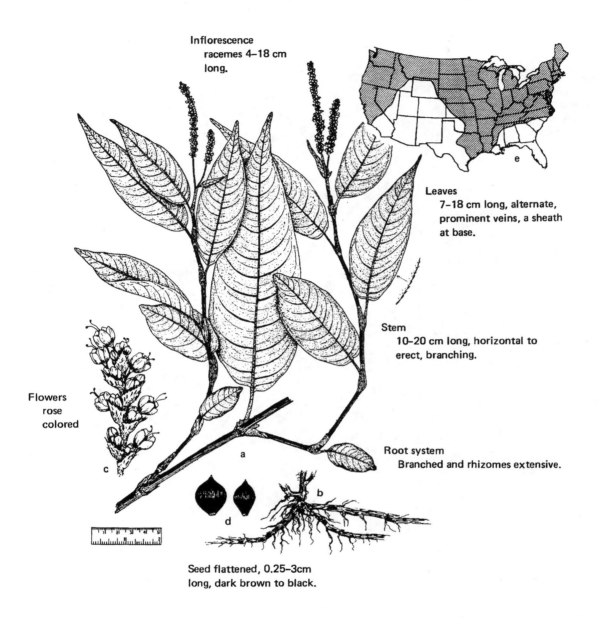

Inflorescence racemes 4–18 cm long.

Leaves
7–18 cm long, alternate, prominent veins, a sheath at base.

Stem
10–20 cm long, horizontal to erect, branching.

Flowers rose colored

Root system
Branched and rhizomes extensive.

Seed flattened, 0.25–3cm long, dark brown to black.

Swamp smartweed, Devil's Shoestring, *Polygonum coccineum* Muhl. a, Habit; b, rhizome; c, raceme; d, seed, 2 views; e, distribution.
Life Cycle-perennial, reproducing by seed and rhizomes.
Habitat-cultivated fields, waste areas, usually in low, wet areas.
Control-prevent production and dispersal of seed and kill rhizomes.

B7. BROADLEAF WEEDS WITH MILKY SAP.

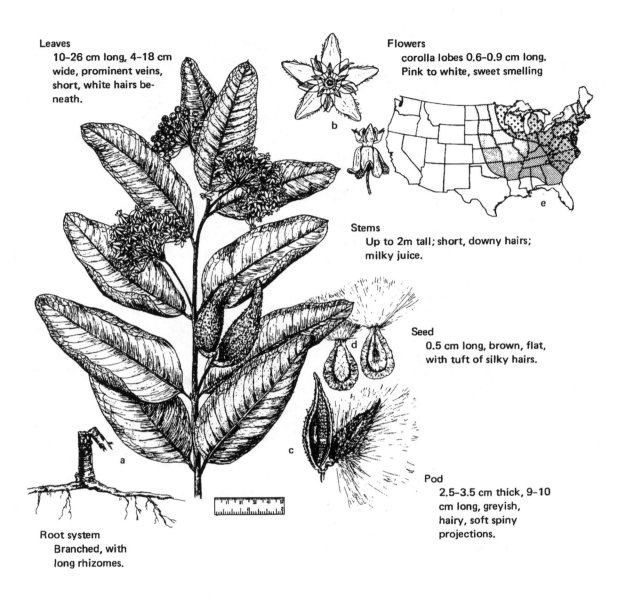

Leaves
10–26 cm long, 4–18 cm wide, prominent veins, short, white hairs beneath.

Flowers
corolla lobes 0.6–0.9 cm long. Pink to white, sweet smelling

Stems
Up to 2m tall; short, downy hairs; milky juice.

Seed
0.5 cm long, brown, flat, with tuft of silky hairs.

Pod
2.5–3.5 cm thick, 9–10 cm long, greyish, hairy, soft spiny projections.

Root system
Branched, with long rhizomes.

Common milkweed, *Asclepias syriaca* L. a, Habit; b, flower, upper view, side view; c, pod; d, seed with hairs; e, distribution.

Life Cycle-perennial, reproducing by seed and long spreading rhizomes.

Habitat-cultivated fields, pastures, waste areas.

Control-prevent production and dispersal of seed and kill rhizomes.

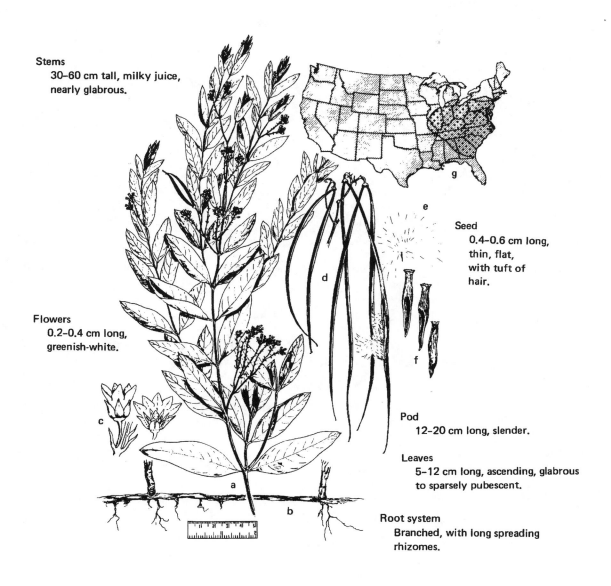

Stems
30–60 cm tall, milky juice, nearly glabrous.

Flowers
0.2–0.4 cm long, greenish-white.

Seed
0.4–0.6 cm long, thin, flat, with tuft of hair.

Pod
12–20 cm long, slender.

Leaves
5–12 cm long, ascending, glabrous to sparsely pubescent.

Root system
Branched, with long spreading rhizomes.

Hemp dogbane, Indian Hemp, *Apocynum cannabinum* L. a, Habit; b, rootstock, c, flowers; d, pods; e, seed with hairs; f, seeds; g, distribution.
Life Cycle-perennial, reproducing by seed and rhizomes.
Habitat-cultivated fields, waste areas, especially low, damp ground.
Control-prevent production and dispersal of seed and kill rhizomes.

ADDITIONAL STUDY QUESTIONS

1. Which of the three foxtail species is least likely to be a problem on a sandy soil with a low amount of available soil water at field capacity?

2. Which "foxtail" species has drooping heads and prominent nodes?

3. The "foxtails", quackgrass, and yellow nutgrass often occur in cultivated row crops. How might control measures differ for these three species?

4. A translocated herbicide, rather than a contact herbicide, may be needed to control perennial weeds that reproduce by rhizomes or stolons. Which species that you have studied fit this category?

5. The natural spread of seed is a much greater problem in the spread of Canada thistle and bull thistle than with horsenettle. Can you explain why?

6. The control of wild buckwheat is usually easier accomplished than control of hedge bindweed and field bindweed. Why is this statement true?

7. Some farmers say a cocklebur will germinate twice. Could this statement be true? Why?

8. A directed application of a herbicide is sometimes used in mid-summer to control velvetleaf, cocklebur, sunflower, and volunteer corn in fields of soybeans. Why is it possible to direct the herbicide to the weed leaves without also applying it to the soybean leaves?

9. The number of lambsquarter or pigweed seed may sometimes be equal to the number of crop seed in a seedlot being planted, without the farmer actually being aware of the problem. Do you believe this statement? Why?

10. A contact herbicide or flame cultivation may control Pennsylvania smartweed, but a translocated herbicide may be necessary for the control of swamp smartweed and curly dock. Why?

11. Vegetative reproduction by way of rhizomes is a serious problem with common milkweed and hemp dogbane. Why is the natural spread of the seed of these two species also a major problem?

SELF-EVALUATION TEST

Weeds

Circle letter corresponding to one best answer.

1. Primary noxious weeds

   a) when established can be controlled by ordinary good cultural practices
   b) are usually annuals
   c) usually reproduce by seeds and vegetative methods
   d) usually reproduce only by producing a large volume of seed
   e) usually do not produce seed

2. "Delayed seedbed preparation" is used in some crops

   a) to provide a better seedbed for crop seedling emergence
   b) to control large-seeded weeds that will emerge from depths of 2 inches or more
   c) to control weeds that will germinate only when they are on or very near the soil surface
   d) because they are perennials and reproduce vegetatively
   e) to compact the soil to form a firm "rootbed"

3. Selective herbicides

   a) kill or stunt all plant species on which applied
   b) kill only parts of the plant receiving application
   c) are always absorbed into the plant and translocated to other parts of the plant
   d) depend on the rate and time of application for their action
   e) do not include specific instructions for application

4. Harvested seed of winter wheat would be most likely to contain seed of a

   a) summer annual weed species
   b) warm season weed species
   c) weed species tolerant to wet soil
   d) winter annual weed species
   e) noxious weed species

5. The successful use of directed herbicide sprays or "wick-type" of application of contact herbicides depends primarily upon

   a) differences in susceptibility of weeds and crops
   b) differences in the size or location of weeds and crop plants
   c) differences in translocation of the herbicide by the weeds and crop plants
   d) temperature at the time of application
   e) soil moisture at the time of application

6. A weedy grass plant was found in a wet area of a field in Central Iowa. It had a fibrous root system, the inflorescence had many 2-4 cm racemes, the lemma and palea had spine-like projections, the culms were 130 cm tall, the leaf sheaths were glabrous with no ligules. This species is probably

   a) giant foxtail
   b) green foxtail
   c) fall panicum
   d) downy brome
   e) barnyardgrass

7. A weedy grass plant in a corn field in Central Illinois has an extensive fibrous root system, extensive rhizomes, culms 100 cm tall, spike type of inflorescence, caryopses enclosed in a lemma and palea, ligules and auricles. This species is probably

    a) fall panicum
    b) Johnsongrass
    c) quackgrass
    d) green foxtail
    e) yellow foxtail

8. A weedy grass in a soybean field in Northern Missouri has a shallow fibrous root system, leaf blades that are often spiraled, long hair at the base of the leaf blade, an open sheath, a dense panicle that looks like a spike, and spikelets with yellowish bristles. This species is probably

    a) yellow foxtail
    b) giant foxtail
    c) yellow barnyardgrass
    d) yellow quackgrass
    e) yellow crabgrass

9. A weedy species is growing in a poorly drained area of a soybean field in Northeastern Nebraska. It looks like a grass and has a umbel inflorescence, a triangular stem, yellowish spikelets, a fibrous root system, and 1-2 cm tubers. This species is probably

    a) yellow foxtail
    b) yellow barnyardgrass.
    c) yellow crabgrass
    d) yellow quackgrass
    e) yellow nutsedge

10. A weed in a corn field in Southern Wisconsin has a branched taproot system, strong rhizomes, white five-lobed flowers, broad leaves with lobed margins and prickles along the larger veins of the leaves and on the stem. This species is probably

    a) Canada thistle
    b) Bull thistle
    c) Horsenettle
    d) Prickly pear
    e) Cocklebur

11. A weed in a fencerow and the adjacent area of a corn field in Eastern Iowa has rhizomes, twining stems, and leaves about 10 cm long, pointed and with large basal lobes. This species is probably

    a) ragweed
    b) field bindweed
    c) wild buckwheat
    d) hedge bindweed
    e) devils shoestring

12. A weed in a poorly fertilized pasture in Southern Iowa has a shallow branched taproot, erect stems that are about 50 cm tall, and leaves that have 5 to 10 or more deep lobes. This species is probably:

    a) common ragweed
    b) sunflower
    c) velvetleaf
    d) giant ragweed
    e) common lambsquarter

13. A weed in a pasture in Northern Illinois has large leaves (15-20 cm long), stems 1.5 m tall that exude milky juice when broken, seed pods 3 cm thick and 9 cm long-containing brown seed with tufts of silky hairs, and a branched root system with rhizomes. This species is probably

    a) hemp dogbane
    b) Indian hemp
    c) common milkweed
    d) swamp smartweed
    e) Pennsylvania smartweed

Chapter 11

Insect Management

Bugs, flies, and bees...
Alas, results of Nature free.
Flowers, birds, and trees...
Suffice, Nature's song to me.

Insects are important organisms in our ecosystem and impact crop growing regions throughout the world. Insects represent approximately 80% of all animal life species. About 1 million insect species are known but only 1%, or 10,000, are classified as pests to animals and plant life. It is estimated that as few as 100 species cause 90% of the damage to world food crops.

Some states in the U.S. have reported 16,000 insect species with approximately 1,000 classified as pests and 600 species as crop pests, lowering crop yields an estimated 5 to 6 % each year. Many scientists believe that the yield loss is considerably higher and additional losses occur in the form of decreased crop quality and from expenses incurred for insect control measures. However, in a broader sense, insects provide many valuable contributions to our natural environment. Because the vast majority of insect species are non-pests, it is extremely important to manage crop insect pests with minimal impact to other insect species.

I. IMPACT OF INSECTS

A. Beneficial Effects

Many people equate the term "insect" with "pest" or something harmful or undesirable. However, insects sustain many important roles in our ecosystem:

1. Natural Pollinators -   Insect species play a major role as natural pollinators of our plant species.

2. Nutrient Cycling -   Insects help break down and recycle animal and plant tissues releasing nutrients for use by diverse organisms in our ecosystem.

3. Natural Predators -   Insects play a vital role in keeping pests populations in check. Many insects harmful to crops are a natural food source for other insects. Predator and parasitic insects often help keep crop pests from causing significant economic losses in yield.

4. Wildlife Diversity -   Insects are an important food source for birds, fish, and many other wildlife. Insects are a vital part of the food chain that maintains the richness and diversity of our world's organisms.

B. Harmful Effects

Insect pests can cause many types of direct or indirect damage to crop plants. Damages can be obvious or subtle resulting in lower yield, poorer product quality, predisposing the plant to disease and/or interfering with normal production practices, such as harvesting. Examples of various damages include:

1. Loss of Leaf Tissue - results in loss of photosynthetic area and possibly lower yields.

2. Stem Damage - results in decreased translocation of water, minerals, photosynthate, and other materials essential for the plant. Stalk lodging (stalk fall from stalk breakage above ground level) may result from severe insect damage and further lower harvestable yield.

3. Seed Damage - results in lower seed viability or in a lower quality seed product.

4. Root Damage - results in lower capacity for nutrient and water uptake. Root lodging (stalk fall at ground level without stalk breakage; occurs from a weak or damaged root system) may result from severe insect damage and interfere with harvesting operations.

5. Premature Death of Plant - may result in lower yield or lower quality because plant functions, including photosynthesis, cease before the desired crop product is completed.

6. Disease Spread - damage to the plant may be a result of an insect being a vector for a disease organism. A vector spreads a disease organism from plant to plant.

7. Disease Entry - Insect wounds on the plant may provide an entry site for disease organisms, which continue to cause damage, possibly more extensive than the actual insect damage previously inflicted.

In what ways are insects beneficial to our environment?

List three obvious and three indirect ways insect damage can increase economic loss in crops.

II. COMPETITIVE CHARACTERISTICS OF INSECTS

Insect pests have a variety of attributes that enable them to survive and flourish in an agricultural environment. They are widely adapted to different environments, persistent and have excellent reproductive potential. Their relatively short life cycles enable rapid generation increase to economically damaging levels. For example, the cotton boll weevil can produce a new generation every 21 days, which unchecked can produce geometric increases in population during a growing season. Short life cycles enable the insect pest to more rapidly develop genetic resistance and adaptability to insecticides and new production practices. In the Midwest, Northern corn rootworm normally has a one-year life cycle and a two-year, maize-soybean crop rotation has been used to help control this pest in maize. However, some rootworm populations have adapted to this rotation through extended diapause (eggs remain viable and dormant for greater than normal periods) and now exhibit a two-year life cycle and can infest the first-year maize crop. This is evidence of the dynamic nature and adaptability of insect populations to crop production practices.

A. Life Cycles

Insects have exoskeletons and grow from eggs into adult forms. As insects develop, they outgrow and shed their old exoskeletons and form new ones (molting) that accommodate their bigger body size. The form of an insect between molts is called an instar. Thus, referring to an insect as a first, second, third, etc. instar is a method of describing its relative age, form, and size during the molting period. Most insects during their life cycle pass through several changes in external form before they become adults. This morphological change in form during an insect's life cycle is referred to as metamorphosis. Insects that damage crops generally exhibit one of two types of life cycles, complete metamorphosis and gradual metamorphosis:

1. Complete metamorphosis - consists of four distinct stages as illustrated in Figure 1. In many instances, chemical control is directed toward the larval stage because of its heavy feeding activity, relative susceptibility, and relatively constant, but slow, mobility.

2. Gradual metamorphosis - consists of three stages and is illustrated in Figure 2. Often control is aimed at early nymph stages before the insect reaches larger body size and consequently, greater feeding capacity.

COMPLETE METAMORPHOSIS

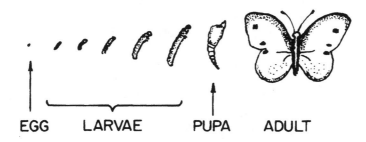

EGG   LARVAE   PUPA   ADULT

Figure 1

GRADUAL METAMORPHOSIS

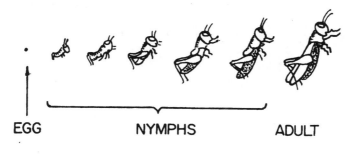

EGG   NYMPHS   ADULT

Figure 2

List the four stages of complete metamorphosis.

List the three stages of gradual metamorphosis.

In which stage are insects with complete metamorphosis usually most susceptible to an insecticide?

III. INSECT MANAGEMENT STRATEGIES

Since their discovery, insecticides have been widely used to control a variety of insect pests. Widespread and indiscriminate use of insecticides has had negative consequences in several ways. Insecticides that kill pests are often broad spectrum and also indiscriminately kill beneficial insects. As natural predator insects are removed from the production environment, populations of insect pests increase forcing even greater dependence on insecticides to control unchecked pest growth. In many instances, regular insecticide use has allowed insect pests to develop genetic resistance to insecticides, posing greater challenges in control. Insecticide chemicals can also be very toxic to other non-targeted organisms in our environment, such as birds, fish, and animals, including humans. Some insecticides that control different metabolic pathways of insect species can also affect similar pathways in higher animals, which increases the health risks associated with their use. Some insecticides can be very persistent in body tissues and in our environment and can reach toxic levels to different organisms at different points in the food chain. Therefore, like weed management strategies, insect management should include preventative control and a variety of non-chemical control methods to help minimize the use of insecticide chemicals. Examples of different control methods are given:

A. Cultural Control

Cultural control can be used to prevent or decrease insect pest infestation. Crop selection, crop rotation, trap crops, and cropping systems can be used to help maintain a large and diverse population of beneficial insects and interrupt the life cycles of insect pests by changing the habitat and/or food source. Crop residue management, mowing and tillage practices can change insect populations by changing survival rates of insect eggs in soil or crop residues. Good planting, fertility, and harvest management can lower the susceptibility of crops to insect damage.

B. Biological Control

Many methods of biological control can be used to help keep insect pests under economically damaging levels. Examples of various types of biological control are given:

1. **Disease organisms**
   A parasitic bacteria (*Bacillus thuringiensis*) has been used to help control European corn borer and other insect species. The bacteria infect and kill the larvae. It is especially effective on young larvae and is non-toxic to mammals, fish, other wildlife, and beneficial insects when used properly.

2. **Animal organisms**
   Cattle egrets, a bird species that has adapted to North America, has been used as natural control of blowflies, fleshflies, horseflies, and deerflies that afflict cattle. They also eat grasshoppers and other crop insects. Scientists have estimated that a female egret will catch over 600 insect prey daily for herself and her brood.

   Beneficial insects, such as predator and parasitic insects and other organisms, have been used to help keep insect pest populations in check. Some examples are:

Predatory Organisms	Insect Prey
Big-eyed bugs	Several small insects and their eggs, including aphids and mites.
Ladybird beetles	Aphids and mites
Green lacewings	Several small insects and their eggs, especially aphids
Spiders	Feeds on most insects
Daddy long legs (Harvestmen)	Most small insects
Damsel bugs	Aphids, lygus bugs
Robber flies	Grasshoppers and bees
Syrphid flies	Aphids
Parasitic Organisms	**Host Insects**
Braconid wasps	Aphids, many species of caterpillars
Sarcophagid flies	Grasshoppers
Ichneumonid wasps	Many species of caterpillars, alfalfa weevil
Tachinid flies	Many species of caterpillars

C. Insect Resistant Cultivars

Cultivars that have some degree of genetically conferred resistance to an insect or its damage can be used as part of an insect pest management program. Cultivar resistance usually implies a certain degree of tolerance or undesirability to an insect, not immunity. Insect resistance in plants may be achieved by several means. Plant may have greater tolerance to damage without severely affecting yield, contain substances that repel or adversely affect metabolic or reproductive functions of an insect, or have morphological traits, such as pubescence, which interfere with feeding or reproductive habits of the insect. For example, genetically resistant varieties have been used in grain sorghum for greenbugs, wheat for Hessian Fly, and alfalfa for spotted alfalfa and pea aphids.

D. Chemical Control

Chemicals used to kill insect pests (insecticides) are widely used and an effective control method. Most of the insects that damage crops can be controlled by the use of insecticides if proper rates, application techniques, and timing are observed. In general, selective chemical control (control without injuring the crop) is easier with insects than with weeds. Insect tissue is quite different from plant tissue and therefore it is easier to kill the insect without damaging or killing the crop plants. However, insecticides can also be more toxic to mammals which have similar metabolic characteristics. Insect populations can become resistant to an insecticide through natural selection. Surviving insects can pass on resistant genes to new generations, eventually producing an insecticide-resistant population. This process occurs much faster with insects than weeds but slower than in disease organisms because of the relative population size (number of individuals in the treated area) and generation time.

Other chemicals have been used to alter insect behavior and disrupt life cycles. A successful example is the use of some pheromones (chemical substances emitted by an organism that influences behavior or activity of another organism of the same species). Some types of pheromones serve as sex attractants (substances emitted by the adult female insect to attract males). These sex attractants have been synthetically produced and used in the field to confuse and disrupt insect mating. Sex attractant pheromones have been used to help control insects in cotton, corn, pears, apple, and other crops.

E. Insect Management Programs

A sound insect management program employs the concepts of integrated pest management involving the use of a combination of environmentally acceptable control methods in a production system including preventative control practices, such as crop selection and crop rotation, and limited chemical control . Using an integrated pest management approach for determining remedial control steps involves scouting fields, establishing economic thresholds for target insect pests, and implementing control procedures:

1. **Scouting**
    Regular scouting of fields should provide:
    a) an accurate identification and population estimate of target insect pests
    b) an accurate identification and population estimate of beneficial insects and status of other natural control agents
    c) crop growth stage and status of injury

2. **Establishing Economic Thresholds**
    Regular scouting of fields provides information on insect population changes and crop injury levels. Crops will tolerate different levels of insect injury without significant yield loss based on factors such as crop type, stage of growth, environment, and yield value. Economic threshold (ET) is the point reached when the insect population (or some index of population) causes enough economic loss to the crop to equal the cost of controlling the insect. The decision to actually implement insect control measures (action threshold) then rests with the producer who must consider, not only continued economic loss from the insect, but also environmental health and safety aspects of the control methods.

    The ET concept assumes that when a pest population reaches a certain density, the cost of remedial control is justified to prevent further increases in pest population that would cause economic loss to the crop. Economic thresholds may vary with different situations. If the cost of control is high in relation to crop value, ET values for a particular pest insect tend to be higher. If environmental conditions favored the pest over the crop, the ET would be lower than normal; and if conditions favored the crop, the ET would be higher than normal. For example, assume the accepted ET for black cutworms in maize is when 3 to 5% of a corn stand has been removed by the insect. However, in years when the temperature is above normal, the development of maize is speeded up more than is the activity of the insect. Thus, the ET during a warm year is higher. The relative development rates of maize and the black cutworm are shown in Figure 3.

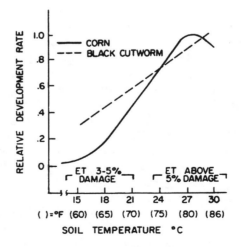

Figure 3

Adapted from S. Elwynn Taylor. Agricultural climatology in integrated pest management. EC-1498h. Cooperative Extension Service. Iowa State University. Ames, Iowa 50011.

3. Implementing Control Procedures

Using scouting and ET information, control tactics can be determined. No remedial control may be necessary if the ET is not reached. Extra control steps may delayed or avoided if the population of beneficial insects is increasing faster than the insect pest. Finally, if remedial control is necessary, then decisions should be made to target insect pest control in an environmentally responsible way with minimal impact to other organisms.

List two general methods of cultural control of insects.

Which pest is generally easier to control using chemicals without damaging crop plants: weeds or insects? Why?

Define the term "economic threshold". What factors influence its derivation?

Insect pests that are unintentionally introduced into a new region frequently exhibit a dramatic, initial population increase followed by a gradual decrease to a more stable population over time. What ecological factor might explain this observation?

IV. INSECT IDENTIFICATION AND CONTROL PRINCIPLES

Proper identification of insect pests and an understanding of their reproductive and feeding characteristics and other traits are essential for developing a sound insect management program. The following section is a description of some of the troublesome insects in crop production, their characteristics and control principles. They are grouped into the following categories:

- A. Leaf feeding (chewing) insects
- B. Leaf feeding (sucking) insects
- C. Insects that damage stems
- D. Insects that damage stored seed
- E. Insects that damage plant roots
- F. Insects that damage planted seed

Be able to identify the species illustrated in this section and to relate characteristics and life cycle to methods and timing of control.

Note: Economic thresholds given are examples only and may vary in different regions.

A. LEAF FEEDING (CHEWING) INSECTS

Grasshoppers

Redlegged Grasshopper (*Melanoplus femureubrum*), Differential Grasshopper (*Melanoplus differentialis*) and many other species.

Color may vary from greenish to brown.

Size may vary from less than 1 cm for nymphs to more than 7 cm for adults

Grasshopper—Adult

Major crops damaged: All crops.

Life cycle: Gradual; eggs laid in soil of ditch banks, stubble fields, fence rows, and other waste areas in late summer and fall. Nymphs hatch from eggs in spring and feed near the hatching area until the third or fourth instar, then they spread into the crop.

Feeding habits: Grasshoppers are voracious plant feeders, devouring the leaves and other tender plant parts. In maize they often feed on the silks, thereby preventing proper pollination, which results in fewer kernels per ear.

Control principles: The most efficient chemical control is to use an insecticide to control the nymphs in the spring near the egg beds soon after they have hatched and have started feeding.

Economic threshold (ET) varies from state to state and crop to crop. 10 to 20 grasshoppers/m^2 along field margins of maize or soybeans is sometimes considered to be the ET, while 3 to 7 grasshoppers/m^2 in the field is considered to be the ET.

Bean Leaf Beetle (*Cerotoma trifurcata*)

Beetles about 9 mm long, yellowish or reddish, usually with dark gray or black markings. A black triangle is located immediately behind the neck section. Major crop damaged: Beans, soybeans, maize.

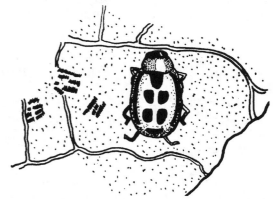

Life cycle: Complete; overwinter as adult beetles in mild climates; fly north and lay eggs at the base of young plants in early spring; eggs hatch; young larvae feed on young roots and may also tunnel into the underground portion of the stalk.

Feeding habits: Adults are severe leaf feeders and also feed on maize silks, hindering pollination. Larvae feed on newly developed roots, especially of maize.

Bean Leaf Beetle—Adult

Control principles: Crop rotations will not control this insect since the adults migrate into an area. Insecticide control may be aimed at leaf feeding adults or at root feeding larvae.

Economic threshold varies. Example-Insecticide may be warranted on soybeans if more than 25% of the leaf area has been destroyed or if pod feeding reaches established economic thresholds based on sweep counts, pod damage level, cost of insecticide, and market value of soybean seed.

Armyworm (*Pseudaletia unipuncta*)

Larvae - Pale green when young. Full grown worms greenish brown with dark stripes, up to 3.5 cm long.

Major crops damaged: Maize, soybeans, small grains, cotton, and forages.

Life cycle: Complete. Does not survive the winter in northern U.S. The moths fly from the South and deposit eggs that hatch in about 5 days. After approximately twenty days of feeding, the larvae enter the soil to pupate. Moths emerge about ten days later. The armyworm may have up to six generations per year in the Gulf States, with fewer generations at more northern latitudes.

Feeding habits: Extensive leaf feeders. May cut the culms of small grains. Larvae often can be seen migrating from rank, lodged small grains or forages to other crops. Often, patches of infested plants appear in a field.

Larvae feeding on an oat panicle

Control principles: Weeds in fields, especially grassy weeds attract adults, which lay their eggs on lower leaves. Armyworms are sometimes heavily parasitized (indicated by white pinhead-sized fly eggs attached to the back). If heavily parasitized, insecticide treatment may not be necessary.

Economic threshold: Example-maize- The ET is sometimes defined as being when 2 or more armyworm larvae per plant occur on 25 to 30% of the plants with 5 to 6 extended leaves or when there is one larvae per plant on 75% of the plants.

Green Cloverworm (*Plathypena scabra*)

Larvae - Light green with faint white stripes, slender and up to 2 1/2 cm long.

Major crops damaged: Mostly legume crops, especially soybeans.

Life cycle: Complete. Moths fly northward each spring and lay eggs on alfalfa, clover, or soybeans. Eggs hatch and larvae continue growth for nearly a month, with damage usually occurring in July. Pupation occurs in a silken cocoon in the plant residue on the ground. There are usually two generations per year in the Northern Midwest.

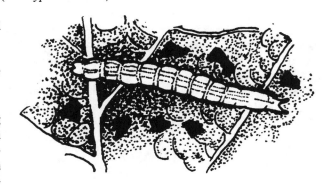

Larvae feeding on soybean leaf

Feeding habits: Extensive leaf feeding, especially by the first hatch in July.

Control principles: Check population carefully before making a decision to apply an insecticide. The economic threshold is about 15 to 20 worms per 30 cm (12 inches) of soybean row. A fungal disease that leaves the sickened white worms attached to the leaves often brings the infestation under control.

Bacillus thuringiensis, a bacteria effective against lepidopterous insects and not harmful to beneficial parasites and predators, can be used for control.

Alfalfa Weevil (*Hypera postica*)

Larvae feeding on alfalfa tip

Adult beetle

Larvae - Grubs about 1 cm long, legless, green with a white stripe down the back.

Adults about 1 cm long, brown, with a darker brown streak down the back.

Major crops damaged: Primarily first growth (first cutting) alfalfa.

Life cycle: Complete. Winters chiefly as an adult, mostly in alfalfa fields. Adults lay their eggs in early spring. Larvae become numerous about the time the first growth produces flowering buds. They pupate soon afterward (usually May and June) and adult weevils remain sexually immature until fall or spring.

Feeding habits: Larvae chew holes in leaves of first growth of alfalfa and proceed to feed on interveinal leaf tissue. May damage basal shoots and retard second growth after first hay cutting.

Control principles: Check the first growth alfalfa frequently for leaf feeding, especially on the tips (or new growth) of the plant. Early first cutting (in the flower bud stage), being careful to mow and rake cleanly, will often prevent excessive damage to the second growth. If adults are numerous, it may be advisable to spray in early spring when the growth is only about 5 cm tall.

Economic threshold -Example- Treat with an insecticide as soon as 25% of the alfalfa stem tips are skeletonized (have a ragged appearance with the leaf veins remaining intact).

B. LEAF FEEDING (SUCKING) INSECTS

Aphids
(Pea aphid-*Acrythosiphon pisum*)
(Spotted alfalfa aphid-*Therioaphis maculata*)
and many other species

Greenish to blue-green in color, soft bodied, adults less than 1/2 cm in length.

Major crops affected: All crops.

Life cycle: Gradual metamorphosis: Overwinters as egg or adult (especially in southern states). Many species reproduce very rapidly by vivipary (live birth) in summer. They reproduce later in the season by eggs, with or without fertilization. Many generations per year may be produced.

Winged adult   Nymph

Feeding habits: Suck juice from the plants and may act as vectors of plant diseases (especially virus diseases). Damaged plants may be stunted or barren especially if plants are also drought stressed.

Control principles: Usually more prevalent when temperatures do not rise above 21°C (70°F). Predator insects, especially lady beetles and their larvae, often bring aphid populations under control.

Economic threshold: Usually not specifically set, but chemical control is seldom used because populations usually decrease with warm, rainy weather and with predator buildup.

Leafhopper
(Potato leafhopper - *Empoasca fabae*)
and many other species

Small, green, wedge-shaped sucking insects, up to 1/2 cm long, may walk sideways.

Major crops affected: Most crops.

Life cycle: Gradual metamorphosis. Egg to adult stage in about three weeks, nymphs pass through 5 stages (instars). Probably does not overwinter in northern U.S. Migrates from the South in May or June.

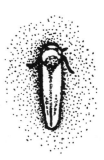

Adult

286

Feeding habits: Sucks juice from underside of leaves. Leaves turn yellow and brown, especially around edges (looks like potash deficiency). May act as a vector for plant diseases.

Control principles: Damage is usually less on plants with dense pubescence. Heavy populations can build up and can cause damage to second and third cutting alfalfa and to new seedings. Economic threshold-Usually not specifically set, but chemicals should be used when insect and damage is prevalent. In a hay crop that has a high population (one or more leafhoppers per sweep), it may be advisable to cut the hay and use an insecticide before the new growth is 15 cm tall.

C. INSECTS THAT DAMAGE STEMS-

European Corn Borer-(*Ostrinia nubilalis*)

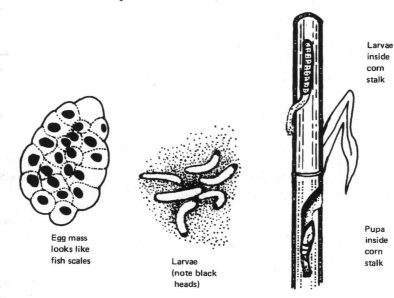

Larvae-Pinkish to grayish white, up to 3 cm long with brownish to black heads.

Major crops affected: Maize, sweetcorn, and other crop species.

Life cycle: Complete (see figure below). Overwinter as larvae inside stalks, cobs, or other debris. Adult is a moth. One generation per year in extreme northern U.S. and up to three generations or more in southern states.

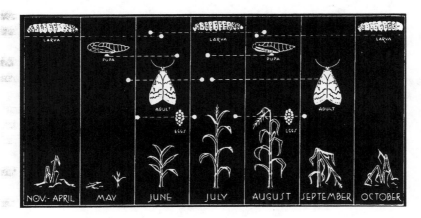

European corn borer seasonal life history for central Iowa. Development is earlier in the south and later in the north.

From The European Corn Borer and its Control in the North Central States. Iowa State University of Science and Technology Cooperative Extension Service and U.S. Department of Agriculture, Pamphlet 176 (Rev.), Ames, Iowa.

Feeding habits: Young larvae feed on leaves and then tunnel into all above-ground plant parts. Stalk lodging and ear dropping plus damage from stalk rotting disease organisms are increased by corn borer feeding.

Control principles:
Cultural-destroy or remove residue before May 15.
Genetic-plant varieties having resistance to first brood larvae or plant stiff-stalked varieties with strong ear shanks (lowers stalk lodging and ear dropping).
Biological-apply *Bacillus thuringiensis* (a parasitic bacteria) in June.
Chemical-treat for first brood in June when the ET is reached. Growing degree days may be used to predict the time of egg laying and larvae hatch.

Economic threshold:
Example-Treatments should be applied to field corn when 35% of the plants show first generation larval feeding in the whorl (unrolling top leaves) and larvae are present. Seed corn fields should be treated when 25% of the plants show first brood larval feeding. Treat seed or canning corn for second generation larvae if plants have not completed shedding pollen and have fresh silks, or have green, juicy stalks and leaves at the time the first eggs are laid (about August 1).

Corn Earworm (Cotton Bollworm)
(*Heliothis zea*)

Larvae -Variable in color-brownish to greenish, sometimes purplish with yellowish lateral stripes and alternating light and dark colored longitudinal stripes. Full grown larvae are about 3.5 cm long.

Major crops affected: Maize, cotton, and many other crops.

Life cycle: Complete. Most moths migrate into the Corn Belt from the south in the spring, lay eggs that hatch in 2 to 8 days. First generation larvae feed on whorls (unrolling top leaves) of corn plants, pupate, and the second flight of moths emerge

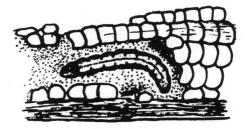

Larva feeding on ear of corn

about the time of silk emergence. Eggs are deposited on the silks, hatch, larvae feed on silks and then bore into the developing ear. Mature larvae eat the husks, crawl down the stalk, enter the soil and pupate. Up to 3 generations per year in the southern part of the North Central States.

Feeding habits: Larvae chew into silks and into ears of maize. They may also eat into the whorls in the top of maize plants, attacking leaves and tassels. Feeding on cotton plants is similar to feeding on maize plants with the larvae tunneling into the bolls.

Control principles: Larvae are easier to control with chemicals before they enter the ear (or boll in cotton).
Growing varieties with long, tight husks may lower damage. The use of a trap corn (rows of maize, which is the preferred host, planted close to cotton in an attempt to attract the egg laying moths away from cotton) has been used to control the cotton bollworm. Economic threshold: May vary from state to state, but is usually based on damage level and larvae and eggs present.

Hessian Fly (*Mayetiola destructor*)

Adult fly

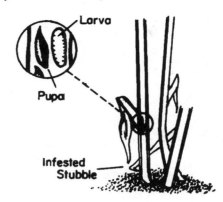

Larvae and Pupa

Larvae at first are small, red maggots. Larvae are glistening white when full grown and about 1/2 cm long. Pupae are brown (look like flax seeds). Adult is a small fly.

Major crops affected: Wheat; some barley and rye. Injury can occur in fall or spring.

Life cycle: Complete (usually two to three broods per year). Eggs deposited on young leaves in fall; maggots -hatch in a few days and crawl down into the leaf sheaths; pupate when larvae are full size (2 to 4 weeks of age); overwinters as pupa (flaxseed stage). Adult flies emerge in early spring and lay eggs. Infestation potential is greater under higher humidity and rainfall conditions.

Feeding habits: Larvae feed on juices under leaf sheaths for about 9 to 10 days stunting the plant and reducing yield.

Control principles: Cultural-plant winter wheat after "the fly-free date" in autumn (date when most of the adult flies have emerged and died). Till the stubble soon after harvest. Destroy volunteer wheat plants. Genetic-use of resistant varieties. No effective control measures can be applied once a field is infested, thus control is based on prevention.

Cutworms
Black Cutworm (*Agrotis ipsilon*) and many other species

Larvae-Light gray to almost black, 6 mm to 5 cm long.

Adults-Moths are nocturnal (night flying).

Major crops affected: All crops, especially maize.

Life cycle: May overwinter as pupae or moths, but outbreaks in maize usually come from moths flying in from the South during late March or April; eggs are laid in low spots in the field, usually before maize is planted; eggs hatch in 5 to 10 days; larvae mature in 28 to 35 days; pupal stage lasts 12 to 15 days; the development from egg to adult requires 47 days at 24°C (75°F) and 62 days at 21°C (70°F)

Black cutworm larvae

Feeding habits: Usually hide in or near the soil during day and feed at night. Cut off plants near or below the soil surface. Small cutworms feed on maize leaves and is evident several days before actual cutting occurs. On rare occasions cutworms may chew holes in maize plants up to 1 meter (3 feet) tall.

Control principles: Outbreaks usually occur first in low, poorly drained areas of fields; most likely to occur in fields that have reduced tillage, with residue on the soil surface-or in fields adjacent to permanent vegetation. The economic threshold is sometimes estimated to be when 3 to 5% of a maize stand has been removed by the insect. The ET may be higher if temperatures are above normal, giving maize a developmental advantage over the insect pest.

D. INSECTS THAT DAMAGE STORED SEED-

Rice Weevil-(*Sitophilus oryza*)
and other weevil species

Larvae in rice kernel

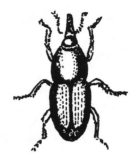

Adult Beetle

Larvae - About 2 mm long, shown in a rice kernel.

Adults - about 3-4 mm long, reddish-brown, with 4 light yellowish spots on the back.

Major crops affected: Stored grain.

Life cycle: Complete (twenty-six days in warm weather). Adult weevils eat small cavities in grain in order to deposit eggs. Larvae hatch and burrow inside kernels. Pupate inside kernels and adults eat their way out.

Feeding habits: Weevils are prevalent in, and spread from, accumulations of old grain around granaries. Burrow and chew cavities in grain kernels.

Control principles: Destruction of waste grain, storage of grain in weather tight bins that are thoroughly cleaned before being filled. Bin fumigation if infestation occurs.

Angoumois Grain Moth (*Sitotroga cerealella*)

Larva in wheat kernel

Adult moth

Larvae - About 3/4 to 1 cm long, white with yellowish heads. Shown in wheat kernel.

Adult - A grayish-brown moth with pointed hair-fringed wings about 1 1/2 cm wide when spread.

Major crops affected: Stored grain. Infests grain in the field in tropical or warm areas (S.E. U.S.).

Life cycles: Complete (thirty days per generation in warm climates). Moths deposit eggs in capped-over round holes in kernels; larvae hatch and bore into grain; pupation occurs inside the grain kernels; and moths emerge to deposit more eggs.

Feeding habits: Larvae bore into grain. Infestation may be continuous in southern U.S.

Control principles: Destruction of waste grain; storage of grain in clean bins, fumigation of bins if infestation occurs.

E. INSECTS THAT DAMAGE PLANT ROOTS-

1. Insects likely to be a problem in crops following a meadow or sod crop-

Wireworms (*Elateridae* spp.)

Larvae-Slick, shiny, brown, six-legged worms, up to 4 cm long.

Adult is the click beetle; 6 to 9 mm in length; brown to black.

Major crops damaged: Most crops, especially row crops following sod or meadow crops.
Life cycle: Complete. Pass the winter in adult or larval stages; eggs deposited in soil among grass roots, eggs hatch and larvae feed on crop roots. Larvae live for 2 to 5 years, then pupate.

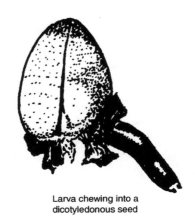

Feeding habits: Larvae chew holes in underground plant parts usually when plants are 2.5 to 30 cm tall. Also bore into seed. Damage is usually more severe in low, poorly drained soils.

Larva chewing into a
dicotyledonous seed

Control principles: Chemical control may be needed in row crops following meadow or sod crops. Bait stations are used to scout infestation levels prior to planting. If an average of one or more wireworms are present at bait stations, a soil insecticide is recommended.

White Grubs
(*Phyllophaga* spp.)

Larvae-2-4 cm long, fleshy, whitish, curved grubs, with light brown heads and six legs.

Adult is known as the May or June beetle.

Major crops affected: Most crops, especially following meadow or sod crops.

Life cycle: Complete. Life cycle usually requires 1-4 years. Eggs are deposited in grass sods; tiny grubs hatch and feed near soil surface until September or October; they then tunnel downward and overwinter at about 46 cm (18 inches); in May they return to surface and feed on crop roots; pupate in early June. The beetles stay in the soil until the following spring.

Feeding habits: Root feeding is prevalent; stand reductions can occur; lodging may result because of weakened root systems.

Control principles: Note wilted or stunted plants, examine roots and dig up grubs nearby. Chemical control may be warranted, especially in crops that follow a meadow or sod crop.

2. Insects likely to be a problem in corn following corn-

Root Worms
(Three species are common)

Northern Corn Rootworm
(*Diabrotica barberi*)

Western Corn Rootworm
(*Diabrotica virgifera*)

Adult beetle

Adult beetle

Northern - Adults are yellowish-green beetles about 4 mm long.

Western - Adults are yellow with a black stripe on the outside of each wing cover, about 4 mm long.

Larvae-Slender, 3 mm to 1 cm long, white with brown heads.

Major crops affected: Maize.

Life cycle: Complete. One generation per year. Eggs deposited in soil in mid- to late-summer by female beetles; overwinter as eggs; hatching begins in May and peaks in June; after about 3 weeks pupation occurs and adults emerge from soil. Development time from larval hatch to adult emergence is 27 to 40 days. Mild winters and drier springs increase egg survival and the infestation potential.

Feeding habits: Larvae feed on roots, often resulting in severely lodged maize. Adults also feed on silks which can interfere with pollination and fertilization.

Control principles: Usually northern and western corn rootworms are a problem on maize following maize; thus, crop rotation is used as control method. Control decisions are based on beetle counts as in the following example:
1. Low beetle counts: no insecticide necessary for beetle control and no insecticide needed for larval control the following spring.
2. Beetle counts exceeding or reaching the economic threshold of 1 beetle/plant: Rotate the field to another crop or use a soil insecticide the next year.
3. If adult control is needed to prevent pollination damage, apply insecticide before 75% of the plants have silked and when beetle counts reach 5 beetles/plant and silk cutting is evident.

Usually not a problem on muck soils or on sandy soil under nonirrigated conditions. It is thought that small larvae are scratched and abraded by the sand.

Southern Corn Rootworm (Twelve-spotted cucumber beetle)
(*Diabrotica undecimpunctata howardi*)

Larvae-Slender, 3 mm to 1 cm long, white with brown heads.

Adult-Beetles are about 9 mm long, yellow to green, with 12 conspicuous black spots on the wing covers.

Major crops affected: Maize-insect referred to as the southern corn rootworm. Insect referred to as the twelve-spotted cucumber beetle when leaf damage occurs to soybeans, cucurbits, and other crops-e.

Adult Beetle

Life cycle: Complete. Overwinter as adults in the South; fly north and lay eggs at base of young plants in early spring; eggs hatch and young larvae feed on young roots and may also tunnel into the underground portion of the stalks; pupate and adults emerge in mid- to late-summer.

Feeding habits: Larvae feed on newly developed maize roots. Adults may feed on silks and are more severe leaf feeders than other rootworm adults.

Control principles: Crop rotations will not control this insect since adults fly in and eggs are laid in the spring. Damage may occur in first year corn. Insecticides have given adequate control where needed.

F. INSECTS THAT DAMAGE PLANTED SEED-

Seedcorn Maggot (*Delia platura*)

Larvae-Pale, yellowish-white, legless maggot, about 6 mm long.

Adults-Grey to brownish flies.

Major crops affected: Maize, beans, soybeans.

Life cycle: Complete. Adults appear early in the spring and lay eggs on moist soil high in organic matter, near decaying vegetation; overwinter as larvae in the soil; pupate in the spring; adults emerge in May. Larval damage to seed is most severe in cool, wet springs.

Feeding habits: Maggots burrow in the seed and eat the germ, resulting in reduced stands.

Larva damaging a corn kernel

Control principles: Dig where plants fail to emerge and examine seed for feeding injury. If replanting is necessary, an insecticide seed treatment should be used.

293

ADDITIONAL STUDY QUESTIONS

1. Spraying one hectare for grasshoppers in the spring may save spraying 50 ha or more later in the summer. Why is this statement true?

2. A general "rule-of-thumb" is that chemical control of a leaf feeding insect on soybeans is not warranted until more than 25% of the leaf area has been destroyed. Why might it be possible for soybeans to lose up to 25% of their leaf area without having the seed yield lowered appreciably?

3. Larvae of armyworms and other species of insects are often observed to have white, pinhead sized objects fastened to their back. How would the occurrence of these white objects be of importance in making insect control recommendations?

4. Give a method of cultural control of the alfalfa weevil.

5. Name two species of insects that are likely to be associated with the spread of virus diseases of crops.

6. How is the incidence of stalk-rot in corn influenced by the European corn borer?

7. A "trap crop" is sometimes used in controlling insects. What is a trap crop?

8. How is the "fly-free date" used in controlling the Hessian fly in winter wheat?

9. What control measures, other than chemical control, may be used to prevent damage by the rice weevil and the angoumois grain moth?

10. Name two insects that are likely to be a problem in maize following a meadow.

11. Which two of the corn rootworm species are likely to be a problem in maize following maize?

12. Is cutworm damage more likely to occur in low, poorly drained areas of a field or in higher, well drained areas?

Crop Science: Principles and Practice

SELF-EVALUATION TEST

Insects

Circle letter corresponding to one best answer.

1. Damage by which of the following would not reduce photosynthetic area?

    a) grasshopper
    b) southern corn rootworm larvae
    c) alfalfa weevil
    d) European corn borer
    e) bean leaf beetle

2. Which of the following is most likely to be a vector?

    a) northern corn rootworm
    b) European corn borer
    c) southern corn rootworm
    d) aphid
    e) grasshopper

3. Types of crop damage by insects would generally not include

    a) loss of leaf tissue
    b) stem or stalk damage
    c) plugging of the translocation system
    d) loss of roots
    e) premature death of the plant

4. Using crop rotations instead of planting the same crop year after year is an example of which kind of control?

    a) chemical
    b) rotational
    c) psychological
    d) cultural
    e) physiological

5. Chemical control of insects that have a complete life cycle should normally be "aimed" at

    a) the pupa stage
    b) the adult stage
    c) the larva stage
    d) the nymph stage
    e) any stage when the insect occurs

6. The following statement about the European corn borer is true.

    a) It overwinters as a larva.
    b) Stalk destruction will eliminate it.
    c) The adult does the actual damage.
    d) There is only one complete generation per year.
    e) It has a gradual life cycle.

7. The following statement about insects that reside in the soil and damage maize is true:

   a) All are more serious in a continuous maize cropping system.
   b) If maize follows a meadow crop, there is no problem.
   c) Western corn rootworms are a greater problem in continuous maize than in maize following meadow.
   d) Cutworms are a greater problem in continuous maize than in maize following meadow.
   e) Western corn rootworms are a greater problem in maize following meadow than in continuous maize.

8. In general, selective chemical control, without damaging crop plants

   a) is easier with insects than with weeds
   b) is easier with weeds than with insects
   c) is easier with diseases than with insects
   d) cannot be accomplished with weeds
   e) cannot be accomplished with insects

9. An insect that lays its eggs in waste areas near crop fields and the nymphs move into the crop fields following hatching is the

   a) leafhopper
   b) aphid
   c) grasshopper
   d) armyworm
   e) cutworm

10. A light green worm with faint white stripes and about 2 cm long was found eating soybean leaves in July. This worm is probably a

    a) green cloverworm
    b) armyworm
    c) cutworm
    d) alfalfa weevil
    e) corn earworm

11. A pinkish to grayish white worm 2 cm long and with a black head was found boring into the stalk of maize. This worm is probably a

    a) corn earworm
    b) cutworm
    c) wireworm
    d) European cornborer
    e) northern corn rootworm

12. A yellowish beetle about 9 mm long with 12 black spots on its back was found feeding on the silks of a maize ear. This insect is probably a

    a) northern corn rootworm beetle
    b) southern corn rootworm beetle
    c) western corn rootworm beetle
    d) click beetle
    e) corn earworm beetle

13. A shiny, brown, six-legged worm, about 3 cm long was found eating a sprouting maize seed. This insect is probably a

    a) corn rootworm
    b) wireworm
    c) seedcorn maggot
    d) cutworm
    e) corn earworm

Chapter 12

Crop Disease Management

Maximum yields of high quality grain are possible when crop plants grow and develop under healthful and disease-free conditions. When plant functions are impaired by organisms or environmental factors beyond normal deviation, the plant becomes diseased. In some cases, the use of modern, disease-resistant varieties may give the impression that crop diseases are not as ominous as in the past. However, widespread use of monocultures using genetically similar varieties, increased mobility of diseases through rapid transport, using pesticides that reduce the potential of natural biological control of disease organisms, and adaptation ability of disease causing organisms to new environments help make the threat of diseases more challenging than ever.

I. DEFINITIONS

A simple definition of a plant disease is "a plant disorder" resulting from some disease-causing factor (pathogen). Under this broad definition, diseases may be caused by pathogenic organisms or by some environmental factor causing plant sickness. Some common definitions used in study of plant diseases (plant pathology) are:

1. **Plant Disease**-an unhealthy condition in the form, function, or processes of the plant that result from continuous irritation by a pathogen. Disease is the condition, not the organisms involved, and is the result of the pathogen and host interacting with each other in a conducive environment.

2. **Disease Symptoms**-the signs or indications of plant disease. Plant diseases are sometimes classified according to the symptoms they cause, such as root rots, wilts, leaf spots, blights, rusts, smuts, etc.

3. **Infectious Diseases**-also called "biotic" diseases. Diseases caused by a biological organism. Common pathogenic organisms include fungi, bacteria, viruses and nematodes. **Pathogenicity** refers to the capability of the pathogen to cause disease. For example, fungal races that can cause a particular disease may differ in their pathogenicity under different conditions and thus, differ in the amount of disease they cause. Crop disease names may include part of the scientific name of the pathogenic organism, for example, Gibberella Ear Rot (caused by the fungus, *Gibberella zeae*) or Phytophthora Root Rot (caused by the fungus, *Phytophthora megasperma* var. *sojae*).

4. **Non-Infectious Diseases**-also called "abiotic" and "physiological" diseases. Diseases caused by some pathogenic factor in the environment, such as nutrient deficiency, oxygen deprivation in the root zone, toxic wastes, air pollution, chemical injury, and many other possible factors.

II. IMPACT OF CROP DISEASES

A. Beneficial Effects of Pathogenic Groups of Organisms

By definition crop diseases have a negative impact on crop production. However, because pathogens are frequently grouped into fungi, bacteria, viruses, and nematodes, one must not assume that all organisms within these groups are undesirable. These groups of organisms are important to us and our environment in the following areas:

1. Decomposition of organic matter and nutrient recycling
2. Production of antibiotics and other medincinal products
3. Food processing and product development
4. Improvement of soil tilth and productivity
5. Involvement in symbiotic relationships with plants to improve legume nitrogen fixation and nutrient uptake by plant roots
6. Natural parasitism and biological control of pathogenic organisms in our envrionment

B. Harmful Effects

Crop diseases cause billions of dollars of loss to farmers every year throughout the world. Crop diseases, in combination with insects and weeds, destroy an estimated one-third of the world's crop production potential. It has been estimated in North America that over 80,000 diseases affect crops caused from parasitism by approximately 8,000 fungal species, 200 bacterial species, 500 viral species, and 500 nematode species. An individual crop may have 100 or more known diseases. Plant pathogens and disease can lower yield, reduce product quality or desirability, and interfere with normal production practices. These losses usually are due to one of the following types of damage:

1. Failure to achieve the proper crop plant population density and distribution because of seed decay and seedling blight.
2. Destruction of leaf area, resulting in decreased photosynthesis.
3. Loss of roots (absorbing tissue) because of "root rot" diseases. Loss of roots can decrease absorption of minerals and water and can result in increased lodging.
4. Destruction-or plugging of the translocation system. These diseases cause plant lodging, wilting, and blight (dying of plant tissue, especially leaves).
5. Production of a toxic or undesirable material. Some toxins are harmful to the crop plant and others may even be harmful to people or animals feeding on the diseased tissue.
6. Premature plant death, resulting in lower yields and lower quality crop products.

What are three desirable contributions of pathogenic groups of organisms?

What are three examples of how pathogens damage crops?

What is the difference between the terms: stalk rot and pathogen?

III. PLANT-MICROORGANISM RELATIONSHIPS

A. Plant-Microorganism Associations

Plants and microorganisms often live together in intimate association with each other. The relationship may be beneficial or harmful to the organisms involved. Two of several definitions used to describe plant-microorganism associations are mutualism and parasitism:

1. **Mutualism** - an intimate association of two different organisms in which the relationship is mutually beneficial to both, e.g. legumes-nitrogen fixing bacteria and plant roots-mycorrhizae. Also referred to as a symbiotic relationship in some fields of study.
2. **Parasitism** - an intimate association of two different organisms in which one organism (parasite) lives on or in the other (host) and obtains nutrients from it. Parasitic relationships are beneficial to the parasite at the expense of the host, e.g. crop plant and a parasitic species of fungi, bacteria, etc..

Plant disease often results from the parasitic relationship of the pathogen and the host plant. During the process of parasitism, plant parasites may extract nutrients, interfere with cellular functions, or harm other plant functions resulting in a diseased condition of the plant host. The severity of the disease will be influenced by the degree of pathogenicity of the parasite.

B. Nutrient Sources For Plant-Associated Microorganisms

Microorganisms can be classified according to their ability to survive and obtain nutrients from their environment. Plant-associated microorganisms range from those that require a living host to grow and reproduce (obligate parasite) to those that can survive and extract nutrients from dead and decaying material (saprophyte). However, some microorganisms have the ability to adjust and survive on living or dead and decaying tissue during some or all of their life cycle (facultative microorganisms). These characteristics influence the persistence and survival characteristics of a pathogen.

1. **Obligate parasites** can live and complete their life cycle only in living plant tissues. Nutrients in the host are absorbed by or diverted to the parasite. Obligate parasites can be carried from one growing season to the next in living crop host plant tissue (including seeds) or in living tissue of alternate hosts (possibly weed species). However, some obligate parasites can persist overseason in the absence of living host tissues by producing good survival structures (e.g. eggs of many nematodes can survive in soil for several years). Plant viruses, several fungi (including mildews, smuts, and rusts), and plant parasitic nematodes are obligate parasites. Generally, obligate parasites have a specific host range that they attack.

2. **Facultative saprophytes and facultative parasites** can live and complete their life cycles on living or dead plant tissue. Facultative saprophytes have the ability to live saprophytically on decaying organic matter if living hosts are not present. Facultative parasites usually live on decaying matter but can attack living plants and become parasitic. These organisms can infect plants and cause diseases or they can live in crop residue in the soil. Disease organisms in these two classes consist of many species of fungi and bacteria. Facultative pathogens frequently attack a wider range of plant hosts than obligate parasities.

3. **Obligate saprophytes** can live only in dead or dying tissue. The vast majority of micoorganisms are obligate saprophytes and are not pathogenic. Most of the beneficial microorganisms are in this group, which include the primary decomposers. Some can infect plant tissues as secondary invaders and live on the dead or decaying tissue previously damaged by other pathogens, insects, or by mechanical means.

IV. PATHOGENIC MICROORGANISMS AND COMPETITIVE CHARACTERISTICS

Plant diseases are often classified or described according to the type of organism causing the plant disorder, i.e. fungal diseases, bacterial diseases, etc.. In a literal sense, insects and larger animal species that cause plant disease could be called pathogens but they are often referred to as predators. In this unit we will focus on some of the more common pathogenic microorganisms:

A. Fungal Pathogens

Fungi are usually multicellular organisms and produce threadlike strands called mycelium. Fungi obtain food by secreting enzymes into host cells and absorbing the nutrients resulting from enzymatic breakdown. The mode of reproduction may be sexual or asexual (analogous to seed production or vegetative propagation in plants, respectively). Fungal diseases can spread rapidly and widely by wind blown spores or conidia.

B. Bacterial Pathogens

Bacteria exist as single celled organisms and reproduce by binary fission (one mature individual cell divides into two equal, smaller individual cells). Pathogenic bacteria colonize and parasitize host tissue. Bacteria are able to exchange and transfer genetic material to other cells and new races can be produced through genetic exchange and genetic mutations.

C. Viral Pathogens

Viruses are usually not considered a living organism. Virus "particles" do not have a cellular structure and consist of strands of nucleic acid encased within a protein coat. They can only reproduce within living cells. Pathogenic viruses can invade living cells and seriously disrupt normal cellular functions.

D. Pathogenic Nematodes

Nematodes are minute wormlike organisms and are classified in the animal kingdom. There are thousands of species and relatively few are pathogenic to plants. Nematodes sexually reproduce by means of eggs. Nematodes range in size from barely visible to microscopic. Pathogenic nematodes penetrate and parasitize host tissue resulting in plant disease. Figure 1 illustrates the common symptoms of the "rootknot" nematode which affects several crop species.

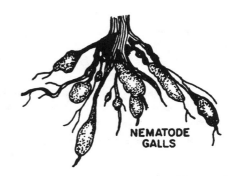

Figure 1. Symptoms of the Rootknot Nematode. Note the swollen "knots" on the roots, which interfere with normal translocation.

E. Competitve Characteristics

1. Reproductive Potential: Pathogenic organisms have tremendous growth and reproductive potential which enable them to colonize host tissue and to survive and adapt to different conditions. For example, many fungi can produce billions of spores per plant; bacterial populations can double in a few minutes; up to 10 million virus particles can be present in a single plant cell; and nematodes can have up to 10 or more generations per year with a single female laying 300 to 600 eggs each time. Pathogenic organisms can produce many races (or strains) causing a particular plant disease and show a great deal of variability in their populations. Due to extremely short generations times and high reproductive capacity, surviving pathogenic organisms can produce populations that are resistant to chemical control agents or adapted to new host or environmental conditions.

2. Dissemination and Survival Potential: Many pathogenic organisms can be widely distributed by various means, such as air, water, insects (vectors) and other animals, and by mechanical means. Many pathogens survive during winter or during unfavorable periods in tissues of different hosts, organic matter, crop residues, seeds, and soil allowing the pathogen to reinfect a crop.

What are four groups of pathogenic organisms that cause diseases in crop plants?

By what process can microorganisms adapt to a new host or chemical control agent?

V. INFECTIOUS DISEASE DEVELOPMENT AND MANAGEMENT

A. Development of Infectious Disease

In order for infectious plant disease to occur three components are necessary: a pathogenic organism, a susceptible host plant, and a favorable environment for disease. The major steps of an infectious disease cycle include:
1. inoculation (coming into contact of the pathogen and plant host)
2. penetration (entry into the plant by direct penetration, natural openings, or wounds)
3. infection (establishment of a parasite within the plant host)
4. invasion (the colonization or spread of a pathogen within the plant host)
5. reproduction, dissemination, and survival of the pathogen

A disease epidemic (disease increase) in a population is influenced by host, pathogenic, and environmental factors. Host factors include type of crop, growth stage, and degree of susceptibility or resistance of the host to the pathogen. Pathogenic factors include level of virulence (degree of pathogenicity), reproductive potential, and mobility and spread of the pathogen. Environmental factors include temperature, relative humidity, soil moisture, wind velocity and direction, soil fertility, and soil pH. Table 1 lists some common crop plant diseases and environmental conditions favoring their occurrence.

Table 1

Crops	Diseases	Conditions Favoring Disease
Maize	-Southern corn leaf blight -Stalk rot -Seedling blights -Ear and kernel rots	-Moist air, frequent heavy dew -Nutrient imbalance-especially high N and low K, high plant populations, hot weather after silking, wet soil, delayed harvesting. -Cold (12°C is optimum), wet soil -Continuous wet weather after corn maturity
Soybeans	-Bacterial blight -Bacterial pustule -Seed and seedling rots -Phytophthora root rot	-Cool, wet weather -Wet, warm weather -Cold, wet soil -Low, poorly drained soil, compacter soil, heavy clay soils.
Small Grains	-Stem rust -Leaf rust -Barley yellow dwarf	-Cool, wet, late spring; continual wind from the south; warm, humid summers -Late planting, moderate temperatures, wet weather. -Cool, moist weather in spring and early summer
Alfalfa	-Bacterial wilt	-Abundant rainfall or irrigation and winter injury.
Alfalfa and Clovers	-Seedling blights	-Cold, wet soil
Smooth bromegrass	-Brown spot	-Cool, wet weather
Orchardgrass	-Scald	-Cool, wet weather

What weather conditions usually favor the development of plant diseases?

Why do areas toward the Gulf of Mexico usually have more problems with diseases of crops?

B. Disease Management Strategies

Because of the relatively rapid spread of many diseases and the difficulty in effectively curing plant diseases after their development, much of the management strategies emphasize methods to prevent and protect crops from disease. Chemical control agents used in disease control can vary in their toxicity and specificity to other organisms in our environment. Thus, non-chemical control methods are important in minimizing chemical use and implementing successful disease management programs. Management strategies include methods to: 1) prevent the pathogen from contacting the host, 2) reduce the inoculum (amount of pathogen) in a plant or field, and 3) protect or cure plants from infection. Examples of different control methods used to achieve these management strategies are:

1. **Regulatory control**- Use of laws and regulatory procedures to prevent importation of a pathogen into an area. Examples include plant and soil quarantines established by an area or country to prevent importation, exportation and use of diseased infected crop material.

2. **Cultural control**- Use of crop management tactics to prevent or reduce disease. Examples include:

   a. Host eradication- May involve removing infected crop plants in an area and alternate hosts (host plants other than the desired crop) that harbor the pathogen.

   b. Crop rotation- Rotating susceptible with non-susceptible crops or including a year of fallow in the rotation can be used to reduce pathogen inoculum in a field. Crop rotation is less effective for pathogens that have wind-borne dissemination, produce long-lived spores, eggs or other structures, or can live saprophytically in the soil for several or more years.

   c. Sanitation- Burning or removing crop debris and cleaning farm equipment and buildings help reduce the amount and spread of some pathogens.

   d. Crop management- Proper planting, fertility, harvesting, and soil management practices can help prevent or lower the susceptibility of crop plants to disease. For example, adjusting planting dates or improving soil drainage can lower the incidence of some diseases.

3. **Biological control**- Microorganisms present in soil or on plants can provide a degree of biological control of some pathogenic organisms. Viruses attack most kinds of microrganisms. Scientists have observed several non-pathogenic bacterial and fungal species that parasitize pathogenic bacteria, fungi and nematodes. For example, some soil-borne, non-pathogenic fungi parasitize fungal pathogens that cause seed and seedling diseases, such as *Pythium* and *Phytophthora*.

4. **Disease-resistant cultivars**- The use of disease-resistant cultivars has been a sucessful and cost-effective method to reduce disease losses and chemical use. However, resistant cultivars are not available for all diseases. Furthermore, new races of a disease pathogen can develop that become virulent on a previously disease-resistant cultivar. In some cases, a disease-resistant cultivar may have a useful life span of only 3 to 5 years before resistance is lost. As new races of a disease pathogen are formed, it becomes increasingly difficult to develop completely resistant varieties. Disease management programs should also include other strategies to prolong the life of a resistant cultivar and reduce the disease pressure.

5. **Physical control**- Use of heat, refrigeration, irradiation, or some other physical means to eradicate or reduce pathogen inoculum.

6. **Chemical control**- Chemical control agents have been used to destroy pathogens and may be foliar, seed, or soil applied. Seed treatments (chemicals used to protect seeds, tubers, bulbs, and other planting stock) are used to protect germinating seeds from fungal pathogens that cause seed and seedling rots. Chemicals used to control diseases are generally classified according to the targeted pathogen:
   1. fungicides-fungal pathogens
   2. bactericides-bacterial pathogens
   3. nematicides-pathogenic nematodes
   4 viricides-viral pathogens

   Fumigants refer to toxic gases or volatile substances that are used to disinfect soil, grain bins, and other areas. Fumigants are usually very toxic, broad spectrum, and are used to eradicate pathogenic organisms and insect pests (as well as beneficial organisms) from a targeted area.

VI. DISEASE IDENTIFICATION AND CONTROL PRINCIPLES

One of the prerequisites in controlling diseases in crops is to recognize the symptoms of the specific disease(s). Once the presence of the disease is recognized and its seriousness assessed, the life cycle and other characteristics of the disease must be studied in order to best deal with the problem. Some identification and control characteristics of a selected few of the many diseases that damage crop plants follow:

Be able to:

    1.   identify the diseases illustrated in this section.

    2.   classify the disease organism(s) involved (obligate parasite, etc.).

    3.   explain how the disease organism overwinters and how it is spread.

    4.   give the possible methods of control.

A. COMMON MAIZE DISEASES

STALK ROTS

Symptoms - A few weeks after pollination dark brown lesions occur near nodes.

By mid-September-Inside of stalk is decayed, sometimes with pink discoloration, vascular bundles may remain intact.

Late season symptoms-Lodging stalks, decaying stalks, decaying ears, dropped ears.

STALK
SHREDDED
VASCULAR
BUNDLES
INTACT

Causal organisms:
    Fungi-*Diplodia zea*
        Gibberella zea
        Fusarium monoliforme (Gibberella fujikuroi)
        Nigrospora oryzae and others
Type: Facultative saprophytes or facultative parasites

Overwintering, spread, and infection: Overwinter in crop residue. Spores are produced in the spring and spread by wind to maize plants. Infection is more serious in fields with previous injury by other diseases, insects, or from mechanical means; inadequate potassium fertility compared to nitrogen; injury by frost or hail; high plant populations; and with hot weather occurring after silking and tasseling.

Control: Some varieties are resistant, crop rotation, destruction of crop residue, grow adapted full-season varieties, avoid exceptionally high population density, control insects, use balanced soil fertility (avoid excess in nitrogen and deficiency in phosphorus and potassium).

EAR AND KERNEL ROTS

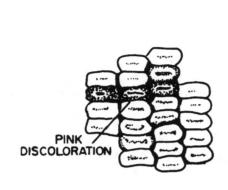

Fusarium kernel rot - white to pink colored mold on kernels. Diseased kernels occur anywhere on the ear and are scattered or clustered.

Gibberella ear rot - Fungal growth from ear tip and adhering husks. Mold is usually pink or red and sometimes white.

Causal organisms: Fungi- *Gibberella zeae*
                              Fusarium moniliforme and others
Type: Facultative saprophytes or Facultative parasites

Overwintering, spread, and infection: Overwinter in crop residue. Spores are produced in the spring and spread to maize plants. Infections are often established where insects such as corn earworm have fed or other injury has occurred. Continuous wet weather after maize maturity may cause more damage.
  Gibberella zea and some other fungi may produce a toxin that is toxic to livestock, especially swine.

Control: Some hybrids are less susceptible, prevent insect or other damage to the ears, harvest as soon as maize is dry enough. Growth of the fungi stops in corn dried to 13% or lower moisture content.

NORTHERN CORN LEAF BLIGHT

First symptoms-On lower leaves. Small elliptical spots, water soaked, grayish green, or dark colored.

Later symptoms-Spots turn greenish-tan and are up to 15 cm long and 3 cm wide. Entire leaves or the whole plant may be killed.
Causal organism: Fungus -*Helminthosporium turcicum*
Type: Facultative saprophyte

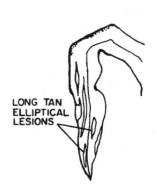

Overwintering, spread, and infection: Overwinters on crop residue in the field, produces spores the next spring, and reinfects maize

Spores are spread by the wind.
Outer layers of ear husks may be infected, but the fungus does not grow through to the kernels.

Control: Plant resistant hybrids. Fungicides give some control, but Environmental Protection Agency (EPA) regulations must be followed.

SOUTHERN CORN LEAF BLIGHT

Leaf blade symptoms-Tan, elliptical lesions approximately 0.5 cm wide and 0.5 to 2 cm long, with a reddish brown border. Leaves may be killed.

Stalk and leaf sheath symptoms-Initially lesions are purple, and develop tan to gray centers (0.5-2.5 cm wide and up to 5 cm long).

Ear symptoms-Gray to black lesions on husks that may extend into kernels.

Causal organism: Fungus-*Helminthosporium maydis* (Race T causes severe damage on hybrids produced by the use of Cytoplasmic-Genetic male sterile system using Texas (T) cytoplasm.)
Type: Facultative saprophyte or Facultative parasite

Leaf Symptoms

Overwintering, spread, and infection: Overwinters in infected maize tissue. Spores are produced in the spring and carried by wind to young maize plants. Race T produces a toxin that kills susceptible T cytoplasm tissue ahead of fungus spread. Under warm, moist conditions, the disease increases rapidly.

Control: Hybrids having normal (N) cytoplasm are resistant to the toxin produced by Race T, but are susceptible to direct damage by the fungus. Till under infected crop residue, use low population densities and early planting dates. Fungicides can help if sprayed on the leaves before the disease is severe.

CORN SMUT

Symptoms - Smut galls on ears, tassels, stalks, and leaves.

First symptoms-Galls are silvery-white.

Later symptoms-The interior becomes a mass of black spores that are exposed when the galls rupture.

Causal organism: Fungus-*Ustilago maydis*
Type: Obligate parasite

Overwintering, spread, and infection: Black spores overwinter in the gall as a part of the crop residue or as single spores in the soil. In the spring, the spores germinate and penetrate the corn plant through stomata, through wounds, and directly through cell walls. The fungus causes maize cells to increase in size and number.

Corn Smut-Ear Infection

Control: Some hybrids are more resistant. Extremely high nitrogen fertility increases the incidence of the disease. Avoid plant damage by cultivation and blowing soil. Crop rotation may help in control.

MAIZE DWARF MOSAIC (MDM)

YOUNG PLANT

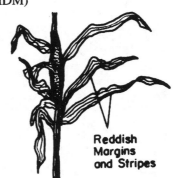

ADULT PLANT

Early symptoms-Shortening of upper internodes, alternating yellow and green stripes on leaves

Later symptoms-Leaves become yellowish-green with red blotches or streaks. Plant is stunted and develops multiple ear shoots that are partially or totally barren.

Causal organism:Maize dwarf mosaic virus
Type: Obligate parasite

Overwintering, spread, and infection: Overwinters in alternate hosts:
  Perennial grasses-Johnsongrass, plumegrass, and gamagrass.
  Annual grasses-Overwintering a problem only in warm climates-crabgrass, barnyard grass, witch grass, goose grass, cup grass, soft chess, Japanese chess, teosinte, and the foxtail grasses.

  Where MDM has been severe, the virus has persisted in Johnsongrass, and has spread to maize. The disease is spread by aphids and mechanically by plants rubbing together in the field.

Control: Control alternate hosts. Isolate infected fields as much as possible. Limit spread by aphids and by mechanical operations. Possibility of resistant varieties in the future.

B.   COMMON SOYBEAN DISEASES

PYTHIUM SEED AND SEEDLING ROT

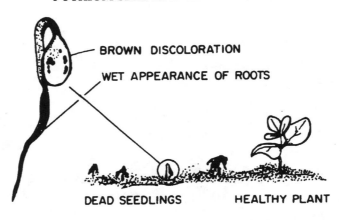

Usual symptoms include seeds decaying in the soil or young seedlings being killed ("Damping off" of young seedlings-infected roots have a brown color and a wet appearance).

Causal organisms: Fungi-*Pythium ultimum* and *Pythium debaryanum*
Type: Facultative parasite

Overwintering, spread, and infection: Fungi are found in most cultivated soils and survive in the soil or in crop residue. Cold, wet soil conditions increase the incidence. Diseased plants may occur singly in small areas-especially in low spots in the field, or uniformly over the entire field if there has been a rainy period.

Control: Plant high quality seed with a low percentage of cracked seedcoats, use a fungicide seed protectant if quality of seed is in doubt, provide for good water drainage from the field.

PHYTOPHTHORA ROOT ROT

Usual symptoms-Brown discoloration of stem and lower branches, extending from below the soil surface to several centimeters above the soil line. Tap-root is dark brown and the entire root system may be decayed. Infection may occur at any stage of plant development. Sometimes no obvious symptoms will occur and plants will be reduced in vigor and stunted.

Causal organism: Fungus -*Phytophthora megasperma* var. *sojae*- Many races have been identified.
Type: Facultative saprophyte

Overwintering, spread, and infection: Survives in the soil or in crop residue buried in the soil. Disease is most common in low, poorly drained areas, in compacted soils, and in heavy clay soils.

BROWN DISCOLORATION
OF STEM ABOVE
GROUND LINE

Control: Plant resistant varieties. Crop rotations with 3 or more years between soybeans help to control the disease. Provide for good water drainage from the field.

BROWN STEM ROT (BSR)

Symptoms-Brown tissue in the center of the stem, sometimes only at the nodes. Browning progresses upward during the growing season. Plants die prematurely, usually 2-3 weeks before normal maturity.

Note-The central tissue of the healthy stem is white.

Causal organism: Fungus-*Cephalosporium gregatum*
Type: Facultative parasite

Overwintering, spread, and infection: Overwinters in infected host residue in the soil. Enters the plants through roots and lower stems. Infection progresses most rapidly during cool weather. Alfalfa and red clover are also hosts of BSR.

Control: Use a crop rotation where soybean, alfalfa or red clover are grown only once in the field every 3 or 4 years.

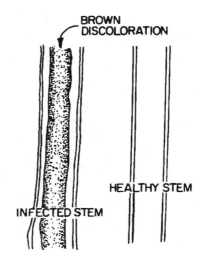

BROWN
DISCOLORATION

HEALTHY STEM

INFECTED STEM

CROSS SECTION THRU
STEMS

BACTERIAL BLIGHT

Early symptoms-Small, angular, water-soaked, yellow spots on leaves. Spots may be surrounded by a small yellowish halo. Symptoms often appear 5-7 days following a storm.

Later symptoms-Lesions become dark brown and cause dead areas in the leaves. Dead areas may be blown out resulting in shredded, badly torn leaves.

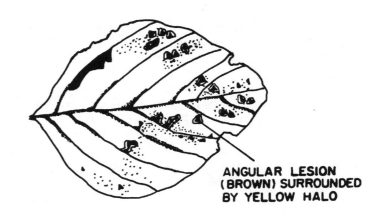

ANGULAR LESION (BROWN) SURROUNDED BY YELLOW HALO

Causal organism: Bacteria-*Pseudomonas syringae* pv. *glycinea*
Type: Facultative saprophyte

Overwintering, spread, and infection: The causal bacteria is seedborne and also overwinters in infected crop residue. Bacteria are splashed from the soil or nearby diseased plants to the lower leaves of healthy plants. Most extensive development is during cool, wet weather in early spring. The disease can also be spread by cultivation if leaves are wet.

Control: Plant resistant varieties (although good resistance is not available), use disease-free seed, crop rotation, till under crop residue, avoid cultivation when foliage is wet.

BACTERIAL PUSTULE

Early symptoms-Small, yellowish-green spots with raised "pustules" in the center. Centers later turn brown.

Later symptoms-Lesions may merge, forming larger dead areas. Dead areas may fall out, giving leaves a ragged appearance.

Causal organism: Bacteria-*Xanthomonas campestris* pv. *glycinea*
Type: Facultative saprophyte

Overwintering, spread, and infection: Bacteria overwinter in diseased leaves and are also seed-borne. Disease usually develops faster during warm, wet weather so it develops later in the season than does bacterial blight.
Bacteria are spread by splashing raindrops, leaf contact, and by cultivation when the leaves are wet.

PUSTULE SURROUNDED BY LESION AND YELLOW HALO

Control: Plant resistant varieties, use disease free seed, crop rotation, till under residue, avoid cultivating when foliage is wet.

PURPLE STAIN

Symptoms (seed)-Purple discoloration of the seedcoat and some-
    times of the hilum only. Seedcoat imperfections (etchings)
    often occur in the purple areas.

Seedlings from infected seeds may have shriveled cotyledons that
    shed prematurely and seedlings may die.

Late in the season symptoms-Reddish-brown spots may appear on
    leaves. Seed yield usually is not lowered.

Causal organism: Fungus-*Cercospera kikuchii*
Type: Facultative saprophyte

Overwintering, spread, and infection: Overwinters in seeds and in crop residue. When diseased seeds are planted,
    the fungus grows from the seedcoat into the cotyledons, then into the stem and remainder of the plant. Spores
    are produced that are wind blown and rain-splashed to leaves of nearby plants.

Control: Plant noninfected seed and some varieties are more resistant. A fungicide applied to the seed or to the
    foliage later in the season may reduce damage.

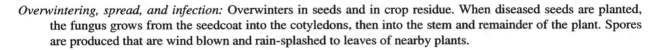

PURPLE DISCOLORATION AND IMPERFECT SEEDCOAT

SOYBEAN MOSAIC

Symptoms-Diseased seedlings are spindly with crinkled uni-
    foliolate leaves that curl downward and become yellow.

Later-Trifoliolate leaves are stunted, mottled with yellow, and
    are crinkled (rugose) and leathery to the touch.

Harvested seed-May have a tannish, brownish, or black dis-
    coloration, depending on the hilum color.

Causal organism: Soybean mosaic virus
Type: Obligate parasite

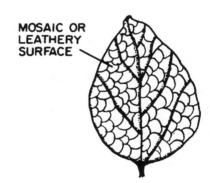

MOSAIC OR LEATHERY SURFACE

Overwintering, spread, and infection: Virus is seed-borne and it can be spread by aphids from infected to healthy
    plants. Symptoms of infection are more severe under cool conditions. Under warm conditions of 31°C (88°F)
    and above, symptoms may be masked and leaves develop normally. Some weed species are alternate hosts.

Control: Plant seed from disease-free fields, practice good weed control, rogue infected plants from seed fields.

C. COMMON DISEASES OF SMALL GRAINS

STEM RUST
(Wheat, Barley, Rye, Oats)

First symptoms-Elongated reddish-brown pustules on stems, leaves, and
    floral parts. Pustules contain brick-red spores.

As plants mature-Pustules and spores become black. Pustules run parallel
    with the leaf veins and rupture the epidermis.

A heavy infection causes poorly filled heads and chaffy, light weight grains.

Pustules on wheat leaf

Causal organism: Fungi-   Wheat- *Puccinia graminis tritici*
                           Barley-*Puccinia gramminis tritici*
                                 and *Puccinia graminis secalis*
                      -Oats- *Puccinia graminis avenae*
                      -Rye- *Puccinia graminis secalis*

Type: Obligate parasite

Overwintering, spread, and infection: Overwinters as black (teliospores) on straw or stubble.

    Sring-Teliospores germinate and produce sporidia that infect common barberry (an alternate host).

    Spring-summer-Red aeciospores are sexually produced on barberry and are blown to reinfect the small grain and red urediospores are produced on the small grain plants.

    Summer-fall-Black teliospores are produced on mature, small grain plants.

    Rust From The South-Most of the stem rust infections are from spores blown in from the South. The stem rust organism overwinters in the red (urediospore) stage in southern U.S. and in Mexico. The damage from wind blown rust is increased if there is more rust in the south, if spring temperatures are higher, and if the small grain is planted later and is later maturing.

Control: Early planted and early maturing varieties tend to escape damage. Resistant varieties have proven useful for a few years and then new races of rust develop. Multiline varieties may reduce grain yield losses. Fungicides will control stem rust but their use is generally not economical.

LEAF RUST
(Oats, Wheat, Rye, Barley)

(Leaf rust of oats is called Crown Rust)

Symptoms: Same as for stem rust except the red spore stages are orange-yellow , more circular, and principally on the leaves, but frequently on stems and inflorescence parts. Pustules often appear to be raised above the leaf epidermis and more easily identifed as individual pustules. Low yields, chaffy or shriveled grain, and lodging accompany infection.

Causal organism: Fungus-Oats-*Puccinia coronata*
                           Wheat and Rye -*Puccinia recondita*
                           Barley-*Puccinia hordei*
Type: Obligate parasite

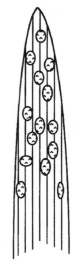

Overwintering, spread, and infection: Life cycle, spread, and infection are similar to stem rust except the alternate host is buckthorn.

Control: Early planted and early maturing varieties tend to escape damage. Resistant varieties have proven useful for a few years and then new races of rust develop. Multiline varieties provide a broad genetic base for resistance and delay the date that the disease reaches epidemic proportions, thus providing some protection for the crop.

LOOSE SMUT
(Oats, Wheat, Rye, Barley)

Early symptoms-A thin, white membrane at first surrounds the smut mass forming where the seed should develop.

Later symptoms-The membrane ruptures and releases black spores.
    Floral bracts as well as kernels are destroyed.

310

Causal organism: Fungus- Oats-*Ustilago avenae*
Wheat-*Ustilago tritici*
Rye-*Ustilago nuda*
Barley- *Ustilago nuda* and *Ustilago nigra*

Type: Obligate parasite

Overwintering, spread, and infection: Loose smut is carried from one season to the next in infected seed. When the infected seed germinates, the fungus grows and develops in the developing plant. The heads of the plant are composed of smut masses. Spores from smutted heads are spread to other plants, germinate in the flowers, grow into the pistils and into developing young kernels. Infected kernels cannot be distinguished from healthy kernels.

Control: Resistant varieties, planting disease free seed, seed treatment with recommended fungicide in oats (seed fungicide treatment is not successful with other small grains).

COVERED SMUT (BUNT, STINKING SMUT)
(Wheat, Barley, Oats, Rye)

Symptoms-Plant may be shortened to one-half of its normal height. Excessive tillering may occur.

Smutted heads are bluish-green and mature earlier than normal heads.

Smutted kernels (Smut balls) Filled with black spores and may have an offensive, fishy odor.

Causal organism: Fungus- Wheat and Rye- *Titletia caries*
and *Titletia foetida*
Barley-*Ustilago hordei*
Oats- *Ustilago kolleri*

Type: Obligate parasite

Overwintering, spread, and infection: In most regions, the fungus is carried from one crop to the next as black spores on the seed or as smut balls. The spores germinate and infect the young seedlings. The fungus grows in the young plant and, at maturity, smut balls are formed in the place of the kernel.

Healthy Plant   **Covered Smut**

Oat heads

Control: Resistant varieties, treatment of seed with fungicide- except that dwarf bunt of wheat cannot be controlled with fungicides.

ERGOT
(Small Grains-especially Rye-and other grasses)

Symptoms-Sclerotia (large purplish-black bodies) develop and replace the kernel in the floret.

Sclerotia are poisonous to livestock and people. May cause sickness, vomiting, abortion.

Causal organism: Fungus-*Claviceps purpurea*

Type: Obligate parasite

Overwintering, spread, and infection: Sclerotia remain in the soil from the previous year. Spores from sclerotia infect the host plant through its open

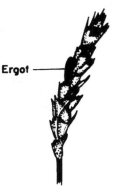

Ergot ——

Rye spike

flowers and the honeydew (sticky) stage is evident about 7 to 14 days later. Spores from the honeydew stage are spread by insects, rain, or wind. Sclerotia are formed on infected plants instead of grain.

Control: Use of ergot free seed and crop rotation (Ergot sclerotia lose their viability after about one year). Mowing of grasses along roadsides, etc. soon after flowering.

BARLEY YELLOW DWARF
(Barley, Oats, Wheat, Rye, and many grasses)

Plant symptoms-Infected leaves have yellowish, reddish, or purple areas along margins, tips, and blades of older leaves. Seedling plants are stunted, have fewer tillers, and may fail to head. Inflorescences are stunted, have sterile florets and aborted or small seeds.

Causal organism: Barley Yellow Dwarf virus

Type: Obligate parasite

Overwintering, spread, and infection: Overwinters in perennial grasses and fall-sown cereals and in the bodies of aphids. Transmitted by aphid vectors, which overwinter as eggs in cold climates and as adults in warm climates. Aphids migrate to temperate areas in spring.

Control: Control aphid vectors. Some resistant cultivars are available but resistance levels vary.

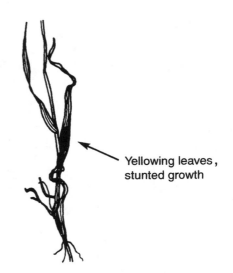

Yellowing leaves, stunted growth

D. COMMON DISEASES OF FORAGES

BACTERIAL WILT
(Alfalfa)

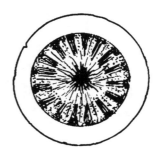

HEALTHY PLANT   **DISEASED PLANT**

Plant symptoms-Reduced stands; dwarfing of infected plants; leaves are small, yellowish and curled. Wilting occurs only in advanced stages of the disease.

Stem symptoms-Cross section shows a yellow to brown ring under the bark. The central woody section becomes discolored during the later stages of the disease.

Causal organism: Bacteria-*Clavibacter michiganense* subsp. *insidiosum*

Type: Facultative saprophyte

Overwintering, spread, and infection: Bacterial wilt infects both roots and crown and is usually more severe in low, poorly drained areas. Infection usually occurs during spring and early summer. Bacteria enter the plant through wounds from winter injury, mowing, or grazing. A great number of plants die the second year after infection.

Control: Use resistant varieties, crop rotation, and provide for good surface drainage in the field.

SCALD
(Orchardgrass)

Symptoms-Lesions on leaves are oval to elongate, 0.5 to 2.5 cm long, light tan to white, and surrounded by a tan to reddish-brown border. Leaf is weakened and may break over.

Causal organism: Fungus-*Rhynchosporium orthosporum*

Type: Facultative parasite

Overwintering, spread, and infection: Overwinters on old dead leaves in the crowns of plants. In the spring, spores infect new leaves to begin the infection. Cool, moist weather increases infection, with the disease usually peaking during May or June.

Control: Resistant varieties, proper management-including balanced soil fertility and good surface drainage of the field.

BROWN SPOT
(Smooth Bromegrass)

Early symptoms-Small, dark-brown, oblong spots on leaves.

Later symptoms-Spots elongated and are dark-purple to brown, with a yellow halo. Lesions may coalesce, forming large yellowed areas on leaves.

Causal organism: Fungus-*Helminthosporium bromi*

Type: Facultative saprophyte

Overwintering, spread, and infection: Overwinters on old leaves and crop residue. Spores are discharged during cool, wet weather and are carried by wind and rain to new leaves to begin the infection. Brown spot develops best during cool, wet weather, reaching a peak in May or June.

Control: Resistant varieties, proper management-including balanced soil fertility and good surface drainage of the field.

E. NEMATODE DISEASES

There are many kinds of nematodes (root knot, cyst, lesion, sting, dagger, etc.) that attack many crops throughout the world. Ectoparasitic nematodes normally feed on the root surface. Endoparasitic nematodes normally enter root tissues and feed internally. Some nematode species are mobile within the plant after entry (migratory nematodes) or are stationary after entry (sedentary nematodes).

313

Root symptoms-appearance of knots, cysts, galls, lesions, excessive root branching, and injured or stunted roots (depending on nematode species).

Plant symptoms-stunted growth, nutrient deficiency symptoms, leaf yellowing, excessive wilting, and reduced yields.

Causal organism: Cyst nematode-*Heterodera* sp. and *Globodera* sp.
　　　　　　　Root Knot nematode-*Meloidogyne* sp.
　　　　　　　and many other species

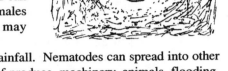

Type: Obligate parasite

Overwintering, spread, and infection: Nematodes are minute worm-like animals that reproduce by eggs, which hatch into larvae and mature into adult worms. Most nematodes live all or part of their life cycle in soil and can complete their life cycle in a few weeks under warm conditions. Females can lay 500 or more eggs. Larvae attack and infest roots. Eggs may remain dormant and overwinter in the soil for one or many years.
Nematodes can be splashed onto aerial plant parts by irrigation and rainfall. Nematodes can spread into other areas by transport of infested plant parts or soil from transportation of produce, machinery, animals, flooding, siltation, dust storms, etc..

Control: In some cases resistant varieties are available which prevent excessive damage from occurring. Long-term crop rotations using non-host crops may lower infestation of more susceptible crops. Fumigating soil, produce, bins, etc. with nematicides or sterilants can reduce nematode populations.

ADDITIONAL STUDY QUESTIONS

Crop Diseases

1. One type of crop damage by diseases is the production of a toxic or undesirable material. Name two diseases causing this type of damage.

2. Controlling a disease by the use of resistant crop varieties is a greater problem if the disease organism reproduces sexually. Can you think of a reason why this statement may be true?

3. Which of the following terms relate to fungi? bacteria? virus?

   single celled organisms-
   mycelium-
   not cellular in structure-
   asexual reproduction-
   sexual reproduction-

4. Would a short (2-year) rotation control corn stalk and ear rot? Why?

5. Why is the control of alternate hosts the major control method recommended for maize dwarf mosaic?

6. Why has early planting of early maturing varieties been a primary control measure for the rust diseases of small grains?

7. Why is phytophthora root rot of soybeans usually more of a problem in the eastern and southern portion of the North Central States than in the western portion?

8. A bag of wheat seed looks almost normal but has a "fishy" smell. What disease do you suspect is present and what further examination of the seed would you perform?

SELF-EVALUATION TEST

Crop Diseases

Circle letter corresponding to one best answer.

1. Wilting of diseased plants is often caused by
    a) loss of leaf area
    b) bacterial blight
    c) virus diseases
    d) destruction of the translocation system
    e) failure of the stomates to close

2. Planting early and using an early maturity variety would help "escape" damage from which disease?
    a) purple stain
    b) soybean mosaic
    c) bacterial blight
    d) maize dwarf mosaic
    e) stem rust

3. Leaf rust of wheat is a good example of
    a) an obligate parasite
    b) a saprophyte
    c) a facultative parasite
    d) a bacterial disease
    e) a facultative saprophyte

4. Multicellular organisms that produce threadlike strands called mycelium and may reproduce either sexually or asexual are known as
    a) angoumois
    b) nematodes
    c) virus
    d) fungi
    e) bacteria

5. Which of the following classes of diseases should be most easily controlled by crop rotations and destruction of alternate hosts?
    a) obligate parasites
    b) facultative saprophytes
    c) facultative parasites
    d) obligate saprophytes
    e) bacteria

6. Grasses growing beside Interstate highways are subjected to a higher level of lead than under normal growing conditions. If lead poisoning symptoms show up, this would be classified as a
    a) nutrient overdose
    b) pH toxicity
    c) non-infectious disease
    d) nutrient deficiency
    e) poisonous plant

7. Which of the following diseases does not damage soybeans?
   a) stem rust
   b) purple stain
   c) Phytophthora
   d) brown stem rot
   e) bacteria pustule

8. Seedling blights of maize are often more of a problem
   a) in droughty situations
   b) in sandy soil
   c) in cool, wet soil
   d) in rotations
   e) in warm, dry soil

9. Scald is a disease that damages
   a) alfalfa
   b) orchardgrass
   c) timothy
   d) maize
   e) red clover

10. Northern corn leaf blight
    a) has larger lesions than southern corn leaf blight
    b) damages corn with T cytoplasm to a greater extent
    c) is caused by a bacteria
    d) has smaller lesions than southern corn leaf blight
    e) is caused by a virus

11. Maize dwarf mosaic and soybean mosaic have the following in common
    a) Both are caused by a bacteria.
    b) Both have Johnsongrass as an alternate host.
    c) Both have alfalfa as an alternate host.
    d) Both are seed-borne.
    e) Both are caused by a virus.

12. Damping off of young seedlings is caused by
    a) pythium seed and seedling rot
    b) crown rust
    c) bacterial wilt
    d) brown stem rot
    e) stem rust

13. The following two diseases may produce substances poisonous to livestock
    a) stem rust and leaf rust
    b) pythium seed and seedling rot and phytophthora
    c) covered smut and loose smut
    d) ergot and corn ear rot
    e) barley yellow dwarf and scald

14. Stunted growth, nutrient deficiency symptoms, and galls on the roots are disease symptoms caused by
    a) brown spot
    b) bacteria
    c) fungus
    d) nematodes
    e) seed and seedling rot

Chapter 13

Crop Harvesting and Storage

Too often, potential yield is not realized because of poor timeliness and incorrect methods of harvest and storage. Understanding basic concepts affecting harvesting of crops can make the difference between profitable crop production and monetary loss. Major considerations in harvest and storage are determining the proper time and method. These two decisions greatly depend on the planned utilization of the crop. Consider the following table.

Table 1. Harvesting and Storage Goals Based on Crop Utilization

Crop	Use	Harvest and Storage Goals
Seed crops	For establishing new stands	Maximum yields of seed with high vigor and germination ability.
Grain crops	Livestock feeding	Maximum grain yields with high energy, protein, and nutrient balance.
Forage and Pasture crops	For ruminant livestock feeding	Maximum vegetative yield with a high protein and digestibility combination.
Special Purpose Crops		
Wheat	Breadmaking	High yields of high protein grain.
Barley	Brewing	High yields of grain with high germinability. High starch and low protein content.
Sugarbeets and Sugarcane	Sugar	Maximum sugar per unit area (optimum tonnage X percent sugar combination).
Cotton	Fiber	Maximum yields of strong, white, trash-free lint with long fibers.

Consider the following:

1. How might harvesting and/or storage operations differ for

    a. alfalfa grown for forage versus alfalfa grown for seed?

    b. barley grown for feed versus barley grown for brewing?

    c. corn grown for silage versus corn grown for grain?

I. CROP MATURITY CONCEPTS

The optimum dates and methods of harvesting and storing crops also depend on crop maturity. The proper maturity stage for harvest and storage of one crop species may be too early or too late for another crop species. Crop maturity can be classified into different stages as crops mature and plant moisture is lost. Thus, maturity classifications are frequently described by the percent moisture of the plant or harvestable product. The following concepts of crop plant maturity are important to understand crop harvest and storage management.

> Using Figure 1, study the relationship of moisture to maturity.

A. Physiological Maturity - Refers to the stage of development when the plant reaches maximum dry weight. In most instances, physiological maturity refers to maximum dry weight of the total plant. However, in grain crops the term physiological maturity is often associated with maximum dry weight in the seeds.

1. Grains stop the accumulation of dry weight when they are at approximately 40% moisture. However, this may vary by 5 to 10% depending on the crop species and variety. The effects of harvesting grain before physiological maturity are lower yield, lower quality due to lower starch content, shriveled kernels and lower test weight.

B. Harvest Maturity -   Refers to the stage of a plant's development at which harvesting will produce the best combination of yield and quality.

1. **Grain crops**
    The moisture content at which grain reaches harvest maturity varies considerably, depending on the crop being harvested and the harvesting machine used. For instance, the ideal harvest maturity of corn (maize) being harvested with a corn combine or picker-sheller may be 26-28% moisture, while soybeans usually cannot be efficiently harvested with a combine until the moisture content is 16-18% or below. For direct combining of small grain crops, the harvest moisture of the grain is frequently 14% or lower to avoid drying costs and allow safe storage of grain.
    Some of the effects of harvesting grain after physiological maturity but before proper harvest maturity could be mechanical damage to the kernels, which are high in moisture and swollen; spoilage in storage if proper drying facilities are not available; and loss in yield due to inability of the harvesting machine to harvest all of the kernels.
    Delaying harvest after grain has reached the proper stage may result in loss of yield due to seed or ear loss and stalk lodging. Loss in quality may result from lower bushel weight, lower germinability, and deteriorated grain because of field weathering.

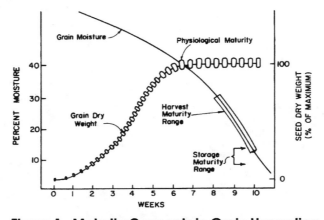

Figure 1. Maturity Concepts in Grain Harvesting

318

2. Hay crops

Color, leafiness, protein content, and digestibility are affected by the stage of maturity at which grasses and legumes are cut for hay. An example of the influence of maturity differences on digestibility of forage is illustrated in Figure 2.

An important item to note is that hay quality as indicated by digestible dry matter (DDM), intake and crude protein decreases with delayed harvest. However, a higher total hay yield often results from some delay in harvest. Thus, the yield-quality combination becomes the important aspect. Another important point in determining the stage of development at which to harvest forages, especially those which will be harvested several times in a season, is maintenance of a stand. The harvest dates should be timed to provide some insurance against the loss of stands. This involves delaying harvest until there is an adequate supply of storage carbohydrates in the storage organs of the plant and harvesting after new growth has begun to develop from the buds in the leaf axils or crown area of the plant.

3. Silage crops

Silage can be made from crops which are commonly considered to be grain crops and also from other forage crops. Therefore, the stage of crop maturity for cutting varies widely.

a.   Grain crop silage-The maturity of corn that would give the best quality-yield combination would be the dent stage, that stage when the kernels dent (at black layer), indicating a large amount of carbohydrates in the grain. The best stage for silage harvest varies with crops:

sorghum-medium to hard dough stage
oats-soft dough stage
barley, wheat-milk stage

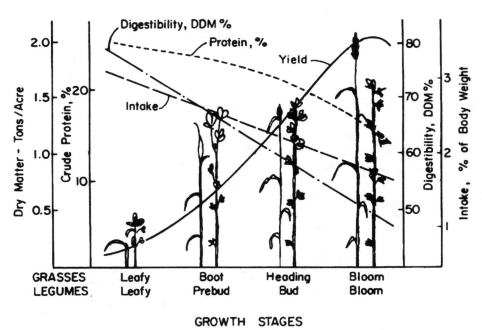

Adapted from R. E. Blaser, et. al., "Challenges in Developing Forage—Analysis Systems", American Forage and Grassland Council, 1980 Conference Proceedings—Louisville, KY.

Figure 2.   For a given species or mixture, growth stage influences digestible dry matter intake and output of meat or milk per head more than any other factor. Crude protein, digestibility and intake decline as herbaceous forage plants become stemmy. Thus, leafy pastures give higher gains per head than hay.

b. **Hay crop silage**-Hay crop silage can be made from any crop from which hay is made. Alfalfa, alfalfa-grass mixtures, sudangrass, and sudangrass-sorghum hybrids are examples. The stage of plant development for cutting hay crop silage would be similar to that for cutting hay (i.e., the best quality-yield combination).

C. Storage Maturity

Refers to plant development or moisture content of plant material related to the probability of maintaining a high quality product in storage. The condition of the plant product that can be safely stored depends to a great extent on the storage facilities (i.e., airtight storage and drying facilities).

1. **Grain storage**-Unless drying facilities are available, grain is safe for storage only if the moisture content is below 14%. Storage at higher moisture contents results in excess respiration, heating, spoilage, and grain quality deterioration.

2. **Forage crop storage**-Forages can be stored as wet silage, regular silage, low moisture silage, or hay. Descriptions of these possible forage uses depending on moisture content are given in Table 2.

Table 2. Possible uses of forage based on moisture content

Moisture content %	Possible use	Previous harvest management
70-80	Wet silage	direct cut
60-70	Regular silage	cut and wilted
40-60	Low moisture silage (haylage)	cut and wilted
25 or lower	Hay	cut and allowed to dry

II. HARVESTING AND STORING GRAIN CROPS

A. Harvest Method

Grain harvesting operations usually involve cutting the plants, threshing and removing the seed from the inflorescence and separating and cleaning dirt and chaff from the seed. The most common machine for harvesting grain in the U.S. is the "combine" which combines cutting, threshing, separating and cleaning into one operation. The combine can be equipped with specially designed headers (cutting and gathering units) to reduce grain loss for different crops. For example, a combine can be equipped with a specially designed header to harvest small stemmed crops and those grown in narrow rows or solid stands, such as soybeans and small grains. The same combine equipped with a different header can be used to harvest individual rows of maize.

Note the various harvesting operations in the combine (Figure 3).

Proper combine operation minimizes losses and damage of grain during harvesting. Improper ground and reel speeds, improper cutting height and dull cutting sickles can cause the loss of grain at the front of the combine while improper sieve setting and fan speeds can cause grain loss in the rear of the combine. The threshing action is done through the beating action of the rotating cylinder. Improper cylinder spacing and clearance can result in incomplete threshing (too wide) or damaged kernels (too narrow).

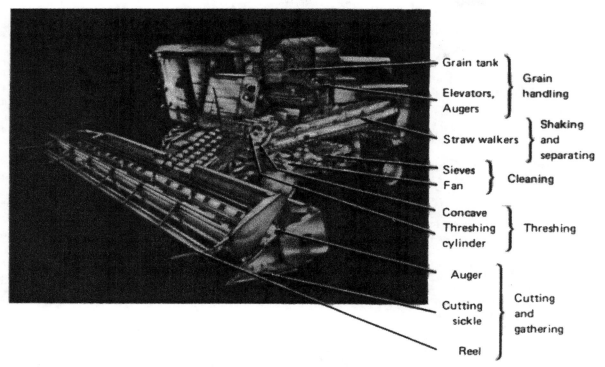

Figure 3. Basic operations of a combine

B. Methods Facilitating Grain Harvest

Allowing crops to unnecessarily remain in the field after physiological maturity can result in harvest losses, both in quantity and quality of yields. Therefore, several methods of facilitating grain harvest have been explored. Some of these are the following:

1. Combining method

Two general methods of combining grain crops are combining standing crops (direct combining) and combining windrowed crops.

    a. Direct combining-Combine harvesting of grain crops that remain standing in the field. Widely used for crops that dry down to harvest maturity in the field, for wide row crops, such as maize and soybeans, and for narrow row or solid seeded stands of wheat, rice, and other small grains when varieties and conditions permit the crop to remain standing until harvest.

    b. Windrow/Combining-A windrower (swather) cuts and places the crop in windrows 2 or more days before combining. A combine equipped with a windrow pick-up attachment is used to feed the grain into the combine. This method is widely used for crops that need additional curing time after cutting for effective combining. It is used for harvesting some forage crops for seed that are ready when the vegetative plant material is still green or for weedy fields where green, high moisture weeds might interfere with normal combine operation. This method also allows one to cut the crop several days earlier than if direct combining, which helps reduce grain loss from plant lodging and pre-mature seed droppage. The more uniform curing of windrowed crops also helps reduce grain damage during combining. This method is frequently used for small grains, forage seed crops, and some edible grain legumes.

2. Chemical aided harvest

Chemical defoliants or desiccants can be used to reduce the amount of green juicy vegetative matter of the crop or from weeds than can interfere with combine operation and reduce product quality.

a. Definitions:

Defoliant- A material that, when applied to plants, causes the leaves to separate and drop from the plant.

Desiccant- A material that causes the plant to dry out and to die.

Defoliation and desiccation have been quite helpful in facilitating the harvest of some crops. For instance, the correct use of chemical defoliants on cotton reduces moisture, objectionable green stains on fibers, and trash from picked cotton. They also facilitate mechanical harvesting of alfalfa seed by reducing the leaf material on the plant and in other crops that have green weeds at harvest time.

3. Different curing and storage systems

Changing the type of curing and storage allows earlier harvesting of some crops:

a. **Airtight storage**-Storage systems that are airtight or those that develop anaerobic conditions allow the plant to be harvested earlier. Airtight structures are involved in high moisture grain storage. Grain of 25-30% moisture is stored in an airtight structure.

b. **Crop drying**-Grains may be dried before or during storage. The rate of grain moisture loss in the field varies with environment and varieties. Waiting until the grain is dry enough for safe storage can result in losses in yield and quality. With drying facilities the crop can be harvested early and later dried to safe storage moisture levels.

C. Grain Storage

Proper storage minimizes losses due to grain respiration, spoilage, molds, heating and insects. Two major factors that must be controlled to ensure proper storage are temperature and moisture.

Observe the relationships of moisture and temperature in grain storage in Figure 4.

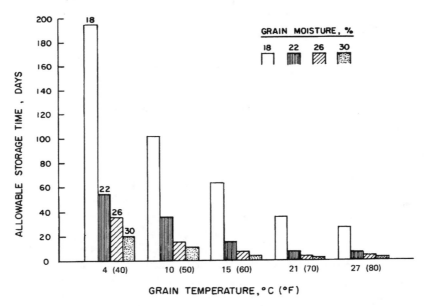

Adapted from L. Van Fossen and D. Hull, *Batch and Continuous Dryers For Shelled Corn*, Pm-382. Cooperative Extension Service, Iowa State University. Data from USDA Corn Harvesting and Conditioning Investigations.

Figure 4. Allowable holding time for field-shelled corn at various grain temperatures and moisture contents without excessive deterioration of grain.

It is evident in Figure 4 that high temperatures and high moisture of grain reduces the allowable storage time. Furthermore, high temperatures and moisture during storage can reduce grain quality:

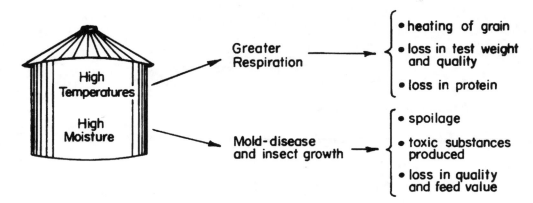

There are several options to help prevent storage problems from occurring:

1. Use air-tight storage-Respiration and spoilage are reduced due to the absence of oxygen.

2. Dry grain to a safe moisture level for storage-retards mold and disease growth. Some precautions concerning drying temperatures should be observed depending on the planned use of the grain:

   a. Grain to be used for planting seed-The drying temperature should not be above 43°C (110°F).

   b. Grain to be used for processed products such as starch and flour for bread making-the drying temperature should not exceed 57° to 60°C (135° to 140°F). Drying at higher temperatures causes changes in the starches and proteins of the grain, resulting in lower quality products.

   c. Grain to be used for livestock feed-present information shows no significant loss in feeding value from drying grain at temperatures up to 88°C (190°F).

3. Use proper ventilation in non-airtight storage-this helps prevent temperature and moisture build-up (Figure 5).

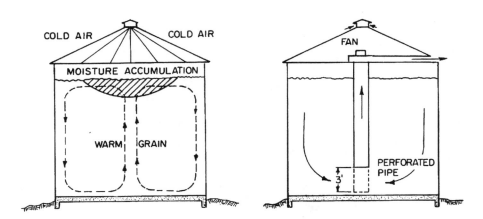

Figure 5. Movement of air and moisture through grain in an unventilated bin (left) and fan ventilated bin (right). Adapted from J. D. Frus, *Aeration of Stored Grain*, Pm-407. Cooperative Extension Service Iowa State University.

1. What is physiological maturity in grain crops? What justification is there in delaying harvest after physiological maturity?

2. What is an important guideline when drying grain for livestock feed versus for planting seed?

3. How does delayed harvest reduce the quality of a forage crop such as alfalfa?

4. Why would airtight storage prevent high temperature buildup in grain?

III. HARVESTING AND STORING FORAGES

Some general methods of harvesting forages include harvesting as hay, silage, greenchop, and pasture.

A. Hay

Hay refers to forages that have been cut and dried for livestock feed. At present most hay is harvested and stored as baled hay. However, some hay is handled as long, loose hay, and some is field chopped.

1. **Baled hay**-Hay baled into pressed "packages" varying from 16 to 1135 kg (35 to 2500 lbs) is the most common method of hay storage. Hay can be baled and stored at moisture percentages up to 25%. Harvest operations usually include mowing and curing hay, raking hay into windrows and baling. Baling hay in round or square bales of 16 to 36 kg (35 to 80 lbs) was traditionally a popular method of harvesting hay but was labor intensive. Efforts to mechanize hay harvesting resulted in the widespread use of large round bales of up to 1135 kg (2500 lbs) in size.

Note the steps in hay harvesting presented below.

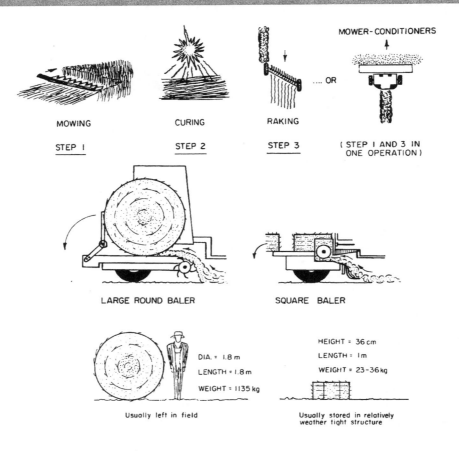

MOWING — STEP 1

CURING — STEP 2

RAKING — STEP 3

MOWER-CONDITIONERS
(STEP 1 AND 3 IN ONE OPERATION)

.... OR

LARGE ROUND BALER

SQUARE BALER

DIA. = 1.8 m
LENGTH = 1.8 m
WEIGHT = 1135 kg

Usually left in field

HEIGHT = 36 cm
LENGTH = 1 m
WEIGHT = 23-36 kg

Usually stored in relatively weather tight structure

2. **Stacked hay**-Before the development of balers, most hay was handled in this manner. Hay was cut, cured (dried), windrowed and placed in buildings or in stacks (Figure 6) on the field. Mechanized stackers which compress hay into stacks has been developed and used in some areas. Stacks may vary in size from .9 to 5 metric tons (1 to 6 tons) or more .

USUALLY LEFT IN THE
FIELD

Figure 6. Hay Stack

3. **Field chopped hay**-This method allows complete mechanization of hay harvesting by reducing hay particle sizes to a size which can be moved by air (Figure 7). Chopped hay can usually be stored safely at moisture contents of 22 percent or lower. Chopped hay may also be ensiled or fed directly to livestock (greenchop).

Figure 7. Harvesting hay with a forage harvester (forage chopper)

4. **Additional methods used in harvesting hay**-The amount of time required for field curing of hay can be reduced by use of a mechanical hay conditioner, artificial hay drying, and by forage dehydration:

   a. Hay conditioners are designed to crush or break the plant stems so they will dry faster. Use of conditioners often results in the drying time being reduced by 50 percent. The faster drying allows the crop to be stored with less weathering, resulting in higher quality hay.

   b. Artificial hay drying-The hay is allowed to dry to 35 to 40 percent moisture in the field, is baled, and then artificially dried in the storage structure. The system allows for a high quality product because the cut hay is removed from the field in a shorter period than in traditional hay operations.

   c. Forage dehydration-The forage is chopped and immediately put through a rotary drum drier (760-815°C (1400-1500°F) which dehydrates the hay in a few minutes. A high quality product results from this system. Farmers may sell their hay crop, especially alfalfa, to a dehydration plant which may package the hay into small pellets.

B. Silage

Silage (ensilage) refers to forage crops which have been preserved in a succulent condition by fermentation in the absence of air (anaerobic conditions). Although maize and sorghum are the two crops that have been commonly used as silage, most crops used for forage purposes can be satisfactorily stored in a silo. Storing forages as silage offers several advantages:

1) Harvesting and feeding operations can be mechanized.
2) Harvesting is less dependent on weather conditions than haymaking because little or no drying time is needed for silage.
3) Silage is usually higher in quality than hay harvested under similar conditions.

1. **Preservation (Ensiling) process**-The following major steps take place during the ensiling process of converting green forage to silage, which can be stored in a preserved condition:

   a. 4 to 5 hours-Plant cells and aerobic bacteria deplete the "free oxygen" in the silo through respiration. Thus anaerobic conditions are created.

   b. 3 to 4 days-Under anaerobic conditions, lactic acid-forming bacteria have increased to several million per gram of silage. These anaerobic bacteria begin converting glucose sugar to lactic acid. As lactic acid accumulates, the pH of the forage material decreases. The following chemical reaction shows the small energy loss in converting glucose to lactic acid.

   (673 kilocalories)   (652 kilocalories)

   $$C_6H_{12}O_6 \xrightarrow{\text{(3.1\% loss)}} 2(C_3H_6O_3)$$

   glucose   lactic acid

   c. 12 days-Although some acid production may take place later, the silage preservation process is essentially completed within 12 to 15 days. The pH has dropped from about 5.5 to 6.5 in freshly chopped forage to approximately 3.6 to 4.6 in good silage. The relatively high acidity of finished silage helps prevent the growth of molds and other organisms, which can spoil moist forage during storage.

2. **Silage quality**- Good quality silage has a pleasant alcoholic odor and tastes sour. Poor quality silage often has a strong odor because of its high content of ammonia, volatile fatty acids (especially butyric acid), hydrogen sulfide, and other odoriferous compounds. Figure 8 illustrates the organic acid content in good versus poor quality silages.

Note the relative amounts of lactic acid as compared to butyric acid in the good versus poor quality silage in Figure 8.

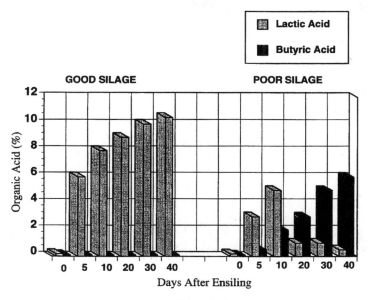

Figure 8

Adapted from Langston et al., Microbiology and Chemistry of Grass Silage. USDA Tech. Bull. 1187

The conversion of lactic acid to volatile fatty acids, such as butyric acid, also results in an additional energy loss in feeding value:

$$2(C_3H_6O_3) \xrightarrow{\text{(19.6\% loss)}} C_4H_8O_2 + 2CO_2 + 2H_2$$

(652 calories)   (524 calories)

lactic acid   butyric acid

a. Reasons for low quality silage:

   1) Low quality of the forage material being stored (e.g., cut at wrong stage of development or containing foreign matter).

   2) Material stored with a high moisture content such as fresh cut forage grasses and legumes (75 percent or above)-This material contains less food material per pound and may result in more objectionable acids being formed since the carbohydrate percentage is lower and an acceptable low pH may not be developed.

   3) Material stored with a low moisture content-Forages with moisture percentages below 60 percent may not develop anaerobic conditions unless stored in airtight structures. Therefore, formation of molds and low quality silage results.

b. Ways of improving silage quality:

   1) Silage additives-Additives such as acids or materials which will be converted to acids are often used to help ensure preservation.

   2) Ground grains and molasses-These materials increase the carbohydrate content of chopped forages such as forage legumes and grasses. The greater carbohydrate content is used for bacterial fermentation and may result in a higher quality silage.

3) Fine chopping and compaction of the plant material-These two precautions in silage making are probably the best insurance of producing a high quality feed. Excluding the air is very important in silage making.

4) Wilting forage legumes and grasses-Silage made from direct cut forage legumes and grasses is high in moisture (usually above 75 percent) and is usually high in protein. The high moisture results in low carbohydrate concentration. Therefore a desirable pH is often not achieved. In addition, the organisms which break down the proteins cause odoriferous low quality silage. The quality of legume and grass silage can often be improved by wilting the forage to a desirable moisture content (60-70 percent) before chopping and storage.

3. **Storing silage**-Silage is usually stored in upright or horizontal silos.

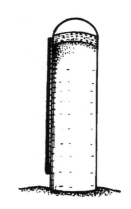

a. Upright (tower) silos-Size can vary, with some silos holding more than 907 metric tons (1000 tons) of silage. Some models of upright silos are airtight. Storage losses are usually lowest with upright silos.

b. Horizontal silos-Width and length of horizontal silos vary widely and they may hold up to 4536 metric tons (5000 tons) or more. Three types are commonly found:

1) Bunker silos- The floor is usually built at ground level with concrete or wood sidewalls extending above ground.

Bunker Silo

2) Trench silos- The floor and sidewalls are located below the ground level.

Trench Silo

3) Stack silos- Silage is simply packed in outside stacks,using no sidewalls and requiring no silo construction. Plastic is commonly used to cover the stack to reduce the spoilage. Although least expensive, stack silos are usually the most inefficient storage method. Storage losses may average 20 percent or more for uncovered or exposed stacks..

Stack Silo

4. **Silage Safety**

Caution should be used when working near or in silos. The ensiling process is an anaerobic process that consumes oxygen and replaces it with carbon dioxide, a suffocating gas. Carbon dioxide is heavier than air and accumulates in low places in the silo. Nitrogen dioxide (silage gas) is also a natural product of the ensiling process and is toxic at concentrations that are too low to be identified by sight or smell (25 ppm). Nitrogen dioxide is yellow-brown and has a "bleach" odor at high and extremely toxic levels (100 ppm). Some important precautions to prevent injury and death are:

a. Stay away from the silo right after filling and the following day. Be careful for 10-14 days after filling.

b. Be alert for signs of bleachlike odors and yellowish-brown fumes. Also, realize that gas toxicity and suffocation dangers exist that cannot be detected by sight or smell.

c. Be extremely cautious near unventilated silage. Thoroughly and forcibly vent and remove air in confined silage to remove dangerous air pockets. Operate the blower for 20 minutes before entering. Never enter a silo alone during the danger period.

d. If exposed to silage gas, seek medical treatment to prevent lung damage and pneumonia.

C. Grazing

Grazing land refers to any land with vegetation that is grazed by livestock. The growth from much of our forage and range crops is harvested directly by grazing livestock. The advantages of grazing include: 1) source of green succulent feed, 2) harvesting costs are minimized, 3) forage can be utilized on land too steep for mechanical operations, and 4) livestock are not confined in a small area, so sanitary conditions are usually easy to maintain.

The major disadvantage of grazing is that the amount of dry matter harvested per hectare is less than if the forage was cut for greenchop, hay, or silage.

1. **Kinds of grazing lands**-Grazing lands may be divided into two major types: range lands (natural grasslands) and pasture lands (improved or "tame" pastures).

   a. Rangeland (natural grassland) is usually relatively undeveloped land in which native plant species are used as forage for grazing livestock. A major portion of the rangeland of the United States is in the western and southern states. They are found in areas that are unsuited for grain crops or improved pastures because of topography, low soil fertility, lack of precipitation, and poor drainage.

   b. Pastureland (improved or "tame" pastures) most commonly refers to land that had been tilled and where native species were replaced by introduced species. The term "pasture" is used to describe a confined or fenced grazing area. Pastures can be further described as permanent, rotational, and supplemental pastures.

      1) Permanent pastures are usually seeded to perennial plants or annuals which reseed themselves and are kept indefinitely for grazing. They are usually found on land that is unsuited for use in a crop rotation system.

      2) Rotational pastures may be seeded to perennials or annuals but fit into a rotation system and have other crops growing on the fields in other years. Rotational pastures are usually tilled and planted to other crops at least once every five years.

      3) Supplemental pastures are used to furnish forage for livestock during periods when permanent or rotational pastures are lacking. Crops used for supplemental pasturing include annuals such as small grains, sudangrass (or sudangrass-sorghum hybrids), rape, lespedeza, and crimson clover or biennials such as sweetclover.

2. **Grazing management**-Grazing management refers to the management of the grazing animals and includes the consideration of number of animals per unit of land (stocking density) per unit of grazing time (stocking rate or grazing intensity) and type of grazing (controlled or uncontrolled). Grazing systems may range from zero grazing to continuous grazing. Four grazing systems are compared in probable liveweight steer gains per hectare in Figure 9.

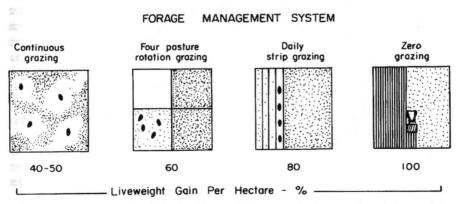

Figure 9. **Steer gains per hectare in four fresh forage management systems. Zero grazing (green chop) is considered to be 100 percent efficient.**

a. Zero grazing (greenchop)-In this system the forage is chopped and immediately transported to the live-stock. This system is used more often on rotational and supplemental pastures than on permanent pastures. The highest production of livestock per hectare should be possible using this management. However, it does involve more harvesting expense than other systems. Greenchop is usually used only in larger operations in which a large number of livestock are fed.

b. Rotational grazing (rotational stocking)-This system involves subdividing pastures into units called paddocks and the livestock are shifted from one paddock to the next as needed. Strip grazing is inten-sified rotational grazing in which the animals are moved daily or weekly. Rotational grazing usually results in more production per hectare than continuous grazing.

c. Continuous grazing (continuous stocking)-In this system livestock remain on a given acreage and have unrestricted and uninterrupted access to forage throughout the grazing season. Continuous grazing is most frequently used on permanent, improved pastures and rangeland. Harvesting costs are low using continuous grazing. However, production per hectare is probably lower than the previously discussed systems.

d. Deferred grazing-Forage growth is allowed to accumulate (this is called stockpiling forage) by delay-ing grazing to some later date. This method can extend the normal grazing season of a species or pro-vide extra grazing during unfavorable growth periods. It is often used for fall and winter grazing.

1. If hay from the second harvest of a 4 hectare (10-acre) field yielded 800 23 kg. (50 lb.) bales, what would be the equivalent number of large round bales?

2. How can hay conditioners improve hay quality?

3. What is the likely cause of silage that had mold throughout the interior of the stack?

4. What changes occur during the first 4 to 5 hours of the ensiling process?

5. Why is it usually more difficult to produce high quality silage from grass-legume crops than from grain crops?

6. How do rotational pastures differ from supplemental pastures?

7. Define:

greenchop

rotational grazing

strip grazing

SELF-EVALUATION

Crop Harvesting and Storage

Circle letter corresponding to one best answer.

1. The most economical way to make high quality silage from alfalfa is

    a) to add lime to the silage
    b) to add water when filling the silo
    c) to add sugar-forming materials to the silage
    d) to allow the plant material to wilt in the field
    e) to store the silage in a broad trench to allow aeration

2. Which of the following grazing management practices involves the most harvesting expense?

    a) zero grazing
    b) rotational grazing
    c) continuous grazing
    d) maximum grazing
    e) intermittent grazing

3. Harvest maturity for grain crops is most dependent upon

    a) plant age
    b) plant weight
    c) seed moisture content
    d) plant species
    e) plant location

4. The major portion of the breakdown of carbohydrates in silage is the result of

    a) high nitrogen content
    b) anaerobic respiration
    c) excess acid
    d) excess sugar
    e) transpiration

5. Seed to be used for planting purposes should never be artificially dried at temperatures exceeding

    a) 10°C (50°F)
    b) 32°C (90°F)
    c) 43°C (110°F)
    d) 63°C (145°F)
    e) 88°C (190°F)

6. Grazing the material from a pasture

    a) improves the quality of harvested feed
    b) costs more to harvest than other methods
    c) is an important contribution to pollution
    d) results in less harvest loss than other methods
    e) results in less dry matter harvested per hectare than harvesting as greenchop

331

7. Percent protein in forages

   a) increases in grasses with plant age
   b) does not change with plant age
   c) decreases with plant age
   d) increases in grasses as seeds are produced
   e) increases in legume plants with age

8. Permanent pasture

   a) refers to unrestricted and uninterrupted access to forage by livestock throughout the growing season
   b) refers to the number of animals per unit of pastureland
   c) are usually found on land that is suitable for row crops
   d) usually have introduced and improved forage species
   e) are usually divided into paddocks

9. The moisture content of most grains at the time of storage, without artificial drying should be

   a) 12% to 14%
   b) 16% to 18%
   c) 18% to 22%
   d) 22% to 24%
   e) 26% to 28%

10. A defoliant

   a) is a weed killer
   b) is a stem killer
   c) causes leaves to drop
   d) kills leaves
   e) increases moisture in plants

11. Kernels that are damaged and broken during the combine harvesting operation are the result of

   a) improper ground speed
   b) improper reel speed
   c) improper cylinder spacing and clearance
   d) improper sieve setting
   e) dull cutting sickles

12. Grain spoilage in an unventilated bin is most likely to occur initially

   a) in the top, center portion of the bin
   b) in the lower center portion of the bin
   c) in the middle center portion of the bin
   d) along the upper side walls of the bin
   e) along the lower side walls of the bin

Glossary

Allele, 186: One of the forms of a gene that may be located at a particular locus (position) in homologous chromosomes.

Anatomy, 1: A study of plant structure with an emphasis on tissues and their components within a plant body.

Anther, 20,23: The sac like structure containing the pollen of a flower.

Arid, 100: A humidity province receiving less than 25 cm of precipitation per year.

Auricle, 14,44: Appendages of the leaf sheath located at the basil end of the sheath near the leaf collar of grass leaves. Auricles may vary in shape and size or may be absent in grass leaves.

Axillary buds, 9: Buds located in the junction of the leaf petiole and the stem.

Azospirillum, 87: A genus of aerobic symbiotic bacteria capable of fixing atmospheric nitrogen.

Azotobacter, 87: Aerobic, heterotrophic bacteria of the genus *Azotobacter* found as nonsymbiotic nitrogen fixers in the soil.

Blue-green algae, 37,87: A class of algae in which the chlorophyll is masked by bluish pigments.

Boerner divider, 225: A device to divide samples of grain into equal halves.

Branch roots, 19: Roots that are formed from the pericycle.

Breed true, 197: Reproducing itself exactly, such as would occur when a homozygous plant is self-pollinated.

C4 plants, 83: Plants that have C4 photosynthesis where the first stable product fanned is a 4-carbon compound.

C3 plants, 83: Plants that have C3 photosynthesis where the first stable product formed is a 3-carbon compound.

Calyx, 23: The collective term for sepals of a flower.

Canopy, 78: The space above the ground surface that is occupied by the aerial portion of plants.

Cardinal temperatures, 102: The minimum, optimum, and maximum growth temperatures of a crop.

Caryopsis, 3: A fruit typical of cereals and grasses in which the seed coat fuses with the ovary wall during its development.

Cell, 1: The fundamental structural and physiological unit of a plant or animal organism.

Chloroplast, 2,12: An organelle in the cell which contains chlorophyll where light energy is changed into chemical energy (photosynthesis).

Chromosome, 186: A structural unit of the nucleus that carries the genes in a linear sequence.

Clostridium, 87: Spore-forming anaerobic bacteria found in soil and animal intestinal tracts.

Collar, 14: The junction area of the sheath and blade of a grass leaf.

Complete flowers, 23: Flowers that contain the corolla, calyx, male and female parts,

Corolla, 23: The collective term for the petals of a flower.

Corolla tube, 23: Fused portion of the petals in a legume flower.

Cortex, 19: The primary tissue of a stem or root between the epidermis and phloem in the stem or between the epidermis and pericycle in the root.

Crown area, 89: A general term usually referring to the basal area of plants near the soil surface.

Crude protein, 319: An estimate of the percent protein on a dry weight basis in feeds.

Cultivar, 185: A group of individuals within a species developed by plant breeding methods, that are unique in characteristics and/or functions. Variety is commonly used to denote cultivar.

Curing hay, 324: The drying of mowed hay to a moisture content low enough for handling and storage.

Dioecious, 20: Plants of species that have imperfect flowers with male and female flowers on separate plants.

Diseases-Infectious, 297: Diseases caused by a biological organism. Also called "biotic" diseases.

Diseases-Non-infectious, 297: Diseases caused by some pathogenic factor in the environment. Also called "abiotic" and "physiological" diseases.

Diploid, 186: The condition in which a cell, or an individual, has two sets (genomes) of chromosomes; the nonreduced number (2n) as in a zygote.

Dominant, 186: An allele or character that, when in a heterozygous situation, expresses itself to the exclusion of its contrasting allele or character.

Donor parent, 200: The parent from which one, or a few genes are transferred to the recurrent parent in the backcross method of breeding.

Double cross (four-way cross), 203: The cross pollination of two single crosses.

Double fertilization, 188: Refers to the two fertilization steps in seed formation where the 1) egg and sperm unite to form the zygote and 2) second sperm unites with the two polar nuclei to form the endosperm.

Drilling, 175: A widely used term referring to seeding with a grain drill and should not be confused with planting with a row crop planter in a drill pattern.

Embryo axis, 4,7: The seed tissue made up of the embryonic root and shoot.

Ensilage, 326: Another term for silage. The process of converting green forage to silage is called ensiling.

F$_1$, F$_2$, etc., 189: The notation that is used to indicate the first generation, second generation, etc. following hybridization.

Fertilization, 188: The fusion of the egg nucleus (In) and the sperm nucleus (in) to form the 2n nucleus of the zygote.

Filament, 20,23: The stalk-like tissue supporting the anther.

Four-way cross (double cross), 203: The cross pollination of two single crosses.

Gametogenesis, 188: Formation of male and female gametes.

Gene, 186: The unit of inheritance; located at a fixed position (locus) in a chromosome. It affects or controls the development of a character and can exist in alternate forms (alleles).

Generative nucleus, 188: One of two nuclei of the pollen grain. The nucleus that gives rise to the two sperm nuclei.

Genome, 187: A set of chromosomes obtained from a parent. A diploid individual has 2 sets (genomes), one from each parent.

Genetic engineering (gene transfer, gene splicing, recombinant DNA technology), 205: The process of identification, duplication, and insertion of genes or pieces of DNA from one genome into another.

Germination (Warm) test, 214: Estimates the maximum percentage of seed capable of developing healthy seedlings.

Glabrous, 14: Smooth; without pubescence (hairlike structures).

Greenhouse effect, 109: The temperature buildup in the atmosphere due to the trapping of infrared (heat) radiation emitted from earth.

Gynoecium, 20,23: Commonly referred to as the pistil or female portion of the flower.

Haploid, 186: The condition in which a cell, or an individual, has a single set (genome) of chromosomes; the reduced number (n) as occurs in a gamete.

Haylage, 320: Silage that has been stored at low moisture contents (40-60%).

Heterogeneous, 189: The plants within a population differ.

Heterozygous, 187: Having unlike alleles at a locus on the homologous chromosomes.

Homogeneous, 189: All plants within a population are identical.

Homologous chromosomes (homologs), 187: Chromosomes that pair during meiosis.

Homozygous, 187: Having like alleles at a locus on homologous chromosomes.

Humid, 100: A humidity province receiving 75 to 100 cm of precipitation per year.

Humidity province, 98: Areas of the world classified on the basis of the precipitation.

Hybrid, 189: The first generation product (Fl) of a cross (hybridization) between genetically dissimilar parents.

Hybridization, 194: See hybrid. One of the three principal methods of plant breeding.

Incomplete flowers, 20: Flowers that lack either a corolla, calyx, male or female parts.

Inflorescence, 20-27: The flowering part of the plant.

Inoculant, 87: Any material used for inoculation purposes (usually applied to the seed).

Intercalcary meristem, 18: An area of actively dividing cells located at the base of each node that stimulates internode elongation in grasses.

Introduction, 193: See plant introduction.

Leaf morphology, 14: The external structure and form of plant leaves.

Leafbud characteristics (vernation), 14: Refers to the structural arrangement of newly formed leaves that are not yet visibly emerged from the main part of the plant. Young leaves may develop and emerge in a folded or rolled characteristic.

Leaflet, 15: The individual component, or the blade, of a compound leaf.

Lemma, 20 . The outer and lower bract of a grass floret lying next to the caryopsis.

Ligule, 14,44: A membranous or hairy projection on the inner side of the leaf at the junction of the sheath and blade. Present in many grasses but also may be absent.

Locus (plural=loci), 186: The position of a particular gene in a chromosome.

Megaspore, 188: One of four haploid (1n) cells produced from the meiotic division of the megaspore mother cell.

Megaspore mother cell, 188: A diploid (2n) cell in the ovary that, through meiosis gives rise to four haploid (1n) nuclei.

Meiosis, 187: A process in the reproductive steps of a sexually reproducing plant in which two successive nuclear divisions reduce the diploid (2n) chromosome number to the haploid (1n).

Microspore, 188: One of the four haploid (1n) cells produced from the meiotic division of the microspore mother cell

Microspore mother cell, 188: A diploid (2n) cell in the anther that, through meiosis, gives rise to four haploid (1n) nuclei.

Mitosis (mitotic division), 187: A division in which the nucleus is divided into two nuclei having equivalent chromosome complements.

Monoecious, 20: Plants having imperfect flowers with the male and female flowers in different locations on the same plant.

Mower-conditioner, 324: An implement that is designed to mow hay and to crush or break plant stems so that they will dry faster. The implement may or may not leave the hay in windrows.

Multiple Cropping, 40: Growing 2 or more crops on the same field within the same year or growing season.

Nodule, 9,87: A swelling (tubercle) formed on legume roots by symbiotic nitrogen-fixing bacteria.

Osmotic potential, 136: The potential energy of water as influenced by solute (salt) concentration. Solutes lower the potential energy of water.

Ovary, 20,23: The maternal tissue that surrounds and contains the ovules in a flower.

Ovule, 8,20,23: The reproductive part that contains the embryo sac, including an egg cell, and its internal tissue.

Palea, 21,22: The inner and upper bract of the grass floret lying next to the caryopsis.

Panicle branch, 26: The stalk that connects the pedicel and the rachis, in a panicle inflorescence.

Pedicel, 23,26: The stalk that supports the individual flower in an inflorescence.

Perhumid, 100: A humidity province receiving in excess of 100 cm of precipitation per year.

Perianth, 23: The collective term for the calyx and corolla combined.

Pericycle, 19: A specialized layer of tissues that encircles the vascular system in roots. This area gives rise to branch roots.

Pesticides: A general term referring to chemicals developed to control weed and insect pests and disease pathogens.

Petiole, 15: The stalk that supports a leaf.

Petiolule, 15: The stalk that supports a leaflet in a compound leaf.

Photosynthate, 13: The simple products of photosynthesis (sugars).

Pith, 16: The placental portion of a stem made up of parenchymatous tissue.

Pit, 16: The placental portion of a stem made up of parenchymatous tissue.

Plant growth regulators, 72: Organic substances found in minute amounts in plants that regulate plant growth and development.

Plant introduction, 193: The transport of plants, seeds or vegetative propagating materials from one area into another. One of the three principal methods of plant breeding.

Plumule (epicotyl), 4: The embryonic leaves and shoot in seed and young seedling tissue.

Pollination (pollinate), 188: The transfer of pollen from the anther to the stigma.

    cross, 198: The transfer of pollen from the anther of one plant to the stigma of another.

    open, 198: Natural cross pollination.

    self, 197: The transfer of pollen from the anther of one plant to the stigma of the same plant.

Pubescence, 14: Hairlike structures on plant surfaces.

Pure line, 194: The progeny of a homozygous plant. All plants of a pure line are identical.

Raking, hay, 324: The field operation of arranging mowed and cured hay into windrows or piles.

Recessive, 186: An allele or character that, when in a heterozygous situation, is not expressed.

Recombination, 189: Formation of new combinations of genes in the progeny from crosses of genetically unlike parents.

Recurrent parent, 200: The parent to which successive hybridizations are made in the backcross method of breeding.

Relative humidity, 104: The amount of water vapor in the air expressed as a percentage of the amount of water vapor the air could hold at the same temperature.

Reproductive cells, 187: Female and male gametic cells (egg and sperm cells) of an individual that are formed through meiosis.

Root hairs, 19: A single-celled extension of an epidermal cell of a young root.

Rotary hoe, 165,166: A tillage implement designed to uproot small weed seedlings and to break up the soil.

Scutellum (cotyledon), 4: In grass species, the single cotyledon within the seed.

Seed coatings, 214: General term for substances that coat the seed.

Seed treatments, 214: Refers to fungicides/insecticides adhered to seeds.

Seed viability, 211: The ability to germinate, indicates the capacity of nondormant seeds to germinate under favorable conditions.

Seed vigor, 211: The vitality or strength of germination.

Self-incompatibility, 203: A genetically controlled situation in which the pollen of a plant will not effect fertilization on the same plant.

Self-sterility, 203: The lack of the capability of fertilization and setting of seed after self pollination.

Semiarid, 100: A humidity province receiving 25-50 cm of precipitation per year.

Single cross (two-way cross), 202: The cross pollination of two distinct lines, usually two inbred lines.

Sodium hypochlorite test, 218: A test to indicate mechanical damage in soybeans,

Solid seeding, 175: Seeding in rows that are too narrow for mechanical cultivation or other cultural practices requiring interrow operations.

Somatic cells, 187: Non-gametic (non-reproductive) cells of an individual that reproduce by mitosis.

Staminal column, 23: Stamens in a legume flower that are fused together to form a protective column enclosing the pistil.

Stigma, 20,23: The part of the pistil) that receives pollen.

Stipule, 15: A leaf-like structure located at the leaf base near the junction of the petiole and the stem. May vary in size and shape and is useful in identifying legume species,

Stomatal apparatus, 13: Refers to the stoma (leaf opening) surrounded by guard cells (two cells surrounding the stoma).

Stoma, 13: Stoma (singular) and stomata (plural). An opening in the leaf surrounded by guard cells.

Style, 20,23: The stalk-like structure supporting the stigma of a flower.

Subhumid, 100: A humidity province receiving 50-75 cm of precipitation per year.

Tendril, 15: A tiny, coiling stem-like tissue found at the terminal end of leaves of some species. Used for climbing or anchorage.

Tiller, 18: Stems that develop from lower nodes near the base of the plant.

Triple fusion, 188: The fusion of a sperm nucleus with the two polar nuclei to form 3N endosperm cells during seed formation.

Tube nucleus, 188: One of two nuclei of the pollen grain. The nucleus that controls the growth of the pollen tube.

Two-way cross, 202: See single cross.

Unifoliate leaf, 73: A leaf that is compound in structure, but having only one leaflet.

Varietal purity, 211: A percentage measure of varietal contamination in a seed lot of a crop species.

Variety, 33: A subdivision of species. A group of individuals within a species that are unique in characteristics and/or functions. Variety is commonly used to denote cultivar (see cultivar).

Vascular bundle, 16: Tissue containing the primary xylem and primary phloem.

Vernation, 43: The manner in which grass leaves are arranged (rolled or folded) in the growing point (budshoot).

Water holding capacity, 134: The ability of the soil to hold water, usually expressed in cm/m or in/ft.

Windrows, 324: A crop that has been raked into rows.

Index

Gravitational water, 136
Gravity (surface) irrigation, 141
Grazing,
    continuous, 330
    deferred, 330
    intensity, 329
    management, 329
    rotation, 330
    strip, 330
    zero, 330
Greenchop, 39,330
Greenhouse effect, 109
Greenhouse gases, 110
Green clover worm, 285
Green foxtail, 243
Groundnut (goober, peanut), 50
Growing degree day, 103
Growing point (apical meristem), 4,9,75
Growth type, 89
Gynoecium, 20,23

Hairy vetch, 61,64
Haplocorm, 18
Haploid, 186
Hard seed, 213
Harvest,
    grain crops, 318
    grain crop silage, 319
    hay crop silage, 320
    hay crops, 319
    maturity, 319
Harvesting forages, 324
Harvesting methods, 320
Hay, 324
    baled, 324
    conditioner,
    field chopped, 325
    stacked, 325
Haylage, 320
Head inflorescence, 27
Heat unit, 103
Hedge bindweed, 256
Hemp dogbane (Indian hemp), 271
Herbicide,
    banded,238
    broadcast, 238
    contact, 239
    directed, 238
    foliar applied, 238
    non-directed, 238
    nonselective, 238
    postemergence, 239

    preemergence, 239
    preplant, 239
    selective, 238
    soil applied, 238
    systemic (translocated), 239
Hessian fly, 289
Heterogeneous, 189
Heterosis (hybrid vigor), 201
Heterozygous, 187
Hill-drop-pattern seeding, 174
Hilum, 8
Homogeneous, 189
Homologous chromosome (homologs), 197
Homozygous, 187
Hopkins bioclimatic law, 103
Horsenettle (sand brier, Carolina nettle), 253
Humid, 100
Humidity, 104
Humidity province, 98
Humus, 130
Hybrid, 189
Hybrid vigor (heterosis), 201
Hybridization, 194
Hygroscopic water, 136
Hypocotyl, 8,75
Hypocotyledonary arch (crook), 9
Hypogeal emergence, 4

Immature embryos, 213
Imperfect flower, 20
Inbred, 202
Incomplete flowers, 20
Indeterminate growth, 89
Indigenous crop, 38
Inert material (foreign material), 215
Infared rays, 79, 109
Inflorescence, 20-27
Inflorescence types, 45
Inoculant, 97
Insecticide, 281
Insects,
    biological control, 280
    chemical control, 281
    complete metamorphosis, 279
    competitive characteristics, 278
    cultural control, 280
    economic threshhold, 282
    gradual metamorphosis, 279
    impacts, 277
    integrated pest management, 282
    life cycles, 279
    management strategies, 280-283

TZ (tetrazolium)
   test, 215
   procedures, 216
Tall fescue, 56,59
Taproot, 20
Temperature, 101
Tendril, 15
Test weight, 227
Testa, 8
Tetrazolium test (see TZ test)
Thermosphere, 98
Till-plant system, 162
Tillage 149
   implements, 150
   methods, 156-164
   systems, 149
Tiling, 143
Tiller, 18
Tillering, 89
Timothy, 56,58
Tine-tooth harrow, 155
Tip (kernel), 4
Topography, 115
Translocation, 83
Transpiration, 84
Transpiration (evapotranspiration) ratio, 84
Trap crop, 40
Trickle (drip) irrigation, 141
Triple fusion, 188
Troposphere, 98
Tube nucleus, 188
Tuber, 18
Two-way cross (single cross), 202
Two-zone tillage, 237

Ultraviolet rays, 79
Unifoliolate leaf, 73

Vacuole, 2
Vapor pressure, 104
Vapor pressure deficit, 104
Variability (genetic), 189
Varietal purity, 211
Variety, 33
Vascular bundle, 16
Vavilov, Nikolai, 38
Velvetleaf (buttonweed, butterprint, Indian mallow), 259
Vernalization, 41
Vernation, 43
Viricides, 303
Viruses, 38,300

Warm germination test, 214
Water holding capacity, soil, 134
Water requirement, 85
Wavelength, 79
Weather front, 107
Weeds,
   competitive characteristics, 234-235
   definition, 233
   identification and properties, 240
   impact, 233
   management programs, 240
   management strategies, 236
   resistance to herbicides, 236
Wheat, 46,47
White alkali, 142
White clover, 61,63
White grubs, 291
Wild buckwheat, 258
Wild sunflower, 261
Wilting range, 136
Windrows, 234
Wing petal, 23
Winter annual, 41
Wireworm, 291

X-rays, 79
Xylem, 12

Yellow foxtail, 244
Yellow nutsedge (yellow sedge, yellow nutgrass), 252
Yield, 71

Zero grazing, 330

Conversion Charts

CONVERSION FACTORS FOR COMMONLY USED UNITS

Length	Å	in.	m	cm
1 ångström (Å)	1	3.94×10^{-9}	10^{-10}	10^{-8}
1 inch (in.)	2.54×10^8	1	2.54×10^{-2}	2.54
1 meter (m)	10^{10}	39.37	1	10^2
1 centimeter (cm)	10^8	.3937	10^{-2}	1

Mass	lb	oz	kg	g
1 pound (lb)	1	32	.4536	453.6
1 ounce (oz)	.0625	1	2.836×10^{-2}	28.36
1 kilogram (kg)	2.204	35.3	1	1000
1 gram (g)	2.204×10^{-3}	.0353	.001	1

Pressure	atm	Pa	mm Hg	dyn cm^{-2}	lb in.$^{-2}$
1 atmosphere (atm)	1	1.013×10^5	760	1.013	14.70
1 pascal (Pa)	9.872×10^{-6}	1	7.502×10^{-3}	10^{-5}	1.451×10^{-4}
1 torr (mm Hg)	1.32×10^{-3}	1.333×10^2	1	1.33×10^{-5}	1.93×10^{-2}
1 bar (dyn cm^{-2})	9.872×10^{-1}	10^5	7.502×10^2	1	1.451×10^1
1 pound per square inch (lb in.$^{-2}$)	6.803×10^{-2}	6.891×10^3	5.17×10^1	6.891×10^{-2}	1

Temperature	°K	°F	°C
1 degree Kelvin (°K)	1	$^9/_5$(°K) − 459.7	°K + 273.16*
1 degree Fahrenheit (°F)	$^5/_9$(°F) + 255.4	1	$^5/_9$(°F − 32)
1 degree Centigrade (°C)	°C − 273	$^9/_5$(°C) + 32	1

Energy	J	erg	cal	kWh
1 joule (J)	1	10^7	.2390	2.8×10^{-7}
1 erg (erg)	10^{-7}	1	2.390×10^{-8}	2.8×10^{-14}
1 thermochemical calorie (cal)	4.184	4.184×10^7	1	1.162×10^{-6}
1 kilowatt-hour (kWh)	3.6×10^6	3.6×10^{13}	8.604×10^5	1

Volume	ml	cm^3	qt	oz
1 milliliter (ml)	1	1	1.06×10^{-3}	3.392×10^{-2}
1 cubic centimeter (cm^3)	1	1	1.06×10^{-3}	3.392×10^{-2}
1 quart (qt)	943	943	1	32
1 fluid ounce (oz)	29.5	29.5	3.125×10^{-2}	1

*Absolute zero (°K) = −273.16°C.

©Burgess Publishing Co.

RULES FOR ESTIMATING QUANTITIES OF GRAINS AND ROUGHAGES

(1) **To Measure Grain in a Bin.** Obtain the cubic feet of level grain in a bin by multiplying the length by the width by the depth of level grain. Divide by 1¼ (or multiply by 0.8) to find bushels of level grain. Multiply this total by the test weight and divide by the standard weight to find the number of bushels of standard weight.

(2) **To Find Bushels of Ear Corn in a Crib.**

Rectangular Crib—Find the cubic feet of ear corn by multiplying the length by the width by the depth of corn. To find the bushels of corn, divide the cubic feet by the conversion factor which applies from the table below.

Round Crib—Find the cubic feet of ear corn by squaring the circumference (distance around the crib) and multiplying by the depth of corn inside. Multiply this figure by 2/25. (This is the same as πr² x depth of corn.) To find the bushels of corn, divide the cubic feet by the conversion factor which applies from the table below. Another formula is: Square the diameter and multiply by .628 to find bushels of small grain and shelled corn or by .314 to find the bushels of ear corn.

Volume of Ear Corn with Different Moisture Contents Needed to Make 56 Pounds Dry Shelled Corn	
Moisture content of kernels	—Cubic feet
13-15%—sound dry corn	2.50
20%—corn as husked when fully mature	2.75
25%—a few ears spongy or immature	3.10
30%—most ears spongy but kernels well dented	3.60
35%—most ears spongy and a considerable proportion of kernels not dented	4.20
40%—very soft immature corn	5.00

(3) **To Find Tons of Hay.**

Loose in Mow—Find the cubic yards of hay in the mow and divide by 15, if hay is well settled, or 18 if loose or not very deep, to estimate tons. If you find the cubic feet in the mow, divide by 450 to 512, depending on the condition of the hay and its depth.

Loose in Stack—Find the cubic feet of hay in the stack by multiplying the length by the width by the distance "over". Divide the cubic feet by 450 to 512 to find the number of tons.

Bales—Weigh ten or more bales from each stack and cutting to determine an average weight per bale. (If possible, weigh after the hay has dried in the barn or stack.) Then multiply the number of bales by the average weight per bale and divide by 2000 to find the number of tons.

Chopped Hay—Find the cubic feet of chopped material. Divide by 200-250, depending on the length of cut and depth of hay, to find the number of tons.

(4) **To Find Tons of Silage.**

If no silage has been removed since filling, the tonnage can be determined directly. If some silage has been fed, the amount remaining can be determined by subtracting the amount fed from the total settled silage originally in the silo. For example: A 20 foot silo had 45 feet of settled silage, or 350 tons. The top 10 feet were fed by January 1, or 41 tons. The difference, 309 tons, is the quantity of silage on January 1 in the bottom 35 feet of the silo.

To find tons of haylage divided by 2 equals tons of corn silage.

To find tons of hay equivalent of haylage using the corn silage tables, use 28% of the tons of corn silage.

STANDARD WEIGHTS PER BUSHEL IN POUNDS (MINNESOTA)

Alfalfa	60	Oats	32
Barley	48	Onions	52
Brome grass	14	Peas, dry	60
Clover	60	Potatoes	60
Corn, shelled	56	Rye	56
Corn, dry ear	70	Sorghum grain	56
Flax	56	Soybeans	60
Kentucky blue grass	14	Timothy	45
		Wheat	60

SILO CAPACITY CHART FOR GROUND EAR CORN*

Size of Silo	82.8 lbs. per bu. 2.15 cu. ft. per bu. 24% ground ear corn bushels	89.2 lbs. per bu. 2.25 cu. ft. per bu. 28% ground ear corn bushels	94.6 lbs. per bu. 2.34 cu. ft. per bu. 32% ground ear corn bushels
12x30	1,576	1,507	1,449
12x40	2,101	2,009	1,932
12x50	2,627	2,511	2,415
14x30	2,148	2,053	1,974
14x40	2,865	2,738	2,632
14x50	3,581	3,422	3,291
14x60	4,297	4,107	3,949
16x30	2,804	2,680	2,577
16x40	3,739	3,573	3,436
16x50	4,674	4,467	4,295
16x60	5,609	5,360	5,154
18x40	4,726	4,516	4,342
18x50	5,907	5,644	5,427
18x60	7,088	6,773	6,513
18x70	8,270	7,902	7,598
20x40	5,842	5,582	5,367
20x50	7,320	6,978	6,709
20x60	8,763	8,373	8,051
20x70	10,223	9,769	9,393
22x40	7,070	7,756	6,496
22x50	8,837	8,444	8,119
22x60	10,605	10,133	9,744
22x70	12,372	11,822	11,368
24x50	10,512	10,044	9,658
24x60	12,614	12,053	11,590
24x70	14,716	14,062	13,521
24x80	16,819	16,071	15,453

* Adapted in part from information in *Doane's Facts and Figures*, published by Doane Agricultural Service, 8900 Manchester Road, St. Louis, Missouri.

CAPACITY IN TONS PER FOOT OF LENGTH FOR TRENCH OR BUNKER SILOS

Average width, feet	5 Cu. ft.	Tons corn	Tons grass	6 Cu. ft.	Tons corn	Tons grass	7 Cu. ft.	Tons corn	Tons grass	8 Cu. ft.	Tons corn	Tons grass	9 Cu. ft.	Tons corn	Tons grass	10 Cu. ft.	Tons corn	Tons grass
8	40	.70	.90	48	.84	1.08	56	.98	1.26	64	1.12	1.44	72	1.25	1.62	80	1.40	1.80
10	50	.88	1.13	60	1.05	1.35	70	1.23	1.58	80	1.40	1.80	90	1.58	2.03	100	1.75	2.25
12	60	1.05	1.35	72	1.26	1.62	84	1.47	1.89	96	1.68	2.16	108	1.89	2.48	120	2.10	2.70
14	70	1.23	1.58	84	1.47	1.69	98	1.71	2.21	112	1.96	2.52	126	2.21	2.84	140	2.45	3.15
16	80	1.40	1.80	96	1.68	2.16	112	1.96	2.52	128	2.24	2.88	144	2.52	3.24	160	2.80	3.60
18	90	1.58	2.03	108	1.89	2.48	126	2.21	2.89	144	2.52	3.24	162	2.89	3.64	180	3.15	4.05
20	100*	1.75	2.25	120	2.10	2.70	140	2.45	3.15	160	2.80	3.60	180	3.15	4.05	200	3.50	4.50
22	110	1.93	2.48	132	2.31	2.97	154	2.69	3.47	176	3.08	3.96	198	3.47	4.45	220	3.85	4.95
24	120	2.10	2.70	144	2.52	3.24	168	2.94	3.78	192	3.36	4.32	216	3.78	4.85	240	4.20	5.40
26	130	2.28	2.92	156	2.73	3.51	182	3.19	4.09	208	3.64	4.68	234	4.10	5.26	260	4.55	5.85
28	140	2.45	3.15	168	2.94	3.78	196	3.43	4.41	224	3.92	5.04	252	4.41	5.67	280	4.90	6.30
30	150	2.63	3.38	180	3.15	4.05	210	3.68	4.73	240	4.20	5.40	270	4.73	6.05	300	5.25	6.75

* From *Doane's Facts and Figures*, published by Doane Agricultural Service, 8900 Manchester Road, St. Louis, Missouri.

Conversion Factors for Acceptable Units

To convert Column 1 into Column 2 multiply by	Column 1 Acceptable Unit	Column 2 SI Unit	To convert Column 2 into Column 1 multiply by
	Length		
0.304	foot, ft	meter, m	3.28
2.54	inch, in.	centimeter, cm (10^{-2} m)	0.394
25.4	inch, in.	millimeter, mm (10^{-2} m)	3.94×10^{-2}
1.609	mile, mi	kilometer, km (10^3 m)	0.621
0.914	yard, yd	meter, m	1.094
	Area		
0.405	acre	hectare, ha	2.47
4.05×10^3	acre	square meter, sq m	2.47×10^{-4}
9.29×10^{-2}	square foot, sq ft	square meter, sq m	10.76
6.45	square inch, sq in.	square centimeter, sq cm (10^{-4} m)^2	0.155
645	square inch, sq in.	square millimeter, sq mm (10^{-6} m)^2	1.55×10^{-3}
2.590	square mile, sq mi	square kilometer, sq km (10^3 m)^2	0.386
	Volume		
102.8	acre-inch	meter^3, m^3	9.73×10^{-3}
35.24	bushel (dry), bu	liter, L (10^{-3} m^3)	2.84×10^{-2}
28.3	cubic foot, cu ft	liter, L (10^{-3} m^3)	3.53×10^{-2}
2.83×10^{-2}	cubic foot, cu ft	cubic meter, cu m	35.3
1.64×10^5	cubic inch, cu in.	cubic meter, cu m	6.10×10^4
3.78	gallon, gal	liter, L (10^{-3} m^3)	0.265
2.96×10^{-2}	ounce (liquid), oz	liter, L (10^{-3} m^3)	33.78
1.82	pint (dry), pt	liter, L (10^{-3} m^3)	0.55
0.473	pint (liquid), pt	liter, L (10^{-3} m^3)	2.11
0.908	quart (dry), qt	liter, L (10^{-3} m^3)	1.101
0.946	quart (liquid), qt	liter, L (10^{-3} m^3)	1.057
	Mass		
454×10^{-1}	hundredweight (short), cwt	kilogram, kg	2.20×10^{-2}
28.4	ounce (avdp), oz	gram, g	3.52×10^{-2}
454	pound, lb	gram, g (10^{-3} kg)	2.20×10^{-3}
0.454	pound, lb	kilogram, kg	2.205
907	ton (2000 lb), ton	kilogram, kg	1.10×10^{-3}
0.907	ton (2000 lb), ton	megagram, Mg (tonne)	1.102
	Yield and Rate		
35.84	32-lb bushel per acre, bu/acre	kilogram per hectare, kg/ha	2.79×10^{-2}
53.75	48-lb bushel per acre, bu/acre	kilogram per hectare, kg/ha	1.86×10^{-2}
62.71	56-lb bushel per acre, bu/acre	kilogram per hectare, kg/ha	1.59×10^{-2}
67.19	60-lb bushel per acre, bu/acre	kilogram per hectare, kg/ha	1.49×10^{-2}
9.35	gallon per acre, gal/acre	liter per hectare, L/ha	0.107
1.12×10^{-2}	hundredweight per acre, cwt/acre	kilogram per hectare, kg/ha	0.892×10^2 or 893
1.12	pound per acre, lb/acre	kilogram per hectare, kg/ha	0.893
1.12×10^{-1}	pound per acre, lb/acre	megagram per hectare, Mg/ha	893
12.87	pound per bushel, lb/bu	kilogram per cubic meter, kg/cu m	7.77×10^{-2}
16.02	pound per cubic foot, lb/ft	kilogram per cubic meter, kg/cu m	6.25×10^{-2}
2.24	ton (2000 lb) per acre, ton/acre	megagram per hectare, Mg/ha	0.446
	Angles		
1.75×10^{-2}	degree (angle)	radian, rad	57.296
	Pressure		
0.101	atmosphere, atm	megapascal, MPa (10^6 Pa)	9.90
0.1	bar	megapascal, MPa (10^6 Pa)	10
47.9	pound per square foot, lb/sq ft	pascal, Pa	2.09×10^{-2}
6.90×10^3	pound per square inch, lb/sq in.	pascal, Pa	1.45×10^{-4}
6.90	pound per square inch, lb/sq in.	kilopascal, kPa	0.145
	Temperature		
5/9 (°F − 32)	Fahrenheit, °F	Celsius, °C	(9/5 °C) + 32

(continued on next page)

© 1994 American Society of Agronomy.

To convert Column 1 into Column 2 multiply by	Column 1 Acceptable Unit	Column 2 SI Unit	To convert Column 2 into Column 1 multiply by
Energy, Work, Quantity of Heat			
1.05×10^3	British thermal unit, Btu	joule, J	9.52×10^{-4}
4.19	calorie, cal	joule, J	0.239
4.19×10^4	calorie per square centimeter (langley), cal/sq cm	joule per square meter, J/sq m	2.387×10^{-5}
698	calorie per square centimeter per minute, cal/sq cm/min	watt per square meter, W/sq m	1.43×10^{-3}
1.36	foot-pound, ft-lb	joule, J	0.735
Water Measurement			
102.8	acre-inch, acre-in.	cubic meter, cu m	9.73×10^{-3}
101.9	cubic foot per second, cu ft/s	cubic meter per hour, cu m/h	9.81×10^{-3}
0.227	U.S. gallon per minute, gal/min	cubic meter per hour, cu m/h	4.40
0.123	acre-foot, acre-ft	hectare-meter, ha-m	8.11
12.33	acre-foot, acre-ft	hectare-centimeter, ha-cm	8.1×10^{-2}
1.03×10^{-2}	acre-inch, acre-in.	hectare-meter, ha-m	97.28
9.35	U.S. gallon per acre, gal/acre	liter per hectare, L/ha	0.107
10^2	bar (water potential)	joule per kilogram, J/kg	10^{-2}
10	water content of plant, %	gram water per kilogram wet or dry (specify) tissue, g/kg	0.1
10	water content of soil, %	kilogram water per kilogram dry soil, kg/kg	0.1
Speed			
0.447	miles per hour, mi/h	meter per second, m/s	2.237
Light			
10.764	foot-candle, ft-c	lux, lx	0.0929
Density			
12.87	grain test weight, pound per bushel, lb/bu	kilogram per cubic meter, kg/cu m	7.78×10^{-2}
1.0	soil bulk density, gram per cubic centimeter, g/cu cm	megagram per cubic meter, Mg/cu m	1.0
Concentration			
$10^4/(\text{mol wt})$	percent, % [must specify the base and if by weight (w/v or w/w) or volume (v/v or w/v)]	liquid, known molar mass mole per cubic meter, mol/cu m	$10^{-4} \times (\text{mol wt})$
10^4	percent, % (must specify the base and if by weight or volume)	liquid, unknown molar mass gram per cubic meter, g/cu m	10^{-4}
$10^4/(\text{mol wt})$	percent, % (must specify the base and if by weight or volume)	ion uptake, mole per cubic meter, mol/cu m	$10^{-4} \times (\text{mol wt})$
$10/(\text{mol wt})$	percent, % (must specify the base and if by weight or volume)	known molecular weight in fresh or dry (specify) plant material, mole per kilogram, mol/kg	$0.1 \times (\text{mol wt in g mol}^{-1})$
10	percent, % (must specify the base and if by weight or volume)	unknown molecular weight in fresh or dry plant material, gram per kilogram, g/kg	0.1
10	percent, % (must specify the base and if by weight or volume)	soil texture composition, gram per kilogram, g/kg	0.1
1.0	parts per million, ppm	extractable ions, milligram per kilogram, mg/kg	1.0
0.5	pounds per acre, lb/acre	extractable ions, milligram per kilogram, mg/kg	2.0 (assume 2×10^6 lbs soil per acre 6⅔ in.)
1	milliequivalents per 100 grams, meq/100 g	centimole per kilogram, cmol/kg (ion exchange capacity)	1
10	percent, %	gram per kilogram, g/kg	0.1
1	parts per million, ppm	milligram per kilogram, mg/kg	1

Plant Nutrient Conversion

	Oxide	Elemental	
0.437	P_2O_5	P	2.29
0.830	K_2O	K	1.20
0.715	CaO	Ca	1.39
0.602	MgO	Mg	1.66